MERCHANDISE BUYING AND MANAGEMENT

THIRD EDITION

MERCHANDISE BUYING AND MANAGEMENT

THIRD EDITION

John Donnellan

FAIRCHILD PUBLICATIONS, INC.
NEW YORK

Executive Editor: Olga T. Kontzias

Director of Sales and Acquisitions: Dana Meltzer-Berkowitz

Acquisitions Editor: Joe Miranda

Senior Development Editor: Jennifer Crane

Art Director: Adam B. Bohannon

Production Manager: Ginger Hillman

Production Editors: Beth Cohen and Jessica Rozler

Copyeditor: Joanne Slike

Cover Design: Adam B. Bohannon

Photo Credits:

    Top: Fancy Photography/Veer

    Middle: Catherine Leuthold

    Bottom: R. P. Kingston/Index

          Stock/Veer

Text Design: Adam B. Bohannon

Composition: Jack Donner, BookType

Library of Congress Catalog Card Number: 2006935252
ISBN: 978-1-56367-521-8
GST R 133004424
Printed in China
TP15

CONTENTS

EXTENDED CONTENTS

PREFACE

The third edition of *Merchandise Buying and Management* combines the successful elements of the first and second editions with helpful suggestions for improvement from reviewers and adopters. Written for college-level courses dealing with retail buying and the management of retail inventories, the text covers topics that are important to those aspiring to become buyers within retail organizations and to those who will become store management personnel with responsibilities for managing retail sales and inventories. The material is presented within the context of a contemporary retail environment in which buyers often act as fiscal managers as well as product developers, and store managers play important roles in sales productivity and assortment planning. Retail technology is a theme that runs throughout the book, tied to topics such as space management, electronic data interchange, point-of-sale systems, and floor-ready merchandise. Completely revised images and new supporting examples ensure that the third edition of *Merchandise Buying and Management* is in step with the times.

Sixteen chapters are organized into five parts. The five chapters that compose part one explain the structure of the retail industry. *Retail Merchandising* covers the retailer's role in bringing products from their point of production to their point of consumption and the merchandising functions of a retail enterprise. *Retailing Formats* categorizes retail stores by their merchandising strategies, while *Retail Locations* covers the various settings in which retail stores operate. *Retail Growth and Expansion* is a discussion of the strategies that retailers use to grow and remain competitive in the marketplace. *Communicating with Consumers* looks at the various groups of consumers that retailers cater to and some of techniques that retailers use to attract customers to their stores.

The three chapters in part two are product oriented. *Fashion Merchandising* contrasts the merchandising of fashion goods with basic goods, while *Brands and Private Labels* contrasts the merchandising of nationally distributed products with goods developed for exclusive distribution by a single retailer. *Merchandise Resources* describes the wholesale market-place and the various types of suppliers from which retailers buy their merchandise.

Part three includes chapters that deal with inventory performance and the fiscal aspects of retail merchandising. *Measures of Productivity* covers the critically important concepts of turnover and sales per square foot. *Merchandising Accounting* interprets fundamental accounting concepts from a retail perspective, while determining the value of retail inventories as organizational assets is the topic of *Inventory Valuation*.

The three chapters in part four involve planning, purchasing, and pricing retail inventories. *Pricing* covers the concepts of markup and markdowns, as well as promotional pricing strategies. *Planning* covers several mathematical procedures for determining the amount of inventory needed to achieve an organization's sales goals. Price, delivery, and payment negotiations between retail buyers and their suppliers are covered in *Purchase Terms*.

Part five comprises two sections. *Merchandising Controls and Report Analysis* is an explanation of various reports that are used to evaluate sales and inventory performance. *Store Layout and Merchandise Presentation* deals with some fundamental store design and merchandise presentation concepts with which both buyers and store managers should be familiar.

Many chapters include sidebars with pertinent information supplemental to the chapter's core content. Company profiles with "real-world" examples of concepts introduced in the text are a feature of most chapters.

End-of-chapter elements have expanded considerably in this third edition. As in prior editions, summary points and a list of key terms and concepts appear at the end of each chapter. Key terms are introduced in bold type within each chapter and defined in the glossary at the end of the book.

Three new end-of-chapter elements have been added to this edition:

- *Thinking About It*—Thought-provoking questions and exercises designed to hone critical thinking with generative thought beyond the textbook.

- *Teaming Up*—Activities that foster group interaction and the cultivation of the people skills that employers often look for in today's college grads.
- *Searching the Net*—Exercises designed to promote information literacy, another skill very much in demand in today's business environment.

Quantitative chapters (9, 10, 11, 12, 13, 14, and 15) include two additional end-of-chapter sections:

- *Solving Problems*—Problem-solving exercises to cultivate numeric reasoning and quantitative decision-making.
- *Using Excel*—Spreadsheet software exercises to link chapter content with informational report design.

Prepared by Patricia Mink Rath, the Instructor's Guide for *Merchandise Buying and Management* is another highlight of the third edition. The guide includes teaching tips; references; case studies; enrichment activities; suggestions for conducting group activities; helpful hints for teaching information literacy and spreadsheet software; and answers to end-of-chapter discussion questions and problems. The Instructor's Guide also includes chapter examination questions in the form of multiple choice, true and false, and essay questions, and a set of PowerPoint slides to aid instructors in classroom presentation.

ACKNOWLEDGMENTS

I extend sincere thanks to members of the editorial staff at Fairchild Books for their support in preparing this third edition: to Olga Kontzias, executive editor, for her sage advice over the many years this book has been in print; to Joe Miranda, acquisitions editor, for his expedient response to my informational queries; to Dana Meltzer-Berkowitz, editorial acquisitions and sales director, for her valuable input on the end-of-chapter elements and other new aspects of the present edition.

I am also grateful to Shaie Lively of Photosearch for her painstaking photo research efforts and her many contributions to the visual aspects of this work; and to Patricia Mink Rath of the International Academy of Design and Technology, for once again composing a pedagogical masterpiece in the form of the Instructor's Guide. I am also indebted to Richard Finn for demonstrating his mastery of the English language in proofreading the final draft of this edition.

This book is dedicated to the memory of Donald I. Klein, merchant, mentor, and dear friend.

JOHN DONNELLAN

PART ONE

The Structure of the Retail Industry

- RETAIL MERCHANDISING
- RETAILING FORMATS
- RETAIL LOCATIONS
- RETAIL GROWTH AND EXPANSION
- COMMUNICATING WITH CONSUMERS

CHAPTER ONE

Retail Merchandising

After reading this chapter, you will be able to discuss:

● The role of retailing in the marketing channel.

● The merchandising functions within a retail organization.

● The skills needed for success in merchandising careers.

The task of assembling an assortment of merchandise that appeals to a store's customers is a challenging proposition. Meeting this challenge requires knowledge of consumer products, consumer behavior, and the store's strategy for growth and profit. Fundamental to this knowledge is an understanding of the role that retail stores play in channeling products from producers to consumers and the ways in which retail enterprises are structured to perform this function. This chapter covers these two topics, as well as the personal qualifications necessary for individuals who wish to pursue careers in the exciting field of retail merchandising.

THE MARKETING CHANNEL

The marketing channel represents the flow of goods from point of production to point of consumption. The model traces the distribution of a product from the manufacturer, or producer, to the final consumer, or ultimate user of the product. The marketing channel is sometimes referred to as the *distribution channel, distribution pipeline,* or *supply chain.*

The marketing channel comprises *channel members* who are classified according to the function they perform. A producer converts materials (such as fabric) and/or component parts (such as zippers) into products (such as jackets). A wholesaler facilitates the distribution process by buying large quantities of goods from producers and reselling smaller quantities to other channel members, a process called *breaking bulk.* A retailer sells products and/or services to final consumers who actually use the product, or derive personal benefit from the service.

It is important to note that retailers sell services as well as products. Hairstylists and residential interior decorators are service retailers. A bank that offers financial services to consumers, such as home mortgages, car loans, and checking accounts, performs a retail banking function. The same bank may provide similar services to businesses but, in so doing, performs a commercial banking function. Wholesalers and retailers do not physically change the products that they buy and sell. Because they link producers and consumers, wholesalers and retailers are often called *channel intermediaries*. This textbook focuses on the channel interactions that occur between retailers of non-food products, such as apparel and home furnishings, and other channel members.

Retailers perform an indispensable function in the distribution of goods to final consumers. A consumer who pays $65 for a blouse is getting far more than fabric, buttons, and workmanship for her money. Inherent in the retail price are the costs associated with assembling a selection of blouses in an assortment of fabrications, styles, colors, brands, and prices at a single location. A retail price also covers the cost of amenities, such as attractive facilities, salesperson assistance, and payment options that may include a store charge account, personal checks, or third-party charges, such as Visa and MasterCard. Without retailers as points of distribution, consumers would need to travel to production sources all over the world to purchase goods.

Retailing is an important segment of the U.S. economy. The industry accounts for 10 percent of the nation's gross domestic product.[1] Between 2002 and 2012, retailing is projected to expand by more than two million jobs, a growth rate of 14 percent.[2]

Streamlining Distribution

Channel members are sometimes bypassed in the distribution process for the sake of expediency. Because of less handling, goods purchased by a retailer directly from a producer spend less time in the distribution pipeline than goods distributed through a wholesaler. Time is a critical factor when dealing with perishable goods, such as food, or goods with short selling cycles, such as fashion apparel.

Cost is another reason retailers bypass wholesalers. The selling price of a product increases as it passes from one marketing channel member to another in that each channel member's selling price must cover the channel

FIGURE 1.1
The marketing channel represents the flow of goods from producers to consumers.

member's operating costs and profit. A retailer can circumvent wholesalers' operating costs and profits by buying directly from producers. The retailer then has the option of selling the products more profitably or passing the savings on to consumers in the form of low competitive prices.

Wal-Mart, the world's largest retailer, is a model of streamlined distribution. By bypassing intermediaries, Wal-Mart is able to price its offerings lower than many of its competitors.[3] Though buying directly from producers is advantageous for many retailers, wholesalers play an important role in the distribution of certain categories of merchandise to certain types of retailers, a topic covered in Chapter 8.

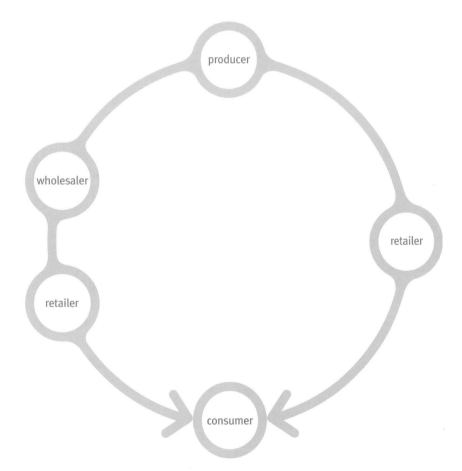

FIGURE 1.2
Retailers bypass wholesalers in the marketing channel to streamline the distribution process.

Vertical Integration

Performing more than one channel function is called vertical integration. Companies vertically integrate for increased channel control and for the fiscal advantages associated with performing multiple channel functions. A producer that sells its product lines directly to consumers through manufacturer-sponsored specialty stores, or *signature stores*, is vertically integrated. These stores facilitate direct contact between producers and consumers and permit producers to retain control over the presentation and sale of their product lines. Some producers also use signature stores as laboratories to test new items. Coach is a producer of a line of fine handbags and small leather goods distributed through prestige department and specialty stores. Coach also operates an international retail division of more than 200 signature stores.[4] Liz Claiborne, DKNY, and Godiva are other examples of vertically integrated producers that operate signature stores.

Retailers vertically integrate when they develop their own product lines for exclusive distribution in their stores, a merchandising concept called

private labeling, covered in Chapter 7. Limited Brands, Inc., is a vertically integrated retailing organization. Through an independent operating division called Mast Industries, Limited Brands develops and sources many of the products sold at Limited Brands stores, including Bath & Body Works, Express, and Victoria's Secret. Gymboree is distinctive among childrenswear retailers because of its fashionable private label lines developed

FIGURE 1.5
Polo/Ralph Lauren
and DKNY are vertically
integrated producers
that act like retailers by
operating their own
specialty stores.
Polo/Ralph Lauren ©
Spencer Grant/PhotoEdit.
DKNY courtesy Fairchild
Publications, Inc.

by the company's own designers who work directly with factories in the Far East to produce goods for more than 600 Gymboree stores.[5]

Companies that vertically integrate risk alienating other channel members. Producers that operate manufacturer-sponsored specialty stores compete directly with the retailers that sell their products through conventional distribution channels. Similarly, producers resent retailers that develop private label goods that are often imitations of products that producers have painstakingly developed.

RETAIL ORGANIZATIONAL STRUCTURES

A table of organization, or *organizational chart*, is a diagram that depicts a company's corporate structure. An organizational chart reflects the various functions performed by an organization and the way in which organizational activities are *departmentalized*, or grouped into organizational units.

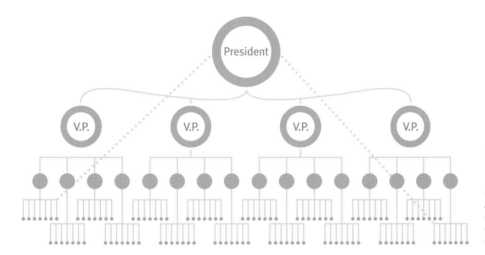

FIGURE 1.7
A table of organization
depicts a company's
corporate structure and
chain of command.

A table of organization defines the hierarchy, or *chain of command*, in an organization, as well as lines of communication and responsibility. Chairman of the board, president, chief executive officer (CEO), chief financial officer (CFO), chief operating officer (COO), and vice president are some of the *top management* titles that appear at the top of a table of organization. These functions have a broader scope of authority and responsibility and a higher salary than lower-level functions. Because the number of functions decreases as one proceeds from the top of a table to the bottom, tables of organization are often called *organizational pyramids*.

As organizations grow, organizational functions with a broad range of responsibility are often split into more specialized functions. An apparel retailer may split the function of buyer of junior sportswear into two more specialized functions, buyer of tops and buyer of bottoms, when business reaches the point that it requires and can support two distinct functions. In general, the tables of organization of large retail organizations have many specialized functions, while the tables of organization of small retail organizations have fewer functions that are more general in scope.

In 1927, Paul Mazur, an investment banker, was commissioned by the National Retail Dry Goods Association, now the National Retail Federation, to develop a model organizational structure for retail stores. Mazur proposed a table of organization with four major functions:

- *Merchandising*—Responsible for procuring merchandise to be resold to customers. These duties were primarily performed by buyers.
- *Publicity*—Responsible for stimulating sales through advertising, display, and other promotional vehicles.
- *Control*—Responsible for the fiscal functions typical of most organizations, such as accounts payable, accounts receivable, and payroll.
- *Store management*—Responsible for sales support functions, facilities management, and the warehouse functions of receiving, checking, and marking goods.[6]

Mazur's proposed structure is still the core of most contemporary retail tables of organization. The organizational growth and the need for a higher degree of specialization, however, have required several enhancements to Mazur's plan. For instance:

- The territorial expanse of multi-unit retail operations spurred the creation of geographically defined pyramids of *regions* and *districts*, an organizational concept discussed later in this chapter.
- As retailers began to recognize the importance of people as an organizational resource, *personnel*, originally a store management function, evolved into a separate organizational function called *human resources*.
- Because the first computer applications in retail stores were fiscal in nature, most retailers relegated computer operations to the finance division. As computer applications spread throughout the entire organization, most retail companies spun off *information systems* (IS) as a freestanding organizational function.

The Separation of Buying and Selling

In Mazur's day, most retail organizations were single-store operations in which buying and selling occurred under one roof. Because Mazur identified *buying* and *selling* as related activities, he proposed a merchandising function that included responsibility for both merchandise procurement and sales floor activities, such as customer service and stock keeping.

As single-unit retail operations evolved into multi-unit chains, buying became a centralized corporate-level function performed independently from the operation of stores. The store-level merchandising activities once orchestrated by buyers became store management functions. Today, the

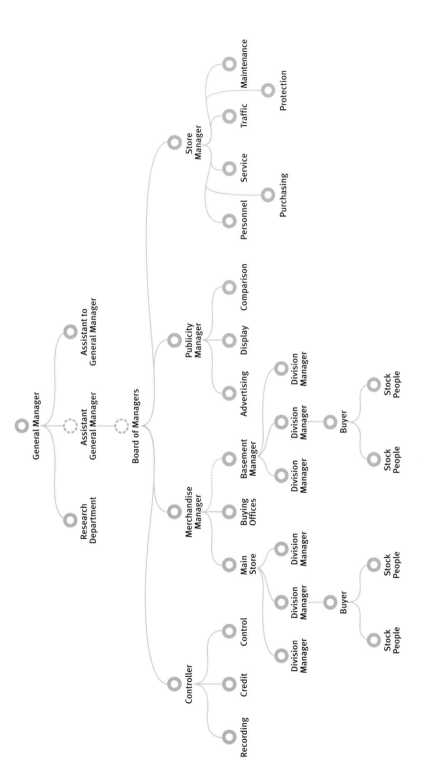

FIGURE 1.8
The table of organization
developed for retail stores
by Paul Mazur in 1927.

store operations, or *store administration*, function in a retail organization is a descendant of Mazur's store management function, but a far cry from the facilities management function that Mazur originally proposed. The contemporary store operations function is likely to include merchandising responsibilities, such as assortment planning, merchandise presentation, and inventory management.

Line and Staff Functions

Organizational functions can be grouped into two categories based on the type of activities performed. A line function performs mainstream activities fundamental to an organization's mission. Buying and selling merchandise are a retailer's mainstream activities, thus merchandising and store operations are a retailer's line functions. These functions are sometimes referred to as the *store line* and the *buying line.*

A staff function supports or advises line functions and/or other staff functions but is not directly involved in an organization's mainstream activities. A retail organization's legal department is an example of a staff function that supports both line and staff functions by performing activities such as negotiating leases and interpreting statutes that govern truth in advertising. The legal department, however, is not directly involved in a retail organization's mainstream activities of buying and selling.

Authority is clearly defined through a chain of command in a line function. Within store operations, an assistant store manager reports to a store manager, who reports to a district manager, who reports to a regional manager, who reports to a director of stores. Staff authority is not as clearly defined. Though the managers of staff functions have authority within their departments, staff managers merely "advise" the managers of other functions without having formal decision-making authority over them. Staff managers sometimes have *functional authority* over other managers in matters that involve their areas of expertise.

Different managerial perspectives are often the source of organizational conflict between staff and line managers. Though the ultimate goal of every retail organization is to make a profit, line and staff managers sometimes adopt divergent strategies for attaining this common goal. For instance, a store manager maximizes profit by employing a competent selling staff. A corporate-level human resource department maximizes profit by establishing salary ranges for various organizational functions. Thus, a store manager's ability to hire top-notch salespeople may be constrained by the human resource department's salary structures.

This is not to say that organizational conflict between line functions in retail organizations is nonexistent. The following is an example of a common dispute between a store manager and buyer.

The dress department of a store within a chain of department stores fell short of its monthly sales goal. When asked to explain the shortfall, the store manager listed the following reasons:

- The styles were too dressy. The store caters to career women, yet social-occasion looks dominated the assortment.
- The prices were too high. The store serves a middle-income market where good value is the primary purchase criterion.
- Size assortments were skewed. The assortment included an overabundance of larger sizes (12s and 14s) and too few smaller sizes (4s and 6s).

Based on observations made during periodic store visits, the buyer retorted with the following reasons for the sales shortfall:

- The merchandise was poorly presented. Looks were not pulled together in any cohesive fashion by color, fabric, or vendor, and customers were likely frustrated by racks of sale goods that were not sized. Furthermore, the store's alterations department should be steaming goods wrinkled in shipment.
- Staffing was inadequate. To conserve expenses, the store manager reduced the selling staff, thereby hampering customer service. Also, newly hired sales associates were poorly trained and unmotivated.

In essence, the store manager blamed the buyer for the sales shortfall, and the buyer blamed the store manager.

Conflict between buyers and store managers has become legendary in retail organizations. Some companies promote empathy between the store line and the buying line by including training stints in both the buying office and stores in their executive training programs.

RETAIL MERCHANDISING

The term *merchandising* has many connotations. In the apparel industry, merchandising involves the planning, development, and presentation of a product line suitable for a firm's intended customers. Mazur cited a classic definition of retail merchandising: "to have the right goods, at the right time, in the right quantities, and at the right prices."[7]

In a broad context, "retail merchandising" includes all of the activities directly or indirectly associated with procuring and reselling merchandise. In a narrow context, retail merchandising embraces only the merchandise procurement function. In this textbook, retail merchandising will be defined in the broader context to include all of the activities associated with buying, pricing, presenting, and promoting merchandise.

Corporate and Field Functions

Organizational functions can be classified by where the function is performed. A corporate function is performed within a company's central organization or corporate office. In a retail organization, buying, sales promotion, and finance are all corporate functions performed in a corporate office. A field function is performed in a remote or satellite operation away from the corporate office. In a retail organization, the store operations function is a field function performed in stores. Within the broad context of retail merchandising, merchandising functions are performed both corporately and in the field.

Though some merchandising functions are common to all retailers, the job titles associated with these functions often differ from one organization to another. The titles and responsibilities described in the following sections are common to most retailers.

Corporate-Level Merchandising Functions

Buying is the main function of a corporate merchandising division. Traditionally buyers were responsible for a diverse group of activities that included inventory planning, selection, and allocation. However, the growth of large retail chains has fostered greater specialization in executing the buying function. Many retailers have split buying into four specialized functions: buying, planning, distribution, and product development.

A buyer buys and prices merchandise for resale. A buyer's challenge is to compose assortments that will appeal to the organization's intended

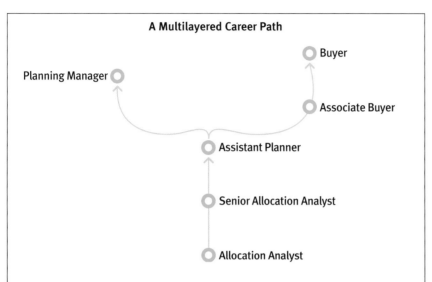

A Multilayered Career Path

Buyer

Planning Manager

Associate Buyer

Assistant Planner

Senior Allocation Analyst

Allocation Analyst

Allocation Analyst: This is your first opportunity to impact our stores across the country by analyzing sales trends, making crucial distribution decisions, and acting as a liaison between our Distribution Centers and our Buyers. Every step of the way you'll apply and develop your analytical, strategic, and creative problem-solving skills.

Senior Allocation Analyst: Handle a greater volume of merchandise allocation, and develop your leadership skills as you train and supervise Allocation Analysts, ensure that work flow within the department is evenly balanced, and see that timely decisions are being made.

Assistant Planner: Enhance your management skills as you work closely with the Planning Manager to create and implement seasonal merchandising plans, assess developmental needs, and train Analysts and Senior Analysts in the development of distribution strategies.

Planning Manager: As a Planning Manager, you'll enjoy full empowerment to build, in essence, your own business worth approximately $150 million. You will work with a Divisional Merchandise Manager and Buyers to determine short and long-term strategies, create seasonal merchandising plans, and partner with other Merchandising executives to ensure that objectives are being met. You will also manage a staff of five to eight Associates and participate in the development of our future Planning Managers and Buyers.

Associate Buyer: Team up with an experienced Buyer as you become increasingly involved in buying decisions. You'll get a first-hand view of our operations, identify strategies for buying trips, and after acquiring the necessary experience, travel to vendor sites and develop negotiating skills.

Buyer: Enjoy full autonomy to handle a sales volume averaging $55–75 million annually. Traveling frequently to New York City and other domestic and international centers, you'll maintain vendor relationships and purchase merchandise for T.J. Maxx and Marshalls stores nationwide.

FIGURE 1.9
Corporate-level merchandising responsibilities at TJX Companies include distribution, planning, and buying functions. Courtesy of TJX Companies, Inc.

MERCHANT TRAINING PROGRAM AT WAL-MART

This Merchant Training Program at Wal-Mart is a one-year preparation that focuses on teaching buyer trainees the operational functions of a store. The program is customized based on the experience of the trainee. The option to test out of components of the program based on prior experience and proficiency is also available.

The First Four Months

During this time, the trainee, under the direction of a store manager, will complete the Retail Leadership School in a designated store. Primary responsibilities include the following:

- Responding to customer complaints and inquiries
- Directing associates' compliance with company policies, procedures, and standards
- Ensuring compliance with established security, sales and record-keeping standards and practices
- Developing leadership ability and customer service skills
- Learning and demonstrating company culture and Our Three Basic Beliefs
- Learning the process of merchandise flow
- Learning the basics of signing, pricing, and merchandise presentation

The Next Seven Months

The trainee works with a buyer and attends merchandise training classes. Primary responsibilities are:

- Making merchandise assortment decisions
- Executing modular assortments and promotional tasks
- Learning how to effectively communicate
- Gaining a basic understanding of retail math by identifying, gathering and performing data analysis
- Reviewing daily financial results to identify variances and issues
- Learning negotiation skills and buying a limited category of merchandise
- Presenting merchandise at the Merchandise Meeting

SOURCE
Wal-Mart. (2006). Merchant Training Program. www.wal-martstores.com.

customers, obtaining the best possible goods at the lowest possible prices. Buyers explore the offerings of the wholesale marketplace by visiting domestic and foreign markets and through frequent interaction with producers' sales agents. Buyers are also responsible for pricing goods low enough to be competitive with other retailers, yet high enough to meet an organization's profit objectives.

The magnitude of a buyer's responsibility is defined by annual sales volume, thus, as might be expected, the buyer of a department with an annual sales volume of $100 million is paid a higher salary than the buyer of a department with $1 million in annual sales. The importance of a buying position may also be linked to the complexity of the wholesale market or the risk associated with purchase decisions. A purchase decision for fashion goods, such as dresses, involves higher risk than a purchase decision for basic goods, such as hosiery. Buying decisions for fashion goods are based on uncertain predictions of consumer acceptance of new styles. An inaccurate prediction will result in poor sales and the need to sell off the inventory at profit-threatening prices. Buying decisions for basics are often just reorders of historically best-selling brands, styles, colors, and sizes.

A planner projects sales and inventories based on an analysis of sales history, current market trends, and the organization's performance objectives. Planning is a statistical function that requires astute analytical aptitude and the ability to make multi-dimensional decisions. A distributor allocates arriving shipments of merchandise to individual stores based on each store's capacity, current sales trends, and inventory levels. Often called *allocators*, distributors correct stock imbalances in stores and are a critical link between stores and the corporate merchandising division. A product developer determines which products to develop internally with the store's private label. Product developers establish specifications for the design, production, and packaging of these goods. They are also responsible for contracting producers to manufacture the goods according to the specifications.

The interdependence of the activities of buyers, planners, distributors, and product developers requires harmonious interaction among all four functions. In some retail organizations, the planning and distribution functions are combined. In small, conventionally structured organizations, the buyer is responsible for planning and distribution, as well as buying. The product-development function exists only in stores that engage in private labeling.

Many organizations use titles such as *senior planner* or *lead analyst* to indicate seniority or level of responsibility. An *assistant buyer*, as the title suggests, assists a buyer with various day-to-day activities and is often being groomed for a buying position. An *associate buyer* is one step closer to being a buyer and often assumes responsibility for buying a category of goods within the buyer's total area of responsibility.

Buying, planning, allocation, and product development responsibilities typically are assigned by merchandise department. A department is a group of related merchandise. A division is a group of related departments. Divisions and departments are identified by product line. A men's division comprises several men's departments, such as men's outerwear, men's suits and sport coats, men's designer collections, and men's accessories. A divisional merchandise manager (DMM) is responsible for a merchandise division. The DMM monitors the sales, inventories, and assortments of the departments within the division to ensure consistency with the organization's merchandising and profit objectives. Divisional merchandise managers report to a general merchandise manager (GMM), who manages a group of related merchandise divisions. A GMM typically is at the senior management level of an organization, often with "vice president" in his or her title. Organizational hierarchies for planning and distribution often parallel organizational hierarchies for buying.

Visual merchandising is a corporate-level merchandising function responsible for store decor, signage, display, fixturing, and standards for presenting merchandise. Visual merchandisers work with buyers to develop *planograms*, or floor layouts, and with store planning to design new stores or renovate existing ones. A store's fashion director is responsible for researching dominant color, style, and design trends in apparel, accessories, and home furnishings markets. The fashion director communicates this information to buyers, so that they can strategically select assortments consistent with current trends, and to other departments where fashion-trend information is critical, such as advertising and visual merchandising.

Store-Level Merchandising Functions

In general, store-level merchandising functions ensure that merchandise is presented on the selling floor in a manner consistent with a company's visual standards and that inventory levels and assortments are appropriate for the store's sales objectives. Store merchandising functions sometimes include

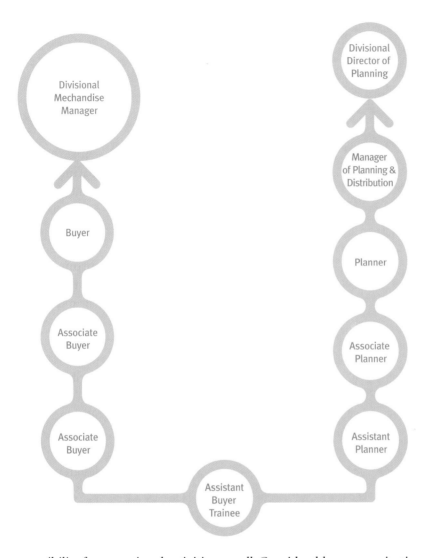

FIGURE 1.10
Organizational hierarchies
for planning and
distribution often parallel
organizational hierarchies
for buying.

responsibility for operational activities as well. Considerable communication occurs between store and corporate merchandising functions.

A general manager, or *store manager*, ultimately is responsible for the merchandising and operations of a store. A general manager sometimes is assisted by an operations manager, a human resource manager, and/or a store merchandise manager. Large stores may have more than one store merchandise manager, each responsible for specific merchandise divisions. There is little consistency among the titles for this function. Titles synony-

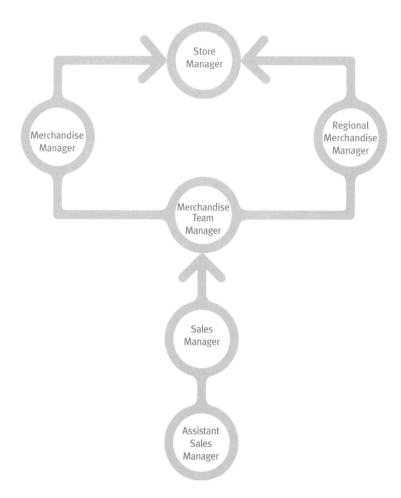

FIGURE 1.11
A hierarchy of store-level
merchandising positions.

mous with store merchandise manager include divisional sales manager and assistant store manager of merchandising. A department manager, or sales manager, usually reports to a store merchandise manager and is responsible for an area defined by department or division. This position usually includes both merchandising and operational responsibilities.

The store merchandising hierarchy just described is typical of large stores, such as department stores like Macy's, and full-line discounters, such as Target. The management structure of a specialty store, such as Banana Republic, is much simpler, usually comprising a store manager and one or more assistant managers. The responsibilities associated with these positions are very general in nature, encompassing both merchandising and operational duties.

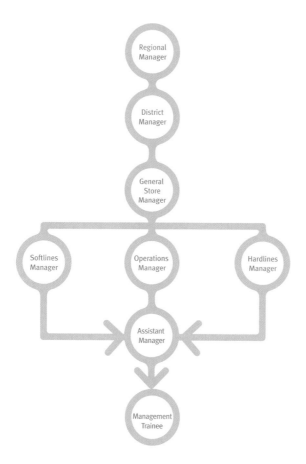

FIGURE 1.12
Multistore retailers have a
geographically defined
organizational hierarchy
that links stores to the
corporate office.

Multi-store retailers have a geographically defined organizational hierarchy that links the stores to the corporate office. A district manager is
responsible for a group of stores located within a defined geographic area.
The number of stores in a district varies from one retail organization to
another, and even within the same organization depending on the distance
between stores. In the densely stored areas of the Northeast, a district may
include 12 stores within a 50-mile radius. A district in the Southwest may
have eight stores within a 100-mile radius. The amount of time required
to travel to the stores in the Southwest is compensated for by responsibility
for fewer stores. A regional manager supervises a group of district managers
and reports to a corporate level person, such as a vice president or director

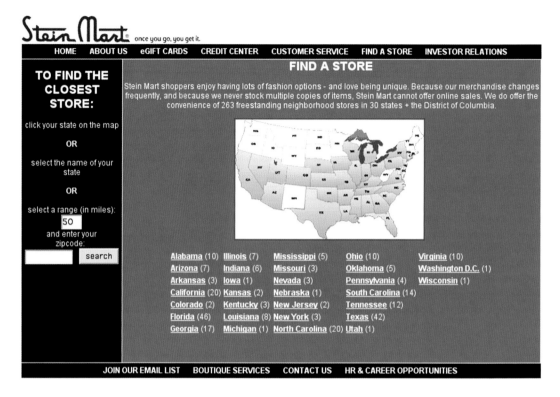

FIGURE 1.13
Stein Mart is an example of
a multistore retailer.
Source: www.steinmart.
com.

of stores. Some organizations link stores to the corporate office with only one managerial level, typically the regional level.

Because merchandising activities occur at both store and corporate levels, the topics covered in this textbook are relevant to students wishing to pursue either corporate merchandising or store administration careers. Though industry restructuring has diminished the number of corporate merchandising career opportunities, considerable opportunities remain for store management executives with merchandising savvy. Knowledge of retail merchandising is also important for students interested in retail sales promotion, shopping center administration, or any phase of the distribution of consumer goods.

Qualifications for Merchandising Positions

There is rigorous competition for the highest paid and most gratifying retail merchandising positions. Merchandising functions at all levels of an orga-

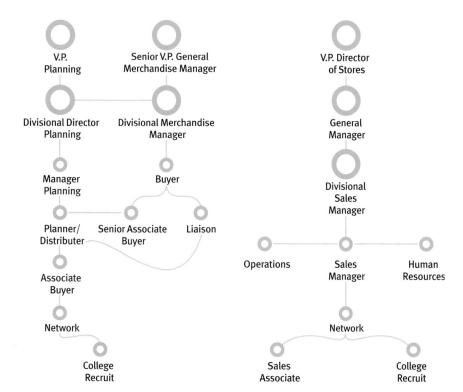

FIGURE 1.14
The store line and buying line at one department store chain.

nization require dynamic, productive individuals, challenged by aggressive goals and committed to standards of excellence. Specific qualifications for merchandising positions differ from one retail organization to another, depending on factors such as a company's size, culture, merchandise mix, and operational strategy. Although there is no set of qualifications universally required by all retailers, the following summarizes a few skills that major retailers have cited as fundamental to success in their organizations.[8]

Decision-Making Skills

Buyers must make decisions frequently and quickly. Retail merchandising requires the ability to evaluate information from multiple sources as a basis for making decisions with far-reaching implications. Planners determine the weighted importance and interaction of market trends, the economy, competition, and consumer behavior to project the amount of inventory that a buyer should purchase. An understated projection will yield inven-

WHAT A BUYER DOES AT WAL-MART

A Wal-Mart buyer's primary responsibility is the selection and maintenance of the best possible merchandise assortment, while giving our customers the best value for their money. There are constants in every buyer's job, from reviewing item movement or replenishment methods, to meeting with suppliers. Other responsibilities include:

- Attending trade shows
- Researching markets
- Shopping the competition
- Visiting stores to review merchandise presentation
- Analyzing product packaging
- Providing stores with seasonal display guides
- Talking with customers

Merchants select the products to be sold in Wal-Mart stores, negotiate price with suppliers, and work with marketing and operations to ensure that products are displayed and advertised in accordance with Wal-Mart's everyday low-pricing philosophy.

SOURCE
Wal-Mart. (2006). Merchandising & Product Development.
www.wal-martstores.com.

tories that are too low to meet the organization's sales potential. An overstated projection will result in excessive inventories, a poor investment of the company's fiscal resources.

Communication Skills

The ability to communicate effectively, both orally and in writing, with people inside and outside the organization is fundamental to the success of a merchandising executive. Conveying ideas to superiors, directives to subordinates, and negotiating price, payment arrangements, and advertising allowances with suppliers are just a few of the instances in which carefully honed communication skills are a necessity.

Analytical and Problem-Solving Skills

Computers have reduced the amount of computational and clerical activities associated with merchandising functions, allowing merchandising

KEY COMPETENCIES FOR MERCHANDISING EXECUTIVES

The following is a list of key competencies for merchandising executives as identified by Kurt Salmon Associates, a management consulting firm specializing in retailing and consumers products.

Is visionary: Explores inspiring possibilities; uses insight to create future successes; pursues innovations in products, services, technology, and managerial methods.

Is results oriented: Develops and implements strategies consistent with the company's goals; uses all available resources to accomplish objectives; sets high performance standards.

Takes risks: Has the courage to act when faced with uncertainty or opposition; willing to move beyond the status quo.

Seeks innovative solutions: Actively collects and synthesizes information from diverse sources to maintain a broad, inclusive perspective; continually conducts market research; remains open to new ideas.

Mentors: Recruits and develops new talent; delegates responsibility and relinquishes authority to subordinates; promotes optimal training, compensation, and recognition systems; encourages frequent exchange and feedback; fosters continuous improvements.

SOURCE
Staff. (May 6, 1998). A roadmap for retail training. *Women's Wear Daily.* pp. 9–10.

executives to devote more time to analyzing reports of sales, inventory, and profit. Physical remoteness from stores has increased reliance on these reports. A single store merchant can "eyeball" inventory and see that "mediums are low" and that it's time to reorder. In large multi-unit operations, this type of stock replenishment decision is based on reports that define inventory status quantitatively.

Computer Skills

Merchandising executives use computers to generate orders, retrieve sales and inventory information, and communicate by e-mail. Though it is impossible to be exposed to all of the available software with merchandising applications, a fundamental understanding of computer capabilities and basic computer terminology is highly useful to the aspiring merchandising executive. Retailers increasingly are using the Internet as both a research and a communication tool. Being able to navigate the Internet as well as evaluate and apply information obtained through it is an essential skill for merchants of all types.

FIGURE 1.15
Saks Incorporated's management training program prepares individuals for both store-line and buying-line positions. Courtesy of Saks Incorporated. Photo courtesy of JWG Associates, Inc.

Organizational Skills

Merchandising positions require careful orchestration of the human and fiscal resources of the organization. The administrative skills necessary to manage time, develop procedures, and prioritize tasks are critical to the success of a merchandising executive.

Mobility

Mobility is a requirement for some merchandising positions. Large multi-store organizations sometimes require store executives to relocate, and buyers must be willing to travel to domestic and foreign markets. Though company-paid travel adds to the attractiveness of a buying position, the travel is often not as glamorous as it seems. Buying trips allow little time for sightseeing and other recreational activities, because typically there is much to accomplish in a short time.

Good taste is sometimes considered a qualification for merchandising positions, especially in the area of fashion goods. However, the ability to translate customers' tastes into merchandise assortments is more important than personal taste. Upon reviewing a fashion jewelry line, a buyer of impeccable taste once declared to the sales representative: "This is the ugliest, most ostentatious line that I've seen this season! I'll take it. My customers will love it!"

Many organizations have structured training programs to groom aspiring merchandising executives to fill projected employment needs. Trainees are promoted from entry-level positions to more advanced levels of responsibility upon successful completion of specified levels of training. Because of the desirability of these programs, competition for entrance into them is intense, and the result of an intense screening process. Large retail organizations are more likely than smaller companies to have structured training programs.

macysJOBS.com | About Macy's East | Career Opportunities | Profiles of Success | Learning & Development | Work-Life Benefits | Where to Live, Where to Play

Career Opportunities
Why Here? Why Now?
Careers in the Spotlight
Career Paths
Job Descriptions

🐦 Search Jobs
▶ College Recruitment
❓ Questions
📷 Shop Online

www.retailology.com CAREER CHOICES
www.fds.com

Home >> Career Opportunities >> Planner

Planner

The following job description may or may not reflect an active job opening at Macy's East. Please click on the "Search Jobs" link to view active employment opportunities and submit your applicant profile online.

Overview of Position
The Planner is responsible for developing seasonal plans by analyzing historical data and forecasting trends by store for a specific area of business.

Key Accountabilities
- Developing departmental plans with buying team for a specific are of the business.
- Developing key item plans for inventory level and sales plan.
- Monitoring stock levels for key items and determine sell through and key item impact.
- Allocating merchandise and ensuring proper distribution.
- Monitoring replenishment of inventory and adjust existing models to assist in meeting and exceeding overall sales and margin plan.
- Communicating inventory level to buyer for approved re-orders.
- Training and development of Assistant and/or Associate Planner talent.

Skills Summary
The Planner position requires strong written and verbal communication skills and the ability to work well with all levels in the organization. The Planner must possess strong analytical skills, be detail conscious, and be proficient in basic and advanced computer skills.

⭐ **macy's EAST** | About Macy's East | Career Opportunities | Profiles of Success | Learning & Development | Work-Life Benefits | Where to Live, Where to Play

Career Opportunities
Why Here? Why Now?
Careers in the Spotlight
Career Paths
Job Descriptions

🐦 Search Jobs
▶ Another School of Thought
❓ Questions
📷 Shop Online

www.retailology.com CAREER CHOICES
www.fds.com

Home >> Career Opportunities >> Director of Distribution and Planning

Director of Distribution and Planning

The following job description may or may not reflect an active job opening at Macy's East. Please click on the "Search Jobs" link to view active employment opportunities and submit your applicant profile online.

Overview of Position
The Director of Distribution and Planning (DDP) oversees the management of merchandise at the location level to maximize and achieve financial objectives and profitability for a specific family of business.

Key Accountabilities
- Directing planning team to produce sales and profit through development of by-store strategies.
- Managing, coaching, and developing Managers of Planning (MPD).
- Supporting the execution of sales and profit goals through proper planning and execution of merchandise plans.
- Oversee the development of location plans to support the demographic needs and business opportunities.
- Working with the buying organization to develop by-store assortment plans which support overall business and promotional strategies.
- Fostering a growth environment that promotes professional development of the planners and their business, and sets the example for development of assistant and associate planners.

Skills Summary
- 4-7 years of retail planner or buyer experience.
- 1-3 years of supervisory skills of one or more persons.
- Strong analytical skills.
- Strong written and verbal communication skills.
- Ability to develop strong partnerships.
- Ability to communicate with all levels of the organization.
- Understands competitor strengths and weaknesses.

FIGURE 1.16
The growth of large retail chains has fostered greater specialization in executing the buying function.
Source: macysJOBS.com.

---

macysJOBS.com | About Macy's East | Career Opportunities | Profiles of Success | Learning & Development | Work-Life Benefits | Where to Live, Where to Play

Career Opportunities
Why Here? Why Now?
Careers in the Spotlight
Career Paths
Job Descriptions

🐦 Search Jobs
▶ College Recruitment
❓ Questions
📷 Shop Online

www.retailology.com CAREER CHOICES
www.fds.com

Home >> Career Opportunities >> Assistant Buyer

Assistant Buyer

The following job description may or may not reflect an active job opening at Macy's East. Please click on the "Search Jobs" link to view active employment opportunities and submit your applicant profile online.

Overview of Position:
The Assistant Buyer is the entry level central buying position within Macy's East. The Assistant Buyer is primarily responsible for the execution of a set business strategy and management of the office.

Key accountabilities:
- Financial analysis of the business for all stores.
- Communicating with vendors in their specific family of business.
- Interacting with store executives to discuss best sellers and merchandise placement.
- Presenting advertising layouts for future publications.
- Monitoring stock levels by door.
- Tracking departmental receipt flows for new and re-ordered merchandise.

Skill Summary
The Assistant Buyer position is both fast paced and dynamic. Individuals need to be multi-task oriented, detail conscious, and have strong communication skills. The position includes financial analysis and requires an understanding of basic computer skills.

SOURCE
Macy's. (2006). Macy's Northwest, Learning and Development.
www.retailology.com/macysnorthwest/training/index.asp.

THE MACY'S NORTHWEST ACADEMY

Macy's Northwest Academy was created to provide consistent, high quality, skill-based training, motivation, and leadership to all participants. It is a corporate university that not only administers and delivers training designed to develop future leaders, but also provides the tools and knowledge necessary for our employees to be successful in their jobs. Outside the classroom, our faculty serve as internal consultants, whether it is providing assistance in focusing on important issues and translating resolutions into actionable plans, or collaborating with managers to achieve their objectives by building effective, diverse teams. While a corporate university is a known concept among business organizations, many members of the training team have advanced their credentials further by becoming state-certified vocational instructors. All of them demonstrate a commitment to lifelong learning through on-going professional and skill development. The faculty is a combination of training consultants and employees representing all facets of the business who facilitate delivery as subject matter experts.

There are a number of certificate programs offered:

- Corporate Management Skills Development Program
- Merchant Development Program
- Planner Development Program
- Store Executive Development Program
- Furniture Sales Executive Program
- Product Knowledge Training and Vendor Seminar Program

Curricula focus on outcomes, and are updated to ensure optimum professional and personal growth. Macy's is committed to supporting and increasing each person's productivity, while meeting the needs of the "whole person" in the process.

Our promise is to provide professional, service-focused training and learning opportunities consistent in quality and execution to every employee participating in the programs. To this end, our goal is to be proactive, seeking new opportunities and avenues to grow the people who grow our business.

Colleges and universities have responded to students' growing interest in retailing careers. Funded in part by a grant from Sears, Indiana University developed a Center for Education and Research in Retailing. The center's goal is to forge alliances between the retail industry and the university by involving retail executives in curriculum planning and development, and by sponsoring conferences on topics of interest to retailers nationwide. Retail organizations have been highly supportive of higher education's outreach endeavors. Founded in 1983, the Center for Retailing Studies at Texas A&M University is sponsored by more than 50 prominent retail organizations.

SUMMARY POINTS
- The marketing channel represents the flow of goods from point of production to point of consumption.
- Marketing channel members are sometimes bypassed in the distribution process in the interest of time or cost.
- Performing more than one function in the marketing channel is called vertical integration.
- A table of organization depicts a company's corporate structure and defines an organization's lines of communication and responsibility.
- Paul Mazur proposed a table of organization for retailers that included four major functions: merchandising, publicity, control, and store management.
- Line functions are fundamental to an organization's mission. Staff functions are support functions. Merchandising and store operations are a retailer's line functions.
- Retail merchandising includes all of the activities associated with buying, pricing, presenting, and promoting merchandise at both store and corporate level.
- Merchandise procurement responsibilities are defined by four functions: planning, buying, distribution, and product development. The responsibilities associated with these functions are typically defined by department.
- Store-level merchandising ensures that merchandise is presented in a manner consistent with a company's visual merchandising standards and that inventory levels and assortments are appropriate for the store's customers and sales objectives.

• Decision-making skills, communication skills, analytical skills, computer skills, and organizational skills are necessary for those pursuing merchandising careers.

KEY TERMS AND CONCEPTS

buyer	general manager	retailer
consumer	general merchandise	retail merchandising
corporate function	manager	staff function
department	line function	store merchandise
department manager	manufacturer-	manager
distributor	sponsored specialty	store operations
district manager	store	store planning
division	marketing channel	table of organization
divisional merchandise	planner	vertical integration
manager	producer	visual merchandising
fashion director	product developer	wholesaler
field function	regional manager	

THINKING ABOUT IT

1. Wal-Mart has become the world's largest retailer by consistently offering quality merchandise at low prices. Clean, convenient, customer-friendly environments have further enhanced the company's growth both domestically and abroad. Wal-Mart's ability to cut operating costs by streamlining distribution and eliminating intermediaries has been instrumental in increasing its profitability, and creating its reputation as a Wall Street sweetheart. Yet some have criticized Wal-Mart for eliminating intermediaries. What do critics have to say about streamlined distribution at Wal-Mart? What are the advantages and disadvantages? Who wins, and who loses?

2. Except in the case of small, independently owned specialty stores, the buying and selling functions within retail organizations typically are separate. In large, multi-unit retail operations, the buying function is performed at a central office, remote from the stores. Essentially, these buyers create assortments of merchandise for stores they have never seen and customers they will never meet. Consider the separation of the buying and selling functions in retail stores. What are the advan-

tages and disadvantages of splitting or combining the two functions? How does the role of buyer in a small specialty store different from the role of buyer in a large organization?

3. Which corporate merchandising position is most appealing to you? Which store merchandising position? Why? Is there a great demand for candidates for these positions?

4. Compare your aptitudes to the qualifications for success in retail merchandising. What are your strengths and weaknesses? How can you improve the areas in which you perceive yourself as weak? Does the academic program in which you are enrolled adequately prepare you to become a merchant? If not, can course electives or experiential learning opportunities, such as an internship or cooperative education experiences, augment your program of study?

5. Jennifer is the general manager of the local Macy's. Jason is the store manager of a Gap store in the same mall. How do their jobs differ in terms of responsibilities, required skills, and compensation?

TEAMING UP

1. Form teams of at least three members. Each member of your team should then choose a brand-name product line sold at manufacturer-sponsored specialty stores, outlet stores, and department stores. Visit the stores and compare shopping experiences relative to price, assortment, merchandise quality, service, and ambience at each type of store. From the perspective of a consumer, what are the differences among the three types of shopping venues? What are the similarities? Share your observations as a group.

2. Each member of the team should choose and then research a vertically integrated producer that distributes its product line through manufacturer-sponsored specialty stores and/or outlet stores, as well as through traditional retailing channels such as department stores. Does it seem that this type of vertical integration is growing? That is, are more and more producers of brand-name product lines choosing to be their own retailers? If yes, what reasons can you cite to explain why this is happening?

3. Each member of the team should find information on a major retail organization with an executive training program. The team should create a grid listing each retailer and pertinent training program infor-

mation, such as qualifications for acceptance, the type of training involved, the duration of the training program, and ultimate job placement objectives. The grid can serve as an informational source for students pursuing jobs upon graduation.

4. Many executive training programs have two career tracks: one to prepare trainees for managerial positions in stores and the other for corporate-level positions. Each member of your team should find a major retail organization with a dual-track executive-training program and answer the following questions. What are the qualifications for each track? How do the tracks differ? How does the training for each track differ? To what degree does each track require decision making skills, communication skills, analytical/problem-solving skills, computer skills, organizational skills, and mobility? Consider other skills that would be valuable in one or both tracks, such as people skills and negotiation skills. Explain how someone might be qualified for one track and not the other.

SEARCHING THE NET

1. Search for retail growth projections for the next decade. Do the projections differ by category of merchandise? Which categories seem to be growing fastest? Which seem to be stagnating?

2. Search for job descriptions for product developers at various retail stores using the "careers" buttons on their web sites. Are the job descriptions consistent? How do they differ among different types of stores? Just what do product developers do?

3. Search for job openings at some large retail organizations using the "careers" button on their web sites. For which types of jobs does it seem that there is the greatest demand for candidates?

CHAPTER TWO

Retailing Formats

By definition, all retailers sell goods and/or services to final consumers. However, retailers differentiate themselves from each other by factors such as the type of merchandise offered, pricing strategies, and the size and location of their facilities. Though every retail organization struggles for uniqueness in the marketplace, many adopt similar merchandising and operational strategies. This chapter classifies retailers according to those similarities.

DEPARTMENT AND SPECIALTY STORES

Some retail stores are classified by characteristics of their assortments. Breadth refers to the number of unique items in a selection of merchandise. An extensive selection is described as *wide* or *broad* in terms of breadth. A limited selection is described as *narrow*. Depth refers to the assortment within a selection. An extensive assortment is described as *deep*. A limited assortment is described as *shallow*. Wal-Mart offers its customers a broad selection of merchandise that includes sporting goods, office products, and hardware. The assortments within these categories are shallow, however, when compared to assortments at stores dedicated exclusively to these merchandise categories, such as Sports Authority, Staples, and Home Depot. None of the three can match Wal-Mart in terms of overall breadth, but within the categories in which they specialize, they carry deeper assortments than Wal-Mart.

There is often a trade-off between breadth of selection and depth of assortment for the obvious reason that having extensive breadth *and* depth would require a mammoth store. A retailer that increases a store's breadth by adding new categories of merchandise consumes space that might otherwise be dedicated to maintaining deep assortments within categories. A retailer that decreases a store's breadth by eliminating categories of merchandise frees space to deepen assortments. Such decisions have considerable profit implications. Limited Brands, Inc., the parent organization of

FIGURE 2.1
Department stores have
considerable breadth in
that they offer multiple
categories of merchandise.
Macy's courtesy Fairchild
Publications, Inc.; JC
Penney courtesy Altoon +
Porter.

Express and Victoria's Secret, has improved its profit performance over the years by carrying deeper assortments of fewer but more profitable items in its stores.

Some retail stores are identified by the breadth or depth of their offerings. A department store has considerable breadth in that it carries many categories of merchandise. Softlines, such as apparel and household-textile products, are the mainstay of department store offerings. *Full-line* department stores also offer hardlines, or nontextile products, such as furniture and consumer electronics.

A department store satisfies the shopping needs of a diverse group of consumers, including men, women, and children, with goods at more than one price level. Department store prices are based on conventional pricing strategies for the products and/or manufacturers' suggested retail prices.[1] Department stores carry well-known, nationally distributed, brand-name merchandise, such as Estée Lauder cosmetics, Dockers menswear, and Calphalon cookware, and complement their selections of brands with private labels. Some highly recognized department store names include Bloomingdale's, Dillard's, and Macy's.

A specialty store has limited breadth in that it carries a single or limited number of merchandise categories such as casual apparel, footwear, jewelry, or tableware. Specialty stores cater to a narrowly defined group of customers often characterized by gender, income, or lifestyle segment. Career women, gourmet cooks, and trend-conscious teens are some of the customers to whom specialty stores cater. Specialty stores can be single-unit, privately owned operations or they can be part of a chain of several hundred stores, such as Ann Taylor, Banana Republic, and Pottery Barn.

In general, specialty store offerings are characterized as narrow and deep. Though their selections are limited to one or a few categories of merchandise, the assortments within these categories are usually extensive. Department stores offer greater breadth than specialty stores, but typically not as much depth. However, in recent years, most department stores have deemphasized their hardlines categories, thus permitting greater depth within their softlines offerings. The depth/ breadth gap that once separated department stores and specialty stores has narrowed, so that many department stores rival the deep assortments of their specialty store competitors.

The Status of Department Stores

Department stores can trace their origin to major cities in the nineteenth century and had humble beginnings as dry-goods stores. Eventually these stores grew to dominate city blocks as multifloor emporiums with hundreds of categories of merchandise, including toys, sporting goods, and major appliances. Department stores became centers of fashion. Apparel was departmentalized by price, ranging from "bargain basement" and "main floor," to the higher-priced goods on upper floors. Services, such as hair salons, restaurants, and travel agencies, were typical department store offerings.[2] Nearly every city boasted at least one major department store. In larger cities, multiple department stores evolved, typically competing with one another to become preeminent in terms of prestige. Department stores became symbols of modern living and upward mobility, their buyers arbiters of taste.[3]

As customers flocked to the suburbs, department stores followed with scaled-down versions of their urban stores called "branches." Over time, many

FIGURE 2.2
Specialty stores cater to a specific need of a narrrowly defined group of customers. Courtesy Fairchild Publications, Inc.

hardlines were eliminated from department store assortments. Low-end price points in softlines were dropped to make room for the moderate price points that have become the staple of a department store's business. Today, department stores are almost universally anchors, or major tenants, within suburban malls. Except in tourist destination cities, such as Chicago, New York, Seattle, and San Francisco, most urban department stores have closed.[4]

The department store industry has experienced considerable decline in recent decades. Many venerable department stores have closed, including Gimbel's of New York, Frederick & Nelson of Seattle, Garfinkel's of Washington, D.C., and Joske's of San Antonio, to name a few. Still others have lost their local identity through corporate mergers and acquisitions.

FIGURE 2.3
Macy's on State Street in Chicago is among the few remaining department store "emporiums." © AP Photo/Brian Kersey.

The monikers of Burdines of Miami, Dayton's of Minneapolis, Hudson's of Detroit, Marshall Field's of Chicago, and Rich's of Atlanta are merely memories. Because of store closures, an aging customer base, intense competition from specialty stores, and a declining market share, analysts question the long-term viability of department stores. From 1995 to 2005, department store market share dropped from 11 percent of all retail sales to 7 percent.[5]

The department store remains, however, an important segment of the retail industry. Producers rely on department stores to give credibility to their brand names and introduce new products and innovative styles. Customers appreciate the convenience of one-stop shopping at department stores, and shopping centers rely on department stores to draw shoppers and to define their image. The department store, though greatly changed from what it was a century ago, is likely here to stay.[6]

Hard-to-Classify Stores

Some stores fit neither the department store nor the specialty store mold, catering to too few customer needs to be a department store or to too many

SOURCE
Kooker, N. (August 27, 2006). Implementing Change in the Kitchen. *Boston Globe*. p. E3.

IMPLEMENTING CHANGE IN THE KITCHEN

The founder of Williams-Sonoma claims that a zester is a necessity in any kitchen with so many recipes calling for the grated rind of some kind of citrus; and it was Chuck Williams who introduced zesters to the United States. At a time when French, Italian, Spanish, and Chinese cooking were foreign to the U.S., Williams opened the first Williams-Sonoma store just north of San Francisco with a product line that included French soufflé dishes, Spanish paella pans, Chinese woks, and Italian pasta machines. Williams' store design was unique. People compared his displays of table- and cookware to art gallery displays. And his business sense was as keen as his artistic sense. When cookie cutters didn't sell, he built a "cookie tree" on which to hang the various molds. And they sold. Williams began selling cookbooks at a time when bookstores were the only venue through which cookbooks were distributed.

A 1953 trip to Paris was Williams' inspiration. There he found that sturdy, thick-bottom pans used commercially in restaurants in the U.S. were used in homes in France. He thought, "So why not in the U.S.?" Three years later he opened the first Williams-Sonoma store with everything from Swedish cup-and-saucer sets to heavy cotton aprons designed by his mother, Nettie Marie Shaw Williams, a restaurateur in her own right.

customer needs to be a specialty store. These stores are crossbreeds that fall somewhere in the middle of a continuum defined at one end by department stores and the other end by specialty stores. Stores such as Saks Fifth Avenue, Neiman Marcus, and Nordstrom are consistent with the department store paradigm in that they are large, multi-departmental units that often anchor shopping centers. These stores resemble specialty stores, however, in that their offerings are almost exclusively apparel. In spite of their limited breadth, these stores typically are classified as department stores, though they sometimes are called *departmentalized specialty stores* or *specialty department stores*. The stores often are referred to as *upscale* or *high-end* department stores, indicative of the quality and price of their offerings, while larger department store formats are often referred to as *moderate*.

Because of their coast-to-coast expanse of hundreds of broadly assorted stores, J.C. Penney and Sears have been called *general merchandise chains* or *national department stores*. These terms are dated, however, and seldom used. Though lacking the panache of many of its competitors, J.C. Penney generally is considered a department store. Likewise, Sears is a department store with greater breadth than other department stores.

FIGURE 2.4
Some stores, such as Neiman Marcus, seem too large to be specialty stores but too small to be department stores.
Courtesy Fairchild Publications, Inc.

DISCOUNTING

A discounter is a retailer that sells goods at prices that are lower than the conventional prices of other retailers. Buying goods at low wholesale prices and maintaining low operating expenses are fundamental to a discounter's low-price strategy. Discounters procure goods at favorable prices by buying large quantities of first-quality goods or by buying manufacturers' close-outs, end-of-season merchandise, and overruns. They maintain low operating expenses with operationally efficient, "no-frills" facilities. Self-service is another concept that contributes to operational efficiency at discount stores. Customer purchases are processed at a centralized checkout area, or *front end*. This approach to customer service is more economical than the decentralized type of customer service at conventional stores. Labor-intensive supplementary services, such as gift wrap and alterations, are also absent at discounters.

The emergence of discounting as a significant sector of the U.S. retail industry did not occur until after World War II; however, discounters can be traced back to the turn of the twentieth century when "undersellers," such as S. Klein of Manhattan and J.W. May of Brooklyn, sold apparel at prices that undercut department stores.

Types of Discounters

Discounting is a highly diverse retail industry segment. There are several types of discounters, each unique in terms of merchandising strategy:

Full-Line Discounter   A full-line, or *general merchandise*, discounter offers a wide selection of merchandise that often includes apparel, home accessories, consumer electronics, housewares, health and beauty care products, and toys. Offerings sometimes include automotive and hardware. Full-line discounters feature low-price brands not offered by department stores, including Hanes underwear, Wrangler jeans, and Maybelline cosmetics. Like department stores, full-line discounters complement their branded offerings with private label merchandise, especially in apparel categories. Some full-line discounters have tried to create a more upscale image by offering higher-priced brands and by emulating the decor, fixturing, and merchandise presentation strategies of department and specialty stores.[7]

The full-line discounting sector once comprised dozens of regional operators with stores in a few states or a specific region of the country. Most regional discounters did not withstand the competition from the "Big Three" discounters—Wal-Mart, Kmart, and Target—as they emerged to become national discounters with coast-to-coast stores. ShopKo in Green Bay, Wisconsin, is the exception. With more than 150 stores in 13 states, the regional full-line discounter is alive and well at this writing.

Category Killer   A category killer, or *specialty discounter*, offers a deep assortment of brand-name merchandise within a single merchandise category. Category killers "kill" the category of business for more generalized

retail formats, such as department stores and full-line discounters, whose assortments are shallow by comparison. Circuit City (consumer electronics), Home Depot (home improvement), Sports Authority (sporting goods), and Staples (office products) are well-known category killers. Although many category killers specialize in hardlines, some specialize in softlines. Operating more than 700 stores nationwide, Men's Wearhouse is a Houston-based category killer, offering deep assortments of men's tailored clothing at prices 20 to 30 percent less than department stores.[8]

A category killer's success often is rooted in identifying an unsatisfied need in the marketplace. The founders of Home Depot determined that consumers bought do-it-yourself (DIY) merchandise at either full-line discount stores, where prices were low but service was poor, or at small, privately owned "mom-and-pop" hardware stores, where service was good but prices were high. Arthur Blank and Bernard Marcus developed a 100,000-square-foot home improvement store with 40,000 products, trademark service, and guaranteed low prices, combining the attributes of both full-line discounters and mom-and-pop stores.[9]

Within recent decades, there has been a proliferation of category killers in nearly every category of merchandise. *Chain Store Guide*, a provider of sales and marketing information for retailers, tracks the locations of more than 300,000 retail stores nationwide. Nearly 50,000 of the tracked stores are category killers, a count that exceeds any other store classification other than convenience stores.[10]

Off-Price Discounter   An off-price discounter, or *off-pricer*, buys manufacturers' irregulars, seconds, overruns, closeouts, canceled orders, and

FIGURE 2.6
Category killers are discounters that offer deep assortments of a single category of merchandise. Bed, Bath & Beyond © Alan Schein Photography/ Corbis; Home Depot © Don Smetzer/PhotoEdit; Best Buy © Susan Van Etten/PhotoEdit.

returns from other retailers. Off-pricers also buy end-of-season and closeout merchandise from other retail stores. Though off-pricers have the reputation of carrying damaged goods and last year's styles, many now offer first-quality in-season merchandise. Some manufacturers make goods especially for off-price stores making productive use of extra reams of fabric and slack production time. Positioned as department store competitors, off-pricers sell department store brands at prices 20 to 60 percent less than regular-price retails. TJX Companies, based in Framingham, Massachusetts, operates several leading off-price retail chains including Marshalls, T.J. Maxx, and A.J. Wright.

Closeout Store   A closeout store is a clearance operation through which a retailer eliminates slow-selling or end-of-season merchandise from its regular-price stores. Closeout stores are sometimes criticized for salting their offerings with manufacturers' closeouts that were never part of their regular-price stores' offerings. Nordstrom Rack and Off 5th Saks Fifth Avenue are examples of closeout stores.

Manufacturer's Outlet   A manufacturer's outlet originally was conceived as a "no-frills" break-even operation for unloading a producer's overruns and irregulars. Some outlet stores remain true to the concept, using outlets to sell imperfect, residual, and discontinued goods. Lenox sells dinnerware with flaws at its outlet stores; Coach offers goods sold at regular-price stores in previous seasons at its outlet stores. But today, most manufacturers' outlets are profitable operations in attractive settings with first-quality merchandise. The shift in the outlet concept evolved as producers who operated at less-than-full production capacity found that they could increase production to 100 percent and profitably sell the additional merchandise in outlet stores.

As in the case of manufacturer-sponsored specialty stores, producers that operate outlet stores run the risk of channel conflict by competing with the conventional retail channel members that they supply. The National Shoe Retailers' Association, a trade group of independent shoe retailers, once adopted a resolution criticizing shoe manufacturers that channel first-run merchandise to factory outlet stores in direct competition with their retail accounts, giving the impression that independent shoe retailers are over-priced. To minimize such conflict, some producers, such as Eddie Bauer,

Brooks Brothers, and Tommy Hilfiger, create outlet-only merchandise that is slightly different from the goods distributed through traditional retail channels.[11]

Warehouse Club   A warehouse club, or *membership club*, is a wholesale/retail hybrid that offers deep discounts on a number of food and general-merchandise items. About two-thirds of a warehouse club's business is from small businesses; the other third is from consumers. Customers pay a membership fee to shop in a warehouse club. Thus, a warehouse club generates income even before customers make a single purchase. Operating at the lowest profit margin of any retailer, warehouse clubs epitomize the "no-frills" concept with cement floors and steel-rack fixtures. Supermarkets are

SOURCE
Reference for Business. (2006). Company Histories, Stein Mart. www.referenceforbusiness.com.

STEIN MART

Established in 1902, Stein Mart was originally a general merchandise department store founded by Sam Stein, a Russian immigrant, in Greenville, Mississippi. Upon Stein's death in 1932, his son Jake took over the business, redirecting its focus to buying order cancellations and overproductions from clothing mills. In 1977, Jay Stein, Jake's son, assumed the reins at Stein Mart. Under Jay's direction, new stores were opened in Alabama, Georgia, Louisiana, and Texas. Soon after, Stein Marts cropped up in the Midwest with stores in Indiana, Ohio, and Missouri.

Stein Mart carries brand-name merchandise, including apparel, accessories, hosiery, costume jewelry, glassware, tableware, and cookware, at 25 to 60 percent off of department store prices. Stein Mart is unique as an off-pricer in that its stores have a department store ambiance with plush carpeting, marble flooring, soft lighting, and nice fixturing. Like other discounters, Stein Mart maintains low operating costs with a centralized checkout system. (But there are no shopping carts at Stein Mart!) Unlike other off-pricers who opportunistically buy overstocked or returned merchandise, Stein Mart buyers negotiate lower prices with manufacturers by buying late in the season, about a month after department store buyers have placed their orders.

Stein Mart continues to expand to cities with populations of 125,000 or more. The stores are generally anchors in neighborhood shopping centers. The Stein Mart customer is a woman who regularly shops department stores. She's between 35 and 60 and has a higher-than-average education and income. Stein Mart's strategy for the future includes increasing store productivity and relying heavily on marketing to draw new customers. With more than 100 years of history, the company will remain a popular name in retailing for many years to come.

FROM THE ANNALS OF DISCOUNTING HISTORY

The origins of many discounting formats can be traced to entrepreneurial founders:

- In 1908, Edward Filene opened the Automatic Bargain Basement as a clearance operation to rid the upper floors of his family's namesake department store of markdowns and closeouts. Today, Filene's Basement is an off-price retailer with stores throughout Massachusetts.
- Frieda Loehmann gave birth to off-price discounting in the 1920s when she stalked the designer showrooms on New York's Seventh Avenue in search of samples and canceled shipments to sell at bargain prices in her namesake store in Brooklyn.
- Though its origins are obscure, retail history pundits often identify the Ann and Hope Mill Outlet as the first general merchandise discounter. The Rhode Island–based manufacturer of tinsel and corsage ribbons began selling discounted greeting cards and housedresses in a retail store in 1953.
- The warehouse club was pioneered by Sol Price who opened the first Price Club in San Diego in 1978.

FIGURE 2.7
Warehouse clubs epitomize the "no frills" concept. Courtesy Fairchild Publications, Inc.

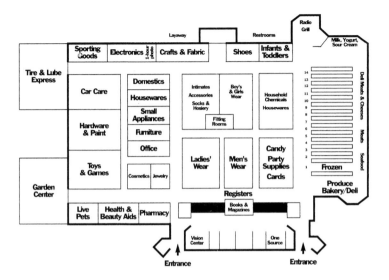

FIGURE 2.8
A supercenter combines
the offerings of a full-
line discounter and a
supermarket under one
roof. Courtesy of Wal-
Mart.

most vulnerable to the competition from warehouse clubs; however, warehouse clubs also compete with general merchandise discounters and category killers. Though a relatively new concept, the format has already matured, leaving little growth opportunity for existing clubs or new entrants. The two largest warehouse club retailers are Costco and Sam's Club, the latter a division of Wal-Mart.

Supercenter   A supercenter, or *combination store*, is a combined supermarket and full-line discount store. The supercenter is actually a scaled-down version of the *hypermarket*, or *les hypers*, an enormous 200,000-square-foot store concept introduced in France in 1960. With assortments ranging from food to fashion, hypermarkets were France's response to a lack of U.S.-style supermarkets, discount stores, and enclosed shopping malls.

A supercenter links the frequency of visit of the food shopper with the higher profit margins of the full-line discounter. Though a relatively new concept in some areas, Meijer of Grand Rapids has been operating in this format for many years, as has Fred Meyer of Portland, Oregon. Epitomizing the concept of one-stop shopping, supercenters are the fastest growing discount store format. Wal-Mart is planning to open 1,500 Wal-Mart Supercenters in the United States over the next several years. Some will be expansions of the company's existing full-line stores.

OTHER RETAILING FORMATS

The retailing formats defined in the previous sections typify most of the retail stores currently operating in the United States. However, the list is in no way exhaustive. Other retailing formats are not as prominent as those just mentioned. Some are specific to a category of merchandise, as discussed in the text that follows.

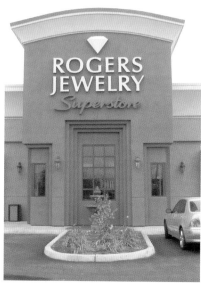

FIGURES 2.9
The term "superstore" is often used to refer to an especially large category killer or specialty store. Rogers Jewelry Superstore courtesy Rogers Jewelry; Niketown © Joseph Sohm, ChromoSohm Inc./Corbis.

Megastore/Superstore   The terms *megastore* and *superstore* often are used to refer to an especially large category killer or specialty store. The 100,000-title book emporiums popularized by Barnes & Noble are called megastores. Located in upscale, high-traffic metropolitan areas, such as New York's Fifth Avenue and Chicago's Michigan Avenue, Niketown is a superstore that features Nike's entire line of athletic footwear in a high-tech, multimedia setting with sports memorabilia displays. Retailers sometimes use the term *superstore* to refer to a store that integrates multiple concepts. Talbots, a specialty retailer of classic women's, men's and children's apparel, defines a Talbots superstore as a store that combines three or more of the seven Talbots concepts such as Talbots Misses, Talbots Petites, Talbots Kids, and Talbots Babies.[12]

Destination Store   A *destination store* is a retailer that has considerable customer drawing power because of a unique or extensive merchandise assortment. Destination stores are attractive as shopping center tenants because of their ability to lure customers. Category killers, such as Home Depot, are considered destination stores. The pharmacies, banks, florists, and quick-processing photo labs in supermarkets are often called *destination services.*

Extreme Value Store   An *extreme value store* is a general merchandise discounter that sells basic household, food, and health and beauty care items. Smaller than other full-line discount stores, extreme value stores cater to low- and fixed-income consumers in locations not often served by larger formats. Family Dollar, which operates more than 5,500 stores, and Dollar General, which has more than 7,000 stores, are the two largest extreme value chains.[13]

Airport Shop   As the name implies, an *airport shop* is located in an airport terminal. These specialty store retailers cater to the many high-income leisure and business travelers who spend considerable time in airports because of flight delays and slack time between check-in and departure times. Sales at airport shops have grown exponentially because of an increase in the amount of time that travelers spend in airports since the September 11, 2001, terror attacks. With more than 100 shops and restaurants, the Greater Pittsburgh International Airport is credited with creating the "airport mall" concept of leasing concourse space to generate a supplemental revenue stream for the airport.

FIGURE 2.11
Spirit of the Red Horse sells Native American jewelry in airports, such as the one in Portland, Oregon. Courtesy CBR Specialty Retail Group.

IF THE SHOE FITS ...

Payless ShoeSource was founded in 1956 in Topeka, Kansas, by two cousins who perfected a revolutionary idea: selling shoes in a self-service environment. The self-service format allowed consumers to browse and try on shoes without waiting for sales help. More than four decades later, the idea continues to provide millions a convenient, friendly shopping experience.

In 1961, Payless became a public company as Volume Shoe Corporation. In 1979, Volume Shoe was acquired by The May Department Stores. In 1996, Payless ShoeSource, Inc. was spun off to shareowners to become an independent, publicly held company. Payless shares trade on the New York Stock Exchange (NYSE) under the trading symbol PSS.

Today, Payless ShoeSource is the largest specialty family footwear retailer in the Western Hemisphere.

The company sold more than 182 million pairs of shoes in fiscal 2005, generating $2.7 billion in net sales. Payless operates stores in all 50 states, plus Puerto Rico, Guam, Saipan, the U.S. Virgin Islands, Canada, Central America, the Caribbean, and South America, and opened its first test store in Japan in 2004. Payless stores feature fashionable, quality footwear and accessories for women, men and children at affordable prices in a self-selection format.

The company's stores are located in a variety of settings, from urban to rural, including malls, strip centers, central business districts, free-standing buildings and, other retail locations.

In addition, Payless ShoeSource operates Payless.com, which cobines the strengths associated with Payless ShoeSource with the convenience of shopping online.

SOURCE
Payless ShoeSource.
(2006). Corporate Info,
About Our Company.
www.payless.com.

Once home to souvenir shops and hot dog stands, airports are now attracting more upscale national retailers such as Gap, Body Shop, and Victoria's Secret. Airport shop offerings sometimes are indigenous to the locale. The retail mix at Washington National Airport includes the National Zoo Store and a Smithsonian Museum Store. Spirit of the Red Horse, a retailer of Native American jewelry, operates a store in the Portland (Oregon) International Airport.[14]

Franchises and Lease Departments

Some retail operations are special types of partnerships between two or more parties. A franchise is a contractual agreement between a *franchisor* and *franchisee* that gives the franchisee the right to sell a franchisor's product line or service. The franchisor often provides a source of supply, a set of operating procedures, and a national advertising program. The franchise is

FIGURE 2.12
Some RadioShack stores
are franchised operations.
© Myrleen Ferguson
Cate/PhotoEdit.

purchased by the franchisee for a price based on the franchise's success record and growth potential. The terms of the franchise agreement are often very rigid, specifying hours of operation, facility design, and so on. This ensures consistency among all franchised operations, a goal fundamental to maintaining the integrity of the franchise. Profits generated from operating the franchise are shared by the franchisor and the franchisee.

The most commonly known franchises are in the fast-food industry. Consumer goods franchises include RadioShack, Athlete's Foot, and Hallmark Cards. Sweets From Heaven is a Pittsburgh-based retailer of bulk and wrapped candy that operates both company-owned stores and franchises. The company's franchising specifications indicate that corner locations in the most heavily trafficked area of shopping centers are preferred sites.

Sometimes franchises are limited to a specific product line. Best known in the retailing of automobiles and gasoline, *product* or *trade franchises* are strategic partnerships between a producer and a retailer to sell a product. The producer provides the retailer with product training and marketing incentives. The retailer, in turn, agrees to maintain specified levels of inventory, sales staffing, and promotional activity. *Authorized dealership* is a term often used to refer to a product or trade franchise. This type of arrangement occurs between many consumer electronics and major appliance producers, such as RCA and Whirlpool, and retailers, such as Circuit City.

A lease department is a retailer that leases space from another retailer to operate as a department within the latter's store. Rent is based on the lease department's sales and the amount of space occupied. The most common types of lease departments include:

- Traffic-generating services, such as restaurants and photography studios.
- Departments with large, difficult-to-manage inventories, such as shoes.
- Departments that require specialized selling, such as fine jewelry.

Some lease departments retain their identity operating as a store within a store. Other lease departments operate anonymously, blending in like any other department adhering to the store's policies, operating procedures, and promotional calendar. Lease departments operate within many different types of retailing formats. Finlay Enterprises operates fine jewelry departments within department stores, including Bon-Ton, Dillard's, and divisions of Federated Department Stores. Cole National Corporation operates more than 800 Sears Optical Centers.[15]

Dying Breeds

Retailing is a dynamic industry within which new formats are always evolving. Constant changes in consumer buying habits, however, have made casualties as frequent as births in the retail industry. The *catalog showroom* and the *variety store* are two long-standing retailing formats that are now virtually extinct.

The catalog showroom was a discount retailer of jewelry, consumer electronics, home accessories, sporting goods, and juvenile products. Catalog showrooms flourished in the decades following World War II by selling department store brands at discounted prices at a time when other discounters sold only low-quality "off-brands." However, catalog showrooms had difficulty withstanding competition from the category killers and full-line discounters offering major brands at competitive prices. Service Merchandise was the last of the major catalog showrooms. Today, Service Merchandise is an online retailer.

S-26— Central Avenue, St. Petersburg, Fla., "The Sunshine City"

FIGURE 2.13
Variety stores once dotted virtually every downtown shopping area. Courtesy National Building Museum.

The *variety store*, also know as the *5&10* or *dime store*, dates back to the nineteenth century when merchants such as Sebastian S. Kresge and Frank W. Woolworth opened stores that sold goods at five- and ten-cent retails. Inflation and expanded assortments that included housewares, linens, fashion jewelry, and cosmetics eventually made "5&10" a misnomer. Variety stores remained a dominant retailing format for many decades, dotting virtually every downtown shopping area and the earliest suburban shopping centers. Variety stores had difficulty competing with a growing number of full-line discounters that offered many of the same merchandise categories in greater depth. Recognizing the dismal future of this format, some of the major variety store chains diversified into areas with greater growth potential. In 1962, the S.S. Kresge Company opened the first Kmart in a Detroit suburb, and eventually abandoned its variety store format. Likewise, F.W. Woolworth became a diversified conglomerate of specialty stores operating under banners that include Foot Locker, Champs Sports, and Northern Reflections.[16] The five-and-dime era came to an end in 1997 when F.W. Woolworth, then owned by the Venator Group, announced the closing of its remaining Woolworth stores.[17]

NONSTORE RETAILERS

Some retailers conduct business without storefront facilities. Direct marketing is a term that defines a direct relationship between a retailer and a customer without the use of a retail store. There are two forms of direct marketing. Direct selling uses personal explanation or demonstration to sell a product. Direct response marketing uses a nonpersonal print or electronic medium to communicate with customers.

Direct Selling

Door-to-door selling and the party plan are two commonly known forms of direct selling. An age-old form of direct selling, door-to-door selling is the practice of canvassing customers at home. The declining number of women at home during the day and an increasing reluctance to open the door to strangers have all but eradicated door-to-door sales. Avon, remembered for its famous "Avon calling" door-to-door campaign, has virtually abandoned door-to-door selling. The company now targets women in the workplace as both sales representatives and customers. To attract younger customers, Avon has developed a new line of cosmetics for women 16 to 24 called Mark. Avon advertises the line on MTV.[18]

The party plan is a form of direct selling in which a demonstrator presents product line to a group of customers in the home of a host/hostess. Proponents of party plans claim that face-to-face selling in a festive atmos-

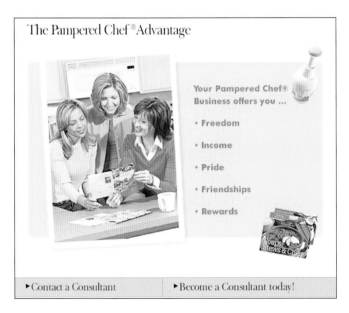

FIGURE 2.14
The Pampered Chef is an example of direct selling in a nonstore retailing format that relies on face-to-face interaction with customers. Source: www.pamperedchef.com.

phere is a sure way to generate sales and build both customer loyalty and repeat business. Though stay-at-home moms are a major customer segment for party plan retailers, Tupperware, a marketer of high-quality plastic storage containers, has taken the party out of the home and into the workplace with "rush-hour parties" held at the end of the workday. Tupperware also targets an increasing number of single households by including men in their market. Other well known party plan retailers include The Pampered Chef, a marketer of cookware and kitchen gadgetry, Southern Living at Home, a marketer of tableware and decorative accessories, and Mary Kay cosmetics. Some retailers use party plans as an adjunct to storefront operations. Body Shop At Home is an offshoot of Body Shop, a retailer of skin- and hair-care products.

Party demonstrators are entrepreneurial retailers who start their own business with an investment in a startup kit that includes a procedure manual and sample products. According to the Direct Selling Association, a trade association of manufacturers and distributors of goods sold directly to consumers through independent sales agents, party plan retailing is the nation's fastest growing direct selling segment, with a stream of constantly emerging new concepts. Based in Orange, California, Footprints International is a new party plan retailer targeted to shoe lovers.[19]

Network marketing, *or multilevel marketing*, is a strategy used by some direct selling organizations to reward sales representatives for recruiting other sales reps. Commissions are based on personal sales as well as the sales of a "downline" of recruits. Among the largest network marketers are Amway household products and Nu Skin skin-care products.

FIGURE 2.15
Talbots is an example of a retailer that uses catalogs to supplement its storefront business. Courtesy Talbots.

wait no more
FALL HAS ARRIVED

Talbots

IT'S A CLASSIC
Misses, Petites and a selection of Talbots Woman and Talbots

Catalog Retailing

Catalog, or *mail-order*, retailing is a form of direct response marketing. Catalogs were originally intended for customers who lacked convenient access to retail stores. However, the focus of catalogs changed as shopping centers and automobiles made stores accessible to virtually all customers. Today's catalogs are intended for time-pressed consumers who want the convenience of shopping at home. The Direct Marketing Association reports the existence of more than 10,000 catalogs of consumer goods.[20] Some of the largest catalog merchants include Lands' End and L.L. Bean.

Full-line general merchandise catalogs were once the hallmark of catalog retailing. However, in 1993, Sears abandoned the publication of its 1,500-page Big Book, marking the end of the general merchandise catalog era. Catalog retailing has evolved into a specialty business targeted to specific customers and specific customer needs. Sears publishes several smaller-than-Big Book catalogs, including its holiday Wish Book and a catalog that features Sears Craftsman hardware and power tools.[21]

Some catalog companies are diversified retailers that publish multiple catalogs. The Williams-Sonoma family of catalogs includes Williams-Sonoma, Pottery Barn, Pottery Barn Kids, PBteen, West Elm, and Williams-Sonoma Home. Some companies spin off storefront operations from their catalogs. Though essentially a catalog retailer of high-end gift items, Sharper Image also operates nearly 100 stores. J. Jill, a subsidiary of Talbots, began as a catalog operation. Today there are nearly 200 J. Jill stores catering to the apparel needs of suburban women age 35 to 55.

Rising paper and postage costs pose constant threats to the viability of catalog retailers. To combat inflation, many catalog retailers have reduced catalog dimensions, number of pages, and circulation.

Electronic Retailing

Electronic retailing is the most contemporary form of direct response retailing. Often referred to as *home shopping*, electronic retailing has three formats that use television as the direct response medium:

- An *infomercial* is a program-length product demonstration. Infomercials have become a popular format for selling cookware, exercise equipment, and various types of services. The Ronco products hawked by well-known pitch man Ron Popeil are familiar to anyone who has ever

SHOWTIME® STANDARD
ROTISSERIE & BBQ OVEN

CREATING HEALTHFUL FOOD
HAS NEVER BEEN THIS EASY.
JUST SET IT AND FORGET IT!

Ron Popeil

FIGURE 2.16
Ron Popeil has become an
infomercial celebrity.
Source: www.ronco.com.

tuned into Saturday daytime television. Some of Ronco's best-selling products are the 5-Tray Electric Food Dehydrator, the Inside-The-Shell Egg Scrambler, and Popeil's Pasta Maker.[22]

- A *television shopping channel* is a cable channel dedicated to talk-show-style programming in which merchandise is presented to viewers who can then order by phone. Analysts once predicted that television shopping would quickly evolve into a $150 billion retail segment that would threaten the viability of conventional retailing. Instead, shopping channels have had problems with a tawdry image and the fact that time-pressed customers are unwilling to adjust their schedules to view the shows. QVC and HSN are the two major shopping channels.

- *Interactive television* is a form of electronic shopping in which consumers take electronic "shopping trips" on their TV screens and then place an order, charge it to a credit card, and choose a delivery option by using a remote and a modem. The availability of interactive television is limited because of the high cost involved in replacing existing cable wire with fiber-optic cable needed for interactive television. As a result, interactive shopping is growing slowly.

Online Retailing

Online retailing, or *e-commerce*, is an increasingly popular form of electronic retailing in which a retailer operates a web site that allows customers to shop over the Internet. The Internet has become the shopping medium for millions of shoppers, generating more than $200 billion in annual sales, a number that has doubled in three years. People are more likely to buy certain products online than others. Some are reluctant to buy apparel online because of concerns over fit; others are reluctant to buy food online. However, most customers are as likely to buy familiar, brand-name products online as they are to buy them at brick-and-mortar stores.[23]

Most retailers use e-commerce to augment other selling formats such as stores and catalogs. Today, there is hardly a major storefront or catalog retailer that does not have a web site for selling online.

A TYPO THAT LIVES ON

Lands' End is a retailer based in Dodgeville, Wisconsin, that specializes in casual apparel and household-textile products. Its name reflects its heritage; the company started as a sailboat equipment retailer in 1963. The misplaced apostrophe in "Lands' End" was a typographical error that the founders elected to ignore since promotional materials had already been printed by the time the error was discovered. Lands' End was purchased by Sears in 2002. Sears continued the Lands' End store, mail order, and Internet businesses, and also began offering Lands' End apparel in Sears stores.

Primarily a cataloger, Lands' End publishes an array of specialty catalogs, including its flagship catalog for men and women; Lands' End Women; Lands' End Women's Plus (for women 16W–26W); Lands' End Men; Lands' End Kids (for newborns to pre-teens); Lands' End for School (with school uniforms and school-appropriate clothing); Lands' End Home; and Lands' End Business Outfitters, which features embroidered company-logo apparel, and gifts and service awards.

Lands' End was an early adopter of e-commerce. The retailer's original web site featured 100 products as well as the stories, essays, and travelogues for which Lands' End has become famous. Today, the web site features every current Lands' End product, as well as an Overstocks section with deeply discounted over-runs. Lands' End has been a leader in developing new tools for enhancing the online shopping experience including:

- My Virtual Model—Customers create an image of themselves by providing personal measurements from which a virtual model is developed to "try on" clothing.
- Lands' End Live—Customers chat online with a Lands' End customer-service representative.
- Lands' End Custom—By answering a few questions about fit preferences and body type, a customer can have tailor-made garments delivered in two to four weeks.
- Swim Finder—A feature that makes a bathing suit choice for the customer relative to style, leg opening, bra type, body shape, and the body areas that should be accentuated or camouflaged.
- Outerwear Headquarters—Customers are guided to the right jacket, coat, or parka based on the weather conditions that prevail where they live.

SOURCE
Lands' End. (2006). About Us. www.landsend.com.

Online retailing is also a vertical integration opportunity for manufacturers who wish to sell their product directly to consumers. The Timex web site has a search feature that sorts watches by gender and end-use categories such as fashion, dress, outdoor, sports and fitness, and technology. The web site also features a store locator for shoppers who choose to browse on the Internet but make their actual purchase face-to-face. A few retailers, such as Amazon.com, have adopted online retailing as their only selling format. With 55 million customers and more than $4 billion in annual sales,

Amazon.com is as well-known as any storefront retailer, selling everything from books to treadmills.

Online retailers encourage Internet shopping with special web-only features and deals such as free shipping. On Best Buy's web site (www.best buy.com), customers can create three-dimensional kitchen or laundry models with Best Buy products.[24] On the Lands' End web site (www. landsend.com), a customer can create a three-dimensional virtual model of him- or herself based on input on hair color, height, and waist and shoulder measurements. The model can then "try on" items that the customer selects from the pages of the web site to get an idea of how the selected items will look on his/her body.[25]

SUMMARY POINTS

- *Breadth* refers to the number of unique items within an assortment. *Depth* refers to the selection within an assortment.
- A department store satisfies multiple customer needs with many categories of merchandise. A specialty store caters to the specific needs of a narrowly defined group of customers.
- Discounters offer low prices in a "no-frills" setting. There are several distinct types of discounters: full-line discounters, category killers, off-pricers, closeout stores, manufacturers' outlets, warehouse clubs, and supercenters.
- Other retailing formats include franchises and lease departments.
- Direct marketing is nonstore retailing; direct response marketing employs a nonpersonal medium to communicate with customers; direct selling involves personal selling.

KEY TERMS AND CONCEPTS

anchor

breadth

catalog retailing

category killer

closeout store

department store

depth

direct marketing

direct response
 marketing

direct selling

discounter

door-to-door
 selling

e-commerce

electronic
 retailing

franchise

full-line discounter

hardlines

lease department

manufacturer's
 outlet

network marketing

off-price discounter

party plan

softlines

specialty store

supercenter

warehouse club

THINKING ABOUT IT

1. What is your impression of department stores? Who shops at them? Compare the merchandise assortments of two competitive department stores. Which of the two do you think has greater hope for survival? Justify your stance.

2. Make a comprehensive list of 50 stores in your area. Classify each by retailing format. Are some stores difficult to classify? Why? Are some hybrids that can be classified as more than one format? Which format is dominant? What do you notice about the locations of stores within the same format?

3. Identify a category of merchandise not sold by a category killer. Discuss what a category killer for this merchandise would look like in terms of assortment. What would set the category killer apart from other retailers of the category?

4. Discuss online retailing. What do you buy on the Internet? Are there products that you won't buy? What web site features would make you more comfortable about buying such products? Discuss the future of online retailing. Should shopping malls and other storefront retailing venues be concerned about competition from Internet retailers?

TEAMING UP

1. Each member of your team should search the Internet for a consumer-product storefront franchising opportunity. Share the information as a group, explaining the purchase requirements of each. Which opportunity is most enticing?

2. Each member of your team should shop an outlet store, and the corresponding department in a department store. Include markdowns in your observations. Share your findings with the group; compare the two stores in terms of price, selection, ambiance, and service. How do they stack up?

3. Each member of your team should shop a warehouse club for a specific category of merchandise, and shop for the same merchandise in a conventional supermarket, full-line discounter, or supercenter. Compare the two stores in terms of price, selection, ambiance, and service. Share your shopping preference with the group.

SEARCHING THE NET

1. Search for the customer profiles of several retailers, not necessarily within the same format but that sell the same categories of merchandise. (Annual reports often are a good source of this information.) Compare the customer profiles of the various stores. How do the customers differ? Which retailers compete for the same customers?

2. As if you were a customer searching for a particular item, search the web sites of several online retailers offering the same category of merchandise. Compare the ease with which you found the product on the various web sites. What web site features facilitated—or hindered—your search?

3. Search for job opportunities as a party plan demonstrator. Assess each job listing in terms of startup costs, earnings potential, and support from corporate. Which party plans provide the best opportunity?

After reading this chapter, you will be able to discuss:

● The various shopping environments in which retailers operate stores.

● The important role that location plays in a retailer's success.

CHAPTER THREE

Retail Locations

An age-old axiom asserts that three factors contribute most to a retailer's success: *location*, *location*, and *location*. Proponents of nonstore retailing might disagree with this posture. However, in spite of the success of many nonstore formats, most retail industry pundits concur that location can make or break a storefront retailer. Chapter 3 considers the synergy between retailing format and retail location along with the various location options available for retail stores.

UNPLANNED SHOPPING DISTRICTS

The earliest retail shopping districts were unplanned clusters of stores that evolved in the centers of cities. Known to many as *downtown*, a central business district (CBD), or *urban core*, is a vital hub of commerce and transportation. The great department store emporiums were founded in CBDs. Many cities had two or more department stores that rivaled each other for market dominance by distinguishing themselves in terms of size or prestige.

Specialty stores were also an important part of the CBD's retail mix. Though many CBD specialty stores were single-unit independent operations, CBDs also were the original home of national specialty chains, including Kay Jewelers and Lerner Shops, which was the predecessor of Lerner New York and New York & Company. Although there was no strategic master plan for locating stores within a CBD, districts defined by categories of goods, such as jewelry, menswear, women's apparel, and furniture, often evolved in large CBDs.

CBDs are no longer major retail shopping districts, except in the case of a few tourist destination cities, such as Chicago and San Francisco. Several factors have contributed to the decline of the popularity of CBDs as retail locations. The proliferation of automobiles meant that readily available public transportation no longer played an important role in drawing shoppers downtown. In fact, traffic congestion and the expense and inconvenience of parking a car diminished CBDs' attractiveness as shopping

destinations. The urban decay that plagued many cities caused many shoppers to perceive cities as unattractive and unsafe places to shop.

The migration of customers to the suburbs, however, is perhaps the factor that has contributed most to the demise of downtown retail districts.[1] Though, as suburbs become saturated with retail stores, some retailers have shown renewed interest in metropolitan locations, including Barnes & Noble, Bed Bath & Beyond, and Gap. TJX Companies, the parent organization of Marshalls and T.J. Maxx, has developed an off-price prototype called A.J. Wright, designed especially for urban areas underserved by other retailers. Because retail space is at a premium in densely populated cities, Staples operates a modified format of its office superstore, called Staples Express, in cities such as Boston, New York, and San Francisco.[2]

Secondary business districts (SBDs), or *subshopping districts*, sprouted in outlying areas of cities as populations migrated to urban perimeters. Likewise, town centers evolved in towns and suburbs peripheral to cities. SBDs and town centers have historically been important locations for independently owned specialty stores and service retailers. Many towns have been aggressive in their attempts to retain a local retail character within their communities. Some guard the local character of their shopping districts by restricting the development of chain stores through ordinance and sometimes legal battles. At least nine California communities have enacted what are called *formula retail ordinances*, which prohibit or cap the development of retail chains, including restaurants. Three towns—Coronado, San Juan Bautista, and Sausalito—make specific reference to non-food chains in their ordinances.[3]

In recent years, chain store retailers that typically locate in shopping malls have shown interest in town centers. About one-third of Gap's stores are in "neighborhood" locations. In Westport, Connecticut, upscale art galleries, antique shops, and specialty stores with names like Gallerie Je Reviens, Table Envy, and Tack Room, operate alongside Banana Republic, Brooks Brothers, Guess, Nine West, and Talbots.[4]

Unplanned commercial districts often evolve on busy thoroughfares in cities and towns. These districts are popular locations for many free-standing stores, stand-alone facilities with their own parking areas. Free-standing stores are typically destination stores, such as car dealerships, furniture stores, supermarkets, movie theaters, fast-food restaurants, or big-box discounters. Traffic congestion is a frequent problem along these thoroughfares.

FIGURE 3.2
Town centers are home to many independently owned specialty stores and service retailers.

PLANNED SHOPPING CENTERS

A shopping center is a commercial complex with on-site parking that is developed, owned, and managed as a unit. Shopping centers blossomed on the retail landscape during the years following World War II as real estate developers responded to the needs of rapidly growing numbers of consuming suburbanites.[5] The International Council of Shopping Centers (ICSC) has identified several distinct types of shopping centers.

Neighborhood Center   A neighborhood center includes approximately 30,000 to 150,000 square feet of retail space. Supermarkets or large drugstores are often major tenants in a neighborhood center. Service retailers, such as dry cleaning establishments and shoe repair shops, characterize the remaining tenant mix.

Community Center   A community center includes approximately 100,000 to 350,000 square feet of retail space. A supermarket and a full-line discounter are often the major tenants in a community center. Specialty and service retailers are typical of the remaining tenant mix. Category killers and off-pricers are sometimes major tenants in community centers.

Regional Center   A regional shopping center has approximately 400,000 to 800,000 square feet of retail space, with two or more department stores as major tenants. Specialty stores of apparel, gifts, and home furnishings and accessories complement the assortments of the department stores.

Superregional Center   A superregional center has more than 800,000 square feet of retail space with three or more department stores as major tenants. The department stores are complemented by general merchandise and specialty retailers that collectively offer broad selections and deep assortments of apparel and home furnishings. Food courts are a common feature of superregional centers, as are various forms of entertainment, such as movie theaters and miniature golf.

Strips and Malls

Most neighborhood and community centers are strip centers, which are linear arrangements of stores with an open-air canopy and off-street parking in front of the stores. J.C. Nichols developed the first strip center, Country

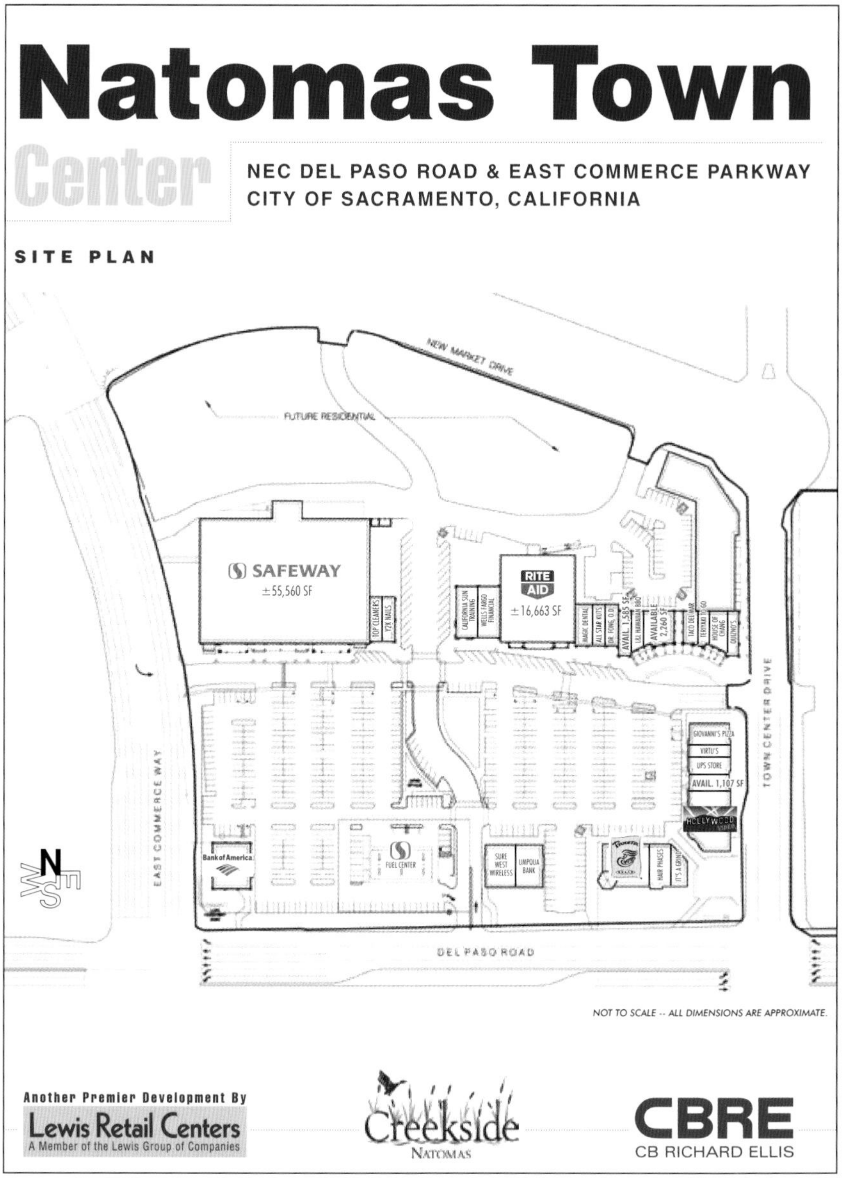

Natomas Town
Center

NEC DEL PASO ROAD & EAST COMMERCE PARKWAY
CITY OF SACRAMENTO, CALIFORNIA

SITE PLAN

NOT TO SCALE -- ALL DIMENSIONS ARE APPROXIMATE.

Another Premier Development By
Lewis Retail Centers
A Member of the Lewis Group of Companies

Creekside
NATOMAS

CBRE
CB RICHARD ELLIS

FIGURE 3.5
Shopping centers are planned retail developments with on-site parking, owned and managed as unit. Source: lewisop.com.

FIGURE 3.6
A superregional center,
such as Crabtree Valley Mall
in Raleigh, North Carolina,
has more than 800,000
square feet and three or
more anchor stores. © Jeff
Greenberg/PhotoEdit.

Club Plaza, in 1922. Built to serve Kansas City's affluent Country Club district, Country Club Plaza featured Spanish-style, tiled-roof, stucco buildings lavishly appointed with Grecian urns, marble statuary, and bronze fountains.[6] Houston-based Weingarten Realty Investors is the nation's largest strip center developer. With more than 300 retail properties across the southern United States, Weingarten's community and neighborhood centers typically are anchored by a supermarket and a value-oriented retailer.[7]

Most regional and superregional centers, commonly referred to as *malls*,[8] are roofed and climate-controlled with an inward orientation of stores connected by a pedestrian walkway. Open-air and/or decked parking surround most regional and superregional centers. With nearly 300 retail properties in 39 states, the Simon Property Group in Indianapolis is the world's leading mall developer. Its portfolio of properties includes the Aventura Mall in North Miami Beach, Barton Creek Square in Austin, the Fashion Valley Mall in San Diego, and the 2.7-million-square-foot Mall of America in Bloomington, Minnesota.[9]

The first enclosed shopping center, Southdale, opened in a Minneapolis suburb in 1956. The development of the Interstate Highway System spurred the growth of regional and superregional centers. Sites at highway interchanges became desirable mall locations because of their high visibility and easy accessibility.

The trading area from which a shopping center draws its customers is a function of its size. Large shopping centers draw from a wider trading area than small centers, in that consumers will travel a greater distance for an extensive selection of stores. The value of space in a shopping center is a function of the number of shoppers that the center attracts. Thus, rent in large, heavily trafficked centers is higher than rent in small centers. For this reason, many regional centers have aspired to become superregional centers by adding new anchors and additional space for more specialty stores.

SOURCES
Bal Harbour Shops. (2006). Our History. www.balhar bourshops.com; Wikipedia. (2006). Bal Harbour Shops; Phipps Plaza. http://en. wikipedia.org; Simon Property Group, Inc. (2006). Phipps Plaza Leasing Sheet. www.simon. com/mall.

Other Types of Shopping Centers

Other types of shopping centers incorporate the characteristics of both strips and malls but are distinct in terms of location and retail composition.

SOUTHERN BELLES

Which is the South's most upscale shopping center? Cast your vote after reading the following:

In 1968, Phipps Plaza opened in the posh Buckhead area of Atlanta as the first enclosed two-level shopping mall in the Southeast. Today, Phipps Plaza is anchored by Saks Fifth Avenue, Nordstrom, and Belk.

With more than 800,000 square feet and 100 specialty stores, the architectural design of Phipps Plaza reflects the aura of the center. Long staircases, high ceilings, glass elevators, and marble floors set the stage for shopping at upscale specialty stores such as Gucci, Jimmy Choo, Bang & Olfusen of Atlanta, Gianni Versace, Giorgio Armani, Barneys New York, and Sisley. Armani Exchange, Tiffany & Co., White House Black Market, and Anne Fontaine further enhance the mix. Five full-service restaurants and a

14-screen AMC theater round out the offerings at Phipps Plaza.

Opened in 1964, Bal Harbour Shops is an upscale shopping mall in Bal Harbour, Florida, a suburb of Miami. The center's anchor stores are Neiman Marcus and Saks Fifth Avenue. Other notable stores include Armani, Prada, Chanel, Dior, Dolce & Gabbana, Cartier, and Tiffany & Co. With an inward orientation of stores, Bal Harbour is technically a mall. However it is unlike other malls in that the center is open-air, there are no kiosks, and the main anchor, Saks Fifth Avenue, has a sidewalk entrance from the town's main street. Bal Harbour has the highest sales per square foot of any mall in the United States, and there is a two-year waiting list for space in the center, which has held a 100 percent occupancy rate for more than two decades.

Table 3.1 ICSC SHOPPING CENTER DEFINITIONS

Type	Concept	Sq. Ft. (Inc. Anchors)	Acreage	Typical Anchor (s) Number	Typical Anchor (s) Type	Anchor Ratio*	Primary Trade Area**
Neighborhood Center	Convenience	30,000–150,000	3–15	1 or more	Supermarket	30–50%	3 miles
Community Center	General merchandise; convenience	100,000–350,000	10–40	2 or more	Discount dept. store; supermarket; drug; home improve.; large specialty/disc. apparel	40–60%	3–6 miles
Lifestyle Center	Upscale national chain; specialty stores; dining and entertainment in outdoor setting	150,000–500,000 (but can be smaller or larger)	10–40	0–2	Not usually anchored in the traditonal sense but may include book store; other large-format specialty retailers; multi-plex cinema; small dept. store	10–50%	8–12 miles
Regional Center	General merchandise; fashion (mall, typically enclosed)	400,000–800,000	40–100	2 or more	Full-line dept. store; jr. dept. store; mass merchant; disc. dept. store; fashion apparel	50–70%	5–15 miles
Superregional center	Similar to regional center but has more variety and assortment	800,000+	60–120	3 or more	Full-line dept. store; jr. dept. store; mass merchant; fashion apparel	50–70%	5–25 miles
Power Center	category-dominant anchors; few small tenants	250,000–600,000	25–80	3 or more	Category killer; home improve.; disc. dept. store; warehouse club; off-price	75–90%	5–10 miles
Theme/Festival Center	Leisure; tourist-oriented; retail and service	80,000–250,000	5–20	N/A	Restaurants; entertainment	N/A	N/A
Outlet Center	Manufacturers' outlet stores	50,000–400,000	10–50	N/A	Manufacturers' outlet stores	N/A	25–75 miles

*   The share of a center's total square footage that is attributable to its anchors.
**The area from which 60–80% of the center's sales originate.

© 2006, International Council of Shopping Centers, Inc., New York, New York. Published in "ICSC Shopping Center Definitions, *Basic Configurations and Types for the United States,*" website at: http://www.icsc.org/srch/lib/USDefinitions.pdf, dated 2004. Reprinted by permission.

FIGURE 3.7
A festival center, such as Faneuil Hall Marketplace in Boston, is often a tourist attraction. © AP Photo/Michael Dwyer.

Mixed-Use Center A mixed-use center, or *MXD*, is a retail, office, parking, and hotel complex that sometimes includes a convention center and/or a high-rise condominium or apartment complex in one sprawling development. MXDs often played a part in revitalization projects to salvage decaying inner cities. The MXD's retail component was an effort to maintain the CBD as a viable shopping district. Airwalks often connected the MXD to local department stores and other retail complexes. Though most urban MXDs have not realized their developers' expectations as retail centers, many have been successful as office and hotel facilities. Encompassing 14 blocks in downtown Atlanta, Peachtree Center is an 18.9-million-square-foot MXD that includes ten office towers, three convention hotels, and a shopping mall.[10]

MXDs also have been catalysts for development in suburban areas as integral parts of planned suburban communities in high-growth, densely populated areas. *Washington Post* reporter Joel Garreau dubbed these areas "edge cities," mini-metropolises that have sprung up along interstate highways within the shadow of urban peripheries.[11] Buckhead, Atlanta's wealthiest neighborhood, is an edge city whose growth was spawned by MXDs that include two famous shopping centers: Phipps Plaza and Lenox Square.[12]

Pedestrian Mall A pedestrian mall is an open-air shopping district created by closing off the streets within a group of blocks to create a parklike ambiance of trees and benches. Pedestrian malls were an attempt by urban planners to recapture the business that downtown shopping districts were losing to suburban centers by emulating the freedom and safety that customers enjoy walking from store to store in enclosed shopping centers. The first pedestrian mall was built in Kalamazoo, Michigan, in 1959. Other examples include Fulton Mall in Fresno, California; the Mid-America Mall in Memphis; Church Street Marketplace in Burlington, Vermont; and Miami Beach's Lincoln Road Mall.[13]

Unfortunately, pedestrian malls were not the answer to declining retail business in CBDs. Critics claim that pedestrian malls hamper retail business by rerouting vehicular traffic and creating confusing traffic patterns. Some pedestrian malls, including one in Eugene, Oregon, have been converted back to conventional paved roadways with sidewalks. A close kin of the pedestrian mall is the *transit mall*, which is a pedestrian mall closed to traffic except public transportation. The Nicollet Mall in Minneapolis and Chicago's State Street Mall are examples of this concept.

Festival Marketplace   A festival marketplace, or urban specialty center, is a shopping center comprising specialty stores, pushcart peddlers, and

FIGURE 3.8
Woodbury Common Premium Outlets. An outlet center's tenant mix includes manufacturer outlet store and off-pricers. ©Robert Brenner/ PhotoEdit.

THE HISTORY OF MANUFACTURERS' OUTLET INDUSTRY

Mid-1800s	Apparel and shoe mill stores on Eastern seaboard begin offering excess and damaged goods to employees. Eventually these mill stores opened their doors to consumers.
1936	Anderson-Little, a manufacturer of men's clothing, opens the first "factory-direct" stores located in remote areas.
1940s	Factory outlets continue to grow, serving mainly as centers for the disposition of overruns and damaged merchandise.
1970s–80s	Several economic factors contributed to the growth of the outlet industry:

- Decrease in consumer discretionary income
- Rising gasoline prices
- Increased desirability of designer labels at low prices
- Consumer importance placed on value

1974	Vanity Fair opens first multi-tenant manufacturers' outlet center in Reading, Pennsylvania.
1980	The first enclosed outlet center opens in a non-metropolitan market to avoid direct competition with retail accounts.
1980s	Outlet centers continue to grow, especially in areas of high tourist trade due to:

- Oversaturation of regional malls
- Outlets becoming profit centers for manufacturers
- Technological advances in apparel manufacturing

Late 1980s	Manufacturers' outlets grow due to increased emphasis on customer service, in-season merchandise, visual merchandising, sophisticated store design, center ambiance and amenities.
1990s	Manufacturers' outlets become the fastest growing segment of retailing, representing a $12.2 billion industry.
2000s	Outlet industry stabilizes with more than 260 centers nationwide and $14.1 billion in gross sales.

SOURCE
Prime Retail. (2006).
Outlet history. http://www.
primeoutlets.com/
corporate/iohistory.asp.

walkaway food merchants that is often a tourist attraction within a city's cultural and entertainment center. Festival centers are sometimes a creative reuse of abandoned warehouses or factories, such as San Francisco's Ghirardelli Square, a converted chocolate factory with a view of the Golden Gate Bridge. Other urban specialty centers include Boston's Quincy Market and Faneuil Hall Marketplace, New York's South Street Seaport, Baltimore's Harborplace, and Miami's Bayside. The Rouse Company of Columbia, Maryland, is the innovator and leading developer of festival marketplaces.

Outlet Center   An outlet center is a strip or enclosed center with a tenant mix composed of manufacturers' outlet stores. Originally attracting retailers of moderately priced goods, such as Van Heusen shirts and Hanes underwear, an increasing number of outlet centers are attracting upscale retail tenants. Woodbury Common in Central Valley, New York, is an example of such an outlet center. The nation's largest outlet center, its tenants include Coach, Dolce & Gabbana, Fendi, Escada, and Off 5th Saks Fifth Avenue.[14]

To avoid conflict between manufacturers and their conventional retail channels, outlet centers are often located in excess of 50 miles from traditional distribution channels, though some recently developed centers fall within this geographic boundary.[15] Outlet centers are destination centers to which customers drive an average of 125 miles and where tour buses are the mainstay of marketing programs. In Ohio, Northcoast Outlet Center is located 50 miles from Cleveland and Toledo, and 100 miles from Columbus. The center benefits from its proximity to the Lake Erie vacation area, which attracts 7.5 million tourists annually. Though manufacturers' outlets represent the majority in an outlet center's tenant mix, off-pricers are also becoming more common in these centers, leading some to refer to an outlet center as an *off-price center* or a *value-oriented center*.

Power Center   A power center is typically an open-air center with a tenant mix of big-box discounters, such as category killers, warehouse clubs, off-pricers, full-line discounters, and supercenters. The mix is sometimes supplemented by a strip of smaller stores as well as a grocery supermarket and/or full-line discounter. Power centers, like strip centers, operate on a low cost-of-occupancy structure. The centers are often located near a superregional center in an effort to feed off its traffic.

FIGURE 3.9
For the most part, the tenant mix at power centers comprises big-box discounters. © Eric P. Martin/Silver Companies.

Power centers rely on the consumer's interest in value shopping versus recreational or fashion shopping. Because each store in a power center is a destination store, there is less browsing, cross shopping, and comparison shopping from store to store than there is in a mall. As destination centers, power centers claim that 85 percent of power center shoppers buy something upon each visit, versus only 50 percent of mall shoppers.[16]

Lifestyle Center   A lifestyle center is an open-air retail development of shops and restaurants designed to create a pedestrian-friendly, town-like atmosphere with sidewalks, landscaping, ambient lighting, and park benches.[17] The village theme is often reinforced architecturally with cedar clapboards, awnings, peaked roofs, and cupolas with weather vanes.[18] Like mixed-use centers, some lifestyle centers include provisions for housing and offices. Lifestyle centers are the newest generation of shopping centers. Super-regional centers perceive lifestyle centers as threats, since both draw from the same portfolio of tenants.[19]

Survival of the Fittest

The growth of the shopping center industry in the United States has been explosive. In 1960, there were 4,500 shopping centers in the country. By 1990, the number had increased to 36,650, a growth rate higher than the growth rate of the population, retail sales, or any other economic indicator. Most observers concur that the marketplace is saturated with shopping centers. Atlanta-based Equitable Real Estate Investment Management, Inc. predicts that several hundred regional malls will close during the early decades of the twenty-first century. Most experts concur that future shopping-center development will be the renovation, expansion, and new use of existing centers, and not ground-up construction of new centers.[20]

Over the years, many shopping centers have had to reinvent themselves to remain solvent in the light of new competition and changing customer

FIGURE 3.10
A lifestyle center, the
newest type of shopping
center, is an open-air center
with chain specialty stores,
restaurants, and
entertainment venues as
tenants. Courtesy Turnberry
Associates.

needs. Strip centers are a good example of the type of resiliency needed to remain competitive in a saturated marketplace. Before the era of enclosed centers, strip centers were often anchored by department store branches, which offered the same breadth of selection as their urban counterparts but considerably less depth. In the 1960s, most department stores abandoned strip centers for larger units at regional or superregional centers. More recently, industry consolidation among full-line discount stores caused additional strip center vacancies.[21]

But as times changed, many strip centers aggressively replaced department stores with emerging discount store formats, such as off-pricers and category killers. Strip center owners touted their heavily trafficked locations and low-cost rent structures, claiming that strip centers attract time-pressed destination shoppers more likely to purchase than the browsers who shop regional or superregional centers. Some strip centers strengthened their

FIGURE 3.11
J. C. Penney conveys a
modest-price image in a
shopping center. Courtesy
Fairchild Publications, Inc.

market position as destination centers by adding office space for physicians and dentists. Others enhanced their image as value-oriented centers by building out-parcel units for big-box tenants such as warehouse clubs.

Landscaping, better signage, and improved ingress and egress have made many strip centers pleasant shopping destinations. Today, strip centers are the preferred location of many retailers, including some that have abandoned malls in favor of strip centers.

Like strip centers, many regional centers have had to reinvent themselves in the light of growing competition from superregional centers. Some regional centers have created a town center–like ambiance with libraries, dry cleaners, post offices, veterinary clinics, and health clubs. The Bergen Mall in Paramus, New Jersey, has a chapel that draws as many as 400 worshipers to daily services. The mall's lower promenade is home to the Bergen Museum of Art and Science, a center dedicated to developing youth interest in the arts.[22] Other regional centers have repositioned themselves as value-oriented centers by replacing shuttered department stores with category killers, off-pricers, and full-line discounters. Based in Coral Gables, Florida, Talisman Companies is a reputed leader in redeveloping and remarketing shopping centers. The company converted the Roswell Mall, a two-story mall in Roswell, Georgia, to Roswell Town Center, a value-oriented strip center that includes tenants such as Burlington Coat Factory and Value City.[23]

The Mix of Stores in a Shopping Center
A shopping center's tenant mix is often the result of a carefully executed marketing strategy. Leasing agents maximize the number of customers

drawn to a center with a synergistic mix of stores that offer a broad selection of merchandise categories, brands, and services.

The strategy for composing a tenant mix is based on the nature of the competition between tenants. Stores that are directly competing offer the same merchandise. Indirectly competing stores offer the same type of merchandise, but different selections of prices and brands. Complementary stores stimulate each other's sales. An apparel store and a shoe store are complementary in that the sale of a new outfit in the apparel store might stimulate the sale of a pair of shoes in the shoe store.

The ideal tenant mix includes indirectly competing and complementary stores. As indirect competitors, J.C. Penney and Lord & Taylor contribute to a center's breadth of selection and attractiveness to a diverse group of customers. Complementary stores enhance customer convenience and one-stop shopping. Direct competition fails to enhance business in a shopping center in that the directly competing stores cannibalize each other's sales.

A tenant mix must be consistent with a center's desired image and the type of customer that the center hopes to attract. A *value-oriented center* is well represented by off-pricers and manufacturers' outlets. The term *fashion*

SOURCE
Weingarten Realty. (2006). About Us. www.weingarten. com.

WEINGARTEN REALTY

The Weingarten story began in 1854 with the birth of Harris Weingarten, a poor villager from a small community in Poland. Seeking new opportunities in the United States, Weingarten eventually settled in the Houston area where he opened a dry-goods store in the 1880s. Weingarten survived the ups and downs of the young town's economy, and eventually became a pioneer in the supermarket industry.

In 1948, under the leadership of Harris' son, the family founded a real estate enterprise known as Weingarten Markets Realty. The company initially built the family's grocery stores, and then began developing shopping centers. In 1980, the family exited the supermarket business to focus on real estate. Following its restructuring as a real estate investment trust (REIT), Weingarten became a publicly-held company in 1985. The company is one of the largest equity REITs listed on the New York Stock Exchange, and has consistently been ranked as one of the nation's leading developers/owners of community shopping centers.

Today, Weingarten's portfolio of more than 300 properties spans the southern half of the United States with new projects constantly underway. And CEO Drew Alexander emulates the entrepreneurial spirit that his grandfather, Harris Weingarten, demonstrated more than a century ago.

center implies the presence of upscale apparel stores, such as Victoria's Secret and Banana Republic. Anchors strongly influence a shopping center's image. A center anchored by J.C. Penney and Sears conveys a moderate-price image. A center anchored by Nordstrom and Bloomingdale's conveys an upscale image.

To ensure compatibility with other stores in a center, some retailers have cotenancy requirements. As an upscale retailer of home furnishings and accessories, Crate & Barrel's cotenancy requirements include the presence of other prestigious stores, such as Ann Taylor, Banana Republic, and Coach, and at least one fashion-oriented department store, such as Lord & Taylor.

SUMMARY POINTS

- Unplanned shopping areas include central business districts, secondary business districts, and town centers.
- Planned shopping centers include open-air neighborhood and community centers, called strips, and enclosed regional and superregional centers called malls.
- Other types of planned centers include mixed-use centers, pedestrian malls, outlet centers, power centers, and lifestyle centers.
- Some shopping centers struggle for survival in the light of keen competition and a saturated marketplace.
- An ideal mix of stores in a shopping center includes indirectly competing and complementary stores.

KEY TERMS AND CONCEPTS

central business district	indirect competition	regional center
community center	lifestyle center	secondary business
complementary stores	mixed-use center	district
cotenancy requirement	neighborhood center	shopping center
direct competition	outlet center	strip center
festival marketplace	pedestrian mall	superregional center
free-standing store	power center	town center

THINKING ABOUT IT

1. Make a list of a dozen or so shopping centers in your area. Classify each. Which format is dominant? Are some centers difficult to classify? Why? Are some hybrids that can be classified as more than one format?

2. Identify a regional center and superregional center in your area. How do they compare in terms of the number of anchor stores and the types of stores? The total number of stores? At which center do you prefer to shop?

3. Identify a mixed-use center in a familiar city. Assess its retail component. Assess the retail environment of the CBD in which the MXD is located. What are your conclusions?

4. As noted, some towns guard the local character of their shopping districts by restricting the development of chain stores through formula retail ordinances. Note the presence of chain stores in a town center with which you are familiar. Do the chains enhance the shopping district? Do they draw customers? Are the chains complementary to the privately owned stores, or do they directly compete?

5. Look at the brand names associated with a nearby outlet center. How close are the brands' non-outlet competitors? Does the outlet center violate the standard of "50 miles from traditional distribution channels"?

6. Power center customers are buyers. Mall customers are shoppers. How do these definitions relate to your personal shopping behavior?

TEAMING UP

1. Have your team shop a local strip center as a customers, taking note of attributes such as access, parking, cleanliness, ambiance, and mix of stores. Compare shopping experiences as a group. Have strip centers made a comeback? Are they good places to shop?

2. Each member of the team should shop for a specific category of merchandise in a superregional shopping center, noting the ways in which the stores differ regarding assortment, price, service, and ambiance. How effectively has the center created a synergistic mix of stores that offers a broad selection of merchandise categories, brands, and services? What is the level of competition among the assigned stores? Which are directly competing? Indirectly? Each team member should share his or her assessment with the group.

SEARCHING THE NET

1. Search the Internet for the web sites of several shopping center developers. Read their profiles. Do you think that shopping center development is a worthwhile real estate venture? Why?

2. Find the web sites of several festival centers and the cities in which the centers are located. Whom do you think is the target demographic for these festival centers?

3. Search the Internet for the web sites of several outlet centers. Look at each center's list of stores. How do the centers differ relative to retail mix? Why?

4. There are several interesting publications with information on the history of shopping centers, including one published by the International Council of Shopping Centers (www.icsc.org/srch/sct/current/page63/html) and another by the University of San Diego (http://history.sandiego.edu/gen/soc/shoppingcenter.html). Read the histories and compare. Are they factually consistent? By searching the Internet, what more information or publications can you find on the history of shopping centers?

CHAPTER FOUR

Retail Growth and Expansion

Bigger is often better in today's retail environment. Large retail organizations have distinct competitive advantages over smaller retailers because of their dominance of the marketplace and the clout that they exert with suppliers. To remain competitive, aggressive retail organizations continually pursue growth opportunities by opening stores in new markets, buying existing retail enterprises, and developing new formats or merchandising concepts. Chapter 4 covers some of the strategies used by retailers to position themselves for continued growth.

CENTRALIZATION

Centralization is an organizational strategy used by companies to enhance fiscal and operational efficiency. Centralization involves performing functions affecting an organization's remote operations from a central location, usually a corporate office. In a retail organization, *centralized buying* means that the process of buying merchandise for resale in a multi-store organization is orchestrated from a corporate office. Decentralization is the opposite. *Decentralized buying* means that individual stores within a multi-store organization are each responsible for buying merchandise.

Centralization is a concept fundamental to the success of many retailers. To understand the impact of centralization, consider the following scenario:

Beth Kyle is the owner of five children's specialty stores in Florida called Monkeys & Pumpkins. She opened her first store on Fort Lauderdale's Las Olas Boulevard in 2005. The store's immediate success spurred the opening of a second store in Palm Beach, and subsequent stores in South Miami Beach, Key West, and St. Augustine. Ms. Kyle's expansion plans are aggressive. She hopes to open stores in other tourist destination locations, including Naples, Florida, Savannah, Georgia, and Charleston, South Carolina. By 2011, she hopes to increase the Monkeys & Pumpkins portfolio of stores to 20.

Beth Kyle always has an eye open for talented people to run new stores. Monkeys & Pumpkins' store managers have considerable autonomy.

After reading this chapter, you will be able to discuss:

● The impact of centralization on operational and fiscal efficiency.

● Retail expansion strategies.

● The importance of international retailing.

● Opportunities for independent retailers.

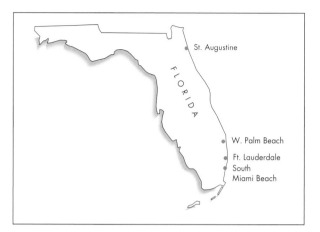

FIGURE 4.1
Existing Monkeys &
Pumpkins locations.

Though the stores have a common identity, they function independently. The manager at each store is fully responsible for merchandising and operating his or her store with the assistance of an office and selling staff.

The organizational strategy that the owner of Monkeys & Pumpkins has adopted to operate her stores is rare. In multi-store retail organizations, functions not requiring customer proximity are often centralized in a corporate office. Individual stores perform only those activities directly related to selling, and the operational activities of maintaining the store and inventory. Functions such as buying, accounting, and sales promotion are executed centrally.

The Advantages of Centralization

The positive results of the decision to centralize the Monkeys & Pumpkins buying functions at an office facility in Orlando exemplify the advantages of centralization. Consider the following:

- Redundancies are reduced. Prior to centralization, five buyer/managers shopped the wholesale childrenswear markets and processed five sets of orders. By centralizing, one buyer can cover the same markets and process a single set of orders for all stores.
- Specialization is fostered. Prior to centralization, five buyer/managers performed a diverse range of merchandising and operational functions. In a centralized organization, buyers devote their undivided attention

FIGURE 4.2
Centralization has laid the
groundwork for future
expansion at Monkeys &
Pumpkins.

to buying. As centralized organizations grow, job functions are often split into more specialized functions. Beth Kyle may find that her expansion plans will require hiring additional buyers. At this point, the single childrenswear buying function might be split into more specialized functions by defining buying responsibilities according to childrenswear market segments, such as boys, girls, and infants and toddlers.

- Expenses are reduced. Though operating a central organization is costly, the owner has more than offset the cost of operating a corporate office by eliminating the merchandising functions in each of the stores.

- Quantity discounts are realized. The buyer/managers wrote orders for *hundreds* of items. The central buyer now writes orders for *thousands* of items, thus qualifying for the price incentives that suppliers offer to companies that place large orders.

- Consistency among stores is enhanced. The selections at Monkeys & Pumpkins were inconsistent from one location to another when each store's assortments were chosen by different buyer/managers. With one buyer maintaining merchandise assortments for all stores, Monkeys & Pumpkins' image is more consistent from one location to another.

· Groundwork for expansion is laid. The inventory needs of the new stores that Beth is planning can be served by the existing central buying structure without having to add additional staff.

Advancements in transportation and communication have facilitated centralization. The Interstate Highway Act of 1955 enabled the construction of an infrastructure to receive goods at national and regional distribution centers and then to expediently transport them to a network of stores. Information technology systems that track sales and inventory activity at hundreds of retail locations, triggering orders for the immediate replenishment of goods as they are sold, have made it possible to orchestrate the buying function for a vast complex of stores from a single location.

In spite of the many positive outcomes that result from centralization, there are some that decry it, claiming that centralization strips stores of their ability to respond to local market conditions. In response to this dilemma, some retailers adopt a decentralized or regional merchandising approach. As part of a reorganization strategy, Federated Department Stores converted the nameplates of its regional operating divisions, including Burdines, Famous-Barr, Foley's, Hecht's, and Marshall Field's, to a single banner, Macy's, with the intent of creating a single centralized buying organization. The identity change caused a stir among the dedicated customers of the regional operators who feared that, as Macy's, the department store to which they had been loyal for a lifetime would lose its local flavor as part of a homogenized national chain likened to Sears or J.C. Penney.

Fearful of losing a faithful customer base, Macy's responded to the outcry by creating seven regional buying offices staffed by planners and buyers who merchandise Macy's stores by region of the country with sensitivity to the geographic distinctions among customers. Macy's also developed a plan to tailor the assortments of individual stores within regions to local markets. Stores in upscale shopping centers, such as the Northpark Mall in Dallas, would be merchandised with high-end brands, while stores in working-class areas, such as Marlo Heights, Maryland, would be merchandised with a moderate-price focus.[1]

Centralization is not a new concept, nor is it peculiar to retailing. Early variety store chains were centralized operations. The strategy is applied in every industry with multi-unit operations, including financial services, manufacturing, and service franchising.

RETAIL OWNERSHIP

Knowledge of a retail organization's ownership structure is fundamental to understanding its competitive position and potential for growth. Type of ownership is often tied to the manner in which a retail organization carries out its merchandising function and the way in which the organization is managed.

Ownership of a retail organization can be either public or private. A public, or *publicly held*, retail organization has many owners or shareholders. A public company's stock is available to the general public and is sold, or traded, on a public stock exchange, such as the New York Stock Exchange (NYSE) or the American Stock Exchange (AMEX). The stock of a private, or *privately held*, retail organization is not traded on a public exchange. A private company has fewer owners than a public company, sometimes only one. The owners are sometimes a family, or they can be a group of investors within or outside the organization. When a publicly held organization is bought by private investors, the organization is said to be *taken private*.

Public companies often evolve from private companies. Private companies "go public" with an initial public offering (IPO) of stock on a public exchange. The money obtained from the sale of stock is used as capital to expand the organization. By going public, the original owners relinquish some of their control over the organization in that, as owners, the new shareholders acquire voting power that can be exercised in the organization's decision making. In 2006, privately held J. Crew offered 18.8 million shares of stock for public trading at $20 a share. The IPO generated about $376 million in capital for J. Crew, and reduced the share of ownership by Texas Pacific, a major J. Crew, shareholder, from 50 percent to 40 percent.[2] The original owners of a public company can retain voting control in the organization by retaining ownership of more than 50 percent of the company's stock. The Dillard family, for example, owns only 10 percent of the stock of Dillard's Department Stores, but that 10 percent represents 99 percent of the voting stock.[3]

The term *independent* often is used to refer to a single, privately owned store; however, privately held multi-store retailers are also considered independent. Though small retail organizations are likely to be private and large organizations are likely to be public, size is not an absolute indication of public or private ownership.

Chains and Conglomerates

A retail organization is often dubbed relative to the number of stores that it operates. A chain of retail stores is two or more stores with the same ownership and identity. The word "chain" often is used to refer to a large group of value-oriented stores, such as Sears or Wal-Mart; however, the use of the term is irrelevant to type of retail format. Chains are classified as local, regional, or national, relative to their geographic span of stores:

- A local chain operates stores within a narrow geographic area, usually defined by a city and its outlying areas.
- A regional chain operates stores within a region or regions of the country, such as the Southwest or Northeast.
- A national chain operates stores in virtually every region of the country.

As retail companies grow, they often become part of organizational structures that further enhance their growth. A conglomerate is an organization that unites the ownership of independently operated subsidiaries, or *operating divisions*. A conglomerate often is referred to as a *parent company*, or

FIGURE 4.3
A regional chain operates stores within a specific region of the country.
Source: www.bon-ton.com.

parent organization. The operating divisions within a conglomerate remain autonomous, each with its own identity and organizational hierarchy. Cincinnati-based Federated Department Stores is one of the oldest retail conglomerates in the United States. Founded in 1929, Federated united the ownership of New York's Abraham & Strauss and Bloomingdale's, Cincinnati's Lazarus Department Stores, and Boston's Filene's. Today, Federated is the largest department store conglomerate in the United States, with nearly 1,000 stores coast to coast. Federated has two major operating divisions: Macy's and Bloomingdale's.

Centralization is fundamental to a conglomerate's success. Though its operating divisions are autonomous, a conglomerate is often organized to perform centralized functions for the sake of economy and operational efficiency. Macy's Merchandising Group (MMG) is the division of Federated Department Stores responsible for developing private label programs for the Macy's and Bloomingdale's operating divisions. MMG provides leadership in the areas of merchandise systems, visual presentation, inventory management, and merchandise distribution. MMG is responsible for coordinating private label programs for all Federated stores.

The level of centralized authority exercised over operating divisions varies from one organization to another. Limited Brands, Inc., is a decentralized conglomerate. Its operating divisions have complete merchandising and operational autonomy; however, its operating divisions themselves are highly centralized. Store operations are rigidly orchestrated through operating manuals, floor plans, and other forms of communication disseminated from each division's Columbus, Ohio, headquarters. Though Limited Brands is a decentralized conglomerate and each division develops its own merchandising strategy independent of the parent company, financial controls are administered centrally.

Lack of centralization can be detrimental to an organization. Federated Department Stores was once a highly decentralized conglomerate. Each of

FIGURE 4.4
The operating divisions at Limited Brands, Inc., have complete merchandising and operational autonomy. Courtesy Limited Brands, Inc.

its many operating divisions operated as distinct retail entities with little control by Federated's headquarters. Federated's failure to eliminate organizational redundancies with a higher degree of centralization, however, led to low profitability and depressed its stock value, making the company ripe for a takeover. The company ultimately was acquired by Campeau Corporation, a Toronto-based real estate company. Shortly thereafter, Federated went into bankruptcy. When Federated emerged from bankruptcy, it was a more centralized, streamlined organization.

RETAIL GROWTH AND EXPANSION

A basic tenet of organizational development is that companies need to grow in order to survive. Mergers and acquisitions are retail growth strategies. A merger occurs when two or more companies are combined to form a new organization. When two organizations are merged, or consolidated, the corporate structure of one company, typically the weaker or smaller, is dissolved, leaving a single corporate structure for both companies. In 2005, Federated Department Stores virtually doubled its size by acquiring St. Louis-based May Department Stores for $10.4 billion. The hope was to combine the strengths of both companies—Federated's merchandising panache and May's operational prowess and its eye on the bottom line—to create a department store powerhouse. By reducing organizational redundancies, Federated hoped to save $450 million in annual operating expenses. Much of the savings was to be achieved by consolidating the corporate offices of both companies in Cincinnati and eliminating redundant newspaper advertising in markets where both May and Federated operated stores. Federated hoped to further reduce merchandise acquisition costs by using its size as leverage for cutting deals with suppliers.[4]

Not every merger is a perfect union. In 2004, Kmart merged with Sears. The $11 billion transaction created Sears Holding Corporation, the nation's third largest retailer, with 3,900 stores and $55 billion in annual sales. The logic behind the Kmart–Sears merger was to maximize the reach of each store's most successful brands: Kmart's Martha Stewart home furnishings and Jaclyn Smith women's apparel lines, and Sears' Kenmore appliance and Craftsman tool lines. Kmart's strip center locations and Sears' mall locations were seen as complementary, and a way for both retail entities to connect to a broader customer base. The opportunity to save $500 million by merging corporate offices at the Sears headquarters in suburban Chicago was yet another rationale for the deal. The wisdom of merging the two companies was questioned, however, in that both Sears and Kmart were weak organizations with troubled pasts. Analysts saw the merger as a melding of weaknesses rather than strengths.[5]

Acquisitions

Some retail organizations grow by purchasing other organizations. An acquisition, or *takeover* or *buyout*, is the purchase of one organization by another. Acquisitions are typical of a department store's growth strategy usually because department stores have reached a saturation point in most markets with few opportunities for building new stores. Bon-Ton, based in York, Pennsylvania, grew to become a regional department store chain with nearly 300 stores in the Northeast and Midwest through a series of acquisitions spanning 50 years. Bon-Ton's first acquisition was Eyerly's in Hagerstown, Maryland, in 1948, followed by its acquisition of McMeen's in Lewistown, Pennsylvania, in 1957. Throughout the 1980s and 1990s, Bon-Ton expanded its presence in Pennsylvania and upstate New York with acquisitions that included Fowler's, Pomeroy's, AM&A, and Hess. Bon-Ton's largest acquisitions occurred in 2003, with the purchase of 69 Elder-Beerman stores, and in 2006, with the 142-unit Northern Department Stores, each a collection of acquired department store chains. The Bon-Ton nameplates reflect the company's acquisition heritage. Bon-Ton operates stores as Bon-Ton, Bergner's, Boston Store, Carson Pirie

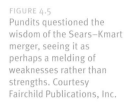

FIGURE 4.5
Pundits questioned the wisdom of the Sears–Kmart merger, seeing it as perhaps a melding of weaknesses rather than strengths. Courtesy Fairchild Publications, Inc.

Scott, Elder-Beerman, Herberger's, and Younkers.[6] Dillard's grew in similar fashion. With its acquisition of Mercantile Stores, Dillard's entered the Cincinnati market and strengthened its market position in Denver.

Some acquisitions are less successful. TJX Companies, the parent organization of T.J. Maxx, Marshalls, A.J. Wright, and HomeGoods, acquired Bob's Stores at a drastically reduced price when the 31-unit, value-oriented, branded-apparel chain was in bankruptcy. The lackluster performance that drove Bob's into bankruptcy did not improve after the acquisition, causing a drop in TJX's earnings, as well as dismay among its shareholders.[7]

Acquisitions can yield happy times when the company being acquired recognizes its organizational or merchandising compatibility with the acquiring organization, and the acquiring organization is in a position to provide financing to an otherwise poorly capitalized or fiscally troubled company. In this case, the acquisition is called a friendly takeover, and the acquiring company a friendly suitor. When the organization being acquired resists being bought out, fearing organizational or merchandising

FIGURE 4.6
Bon-Ton grew to become a regional department store chain through a series of acquisitions spanning more than 50 years. Courtesy the BON TON Stores, Inc.

THE BON•TON STORES, INC.

BON-TON   BERGNER'S   BOSTON STORE   CARSON PIRIE SCOTT   ELDER-BEERMAN   HERBERGER'S   YOUNKERS

BON•TON

Bergner's   Elder-Beerman

Boston Store   Herberger's

Carson Pirie Scott   Younkers

incompatibility with the acquiring organization or the loss of jobs due to organizational streamlining, it is called a hostile takeover. The acquiring organization is then a hostile suitor.

A bidding war can ensue between two or more parties interested in acquiring the same organization. The parties attempt to outbid each other by a series of counteroffers, often resulting in the sale of an organization's stock for a price greater than its worth. In 2005, Liz Claiborne, Inc., made an unsolicited offer to buy J. Jill for $18 a share and threatened a hostile takeover if J. Jill refused to negotiate. As a friendly suitor, Talbots bested the offer at $24.05 a share and acquired J. Jill. Some analysts felt that Talbots paid too much for J. Jill, whose performance had been lackluster for several years.[8]

Acquisitions also can be defined by who the buyers are, or by the terms of financing. An internal buyout is the acquisition of an organization by its employees. In 1986, 348 Macy's executives acquired Macy's from its shareholders in the largest internal buyout of any retail organization in history. An acquisition financed through debt is called a leveraged buyout (LBO). In 2006, two private equity firms, Bain Capital and the Blackstone Group, bought the 600-unit Michaels, an arts and crafts category killer, for more

FIGURE 4.7
Talbots acquired J. Jill in 2005 as a friendly suitor, besting Liz Claiborne's in a hostile takeover move. Courtesy Talbots.

than $6 billion. With borrowed funds, private equity firms buy troubled companies with the intent of resurrecting profitability by cutting costs. When the company becomes profitable, the private equity firm takes the company public with an IPO, effectively selling the company for much more than the firm paid for it.

The Federal Trade Commission (FTC) is a regulatory agency that reviews all proposals for acquisitions and mergers. The FTC monitors unfair competition and determines if the resulting organization will restrict competition by its dominance in the marketplace. In 1998, the FTC blocked the merger of Office Depot and Staples, claiming that the synergies created by merging the two office supply superstores would be an unfair competitive advantage to smaller competitors.

Besides mergers and acquisitions, retail organizations also grow through ground-up expansion, a "start from scratch" strategy. Wal-Mart's rise to become the world's largest retailer happened, for the most part, with ground-up expansion: building new stores and developing new divisions, such as Sam's Club, Wal-Mart's warehouse club division, and new prototypes, such as Wal-Mart Supercenters. Wal-Mart's strategy for foreign expansion, however, has sometimes involved acquisitions.

Divestiture is the sale of an organization's assets. Retail organizations divest themselves of stores or entire operating divisions to unload unprofitable units, generate capital, or concentrate on other areas of business. Federated Department Stores sold off Lord & Taylor, a somewhat

FIGURE 4.8
As private equity firms, Bain Capital and the Blackstone Goup bought Michaels for more than $6 billion. Courtesy Brasher Design.

conservative specialty department store chain that Federated acquired as part of its May Department Stores acquisition. Lord & Taylor was inconsistent with Federated's portfolio of larger, full-line department stores and its intent to appeal to young, trendy consumers.[9] Federated also sold off the bridal specialty division that came as part of the May package which included David's Bridal, After Hours Formalwear, and Priscilla of Boston. In another divestiture action, Federated closed more than 80 redundant department stores in shopping centers where both May and Federated stores coexisted prior to the acquisition.[10]

Diversification

Diversification is an organizational growth strategy that involves entering a line of business that differs from present businesses. Organizations diversify when they perceive limited growth within their existing businesses or when they endeavor to serve the needs of new groups of customers. One approach to diversification is through acquisition. Sears diversified with the purchase of cataloger Lands' End. Talbots, a retailer of classic, career-oriented female apparel, diversified with the acquisition of J. Jill, a retailer of casual female apparel. J. Jill was Talbots' first acquisition since its founding in 1947.[11] Retailers also diversify by developing new merchandising concepts. The Venator Group, formerly the Woolworth Corporation, has a diversified portfolio of stores that includes Northern Reflections, Champs Sports, and the various Foot Locker formats. Through diversification, companies insulate themselves against shifting tides. Though casual female apparel is Limited Brands' core business, it is its newer concepts, such as Victoria's Secret and Bath & Body Works, that have driven the organization's profit in recent years.[12]

Organizations minimize risk when they stay close to a business they know. Related diversification occurs when an organization's various lines of business dovetail with its core business. Classic American casual apparel is the core business of The Gap, Inc., the nation's largest specialty store retailer for apparel. The Gap operates three closely related divisions: Old Navy, Gap, and Banana Republic. The product lines among the three divisions are essentially the same. The distinction is price: Old Navy is value-oriented, Gap is moderately priced, Banana Republic is luxury priced. With related diversification, a retailer can use the same sources of supply and marketing strategies with minor adaptations for multiple divisions.

Having businesses that are too closely related, however, may lead to cannibalization. Limited Brands, whose product lines include intimate apparel (Victoria's Secret), casual female apparel (Limited and Express), and beauty and fragrance (Bath & Body Works), once operated a French-inspired intimate apparel division called Cacique. Cacique's product line was too closely related to the Victoria's Secret product line. Thus, both stores ended up competing for the same customers. Limited eventually closed Cacique. Currently the operating divisions of Limited Brands are not as closely related. With more than 40 female apparel and accessory brands, Liz Claiborne has successfully avoided cannibalization with a portfolio of lines and stores that complement, not cannibalize, one another, including Ellen Tracy (classic), Sigrid Olsen (relaxed), Lucky Brand (denim), Mexx (modern), Prana (active), and Trifari (accessories). Cannibalization also can occur when new stores are geographically close to existing stores.

Some large-format retailers diversify by spinning off scaled-down formats. For areas not large enough to support a full-line store, Saks Fifth Avenue created smaller versions of its prestigious specialty department store: Saks Main Street concept stores for the town centers of affluent communities, and Saks Resort concept stores for prestigious vacation spots, including Southampton in New York and Carmel-by-the-Sea in California. Home Depot developed Expo Design Center, a showroom of decorated room settings targeted to affluent homeowners in need of the services of a designer for home renovation projects.[13] To complement its superstore format, Circuit City developed a mall-based concept called Circuit City Express, which features the store's smaller, gift-oriented items.

Diversification transcends all levels of the marketing channel. Jones Apparel, producer of Jones New York, Evan-Picone, Gloria Vanderbilt, and Nine West, purchased Barneys New York, adding Barneys to its portfolio of stores that includes the Nine West manufacturer-sponsored specialty stores.

Opportunities for Small Stores

The dominance of the marketplace by large retail organizations is obvious even to the casual observer. Large retailers have a definite competitive advantage over small, independently owned retailers. Though a large retailer's broad selections, deep assortments, and competitive prices are unquestionably hard to match, there is still room in the marketplace for independents.

AN HISTORICAL TIMELINE OF LIMITED BRANDS, INC.

1963	The Limited opens its first store in Kingsdale Mall in Columbus, Ohio.
1969	The Limited's first public stock offering is issued.
1980	Limited Express opens in Chicago.
1982	Lane Bryant is purchased consisting of 207 stores and a mail order division.
1982	Victoria's Secret purchased, for $1 million.
1985	Henri Bendel is acquired for $10 million.
1985	Lerner stores are acquired for $297 million.
1987	Express men's brand is sold in 16 Express stores. Two years later the brand is renamed Structure.
1988	Abercrombie & Fitch catalogue is acquired for $46 million.
1988	The Limited Too fashion for girls brand is unveiled in Limited Stores.
1990	First Structure store is opened.
1990	Bath & Body Works opens in Boston.
1995	Intimate Brands, Inc. establishes itself as a fully independent company.
1998	Bath & Body Works Home stores are converted to The White Barn Candle Co.
1998	The Limited, Inc. completes spin-off of Abercrombie & Fitch.
1999	The Limited, Inc. completes spin-off of Limited Too.
1999	The White Barn Candle Co. is launched by raising an old-fashioned barn in New York City's Bryant Park.
2001	The Limited, Inc. announces the integration of Structure into Express as a dual gender brand for both men and women.
2002	Lane Bryant is sold to Charming Shoppes for $335 million.
2002	The Limited, Inc. changes its name to Limited Brands to further emphasize the company's commitment to building a family of the world's best fashion brands.
2002	Limited Brands sells Lerner New York/New York & Company.
2006	The collective value for share-repurchase programs over a ten-year period reaches $6.3 billion.

SOURCE
Limited Brands, Inc. (2006). About Our Company. www.Limited brands.com.

FIGURE 4.9
Three operating division of Gap Stores, Inc., are differentiated based on price: Banana Republic is luxury priced; Gap is moderately priced; Old Navy is value priced. Banana Republic © Rudi Von Briel/PhotoEdit; Old Navy © Dennis McDonald/ PhotoEdit.

FIGURE 4.10
Home Depot diversified
with Expo Design Center,
a showroom of decorated
room settings for the
homeowner embarking on
a home renovation project.
© Michael Newman/
PhotoEdit.

Independents can coexist with large retailers if they differentiate them-selves by complementing, rather than competing with, large stores. In 2005 Ikea, the Swedish home furnishings chain with more than 200 stores in 33 countries, invaded the Boston market with a store the size of six football fields. In response to the competition, Affordable Furniture, an indepen-dent retailer a block away, narrowed its ready-to-assemble furniture assort-ment, the mainstay of Ikea's business, to focus on upholstered furniture, an area in which Ikea is weak.[14] Likewise, after the May–Federated merger, Macy's dropped several popular brands from its merchandise assortments. The jettisoned brands became opportunities for independents to lure the customers disappointed at not finding their favorite brands at Macy's.

Some vendors like dealing with independents because of their ability to respond to local events, regional tastes, and local weather conditions. There-fore, independents can have distinctive assortments by dealing with these suppliers as well as those too small to distribute to large retailers. Vivienne Tam, an upscale female apparel line distributed through department stores such as Neiman Marcus and Saks Fifth Avenue, favors independent specialty stores as a distribution channel because they are more spontaneous and less bureaucratic than department stores.

A LINEAGE OF MERGERS, ACQUISITIONS, AND GROUND-UP EXPANSION

The first Target store opened in 1962 in Roseville, Minnesota, a suburb of St. Paul. Target actually can trace its origins back to 1902, when George Dayton opened a retail store called Goodfellows in downtown Minneapolis. In 1903, the name of the store was changed to the Dayton Dry Goods Company. In 1910, the name changed again to the Dayton Company. In 1956, the Dayton Company opened Southdale, the world's first fully enclosed two-level shopping center, in suburban Minneapolis. And in 1962, the Dayton Company entered the full-line discounting arena by opening Target.

In 1967, the Dayton Company went public, and, in 1969, it merged with the J.L. Hudson Company of Detroit. In 1978, the company, now named Dayton Hudson, acquired Mervyn's, a moderate-price chain department store based in Heywood, California, and thereby became the nation's seventh largest retailer. In 1990, Dayton Hudson acquired the venerable Chicago-based department store chain, Marshall Field's.

By 1979, the Target division had surpassed the Dayton division as a revenue producer. In 2000, Dayton Hudson changed its name to the Target Corporation. By then, more than 75 percent of the company's revenue came from the Target division. In 2001, Target Corporation announced that its Dayton's and Hudson's stores would operate under the Marshall Field's banner. The three brands had until then been operating as the Target Corporation's department store division.

In 2004, the Target Corporation hired the Goldman Sachs Group to analyze options for divesting of Marshall Field's and Mervyn's. Target then sold Marshall Field's to May Department Stores, and sold Mervyn's to an investment consortium that included Sun Capital Partners, Inc., Cerberus Capital Management, L.P., and Lubert-Adler/ Klaff and Partners, L.P. In 2005, Federated Department Stores acquired May Department Stores and announced that it would replace the Marshall Field's nameplates with Macy's.

Today, the Target Corporation is headquartered on Nicollet Mall in Minneapolis, near the site of the original Goodfellows store.

SOURCES
Target. (2006). About Target. www.target.com.
Wikipedia. (2006). Target Stores. en.wikipedia.org/wiki/Target_Stores.

BANKRUPTCY

Unfortunately, a discussion of retail organizations is incomplete without a discussion of bankruptcy. Bankruptcy occurs when an organization becomes insolvent or incapable of paying its debts. In essence, an organization is bankrupt when its liabilities exceed its assets. The Federal Bankruptcy Act was enacted in 1898 to establish guidelines for insolvent debtors to pay their creditors. The act was written in sections or chapters; the chapter most often cited in bankruptcy filings is Chapter 11.

LIKE FATHER(S), LIKE SON(S)

Walk into a BuyBuyBaby store for a sense of déjà vu: floor-to-ceiling shelves stacked with merchandise, a race-track layout, and an A-to-Z assortment of a single product line. Replace the Winnie-the-Pooh lamps and disposable diapers at BuyBuyBaby with Farberware cookware and shower curtains, and what do you get? Bed Bath & Beyond. There's a reason for the similarity. BuyBuyBaby is the brainchild of Jeffrey and Richard Feinstein, sons of Bed Bath & Beyond co-founder Leonard Feinstein. Both sons worked at Bed Bath until Richard, upon becoming a dad, partnered with Jeffrey to open up a Bed Bath & Beyond-type store for new parents.

The apple also fell close to the tree for the other Bed Bath & Beyond co-founder, Warren Eisenberg. His son, Ron, worked at Bed Bath for 15 years before striking out to start an emporium for foodies, Chef Central. Its two suburban New York stores offer gourmet food, upscale kitchenware, and live cooking presentations for the connoisseur.

So why didn't the kids stay in the family business? Eisenberg and Feinstein decided early on that to keep the peace, none of their children would ever run the chain. "I don't want to say that this kid is smarter than that kid, my kid is smarter than your kid," says Eisenberg. Feinstein agrees: "There's no such thing as constructive criticism of someone else's child."

SOURCE
Excerpted from Byrnes, N. (January 19, 2004). Like father, like son. *BusinessWeek*, p. 50.

In 1978, Federal Bankruptcy Laws were rewritten to "protect" companies from their creditors by prohibiting their petitioning a court for liquidation of a debtor's assets to pay its debts. Chapter 11 freezes a debtor's indebtedness to lending institutions, suppliers, and bondholders. The debtor organization retains its assets for use in a plan of reorganization (POR) designed to help the debtor regain profitability. Actions typical of a POR include:

- Terminating the organization's leadership and hiring a "turnaround" leader with a track record of rescuing ailing retailers.
- Closing unprofitable stores.
- Implementing expense-saving measures.
- Selling unprofitable units or divisions. The sell-off infuses the company with cash to reduce debt and generally results in a smaller but better-focused organization.

DRESSED FOR SUCCESS

In 1929, William Sussman opened his doors for business in Daytona Beach, Florida. It was not unusual for chauffeured cars to pull up in front of his Seabreeze Boulevard boutique in those days. And the offerings at Sussman's were quite appropriate for the beachside elite. Elegance and sophistication were the hallmarks of a fine assortment of casual apparel and eveningwear. Sussman was accustomed to catering to the socially prominent. As a tailor, he outfitted British high society before coming to the United States and working for Bergdorf Goodman in New York.

Since 1950, Sussman's daughters, Naomi Frank and Selma Sussman, have run the store. Times have changed since the store's early days. Malls and chains now dominate the retailing picture. However, Sussman's remains the indisputable *grande dame* of Daytona Beach's locally owned boutiques.

Being "special" is the secret of Sussman's success. Independent retailers "can't compete against national chains in terms of price. But they can in terms of unique assortment and customer service," says Barton Weitz, director of the Miller Center for Retailing Education & Research at the University of Florida. Other independent merchants concur including Laurie Schammel, owner of Adornments in Ormond Beach, Florida. "Most importantly, you have to be different from big department stores," claims Schammel. "If Dillard's picked up one of my lines, I'd drop it like a hot potato," she said. But Adornment's motto printed on its hang tags says it all: "It's different here." And being different is what makes the difference.

SOURCE
Excerpted from Callea, D.
(July 30, 2005). Dressed
for success. *Daytona-Beach
News-Journal*. pp. 1E, 2E.

Because its pre-Chapter 11 debts are frozen, a bankrupt retailer starts with a clean slate and can obtain a new line of credit from lending institutions to continue shipments from suppliers. Creditors are willing to extend credit to the retailer because Chapter 11 guarantees that indebtedness incurred after the Chapter 11 filing will receive priority payment, taking precedence over the payment of any old debt. Emergence from bankruptcy occurs when the company becomes profitable. Pre-Chapter 11 debts are settled by offering creditors equity in the company as partial debt payment. Thus, the creditors become the owners of the company.

In 2002, Kmart filed Chapter 11 bankruptcy citing, among other problems, $4.3 billion in debt to vendors. After closing 600 stores and eliminating 67,000 jobs, Kmart emerged from bankruptcy 15 months later with the help of $2 billion in exit financing from banks, led by Bank of America, and a major infusion of capital from ESL Investments, a hedge fund. Vendors ended up with a 37 percent equity share in the newly emerged organization. At that point, stock in the old Kmart corporation was worthless.

Critics of the Federal Bankruptcy Laws claim that the 1978 revisions to Chapter 11 encourage reckless management, who know that the government will shield bankrupt companies from their creditors. Some feel that retailers often file Chapter 11 to rectify poor management decisions. Shopping center landlords are especially critical of Chapter 11, claiming that many retailers who file Chapter 11 do so to get out of bad leases. Why does the federal government seemingly protect organizations that have been haphazard in their fiscal management at the expense of creditors who, in good faith, financed and supplied the debtor? Consider the alternatives to Chapter 11: lost jobs, vacant storefronts, fewer points of distribution for suppliers, and fewer shopping alternatives for consumers.

Bankruptcy is not as foreboding as it sounds. Some of the country's most prestigious retailers, including Federated Department Stores and its subsidiary Macy's, have successfully emerged from bankruptcy. But not every bankruptcy story has a happy ending. Companies that file Chapter 11 but fail to become solvent are forced to liquidate their assets and close. Other companies successfully emerge, only to become victims of a sour economy, rigorous competition, and/or shifts in consumer spending. Some liquidate. Others again file Chapter 11, but a second filing often is the death knell. Such scenarios were the fate of many of the regional full-line discounters mentioned in Chapter 2: Ames, Bradlees, Caldor, and Jamesway, to name few.

INTERNATIONAL RETAILING

Over the past few decades, retail space in the United States has grown exponentially, rising from 8 square feet per capita to a staggering 20 square feet per capita.[15] As the United States marketplace becomes saturated with retail stores, expansion in less competitive foreign markets has become a desirable alternative to domestic growth. Assortment, convenience, and value make U.S. retailing very exportable to countries where limited selection, short shopping hours, and high prices are the norm.

Foreign Growth Opportunities

Several factors have made the global marketplace ripe for retail expansion. The North American Free Trade Agreement (NAFTA) created the world's largest free-trade zone between the United States, Canada, and Mexico, while the European Union (EU) has consolidated the European market-place paving the way for expansion there. Revisions of the General Agreement on Tariffs and Trade (GATT) have lowered tariffs worldwide and have opened doors to other foreign markets. A growing demand for Western goods has presented opportunities for retailers in Asian countries, while emerging middle classes in Thailand, Indonesia, Maylasia, Hong Kong, and Singapore have attracted many U.S. retailers. With a population of 950 million, India holds huge promise as a developing market. China, with a quarter of the world's population, is yet another growth opportunity.

Foreign expansion is not as simple as domestic expansion. Often retailers must adapt their merchandising strategies to local consumer culture.

Wal-Mart Around the World

Mexico was the site of Wal-Mart's first international store, and has the most stores of any country other than the United States.

COUNTRY	TOTAL STORES	TOTAL EMPLOYEES	YEAR ENTERED MARKET
United States	3,499	1,200,000	1962
Mexico	633	100,164	1991
Britain	266	127,800	1999
Canada	225	58,000	1994
Germany	92	13,000	1998
Puerto Rico*	53	11,600	1992
China	31	16,000	1996
Brazil	25	6,600	1995
South Korea	15	2,800	1998
Argentina	11	4,200	1995

*Puerto Rico, a territory of the United States, falls under Wal-Mart's International Division

Source
Weiner, T. (December 6, 2003). Wal-Mart Invades, and Mexico Gladly Surrenders. *The New York Times.* p. A1.

Wal-Mart learned the hard way that Brazilian men do not wear white underwear, and that ice makers are slow-sellers in countries where cocktails are served straight up. In Chile, J.C. Penney misread local taste, which favors understated clothing, and offered expensive lines in the flashy colors popular in more tropical markets such as Miami and Mexico. Gap found that French customers are smaller than U.S. customers, that Germans like dark colors, and that Europeans in general found greeters at the door intimidating.

Expansion to other English-speaking countries often is the safest route for U.S. retailers. For both language and cultural reasons, U.S. companies seeking to enter Europe typically open shop in Great Britain first. Gap's first store was in Great Britain. The company now has stores throughout Europe and in Asia. Foreign expansion is not without risk. Wal-Mart sold off its unprofitable chain of 16 supercenters in South Korea. Low prices were not enough to draw South Korean shoppers, who simply did not find Wal-Mart's warehouse-like, no-frills shopping environment appealing.[16]

Expansion into the United States has become a growth strategy for foreign retailers. In 2000, Swedish retailer H&M entered the U.S. market with a blockbuster grand opening in New York City's Herald Square. Like any foreign retailer, the retailer of fashionable, affordable apparel has made some *faux pas* in translating European fashion to U.S. tastes. Snug-fitting, fluorescent-pink tank tops in the men's line didn't quite make it in the United States.[17] Ikea, another Swedish retailer, has also has met with success in this country. Its hyped openings draw so many customers that it can take hours for crowds to pass through a store. In Atlanta, one man waited in a tent for eight days for the grand opening of a new Ikea in order to win a $4,000 Ikea gift card for being first in line.[18]

Foreign Expansion Strategies

Retailers wary of direct investments in foreign countries sometimes opt for less risky forms of foreign expansion such as joint ventures, licensing agreements, and franchising. In a joint venture, a foreign partner makes an uncharted course more navigable for a U.S. retailer by sharing knowledge of local laws, customs, and industry alliances. Wal-Mart operates more than 50 stores in the Republic of China as joint ventures, and penetrated Mexico as a partner with Cifra SA, Mexico's largest retailing chain.[19] Pier 1 Imports has forged joint venture partnerships in which Pier 1 supplies the merchandise and operational expertise and its joint venture partners develop and operate the stores.

Licensing is a contractual arrangement whereby a retailer allows another company to conduct business under the retailer's name in exchange for a percentage of profit. Saks Fifth Avenue signed its first licensing agreement in 2001 for a store in Saudi Arabia, followed by a license for a store in Dubai, in the United Arab Emirates, in 2004.[20] Saks also has licensing agreements with a company called Roosevelt China Investments to operate stores in China and Macao. J.C. Penney also licenses stores in the Middle East.

Franchising is another option for foreign expansion. Though franchising is not common among product retailers in the United States, many U.S. companies franchise abroad. Gap, Inc., has franchise agreements with the Dubai-based Al Tayer Group to operate 25 Gap stores and 10 Banana Republic stores in Bahrain, Kuwait, Oman, Qatar, and the United Arab Emirates, as well as agreements with other franchisees to operate stores in Maylasia and Singapore. Al Tayer has agreements with other franchisors in addition to Gap, Inc., including Giorgio Armani and Gucci.[21] Franchising has become a popular strategy for foreign expansion for all types of retailers. Build-a-Bear Workshop has franchise agreements with the Murjani Group to operate stores in India. Build-a-Bear also has franchises in Australia, Belgium, Denmark, France, Japan, Luxembourg, the Netherlands, Norway, the Republic of China, South Korea, Sweden, Thailand, and the United Kingdom.[22] A retailer's foreign-expansion strategy can vary by country. For example, Pier 1 makes direct investments in English-speaking countries, but favors joint ventures in non-English-speaking countries.[23]

Shopping centers are another exportable U.S. concept. Burgeoning populations and economies in east and southeast Asia are supporting shopping center development there. Middle-class households in India are projected to grow from 57 million to 153 million over the next decade. For the same period, the number of shopping centers in India is expected to grow from 40 to 250.[24] Favorable demographics have spurred Simon Property Group to develop shopping centers in India, Maylasia, Singapore, and Taiwan.[25] Shopping center development in foreign countries has been facilitated by the enactment of real estate investment trust (REIT) laws that are sweeping the world.[26] An REIT corporation uses the pooled capital of many investors to purchase and manage income property. REITs are traded like stock and are granted special tax considerations.[27]

SUMMARY POINTS

- In a centralized retail organization, functions that do not require proximity to customers are performed collectively for all stores in a central location for efficiency and cost effectiveness.
- Retail ownership can be public or private. Retail organizations can be structured as conglomerates, chains, or single-unit operations.
- Retail organizations expand by developing new merchandising concepts and through acquisitions and mergers. They downsize through divestiture.
- Bankruptcy occurs when an organization's liabilities exceed its assets. Chapter 11 protects a bankrupt retailer from its creditors while it reorganizes to become a profitable organization.
- As the U.S. marketplace becomes saturated with retail stores, retailers are expanding beyond domestic borders into Asia, Europe, and South America.

KEY TERMS AND CONCEPTS

acquisition	divestiture	leveraged buyout
bankruptcy	franchise	licensing
bidding war	friendly suitor	merger
cannibalization	friendly takeover	plan of reorganization
centralization	hostile suitor	private company
chain	hostile takeover	public company
conglomerate	initial public offering	subsidiary
decentralization	internal buyout	
diversification	joint venture	

THINKING ABOUT IT

1. In a retail organization, a high degree of centralization ensures consistency among stores. What are the positive aspects of this consistency? What are the negative aspects?
2. How did the Kmart–Sears and Federated–May mergers impact stores in your area, and you as a consumer?
3. Consider cannibalization relative to a new chain store in your area and its geographic overlap with an existing store or other stores in the chain. What do you think the rationale was for building the new store?

4. Consider a store in your area that closed because of bankruptcy or simply went out of business. What do you think were the reasons for the closure?

5. Consider retailers of various categories of merchandise and retailing formats. Which retailers do you think are most suitable for foreign expansion? To which countries? Why?

TEAMING UP

1. Each member of your team should research the history of a large retail organization. As a group, discuss each company's trail of mergers, acquisitions, divestitures, as well as the development of new concepts. Which were good for the growth and profitability of the organization? Which were not?

2. Each team member should shop for the same item at a chain store and an independent store. How do the stores compare in terms of price, selection, ambiance, and service? Share your findings with the group.

3. Obtain a list of stores at a local mall. As a team, determine the corporate ownership of each store, making a list of retail conglomerates and the stores owned by each. Each team member should discuss a conglomerate relative to diversification. How are the various store concepts and formats related? Do they complement one another? Cannibalize one another? Explain.

SEARCHING THE NET

1. Search for the annual reports of a few of the retail conglomerates mentioned in this chapter. Assess the diversification of its operating divisions.

2. Search for recent news stories on a retail organization filing for bankruptcy under Chapter 11. What factors contributed to the bankruptcy? What are the elements of the POR? When is emergence from Chapter 11 expected?

3. Search for recent news stories pertaining to retail acquisitions. Why did the acquiring organization want the new business? Will the acquisition increase market share? Complement existing lines of business? Was it a hostile or friendly takeover, and did the acquiring organization get a good deal?

4. Search for recent news stories pertaining to retail divestitures. Why did the divesting organization want to sell? To get rid of a poor performer? To concentrate on another line(s) of business? To raise capital?
5. Make a list of major retail organizations. Search for information pertaining to their foreign operations. Consider burgeoning populations, economies, and easy cultural crossover. Into which countries do many U.S. retailers seem to be expanding? Why?

CHAPTER FIVE

Communicating with Consumers

Customers' needs, tastes, and spending power differ relative to factors such as gender, age, income, and lifestyle. To develop a strategy for selecting specific merchandise categories, brands, sizes, styles, items, and colors, buyers need a clear profile of a store's intended customers. Chapter 5 deals with some of the ways in which a retail store defines its customer base and some of the strategies used to draw in customers.

RETAILERS AND THEIR CUSTOMERS

A market is a group of customers with the potential to buy. Claiming that there is "a market" for something implies that there is a group of customers with the desire or need for it, and the financial resources to purchase it. A mass market is a large group of customers with similar characteristics and wants. Mass market characteristics are often described as "typical" or "mainstream"; for example, people who are average height, middle income, or light readers are considered mass market customers. Wal-Mart is a mainstream retailer that caters to the mass market: more than 175 million customers pass through Wal-Mart's doors in 15 countries each week.[1]

A niche market is a small group of customers with characteristics and wants that differ from the mass market. Members of a niche market are not typical or mainstream, and usually are undersatisfied or dissatisfied with mass market offerings. For example, people who are very tall, who are very wealthy, or who read a book a week are considered niche market customers. By virtue of their height, spending power, or passion for reading, the wants and needs of these niche market members differ from the wants and needs of the mass market.

Though niche markets are smaller than the mass market, niche market customers tend to be loyal to retailers that respond to their needs. A man who wears a size 48-extra-long suit will become dedicated to the store that consistently carries a deep assortment of goods in his hard-to-find size. A man of average proportion is not likely to be as dedicated to a specific apparel retailer because his needs can be satisfied by any number of department stores, full-line discount stores, and off-pricers.

Casual Male XL, based in Canton, Massachusetts, is a niche market retailer with nearly 500 stores. The company caters to men 6 feet, 2 inches or taller, with 42-inch waists or larger—a niche market representing about 10 percent of the nation's adult male population.[2] Among the store's popular items are "relaxer" pants with waists that stretch up to 4 inches from their marked size. Former heavyweight boxer champ George Foreman has been a Casual Male XL celebrity endorser.[3]

Market Segmentation

Market segmentation is the process of identifying niche markets. Target marketing responds to the wants and needs of a niche market with a marketing strategy that may include a mix of products, services, or advertising. Markets can be segmented, or defined, based on several types of characteristics. Demographic and psychographic characteristics are the most common bases for segmenting markets.

Demographic segmentation involves identifying markets by objectively measured and quantifiable characteristics such as gender, age, education, and income. For example, off-price retailers target well-educated, discerning consumers who recognize the value of brand-name offerings at lower-than-conventional prices. While high income is a desirable demographic for many retailers, some retailers specifically target low-income markets. Dollar General and Family Dollar appeal to households with annual earnings of less than $25,000 in areas not served by other general merchandise retailers. With its newest off-price concept, A.J. Wright, TJX Companies targets lower- to middle-income, urban, blue-collar customers with family earnings under $40,000 a year.

Because of constant shifts, demographic characteristics warrant continuous monitoring. A significantly low birth rate in the 1970s caused the teenage population to drop off considerably through the end of the 1980s. In response to this demographic trend, department stores significantly downsized their junior departments. Some of the stores that catered to the teen market, including Susie's, Ups 'N' Downs, and Merry-Go-Round, went out of business. In 1992, however, the teenage market began growing at twice the rate of the rest of the population. Retailers of teen apparel, such as Gadzooks, Pacific Sunwear, Hot Topic, and American Eagle Outfitters, have recognized the potential of the teen demographic and catered to the market accordingly. New teen apparel stores continue to emerge. A new division of PacSun, d.e.m.o., offers popular hip-hop brands for teens, including Eminem's Shady Ltd.[4] The nation's teen market is projected to max out at 35 million by 2010, with an estimated buying power of $140 billion.

Apparel merchants are not the only retailers with an eye on the teen market. Home furnishings retailers also target the teen demographic. Decorating shows such as the Discovery Channel's *Trading Spaces: Boys vs. Girls*, a spinoff of the adult version of *Trading Spaces*, have popularized teen decorating. Lowe's, the home improvement category killer based in North Wilkesboro, North Carolina, has responded by promoting bedding, furniture, flooring, lighting, and accessories with surfing, bohemian, and camouflage themes especially popular among teens. In its PBteen catalog, Pottery Barn promotes bedding and window treat-

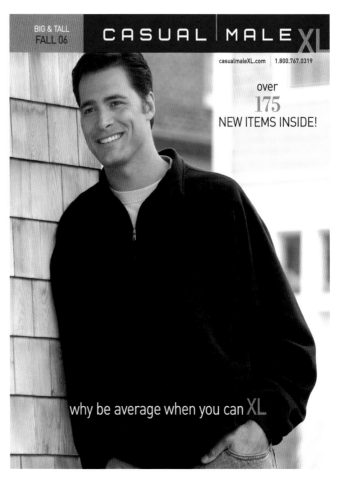

ments with the slogan "You, your friends, your space."[5] Dorm decorating is also big business. Todd Oldham designed a dorm line for Target so that the company could get its share of the $2.1 billion that college freshmen spend on dorm furnishings such as featherbeds, roman shades, and microfridges. Likewise, Best Buy has a college registry, a spinoff of the wedding registry, for first-time dorm shoppers.

Baby boomers, of course, attract considerable attention as a demographic group. Born between 1946 and 1964, baby boomers constitute one-third of the U.S. population. They are a $2 trillion market controlling more than 50 percent of the nation's disposable income and 75 percent of the nation's personal assets. Because of its size, marketing organizations have been

FIGURE 5.1
A niche market retailer caters to customers with characteristics that differ from the mass market. Courtesy Casual Male Retail Group.

FIGURE 5.2
Though high income is a desirable demographic for many retailers, some retailers target low-income markets. Courtesy Fairchild Publications, Inc.

catering to the whims of the baby boom market segment for the past 60 years, identifying its needs at every stage of life through which the boomers have passed. Disposable diapers, junior-size apparel, sugary cereals, minivans, bottled water, and designer jeans are but a few of the products developed with the baby boomers in mind.

For some marketers, baby boomers have become increasingly attractive as they age. Very soon, women over 45 will unseat female teenagers as the

FIGURE 5.3
Some retailers, like Pacific Sunwear, cater to the needs of the teen market. Courtesy Fairchild Publications, Inc.

FIGURE 5.4
Television shows such as *Desperate Housewives* have glamorized older women and given them a new image in the marketplace. Courtesy ABC/Photofest, © ABC, photographer Ron Tom.

biggest spenders on clothing, shoes, and accessories. Pop culture, with television shows such as *Desperate Housewives*, has glamorized older women, giving them a whole new image in the marketplace. Retailers are responding accordingly.[6] Gymboree has a new division called Janeville, and American Eagle has a division called Martin + Osa, both targeted to women 35 and over.[7] Gap developed Forth & Towne, a new concept catering to women over 35, but closed the division in 2007.[8]

Some retailers are already naturally positioned to cater to aging boomers; for example, J. Jill and Talbots have always catered to the over-35 set. Other retailers have aged along with their customers. Pier 1 Imports, the nation's largest retailer of home accessories, once sold incense, beads, and candles to the flower children of the 1960s. Over time, Pier 1's flower children became affluent nesters. Pier 1 responded with more upscale assortments.

Aging along with customers is not always a successful marketing strategy, however. Lord & Taylor, a venerable department store fixture on New York's Fifth Avenue since 1914, once catered to a Junior League–type customer. Over the years, the store remained loyal to its dedicated customers and aged

FIGURE 5.5
The Gap created Forth
& Towne, targeted to
women over 35, but
closed the division in
2007. © James
Leynse/Corbis.

with them. But as its customer base died, Lord & Taylor was left with a shrunken market and dowdy image. By failing to attract young customers, Lord & Taylor now struggles for both identity and survival.[9]

Psychographic segmentation involves identifying markets according to their values, attitudes, and lifestyles. Psychographic characteristics are important to retailers. For example, mothers who work outside of the home shop differently than stay-at-home moms. The former are more pressed for time and spend less time browsing. They place a high value on convenience and service. They embrace one-stop shopping and become dedicated to retailers that satisfy multiple needs.

Americans strive for order in their hectic lives, and catering to the need for order has become a massive industry in and of itself. According to the International Housewares Association, Americans spend more than $5 billion a year on space organizers. The Container Store is an example of a retailer that responds to this need. The Dallas-based storage and organization retailer offers more than 10,000 items to organize closets, laundries,

FIGURE 5.6
Courtesy of King Features
Syndicate.

kitchens, and home offices in nearly 40 stores. The popularity of home organization is evident across many mass media segments: the magazine *Real
Simple*; the book *Smart Storage: Stylish Solutions for Every Room in Your
Home* by Copestick, Lloyd and Wood; and home organization shows such
as TLC's *Clean Sweep* and HGTV's *Mission: Organization*.[10]

Demographic characteristics become more meaningful when coupled
with psychographic characteristics. Baby boomers' psychographic characteristics make them different from previous generations of older Americans.
They are more independent, active, and healthier than their parents. They
fear aging and spend freely on products to help them look young and retain
their youth. Consistent with this psychographic profile, Revlon has developed an age-defying cosmetic line called Vital Radiance for women over 45,
a demographic group that accounts for 69.3 percent of the purchases of
mass market cosmetics.[11] Cover Girl also has an age-defying line called
Advance Radiance.

Psychographic information supplements demographic information to
help marketers accurately predict consumer behavior. Developed by market
research giants RoperASW and Mediamarket Research, LifeMatrix is a
psychographic marketing tool that sorts people into ten psychographic categories based on hundreds of personal variables, including religious and
political affiliations. The categories of like-minded individuals have titles
like "priority parents" and "tribe wired"—each linked to a battery of personality traits and purchasing preferences. A working mom trying to balance
job, family, and cultural activities is a "Renaissance woman"—a category

FIGURE 5.7
The Container Store caters to the need for order in hectic lives. © 2006 The Container Store® Inc. All rights reserved.

comprising involved, caring, and optimistic women who are altruistic rather than hedonistic, who are likely to be Internet users, and who enjoy museums and eschew radio and television.[12]

Many retailers define their customers in both demographic and psychographic terms. The Zale Corporation, the nation's largest fine jewelry retailer, operates six divisions, each distinct in terms of targeted customer: Piercing Pagoda is for the young trendsetter, age 16 to 25; Zales Jewelers targets the classic, traditional customer, age 25 to 65; Mappins/Peoples Jewellers is for the moderate, value-oriented Canadian customer, age 25 to 65; Gordon's is for the contemporary and fashion-forward customer, age 40 to 65; Zales Outlet is for the value- and brand-oriented customer, age 30 and over; and Bailey Banks & Biddle is for the upscale customer, age 35 to 65.

Using demographics without psychographics can be disastrous. Because people between 55 and 64 purchase more greeting cards than members of any other age group, Hallmark Cards created a line of occasional cards that subtly flattered the egos of customers over 50. The Time of Your Life cards were distributed through Hallmark's 43,000 retail distribution points in attractive store displays showing youthful-looking middle-agers frolicking on beaches and in pools. Hallmark discontinued the line three years later, however, because of lagging sales. The reason: baby boomers were too vain to be seen shopping in an "old folks" card section.

Retailers with large-store formats cater to multiple customer segments. Nordstrom organizes itself as a series of lifestyle shops, including Savvy, with cutting-edge lines such as Vivienne Tam, Vertigo, and Theory; t.b.d., a trendy shop; Individualist for contemporary career and casual fashions; and Studio 21, a shop of timeless, sophisticated looks.[13] Even the largest retailer lacks the physical capacity to satisfy every market, however, and attempting to be everything to everyone can result in shallow, disjointed assortments.

FIGURE 5.8
The Zale Corp., the nation's largest fine jewelry retailer, has six operating divisions, each distinct in terms of its target customer. Courtesy Fairchild Publications, Inc.

Micromerchandising

Micromerchandising involves tailoring an individual store's product mix to the local market based on the store's database of customer purchase history and knowledge of local tastes and demographics. Sears sells fringed suede vests and skirts during rodeo season in a handful of Texas stores in January. In New Orleans, Saks Fifth Avenue offers an extensive assortment of long dresses for Mardi Gras. The Kmart in New York's Greenwich Village has a dorm shop to cater to the large number of college students in the area.

Wal-Mart is an industry leader in micromerchandising. The Wal-Mart in Tom's River, New Jersey, responds to the needs of a large senior market with inexpensive canes, large-size women's apparel, and golf equipment. About 80 percent of the goods carried at the Wal-Mart stores in Mountain View and Union City, California, are the same. But the Mountain View store caters to the Silicon Valley crowd with eye-catching displays of mountain bikes and health supplements like echinacea. For the more blue-collar crowd in Union City, there is stronger emphasis on home entertainment, especially televisions.[14]

BIGGER IS GETTING BETTER

Blame it on economic prosperity and sedentary lifestyles. Whatever the reason, the fact remains that two-thirds of the U.S. population is either overweight or obese. Today, 36.8 percent of the female population wears size 14 or larger, a striking contrast to 1985 when size eight was the most popular size. The media has done well in its effort to make a growing majority feel okay about being overweight. Consumer magazines, such as *Glamour* and *Marie Claire*, have featured overweight women, as have "teenzines" *Seventeen* and *CosmoGirl*. Plus-size supermodel Emme was twice annointed by People magazine as among the most beautiful 50 people in the world. Even *Vogue*, the bastion of the willowy models, devoted an entire issue to full-figure women, sending a signal to the fashion industry legitimizing the plus-size demographic as a target market. Entertainment figures such as Oprah Winfrey, Catherine Zeta-Jones, and Kirstie Alley have further enhanced the image of full-figure women.

The $17 billion plus-size apparel business is growing faster than straight-size business. In response to the trend, stores such as Saks Fifth Avenue and Macy's have expanded their plus-size departments with labels such as Ralph Lauren, Calvin Klein, Liz Claiborne, and Tommy Hilfiger. With music diva Queen Latifah as its celebrity model, Lane Bryant has become the nation's largest plus-size specialty retailer with more than 650 stores nationwide. Based in City of Industry, California, Hot Topic operates more than 100 Torrid stores with apparel and accessories for plus-size teens, and such trendy labels as Tyte Jeans, Chica Junior, HotKiss, Dickies, and Paris Blues.

SOURCE
Excerpted from Marton, A. (April 18, 2003). The plus-size woman. *The* (Springfield, MA) *Republican*. p E1.

Other Types of Segmentation

Markets can be segmented other than by demographic and psychographic characteristics. Geographic segmentation involves profiling customers by geographic region of the country. Climate is an obvious reason for this segmentation. Ski parkas are an important apparel category in Minnesota, but not in Louisiana. Consumer tastes are also geographically linked. Observers note that the Dallas unit of Barneys New York failed because it featured black minimalist fashions and low-heeled shoes at a time when Dallas was still into glitz and big hair. The type of geographic area, such as urban, suburban, or rural, is another segmentation factor that affects assortments. When Kmart opened a store in Manhattan, the company strategically edited categories such as lawn-and-garden and automotive.

Family life cycle segmentation is based on marital status and the presence or absence of dependent children in a family. Murphy and Staples have identified 13 life-cycle stages in the Modernized Family Life Cycle shown in Figure 5.9. Purchasing power and spending habits differ at each stage of the family life cycle relative to the number of dependent children. A "middle-aged married without dependent children" has more spending potential than a "young married with children"; however, the latter is a more lucrative target for retailers of toys and juvenile furniture. The Murphy and Staples family life cycle reflects a more contemporary perspective than previous versions of the family life cycle that did not consider the effect of divorce on families. Divorce is an important economic consideration, because divorce breaks families into smaller, usually less affluent units.

Ethnic segmentation has become an important marketing strategy because of the rapid growth of populations of African, Asian, and Latino descent. Once a homogenous "melting pot," the United States has become an ethnically diverse "salad bowl."[15] The Latino population alone grew by 58 percent in the United States in the past decade, making it the nation's fastest growing minority group. Latino purchasing power is now nearly

SOURCE
Excerpted from Reidy, C. (November 15, 2002). Casual Male hoping to don a new image. *Boston Globe.* p. D3.

SIZE MATTERS

Casual Male XL is the nation's largest retailer in the $6.0 billion big and tall men's specialty apparel market. With more than 500 locations throughout the United States, England, and Canada, and substantial e-commerce and catalog operations, Casual Male operates under the trade names of Casual Male XL, Rochester Big & Tall, and Sears Canada-Casual Male. Casual Male's mid-price brands include Perry Ellis America, Geoffrey Beene, Izod, and Reebok, along with its private label, the George Foreman Comfort Zone. The Rochester stores offer more upscale brands, such as Burberry, Ermenegildo Zegna, Polo/Ralph Lauren, and Andrew Marc.

Casual Male has worked hard to attract the nonsedentary, fashion-oriented big and tall customer. Its "Freedom" advertising campaign said it all: "Freedom ... it should belong to all of us. Which is why Casual Male is bringing freedom to big-and-tall guys everywhere. When you're big and tall, it's hard to find clothing that gives you the freedom to enjoy life and look great doing it." The ads' imagery depicted the breadth of the company's apparel assortment through vignettes of big and tall men romping with dogs, playing basketball with their kids, and dressing up for a date.

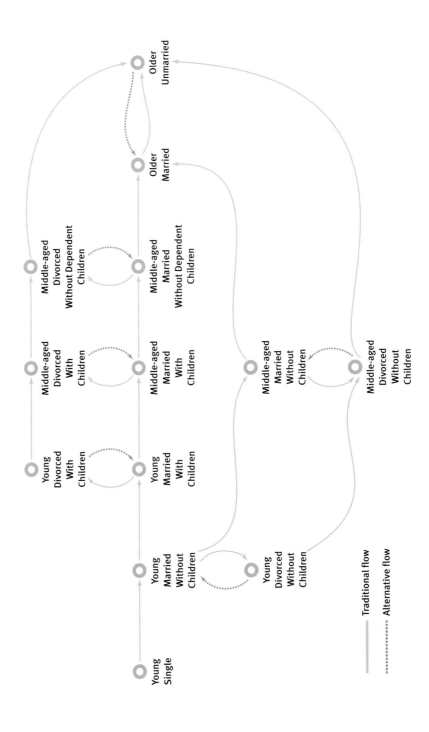

Young Single

Young Married Without Children

Young Divorced Without Children

Young Divorced With Children

Young Married With Children

Middle-aged Divorced With Children

Middle-aged Married With Children

Middle-aged Divorced Without Dependent Children

Middle-aged Married Without Dependent Children

Middle-aged Married Without Children

Middle-aged Divorced Without Children

Older Married

Older Unmarried

Traditional flow

Alternative flow

FIGURE 5-9
The Modernized Family Life Cycle.

TURNING WOMEN ON

Lowe's and Home Depot battle to win female customers. Though Home Depot is about twice the size of Lowe's in terms of number of units and annual sales volume, the home improvement store behemoths compete head-on in many markets.

Lowe's thinks that women are worth focusing on in that women initiate about 80 percent of all home-improvement projects. To woo female customers, Lowe's began designing stores with wider aisles, brighter lighting and larger signs to make products easier to find. The retailer also beefed up its selection of designer brands, such as Eddie Bauer and Nickelodeon paint, while upscaling its major appliance selection with energy-efficient washers, such as Maytag's Neptune and Whirlpool's Calypso.

To remain competitive, Home Depot improved its signage, and installed self-checkouts to expedite customer transactions. Home Depot cultivates women shoppers by holding do-it-yourself workshops for women. But Lowe's has chosen not to emulate its archrival on this one. Its surveys showed that most women don't want women-only workshops.

SOURCE
Excerpted from Matthews, S. (November 23, 2003). Women customers help Lowe's gain on home Depot. *Boston Globe.* p. E3.

$700 billion and growing at an annualized rate of 7.7. percent, nearly three times the 2.8 percent growth rate of total U.S. population.[16]

The impact of Latino immigration to the United States has been significant. Latinos are remaking the face of the country in many areas of culture. They are energizing an aging population, supporting a housing boom, supplying scarce labor to many industries, and forcing the marketplace pay attention to their growth. European immigrants who arrived in the United States in the last century were more anxious to *assimilate* the language, customs, and traditions of their new country, often renouncing the ways of the world from which they came. Latinos tend to *acculturate* rather than assimilate, retaining their language and culture as they adapt to life in the United States.

Accounting for about 9 percent of U.S. apparel sales, Latinos spend more on clothing than other demographic groups. But fashions popular among Latinos are not readily found in mainstream stores. Dressy styles in vivid colors for women and modern versions of the "guayabera," the loose-fitting Cuban-style shirt, for men are hardly staples at Wal-Mart. Recognizing this deficit, some retailers have responded to the demand for distinctively Latin looks. Sears debuted an apparel line developed with Latina lifestyle expert Lucy Pereda. Kmart partnered with Mexican soap opera sensation

Thalía Sodi to create eponymous lines of apparel, accessories, and home accessories. Similarly, Kohl's collaborated with MTV host Daisy Fuentes to create an apparel line with a Spanish accent.[17]

Some retailers attract ethnic customers with special advertising campaigns. To draw African-American and Latino customers, Kmart developed a multicultural advertising campaign under the tag line "Kmart . . . the Stuff of Life" and "Kmart . . . las Cosas Para la Vida." The campaign included television commercials set to original music by Chaka Khan and BeBe Winans shown on BET, and others set to music by José Feliciano shown on Telemundo and Univision. More than one-third of Kmart's customers are African-American or Latino.[18]

Even shopping centers have gotten on the ethnic segmentation bandwagon. Milpitas Square is an Asian-themed shopping center just outside San Jose, California. The mall has Asian restaurants, bakeries, specialty food stores, and an Asian-owned bank.[19]

SOURCE
Excerpted from Staff.
(February 14, 2005).
New Penney: Chain goes
for 'missing middle'.
Wall Street Journal.

J.C. PENNEY'S MISSING MIDDLE

J.C. Penney has carved out a marketplace niche for itself by appealing to the "missing middle." With upscale retailers like Neiman Marcus and Nordstrom attracting the affluent shopper, and with value-oriented retailers like Wal-Mart and Target appealing to the opposite end of the economic continuum, it makes sense that the only space left is the middle. As Mike Ullman, J.C. Penney's CEO, puts it, "The core of America is up for grabs in terms of their heart and soul. This customer is underserved."

According to J.C. Penney, the missing middle customer is:

- female
- age 35–54
- from a $69,000 income household
- married, with kids
- stylish, but not too trendy
- searching for high-quality, form-fitting apparel that isn't too tight

Penney's has worked hard to satisfy the needs of the missing middle. The company partnered with well-known designer Nicole Miller to develop an exclusive line of moderately priced and more than moderately stylish casual women's apparel. Penney's also added an exclusive line of home furnishings from Chris Madden and Colin Cowie to its offerings, and a new private label, W—Work to Weekend, especially designed for the missing middle customer.

COMMUNICATING WITH CUSTOMERS

Positioning refers to a marketplace position that a product or service occupies relative to its competitors. Positioning is often based on price. Price positioning has given birth to terms like "low end" and "high end," and in the automobile industry, categories such as "economy" and "luxury." Positioning can be based on product attributes. Some toothpastes whiten, others control tartar, while still others guard against cavities. Positioning can also relate to the demographic and/or psychographic characteristics of an intended customer.

Estée Lauder is the nation's leading producer of prestige cosmetics lines. The company has several uniquely positioned lines. Estée Lauder is a fragrance-oriented line for older customers. Clinique is a hypoallergenic line for younger suburban types. Prescriptives is a high-fashion line for urban customers. Origins is a "green" line featuring New Age products such

FIGURE 5.10
Iman has a cosmetic line designed especially for women of color. © Sygma/Christian Simonpietri/Corbis.

as aromatherapy oils. To be successful, products must be strategically positioned and clearly differentiated from their competitors.

Retail stores, like consumer products, also are positioned. As noted earlier in this chapter, the operating divisions of Zales are profiled, or positioned, by age of customer and product price. Gap's operating divisions are all positioned as casual apparel stores, but they are further positioned by price. Gap's newest division, Forth & Towne, is positioned by the gender and age of the intended customer: women over 35.

Image is a term closely allied to positioning. A store's image is the way it is perceived by the public. References to a store's image include "value-oriented," "fashion-forward," and "prestigious." Though negative images are never intended, stores also can be perceived as "stodgy," "overpriced," or "boring."

A store's image is the result of a carefully honed marketing strategy involving multiple factors. Location and physical facilities are components of a store's image. Though the lines of demarcation are blurring, mall and strip-center tenants are distinct in terms of service, price, and fashion. A store's architecture, interior decor, fixturing, signage, and merchandise presentation can deliver messages of prestige, service, or price. Marble floors and elegant elevators convey an image distinctly different from vinyl tile

SOURCES

1. Caminiti, S. (March 18, 1996). Will Old Navy fill the gap? *Fortune*. pp. 59–62.

STORE NAME AND IMAGE

A store's name can reflect its image. Long-established retail enterprises often bear the family name(s) of their founder(s). However, more contemporary names often identify a store's offerings or target market. The word "mart" in Wal-Mart and Kmart conveys a discount image. Store names such as Kids "R" Us and Casual Male XL, convey clear images of product line and target markets.

Old Navy was originally known as Gap Warehouse. When Gap, Inc., Old Navy's parent company, decided to expand its value-oriented concept nationally, it hired a marketing company to come up with a name with a little more imagination. Forklift and Monorail were the two top choices. Old Navy came from the side of a building. The name was chosen because it was seen as being "euphonious, unpretentious, suggestive of canvas and discipline."[1]

and shopping carts. Talbots uses architectural elements such as foyers, maple flooring, and wainscoting, as well as antiques and equestrian-themed prints to convey a gracious, residential ambiance in its stores.

The merchandise division of a retail organization plays a critical role in creating and maintaining a store's image. Buyers' choices of brands, styles, fabrics, and colors reflect a store's image. To reinforce an image of fashion, a buyer searches the market for the latest styles and trends. To maintain an image of value, a buyer seeks opportunistic buys of goods that can be retailed at prices lower than competitors'. Buyers are diligent in their efforts to convey a consistent image throughout an entire store or department from season to season. Gap periodically has suffered from an inconsistent image: trendy one season and classic the next.[20] An inconsistent image has been painful for other retailers. The worst performing year in Talbots' history was 1997, the year that the company strayed from its classic tailored looks by trying to attract younger customers with high slits and short skirts.

FIGURE 5.11
Kmart partnered with Mexican soap opera sensation Thalía Sodi to create namesake lines of apparel, accessories, and home accessories. © AP/Wide World Photos/Diane Bondareff.

Sometimes stores "reposition" themselves by creating a new image. Ethan Allen Interiors was long known for its stodgy collections of colonial reproductions. The conservative styles were an anathema to the 20- and 30-year-olds at the heart of the home-buying market. To attract younger customers, Ethan Allen repositioned itself with colorful, contemporary, less formal assortments, even replacing many of its white-column storefronts with art deco façades. Shreve, Crump & Low, Boston's grande dame of jewelry stores, also repositioned itself. The metamorphosis from staid and traditional to chic and trendy happened when the store moved to a new two-story location. First-floor prominence was given to semiprecious stones,

FIGURE 5.12
Abercrombie & Fitch has a
carefully honed image that
makes the store attractive
to teenagers. © David
Young-Wolff/PhotoEdit.

such as pink tourmaline, and avant-garde jewelry lines, such as Barry Kieselstein-Cord and Vera Wang. To avoid alienating its longstanding, change-resistant customers, the entire second floor was dedicated to traditional product, including fine china, Mikimoto pearls, and porcelain Gurgling Cods.[21]

Sales Promotion

In a retail company, sales promotion is the organizational function responsible for inducing customer traffic and sales by communicating information to customers pertaining to assortments, prices, services, and other sales incentives. An effective sales promotion strategy positions a store in the minds of consumers and is thus an important factor in defining a store's image. Sales promotion encourages repeat business and customer loyalty. Sales promotion functions include advertising, publicity, and special events.

Advertising conveys a message to a large group of people through a mass medium, such as newspapers, magazines, radio, television, or the Internet. The cost of delivering the message is paid for by the advertiser or sponsor. Newspapers are a local advertising medium appropriate for retailers with trading areas that parallel a newspaper's circulation. Regional and national retailers reach customers by advertising in many newspapers. Because newspapers attract a diversely demographic readership, retailers that target a diverse group of customers are appropriate newspaper advertisers. An age-old alliance between department stores and newspapers dates back historically to their growth alongside each other in cities populous enough to support both. Department stores and full-line discounters continue to be major newspaper advertisers, though newspapers now share retail advertising budgets with other forms of advertising, such as television.

The preprinted insert has become a popular newspaper advertising vehicle. Often called "circulars," the most common type of insert is the multipage 10-by-15-inch tabloid. The piece is prepared by the retailer's advertising department, printed, and then sent to various newspapers for insertion into the folds of a specific edition, often a Sunday paper. Newspapers charge retailers an insertion fee of approximately 25 cents per insert for inserting the piece and for using the newspaper to carry the advertising message.

Preprinted inserts are an alternative to the conventional practice of placing ads within the paper. Retailers prefer preprinted inserts for two major reasons:

- Preprinted inserts can be printed on paper that reproduces color with greater clarity than newsprint.
- The cost of producing and inserting an insert is less than buying the same amount of space within the paper.

Magazines are a national advertising medium whose major advertisers are producers of nationally distributed consumer products and services. As a national medium, magazines are a popular advertising vehicle among national retailers, but not common for local or regional retailers. Unlike newspapers, magazines are targeted to readers with clearly defined interests, such as sports, fashion, and health. The products and services advertised in magazines reflect their readership. David's Bridal, the 250-unit bridal superstore, advertises in *Modern Bride, Weddings and Brides*, and *Bride's* magazines. Spurred by competition from Target, Wal-Mart hoped to upgrade its fashion image by advertising in *Vogue*.[22] Producer-sponsored magazine advertising sometimes includes the names of retailers at which the product line is available.

Like newspapers, radio is primarily a local advertising medium. Radio's inability to convey a visual message limits its desirability as an advertising medium for retailers who need to convey the physical attributes of their assortments. Radio is an effective advertising medium for events, however, such as a "One-Day Sale." Kmart's "Stuff of Life" campaign included both television and radio components.

As a national advertising medium, television is most appealing to national retailers. J.C. Penney, Sears, and Wal-Mart conduct extensive prime-time advertising on major television networks and cable stations. High production costs and the rising cost of airtime have made television advertising an expensive proposition. By converting multiple regional nameplates to either Macy's or Bloomingdale's, Federated Department Stores stretched its advertising budget by developing national television advertising campaigns for two operating divisions, and buying airtime on a national instead of regional basis.[23] Small independent retailers and regional chains buy television time through local network affiliates and cable companies. The high cost of producing quality television advertising makes it prohibitive for many independent retailers.

Direct response advertising, such as catalogs, bill enclosures, and flyers, is another form of retail advertising. Commonly called *direct mail*, a store's charge customers are the likely recipients of direct response advertising. As noted in Chapter 2, some retailers are exclusively direct mail merchants, using catalogs and other direct response vehicles as their only customer communication. Other retailers use direct response to supplement store-front business by attracting customers who live beyond the store's geographic market area, or who like the convenience of shopping at home.

Internet advertising is a rapidly growing form of direct response advertising. In Internet advertising, ads are strategically placed in close proximity to related searches. Customer purchases are facilitated by links to the advertiser's web site. Internet advertising is distinct from other forms of advertising in that advertisers are only charged for responses, or clicks—on an average, 50 cents per hit. In other forms of advertising, advertisers are charged for merely exposing customers to an ad, and advertisers have no way of knowing how many customers actually respond. Internet advertising is closely allied with direct mail. For convenient ordering, direct mail pieces now often include both a toll-free 800 number and a URL.[24]

Retailers occasionally use out-of-home advertising, such as billboards and transit advertising appearing on various forms of public transportation. Target received the prestigious Obie award for its "Wants– Needs" ad campaign that creatively wedded utilitarian products, such as toilet paper, with items that consumers simply want, such as an attractive scarf, on eye-catching billboards.[25]

Publicity is "free advertising" through a mass medium in the form of news coverage. A retailer's newsworthy events include the announcement of plans for new stores, the appointment of new executives, or the latest quarterly report of earnings. The news media often rely on buyers as news sources for timely comments on fashion, hot items, and consumer purchasing. Eileen Fisher, a 30-unit retailer of upscale female apparel, receives good publicity for a social-consciousness public relations program that supports noble causes such as the well-being of women, conducting business with regard for human rights, and environmentally sustainable business practices.[26]

Sometimes retailers receive negative publicity, as Abercrombie & Fitch did when it unveiled a line of thong underwear for girls 10 to 16 imprinted with phrases such as "wink, wink" and "eye candy."[27] To counter news stories portraying it as a company that pays low wages with few benefits, Wal-Mart bought full-page ads in more than 100 newspapers to tout the fact that the company provides full-time employment with benefits and opportunities for advancement to thousands of employees.[28]

BE AN INSIDER
IT'S EASY TO BECOME AN INSIDER. AND THE BENEFITS START RIGHT AWAY. OPEN AN ACCOUNT SEPT. 8TH-10TH **AND SAVE 20% ON** YOUR FIRST DAY'S PURCHASES.* PLUS YOU'LL RECEIVE PREVIEW SAVINGS DAYS, SPECIAL INVITATIONS, BONUS OFFERS AND MORE. AS YOUR SPENDING INCREASES, SO DO THE REWARDS. ASK ANY SALES PROFESSIONAL FOR DETAILS. YOU CAN SIGN UP ANYTIME.

ON THE INSIDE
OUR HOT EVENT IS JUST FOR INSIDERS AND IT DOESN'T GET HOTTER THAN THIS. EVERYWHERE YOU LOOK: SOMETHING EXCITING DESIGNERS DROPPING BY DJS SPINNING TUNES **A CHANCE TO WIN ONE OF** 32 FREE TRIPS TO SAN FRANCISCO THE TRENDIEST FASHION ON DISPLAY GOODIES TO NIBBLE GOODIES TO TAKE HOME **EXCLUSIVE SAVINGS AND BONUSES**
(WHEN YOU'RE ON THE INSIDE)

FIGURE 5.13
A store's charge customers are likely to be the recipients of direct mail pieces. Courtesy of Bloomingdale's.

Special events, such as informal modeling, "how-to" seminars, and appearances of television and sports celebrities, are promotional attractions that draw customers and create an exciting shopping atmosphere in a store. Cooking demonstrations are popular special events. The State Street Macy's in Chicago has a 150-seat, state-of-the-art demonstration kitchen in which it hosts cooking demonstrations by local celebrity chefs. Cosmetics counters often are abuzz with special events like facial massages, skin care analyses, makeovers, and new product demonstrations. Special events sometimes have a public relations dimension. In its stores in the Pacific Northwest, Macy's sponsored three traveling exhibits to honor the legacies of three ethnic communities—African American, Chinese American, and Latino—as pioneers of the region.[29]

The merchandise division is often the source of ideas for special events. Suppliers frequently offer retailers special event opportunities, such as product demonstrations, appearances by designers, or the use of vintage collections of their product line. Though special events are often considered the domain of department stores, other types of retailers, including discounters, use special events in their promotional strategy. The concept of the "store as theater" was popularized at the Bloomingdale's flagship store in New York City, where "spritzing" by fragrance company models, book signings by famous authors, and cooking demonstrations are everyday occurrences.

FIGURE 5.15
Special events are a traffic-generating promotional strategy often used by department stores. Courtesy of Bloomingdale's.

Types of Retail Advertising

Retail advertising is classified according to the type of goods advertised and/or the message conveyed.

Regular price advertising   Features premier assortments at conventional prices. Brand, quality, styling, and assortment are emphasized in regular price advertising; price typically is downplayed. Regular price advertising reinforces an image of fashion or prestige and is common among department and specialty stores.

Promotional advertising   Commonly called "sale" advertising, promotional advertising features a retailer's regular offerings at discounted prices. Value is emphasized with comparisons of the promotional price to the regular price. The discounted price typically is offered for a specified period stated in the ad.

Clearance advertising   Like promotional advertising, clearance advertising features goods at discounted prices. However, clearance goods are residual assortments of end-of-season, slow-selling, or discontinued merchandise.

BLOOMINGDALE'S, MICHAEL ARAM, & INSTYLE WEDDINGS INVITE YOU TO

The Wedding Party

WEDNESDAY, MARCH 1ST
6:00–8:00PM
CHESTNUT HILL
THE REGISTRY ON LEVEL 1

Meet designer Michael Aram and learn about the craftsmanship behind his designs, followed by a product signing. Discover the magic behind Champagne Taittinger's bubbly, sip cappuccino from Nespresso, get royally pampered, see the best in wedding wear and get tips from the experts. Plus, enter to win a honeymoon getaway from Starwood Hotels*.

BEST OF BLOOMINGDALE'S
See gowns from Yolanda's that will take your breath away and outfit your bridal party in bridesmaid dresses from Bloomingdale's private collection.

GROOM'S GATHERING
Select formalwear for your groomsmen from Armani.

COOKING WITH DANIEL BRUCE
Let Chef Daniel Bruce of the Boston Harbor Hotel tantalize your taste buds while your senses are soothed by the sultry sounds of the April Hall Quartet.

HOME BLISS
Find your inner hostess with domestic accents from Michael Aram, Vera Wang, Villeroy & Boch, Kate Spade, Calphalon, Baccarat, Kosta Boda, Bernardaud and Christofle.

ICING ON THE CAKE
Looking to get in shape for the big day? Let Healthworks Chestnut Hill be your fitness guru.

* No purchase necessary; see store for details.

PLEASE REPLY by February 27TH
617.630.6044

You've found it all in one person, now find it all in one store. The registry is available in stores nationwide, at bloomingdales.weddingchannel.com, and at 1-800-888-2WED.

LIKE NO OTHER STORE IN THE WORLD

Institutional advertising   Often called image advertising, institutional advertising reinforces a store's position as a leader in value, service, fashion, or prestige. Institutional advertising often characterizes the lifestyle of the store's targeted customers, without reference to specific merchandise or prices.

Retail advertising often is tied to a promotional theme or event, such as a Men's Wardrobe Sale, an After Inventory Clearance, or a Fall Fashion catalog. Events are categorized by their scope:

- A storewide event includes virtually all categories of merchandise in a store, such as an Anniversary Sale or Summer Clearance.
- A divisional event includes a single merchandise division, such as a Great Gift Ideas for Dad ad or a Back-to-School sale.
- A departmental event includes a single department or category of merchandise, such as a Fragrance Festival or a Dress Bonanza.
- A vendor event includes a single vendor, such as Liz Claiborne Week. The advertising expense for vendor events is usually shared with the supplier, a topic discussed in Chapter 14.

Though events typically encompass multiple items, some retailers choose to advertise single items. Regular-price ads for single items often are semi-institutional in nature, symbolizing a store's image or prestige. The products featured in single-item promotional ads usually are exceptional values and powerful traffic inducers.

The sales promotion and merchandising functions are closely allied in a retail organization, sometimes falling within the same organizational pyramid. The two work in tandem to develop promotional strategies, budgets, and event schedules. Advertising is responsible for the creative development and production of advertising pieces and for coordinating the purchase of media space and time. The merchandising division is responsible for choosing the merchandise that appears in ads and ascertaining that the goods are consistent with the theme or event. Buyers often obtain photographs or art from their suppliers for ads, or they provide samples to be photographed or sketched. Buyers furnish product information for the copy or wording of ads. They then proofread the copy to ensure that product descriptions and prices are correct. Buyers are also responsible for obtaining support from suppliers to share the cost of advertising their goods, a topic discussed in Chapter 14. A merchandising division is responsible for ensuring the arrival of goods in stores by the time an ad breaks and for ascertaining adequate levels of inventory. There is hardly a more frustrating shopping experience than to travel to a store in response to an ad and find a paltry selection of advertised goods or, worse yet, none at all.

Personal Selling

Personal selling is one-to-one communication between a salesperson and a customer. In manufacturing organizations personal selling is a marketing function. In a retail organization, however, the human resource division typically is responsible for personal selling programs and personal selling training. As a store-level function, the supervision of personal selling falls within the realm of store administration. Though the merchandising division is not directly responsible for personal selling, buyers often are the source of the product information used to train salespeople on the features and benefits of the goods that they are selling in stores.

Retailers have historically attached more importance to procuring goods than to selling goods, a distinction that is obvious when salaries for the two functions are compared. Low wages coupled with the erratic work schedules contribute to a high turnover rate among retail salespeople, who are often not committed to selling as a profession. Customer service in retail stores is often inhibited by sales force reductions to cut operating expenses.

Many retailers recognize that good customer service is a competitive advantage and that good service can influence a consumer's choice of retail outlet. RadioShack favorably positioned itself in the highly competitive consumer electronics market with its "If you've got questions, we've got answers" campaign that ensured easy-to-understand product use instructions for non-technically oriented customers.

Most retailers have some type of customer service program to foster good customer relations and to reward star sellers. Some retailers use a "canned" sales approach, a step-by-step selling technique. The following steps are typical of many canned approaches:

- *Greet the customer.* Avoid closed-ended questions or clichés that will yield a reflexive "no" such as, "May I help you?" "Hi! A little muggy out there today!" is a better icebreaker.

- *Determine the customer's wants and needs.* "Looking for a Mother's Day gift?" or "What's her favorite color?"
- *Explain product features and benefits.* "This blend of polyester and cotton is perfect for a busy person with little time for ironing."
- *Suggest additional merchandise.* "How about a moisturizer to go with the cleanser?"
- *Close the sale.* "Thanks so much, Ms. Jones. No problem with returning the scarf if the match isn't perfect."

The pitch is typical of those used in department and specialty stores. Though discount stores are essentially self-service, discounters convey an image of service through "greeters" at the store entrances, efficient front-end operations, liberal return policies, and various customer services.

Loyalty Programs and Database Marketing

A loyalty program is an individualized mass marketing strategy of tracking customer purchases to anticipate their future needs. The concept involves identifying customers at point of sale by their credit cards or other identification vehicles, such as frequent-shopper cards, and maintaining a database of their brand and style preferences using their purchase histories. Loyalty programs reward shoppers for dedicated patronage with perks, such as advance notice of promotional events, free gift wrapping, and discounts.

The criterion for determining preferred customers is spending over a period of time, typically a year. Macy's Star Rewards program features color-coded cards that represent customer spending level. The Macy's Red Star Rewards is the baseline card that most customers receive. Customers at the next level of spending receive a Macy's Gold Star Rewards card. A Macy's Platinum Star Rewards card is next. Macy's best customers receive a black Macy's Elite Star Rewards card. Each tier is tied to a certain level of benefits, including vouchers for making Macy's purchases based on spending. In addition to being tied to credit card usage, Macy's Star Rewards program includes frequent-purchase benefits in categories such as hosiery.[30]

Loyalty programs are facilitated by sophisticated database systems such as Fidelity Instant Loyalty, a customer profile system that can track the department, category, style number, and brand of a purchase, as well as customer characteristics such as size, occupation, hobbies, and birthday. Targeted mailing lists can be derived from the database using any combination of criteria. The system also can evaluate the effectiveness of promotional mailings by tracking customer purchases resulting from the mailing. A store can take notice when a customer's purchases decline and can decide how to entice her or him back to the store.[31]

Loyalty programs also are used to track brand preference and the frequent purchase of particular items or categories of items, and to identify cross-selling opportunities. For example, a customer who purchases a pillow-top

FIGURE 5.16
Loyalty programs reward dedicated customers. Courtesy of Bloomingdale's.

mattress may be interested in pillows or bed linens. Some loyalty programs track customer demographic information such as family size, age, or household income. Loyalty programs are descendents of the airline industry's frequent-flyer programs, the original loyalty program. Today, more than 75 percent of U.S. consumers have at least one loyalty card. A third have two or more.

Using databases to reinforce relationships with consumers is widely used in direct marketing. The concept is gaining greater acceptance among storefront retailers in an effort to personalize their customer transactions, enhance service, foster long-term customer loyalty, and tap more revenue from core customers.

Stored value cards, known to customers as *gift cards*, are a database marketing strategy. Like warehouse club membership cards, stored value cards provide retailers with up-front cash that the retailer retains whether the card is redeemed or not. When redeemed, shoppers typically spend more than the card's value, and a high percentage of customers reload their cards with additional cash upon redemption. As with loyalty cards, a stored value card's embedded spending data can be mined to predict future purchases so that a retailer can target customers with promotional mailings based on past purchases.[32]

Invitation-only shopping events are a way of rewarding best customers while enticing them to buy. At these events, a retailer promotes products to preferred customers in a clublike atmosphere with free food, giveaways, and discounts. Gap identified best customers in ten top markets, anointing them "Gap ambassadors." The ambassadors composed guest lists for invitation-only events featuring goody bags, refreshments, and experts to help find the perfect-fitting jeans. To stimulate sales, Toys "R" Us holds invitation-only shopping events during holiday seasons, with door prizes, refreshments, special values, and toy demonstrations.[33]

SUMMARY POINTS

- A market is a group of customers with the desire and ability to buy. Retailers develop merchandising strategies to satisfy the wants and needs of markets that are undersatisfied or dissatisfied with current retail offerings.
- Large markets are segmented into smaller markets on the basis of

similar geographic, demographic, ethnic, psychographic, family life cycle, or geodemographic characteristics.

• A store's image is the way that it is perceived by the public. Retailers develop an image to position themselves in the marketplace and to distinguish themselves from their competitors.

• Sales promotion is an organizational function responsible for advertising, special events, and publicity.

• Personal selling involves one-to-one communication with customers.

• Loyalty programs use historical customer purchase data to anticipate future purchases.

KEY TERMS AND CONCEPTS

advertising

clearance advertising

demographic
  segmentation

direct response
  advertising

ethnic segmentation

family life cycle
  segmentation

geographic
  segmentation

image

institutional
  advertising

invitation-only
    shopping events

loyalty program

market

market segmentation

mass market

niche market

out-of-home
  advertising

personal selling

positioning

preprinted insert

promotional
  advertising

psychographic
  segmentation

publicity

regular price
  advertising

sales promotion

special events

stored value card

target marketing

THINKING ABOUT IT

1. Using a mall directory, examine the list of stores within a specific category of merchandise. Determine the demographic and/or psychographic profile of each store's customer. Is each store uniquely positioned? Is there overlap?

2. Which stores or types of stores will benefit as baby boomers age? Which will suffer?

3. As the teen population dwindles, what advice would you give to teen apparel stores? Should they grow older with their customers? Should they reposition themselves for a new group of customers?

4. What are some regional distinctions among consumer markets in the United States? What demographic, psychographic, and ethnic distinctions do you see?

5. Identify regular price, promotional, and clearance ads in a local newspaper. Compare them aesthetically. What differences do you notice?

6. Do you have a loyalty card? Does having the card impact your spending? How "loyal" are you as a customer?

7. Profile yourself as a customer using both demographic and psychographic characteristics.

TEAMING UP

1. Each member of your team should visit a store selling the same category of merchandise at a local mall. Assess each store's image relative to signage, decor, service, music, and so on. Share observations as a team. Are the stores' images clearly defined?

2. Each team member should shop a niche market retailer, and then find the corresponding assortment of goods in a generalized retail format, such as a department store or full-line discounter. How do the two stores compare in terms of selection? Share your findings with the group.

3. Each member of your team should evaluate a preprinted insert from the local Sunday newspaper regarding featured items, photography, advertising copy, and layout. Are you enticed to buy? Why? Share your observations with the group.

SEARCHING THE NET

1. Search for the annual report of a retail conglomerate mentioned in this or a previous chapter. How are each of the company's operating divisions positioned?

2. Search for recent news stories on aging baby boomers. What impact do aging boomers have on consumer products and services?

3. Search for recent news stories pertaining to obesity. Discuss obesity as a lifestyle trend. What is the impact of obesity on consumer products and services?

4. Search for information pertaining to television advertising campaigns by major retailers. Are any campaigns noteworthy? Which retailers appear to be heavy television advertisers? Have any major retailers conspicuously dropped television as an advertising medium?

CHAPTER SIX

Fashion Merchandising

After reading this chapter, you will be able to discuss:

● The pervasiveness of fashion.

● Basic fashion terms.

● The relevance of fashion to retail merchandising.

The world of fashion is a dynamic and highly competitive arena that provides challenging and rewarding careers to millions. Though the word "fashion" often is associated with women's apparel and accessories, the concept is far more pervasive. Fashion is inherent in men's, women's and children's apparel, home furnishings, food, entertainment, and virtually every facet of culture. Fashion is an integral part of our economic system that embraces a host of industries including manufacturing, advertising, and retailing. Entire textbooks and courses are dedicated to a comprehensive study of fashion. The following is an abbreviated discussion of some fashion concepts and their relevance to retail merchandising.

FASHIONS AND TRENDS

Fashion is a form of expression widely accepted by a group of people over time. The group that accepts a fashion is usually defined by the same demographic and psychographic characteristics used to describe markets in Chapter 5. Young marrieds, senior citizens, and urbanites are among the groups associated with particular fashions. The time period that defines the duration of a fashion varies. Something may be fashionable for a short time, such as a month, or remain fashionable for decades.

Fashion surrounds us. It affects the way we eat, dress, decorate our homes, spend our leisure time, and speak. It is difficult to name a category of consumer goods or services that does not, to some degree, reflect fashion. Cars, consumer electronics, and personal fragrances—all are fashion-oriented products.

The acceptance of a fashion by one group is independent of its acceptance by another. Inherent in the concept of fashion is the fact that fashion acceptance changes with time. As a casual apparel line, Tommy Hilfiger was fashionable among the hip-hop set for many years. Tommy endeavored to become fashionable among additional groups of people and, in so doing, created a plus-size line for women. But Tommy alienated urban

FIGURE 6.1
Marketers use advertising
to convey a fashion's
image. Courtesy of Diesel.
Courtesy of Aussie Bum.

teenage customers, who quickly reject anything that looks like something
their grandmothers are wearing. The youth market abandoned Tommy for
lines they felt more "authentic," such as FUBU, Ecko, Phat Farm, J. Lo, and
Sean John.[1]

Trends

A trend implies the direction or movement of a fashion. The word "trend"
often is used synonymously with "fashion." Thus, something that is trendy
is also fashionable. Trends are described in ways that imply degree of acceptance (a "strong" or "key" trend), direction (an "emerging" or "dying" trend),
duration (a "seasonal" trend), or relationship to other trends (a "secondary"
or "background" trend). In addition, trends are ubiquitous. There are trends
in apparel, home furnishings, lifestyles, consumer spending, even weather
conditions. Trends are important to manufacturers and retailers. Because

STYLE VS. FASHION

Style refers to an item's distinctive characteristics or design features. Turtle-neck, mock turtleneck, and crew neck are collar treatments that define the style of a garment, just as cocktail-, ballerina-, and tea-length indicate skirt lengths. The word "style" is not synonymous with fashion, though popular use of the word sometimes implies that it is. Something that is dated is said to be "out-of-style" when, in fact, it is "out-of-fashion." Something said to be stylish is really in fashion. Only when a style is popular is it a fashion. All fashions have at least one style, but not all styles are fashions. Fashions change, styles do not. Safari jackets may be fashionable one season and not the next, however a safari jacket is always a style whether or not it is fashionable.

of their impact on customer purchases, trends tell retailers what to buy, how to price, when to promote, and when goods need to be marked down.

As a society, we have trended more casual and less formal over the last couple of decades. Nowhere is this more evident than in the workplace. When the casual workplace trend blossomed in the 1990s, apparel producers and retailers were quick to respond. Denim giant Levi Strauss created Dockers, a line of relaxed-fit cotton trousers that have become a staple of the casual workplace. Saks Fifth Avenue conducted seminars to help customers adapt to business casual. Other retailers, such as Gap and Lands' End, by virtue of their existing apparel lines, were poised to reap the benefits of a dressed-down workplace.

Overreacting to trends can be as devastating as not reacting to them at all. Brooks Brothers, a long-established retailer of traditional menswear, introduced casual looks into its assortments as the business-casual trend emerged to compete with casual apparel stores such as Banana Republic and J. Crew. But though the workplace in general had definitely become more casual, there were still men in industries that dressed up, and they had no place to shop. Eventually Brooks Brothers recaptured its alienated customers by reversing its casual leaning and resurrecting many of the traditional looks for which the store was known.[2] The timing was right; as the century turned, the casual workplace trend began to reverse itself as more and more companies reinstated dress codes. Target, among other companies, ended its long-standing policy of business casual at its corporate headquarters in favor of one requiring professional attire.[3]

The surf-and-skate trend hit a high at the beginning of this century. Fueled by the surging popularity of rollerblading, and board sports such as surfing, snowboarding, and skateboarding, the teenage lifestyle trend evolved from a sense of individualism and athleticism infused with a laid-back spirit. Pop-culture hits such as the movie *Blue Crush* and the WB television network's reality show *Boarding House* reinforced the trend. Department stores jumped on the trend by featuring brands such as Billabong, Hurley, and Roxy in their junior departments, at the same time that flip-flops and hooded sweatshirts were exploding the trading price of the stock of teen-apparel retailers, such as Pacific Sunwear and Quiksilver.

Cocooning is a lifestyle trend associated with the increasing amount of time that people spend at home relaxing, entertaining, or working, has stimulated the growth of the $103 billion home furnishings and accessories industry, and has given birth to merchandising concepts such as the home theater. Cocooning manifests itself in many ways, including the home office trend. Staples and Office Depot are retailers that cater to the 27 million families with home offices who spend, apart from computers, $2,000 annually on office supplies.[4] Curbside takeout has become the fastest growing segment of the $511 billion restaurant industry. The growth is tied to two trends: time-starved customers preparing less food from scratch and families eating together at home more often that they did five years ago.[5]

FIGURE 6.2
Department stores jumped on the surf-and-skate trends by featuring brands such as Billabong. Courtesy Fairchild Publications, Inc.

Some trends are short-lived. Metrosexual was a lifestyle trend that typified the young, affluent, urban, aesthetically inclined, heterosexual male who indulged in facials, manicures, fine dining, and fine clothing. The term was coined by British columnist Mark Simpson in 1994, but didn't come into popular use in the United States until 2000.[6] By 2005, however, the trend was dead, and advertisers of men's products, such as shaving cream, were eschewing metrosexuality in favor of advertising appeals to manliness.

Trends are as numerous as the products associated with them. Down-aging is a trend defined by the popularity of products from the past among aging baby boomers. Egonomics refers to consumers' desire for personal expression. All types of industries follow trends. Yankee Candle, the producer and retailer of home fragrances based in Deerfield, Massachusetts, identifies trends in food, fashion, and personal fragrances as the basis for developing as many as 30 new candle scents each year.

Some trends relate to consumer behavior. Historically, the peak selling period for the $14 billion back-to-school business in the United States has been the two weeks immediately preceding Labor Day. However, retailers of children's and teen apparel have noticed a trend: sales for the traditional back-to-school selling period have flattened, but sales remain brisk for the few weeks after school starts. The reason: some kids delay the purchase of back-to-school apparel until they have a chance to see what the cool kids are wearing.[7] Not all trends bolster business, however. A victim of business casual, the women's sheer hosiery business declined considerably in the late 1990s.

FIGURE 6.3
Cocooning is a lifestyle trend that has stimulated the sales of products for the home. Courtesy Jim Bastardo Photography.

THE FASHION LIFE CYCLE

The fashion life cycle represents the evolution, culmination, and decline of fashion acceptance. The fashion life cycle has four phases: introduction, growth, peak, and decline.

- *Introduction*—A fashion is *avant garde* during the introductory stage of the life cycle. During this stage, fashion apparel is called high fashion and is available only through designers or very exclusive stores. Prices during the introductory phase are high, but fashion leaders, or *trend-setters,* are willing to pay the price for the sake of exclusivity and novelty.
- *Growth*—A fashion's introduction is followed by a period of rapid growth during which the mass market becomes flooded with knock-offs, or less expensive, mass-produced copies in cheaper fabrications. Growth phase fashions are adopted by fashion followers. Fashion leaders abandon a fashion at this point. Their commitment to exclusivity motivates them to explore the latest fashions. The fashion life cycle is evident in the home furnishings industry. Toile, a French-inspired scenic design, was once prevalent in high-end wallpaper and upholstery fabrics. Over time, the design started appearing in chair pads and tissue boxes sold at Kmart, an indication that the print was in the mass market phase. By then, "contemporary retro," a mishmash of geometric patterns and Marimekko prints, had replaced toile as high fashion.[8]

SOURCE
Wheeler, S. (May 23, 2006). iPod: for teens and adults, a symbol of prestige, hipness. *The* (Springfield, Mass.) *Republican.* pp. E2, 3

A SYMBOL OF HIPNESS

The iPod, Apple's MP3 player, has become a status symbol just like anything Prada, Hummer, or Converse All-Stars. For teens, iPods are the "must-haves" that cell phones and CD players once were. And for adults, the iPod is an accessory to broadcast hipness and youthfulness. As the technology becomes more accessible, however, iPods will cease to be status symbols. Now, more than half of U.S. households have one or more of the different iPod models. Some believe Apple's marketing success can also be attributed to "podification"—the current trend among Americans to insulate themselves from the outside world. The iPod both shields users from the outside world while broadcasting that they are "keeping up with the Joneses."

Avanquest Software USA in Westminster, Colorado, has designed accessories to enhance the iPod experience, including the iPodPresenter, which allows users to run overhead projection presentation from their iPod instead of their laptop, and the iExtend, which transforms the iPod into a portable hard drive letting users back up files. "The iPod is the perfect blend of fashion and technology which plays directly into image and status," said Bob Land, president of Avanquest. "Owning an iPod means peer acceptance, and feeling connected by sharing the same technology. Because of the importance that's placed on popular culture and music in adolescence, the iPod is seen as a requirement for them. When you are 50, you are perceived as having more vitality that you really are young at heart and hip to popular cultural trends."

- *Peak*—A fashion peak is characterized by no new customers. Sales plateau, neither increasing nor decreasing, and are typically replacements.
- *Decline*—Diminishing sales are characteristic of a fashion's decline. During this phase, most retailers have marked down the fashion for clearance in order to make room for fashions in earlier cycle phases. Fashion laggards purchase the fashion during this stage, as well as nonfashion customers who have no interest in fashion.

Though all fashions pass through the various phases of the fashion life cycle phases, the length of the cycle or any of its phases varies from one fashion to another. Something may be fashionable for a single season or for many years. Durability and replacement rates often determine the length of a fashion life cycle. Goods with limited durability, such as apparel, have

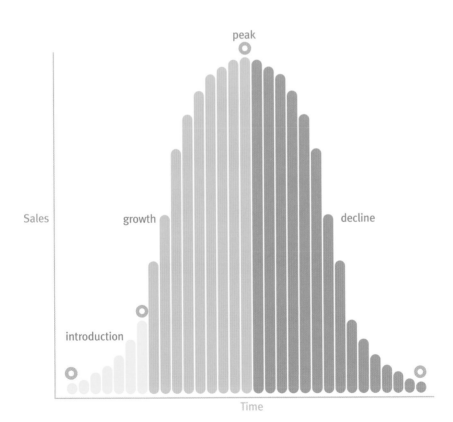

FIGURE 6.4
The fashion life cycle.

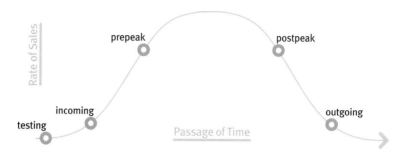

FIGURE 6.5
One store's interpretation
of the fashion life cycle.

shorter fashion life cycles than durable goods, such as home furnishings. Fashions targeted to the young evolve and die so quickly that they are often referred to as disposable. A function of sales and time, the fashion life cycle reinforces the notion that consumer purchases define fashion and that many of the "fashions" that appear on fashion show runways are styles that never really become fashion.

FIGURE 6.6
The growth phase of the
fashion life cycle is
characterized by the
appearance of less
expensive copies of high
fashion called knockoffs.
Source: www.fashion
knockoffs.net.

Fads and Classics

Fads and classics are fashion life cycle extremes. A fad is a short-lived fashion. Fads rise and fall in popularity quickly, enduring for as little time as a few weeks. Some call fads miniature or minor fashions, hesitant to classify fads as true fashions because of their brief acceptance. Fads are especially popular among the young. In particular, the toy industry is prone to fads, and the dream of every major toy company is to release an item that will become the holiday season's toy sensation. In 1996, Tyco came out with Tickle Me Elmo, a plush Sesame Street Muppet character that giggled when squeezed. Unanticipated demand exceeded supply, and "Elmo Mania" ensued. An associate in a Wal-Mart store in New Brunswick, Connecticut, sustained injuries upon being trampled by a crowd of 300 people looking for an Elmo to take home as a holiday gift.[9]

FIGURE 6.7
Poodle skirts were a fad in the 1950s. Source: Sharland/Time Life Pictures/Getty Images.

Fads generate generous revenues for retailers who identify their emergence early. Fads represent a high risk, however. When they die, they die quickly. Fads purchased late in the fashion life cycle must be sold off at drastic price reductions. Some fads have attained historical significance in the annals of U.S. pop culture, including hula hoops (ca. 1958), hot pants (ca. 1971), mood rings (ca. 1975), and fanny packs (ca. 1995).

A classic is a long-enduring fashion. Some are reluctant to classify a classic as a fashion, because the term "fashion" implies change and classics seldom change. When classics do change, the changes are very subtle. Classics remain popular indefinitely, which is why the word "timeless" is frequently associated with classics. Also referred to as traditional, classics typically appeal to customers with conservative taste. Classics include navy blue wool blazers, strings of pearls, and the color black. Unlike fads, classics are low risk, with stable rates of sale season after season. Classic apparel is often promoted as "investment dressing," accentuating the enduring acceptance of classics season after season. Classics saved the day for Brooks Brothers.

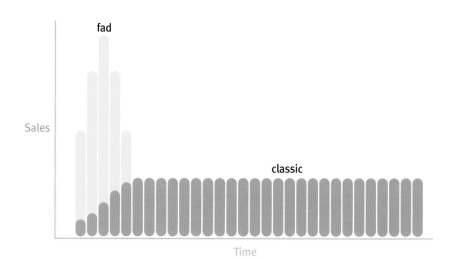

FIGURE 6.8
The fashion life cycle of
fads and classics.

When the retailer returned to its classic roots after its foray into business casual, it brought back items that had disappeared from its racks, including the Shetland sweater introduced in 1904, the sack suit worn by John F. Kennedy, and cordovan shoes made of horsehide.[10]

THE TRICKLE THEORIES

The trickle theories explain the transmission of fashion acceptance from one socioeconomic group to another. There are three trickle theories: the trickle-down theory, the trickle-across theory, and the trickle-up theory.

The trickle-down theory traces the origins of fashion to upper socioeconomic classes. The theory proposes that lower socioeconomic groups imitate the fashions of the upper socioeconomic classes and that the wealthy abandon a fashion when it is mimicked by the lower classes. The popularity of Jacqueline Kennedy's pillbox hat and the open-collar disco shirt sported by John Travolta in "Saturday Night Fever" are examples of fashions of the rich and famous that trickled down to become must-haves for the masses.[11]

The trickle-across, or *diffusion,* theory, suggests that fashion is simultaneously adopted across all socioeconomic groups. Proponents of the trickle-across theory claim that the trickle-down theory is dated because it does not consider the impact of mass communication and computerized design and production capabilities on accelerating the availability of high-fashion knockoffs in mass markets. The trickle-across theory accounts for the fact that similar fashions appear concurrently at stores that cater to diverse socioeconomic groups. A knockoff of a Neiman Marcus fashion may appear concurrently at Wal-Mart. The Neiman Marcus fashion may be 100 percent wool with finished seams and a folded hem. The Wal-Mart fashion may be a polyester blend with unfinished seams and a taped hem. Though fabric and construction are different, the same fashion is available simultaneously at both stores.

Still other fashion theorists find evidence of a trickle-up theory, or *status float phenomenon*. The theory proposes that fashions float up from lower socioeconomic groups to higher socioeconomic groups. It is true that looks with humble origins sometimes end up in the collections of high-end designers.[11] With sleeveless plaid shirts and ragged jeans, the grunge look, pioneered by Seattle rock bands Soundgarden, Pearl Jam, and Nirvana, became part of collections created by maverick designer Marc Jacobs for Perry Ellis.[12]

Some fashions travel in multiple directions. Looks popularized by Gap have simultaneously appeared on the runways of Giorgio Armani and the aisles of Kmart.[13]

THE BASIC–FASHION CONTINUUM

Merchandise often is classified as being either basic or fashion. Basic goods are functional goods that change infrequently and are generally considered necessities. Fashion goods are aesthetically appealing goods that change frequently and are generally considered non-necessities.

Basic goods and fashion goods can be represented at the opposite ends of a continuum. Goods at the far left of the continuum are purely basic. Men's white cotton T-shirts are at this end. Their fabrication, styling, and color do not change from one season to another. A T-shirt is a functional garment worn for warmth and to protect outer garments from body oils and perspiration.

FIGURE 6.9
Talbots is a retailer of classic female apparel. Courtesy of Talbots.

FIGURE 6.10
The grunge look was
evident in the collections of
upscale designers such as
Perry Ellis. Courtesy
Fairchild Publications, Inc.

Goods at the far right of the continuum are purely fashion. Fashion jewelry[14] is at this end. The coloration, composition, and styling of fashion jewelry change each season. Fashion jewelry is not a necessity. It is used for adornment and purchased for its aesthetic value.

Basics are purchased on a replacement basis and out of necessity. A mattress pad is purchased when an old one wears out. Customers do not typically walk by a display of mattress pads and expound: "What a great-looking mattress pad! I think I'll buy one!" Price coupled with need is more likely to be the purchase incentive.

Fashion purchases, however, are based on consumer desire for novelty and change. Unique styling, color, or texture entice consumers to buy fashion goods, as does the way in which the goods are packaged or displayed.

Goods that fall between these extremes have both basic and fashion characteristics. A coat is an apparel necessity in many climates in that it insulates the body from the cold. The functional characteristics of a coat do not change from season to season. Fashion elements, however, such as color, styling, and fabrication, change seasonally.

Merchandise on the left half of the continuum is primarily basic with limited fashion qualities. This includes goods, such as pastel-color bath

FIGURE 6.11
The Fashion–Basic
continuum.

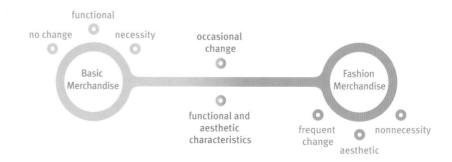

THE IMPRESARIO OF HIP-HOP

There is hardly a major consumer company around that isn't trying to cash in on hip-hop's singular popularity, if not its edgy authenticity. Hip-hop music, and its signature style, emerged from mostly impoverished, largely African-American urban neighborhoods, grew into a way of life, and today dominates youth culture. It's not about race or place. It is an attitude, a state of mind. Marketing experts estimate that one-quarter of all discretionary spending in America today is influenced by hip-hop. The seamy side of hip-hop is what makes it so valuable to mainstream marketers. When Reebok launched the limited edition, $100 S. Carter shoe, it sold faster than any shoe in Reebok's history. The next day the S dot, as it's called, was on eBay going for $250 a pair.

Russell Simmons has brought an urban sensibility to popular culture. He was the first person to design a series of limited-edition Motorola cell phones with his name on them. His wife, Kimora Lee Simmons, who started the Baby Phat women's apparel line, is the second. Russell Simmons also advises Motorola on how to insinuate itself further into the hip-hop community, where a cell phone has become a fashion statement. Simmons has Phat Farm, a highly successful apparel brand described as "classic American flava with a twist," as well as other apparel brands, including Run Athletics, available at Sears and J.C. Penney, and Def Jam University, available at Sears. Phat Farm does its best business in a chain of stores called d.e.m.o., located almost entirely in suburban malls.

towel ensembles, flannel pajamas, and pumps in basic colors, such as black, brown, and beige. These goods are most often purchased as replacements, but uniqueness of color or some minute variation in style will sometimes induce the consumer to buy more frequently than necessary or to buy multiple quantities.

Merchandise on the right half of the continuum is primarily fashion with some basic characteristics. These goods have functional uses. However, their purchase is based primarily on characteristics of styling, prestige, or color.

Transforming Basics into Fashion

Producers transform basic goods into fashion goods by introducing new product features or creating interesting styles, colors, or fabrications. Color

FIGURE 6.12
Athletic footwear was a basic product line that was transformed into fashion. ©*Boston Globe*, June 1, 2006.

is the simplest and least costly product change to implement because it does not require new designs, fabrics or materials, production patterns, or manufacturing setups. *Consumer Reports* found that only one out of five items in new editions of catalogs had *not* appeared in previous editions.[15] The other items were new colors of previously appearing items. Consumers respond positively to color. Louis Vuitton's successful Boulogne Multicolor bag is a remake of a successful LV classic, the Boulogne. The Boulogne Multicolor is, in fact, the Boulogne fabricated in a colorful toile, accented with metal studs.[16] Color invades new areas every day. Presently, 20 percent of the wedding gowns sold at David's Bridal are colors other than the traditional white or off-white. About half of the Vera Wang bridal gown collection is color.[17]

With the help of well-known designers, athletic footwear companies have transformed activewear, historically a basic business, into a fashion business. Stella McCartney, who designed Gwyneth Paltrow's gown for the 2005 Academy Awards, developed the Y-3 line for Adidas. She did it with the help of Yohji Yamamoto, a Japanese designer known for his avant-garde silhouettes and expert pattern cutting. Neil Barrett, who once worked for Gucci and Prada, collaborated with Puma to create the 96 Hours collection. Diane von Furstenberg worked with Reebok to create activewear worn by tennis star Venus Williams at Wimbledon.[18]

The result of transforming a basic category of merchandise into fashion is more sales. Now consumers have activewear wardrobes that they wear as streetwear, buying yoga pants instead of jeans or khakis. Consumers spend $39 billion on activewear, only about a third of which is worn for exercise. Activewear has crossed the line into high fashion. Prada has a sport line and celebrities such as Cameron Diaz and Jennifer Lopez have been seen in tracksuits by Juicy Couture.[19]

Transforming basic goods to fashion is not new. Long before activewear became fashionable, footwear giants such as Nike and Reebok International made athletic footwear fashionable. Because fashion is constantly changing, the process never stops. Reebok continues to promote its product line as fashion with the help of such hip-hop stars as Jay-Z and rapper 50 Cent. Reebok launched its Rbk store in West Hollywood, featuring street-inspired footwear and clothing for the celebrity crowd. The concept reflects the attitude of today's youth: "cool, edgy, authentic and aspirational."[20] Hotel heiress Paris Hilton appeared at the grand opening of Rbk to buy a pink Reebok Princess T-shirt, while a DreamWorks SKG costume designer picked out a few things for starlet Scarlett Johansson to wear in the sci-fi thriller, *The Island*.[21]

Sometimes retailers are responsible for a basic-to-fashion conversion. Victoria's Secret took women's innerwear from basic to fashion by converting basic white and beige bras, slips, and panties in cotton, nylon, and rayon into fashion assortments of coordinated slips, bras, and panties in an array of colors and prints in luxury fabrications. The producers of national innerwear brands and department stores followed suit. Men's underwear went through a similar transformation. Color and sexy styles, such as the bikini, added a fashion dimension to men's underwear, a merchandise category that was once dominated by white cotton and cotton-blend T-shirts

BRING HOME THE FASHION

The elevation of *tchotchkes* to fashion has been fueled by high-end fashion designers whose names have been appearing on mass market home furnishings and accessories. Isaac Mizrahi is one such designer. Subsequent to the success of his female apparel line for Target, Mizrahi has introduced hundreds of furniture, bedding, bath, tabletop, lighting, and kitchen products in Target stores. Mizrahi got his start as a high-end fashion designer almost as famous for his irrepressible personality as his savvy fashions. Since teaming up with Target, Mizrahi has been preaching the gospel of quality design at affordable prices. "All this time, I've been an interior decorator trapped in the body of flamboyant fashion designer," Mizrahi says. "Now I can be both." Isaac Mizrahi is not Target's only reputed home-product designer. World-renowned architect Michael Graves has also brought innovative design to everyday household items at Target. With Mizrahi, Graves shares the belief that people instinctively appreciate great design, and that it should be affordable and accessible to all.

Meanwhile, another hip New York designer, Jonathan Adler, has partnered with mid-price Rowe Furniture to design sofas, tables, and accent chairs. Some of his avant-garde groupings are named for movie characters whose style inspired the collections, including Mrs. Robinson of *The Graduate*, and Anne Welles of *Valley of the Dolls*. Adler, who has also produced bath products for Croscill Home, began as a potter then branched into textiles, lighting, and rugs. "I'm very democratic," he says. "I see no reason why design at reasonable price points shouldn't be as good or better than design at the high end."

SOURCE
Puente, M. (March 18, 2005). Spot-on design. *USA Today*. p. D.4.

and athletic shorts. Men's underwear sales have been further augmented by the transformation of the boxer short, long considered a vestige of the past worn only by older men, into a fashion item, thanks to the influence of Joe Boxer, which introduced glow-in-the-dark boxer shorts in 1988.[22]

Not every attempt to transform a basic business into a fashion business is successful. In the mid-1960s, the menswear industry launched a casual, lapel-less suit with a mandarin collar called the Nehru, confident that the style would be a success as traditional dress standards began to ease. However, men were not ready to replace their conventional suits with this revolutionary fashion. The Nehru was an abysmal failure and became a joke and cautionary tale in the menswear industry. Although men's apparel now undergoes more frequent changes than four decades ago—occasionally vests appear, and lapel and pant widths change, as do the treatment of vents, pleats, and cuffs—the Nehru suit taught the menswear industry a lesson that fashion change should be gradual.

FIGURE 6.13
Victoria's Secret
transformed women's
innerwear into a fashion
business. Courtesy
Fairchild Publications, Inc.

Women also can be resistant to change. In 1957, an unfitted sheath called the sack dress, or *chemise*, made its debut from the houses of a very young Pierre Cardin and Guy Laroche. Fashion forecasters predicted that women would hail the arrival of the sack, preferring it to the less comfortable fitted styles of the day. But it didn't happen. Similar to what would happen to the Nehru suit a decade later, the sack was a failure except in high-fashion circles, derided even in the popular song, "No Chemise Please."[23]

When fashions change, the line between consumer acceptance and consumer rejection is a fine one, contingent upon many factors such as the target market, economic conditions, and the type of merchandise. Consumers may reject drastic change, but they also will not buy unless they perceive an appreciable difference between current and previous offerings. There is no universal answer to the question of how much change is too little and when is it too much. Perhaps the best response is to make something familiar look new. Ironically, elements of the Nehru

FIGURE 6.14
The chemise, or "sack"
dress, was a fashion with
limited acceptance by the
masses. Courtesy Ann
Betters.

suit reappeared in men's fashion a few years later in the leisure suit, and the comfortable, waistless aspect of the sack reappeared in women's fashion in shifts and muumuus in the 1960s.

FASHION INFLUENCES

Fashion change has roots in changes in technology, the economy, and society. Product manufacturers react to these environmental changes by designing or by developing products consistent with these changes.

The technological advances that have contributed to the growth of the fashion apparel industry date back to the Industrial Revolution and the invention of the sewing machine (ca. 1850), which enabled the production of mass-produced ready-to-wear garments that could be purchased from racks in stores. Today's consumer is especially conscious of technology and its attributes. The element titanium was discovered in 1791. For a long time, titanium was used primarily as lunch-bucket material.[24] Today it is known for its strength and light weight and has become synonymous with high tech because of its use in the computer industry. Titanium also has become a symbol of high fashion, with claims of titanium in products ranging from ski parkas to cologne. Using titanium as a symbol of cutting-edge fashion began in Portland, Oregon, when Columbia Sportswear dubbed its high-end skiwear "Titanium." Exactly why the name was chosen is a mystery, but obviously someone thought it would resonate well with consumers.

Fashion is inextricably linked to economics. Fashion sells best when economic times are favorable. When times are tough, consumers stick to the basics, shunning fashion as frivolous and unnecessary. A mill that produces velvet claims that black is the preferred color of apparel manufacturers during trying economic times. Because black is a classic color, consumers feel that they will get more wear out of a black velvet dress, for example, than a fashion color dress that will become dated quickly and worn perhaps only once. Producers of fashion goods are mindful of consumers' conservatism during difficult economic times, and they lean toward the basic end of the basic–fashion continuum as they design and produce their lines.

Fashion also reflects societal trends. Back in the 1930s, Buxton, a small leathergoods company, created the two-toned Lady Buxton billfold in response to the needs of a greater number of women entering the workforce.[25] The fur industry peaked in the 1980s, thanks to the influence of such pop culture icons as Alexis Carrington, a lead character on the popular television series *Dynasty*. But fur sales dropped drastically in the 1990s because of heightened environmental consciousness and the influence of animal rights organizations, such as People for the Ethical Treatment of Animals (PETA), which objects to the use of animals for experimentation, food, or clothing.[26]

All of the sources of fashion influence cannot be addressed here; however, popular entertainment as a fashion catalyst is worth noting. Since the advent of motion pictures, actors, actresses, and other entertainers have had profound influence on fashion. In 1934, in *It Happened One Night*, screen idol Clark Gable took his shirt off, revealing a bare chest instead of an undershirt. Audiences gasped, undershirt sales plummeted, and didn't recover until James Dean made them sexy again in *Rebel Without a Cause* (1955). Elizabeth Taylor popularized blue eye shadow in *Cleopatra* (1963). Richard Gere created a Giorgio Armani sensation in *American Gigolo* (1980). *The Italian Job* (2003) did wonders for the sale of Mini Coopers, a British automobile popular since the 1960s. Realizing the powerful impact of motion pictures, Giorgio Armani created a line of 1920s, 1930s, and 1940s fashion inspired by the Cole Porter biopic *De-Lovely* (2005).[27, 28]

Television is also an important fashion medium. When hosting the television game show *Who Wants to Be a Millionaire*, Regis Philbin created a fashion stir with his monochromatic shirts and ties. The HBO television series *The Sopranos* inspired a necktie line called "Bada Bing," named for a strip club in the series.[29] Bravo's *Project Runway*, a series showcasing competing designers, naturally has an effect on fashion: Designer Michael Kors complimented designer contestant Kara Janx on her silk kimono wrap dress; the next year, she sold thousands of them.[30]

FIGURE 6.15
The dress that Elizabeth Taylor wore in the 1952 film *A Place in the Sun* popularized Dior's "New Look." © Bettman/Corbis.

FIGURE 6.16
The movie *The Italian Job* did wonders for the sales of Mini Coopers. © AP/Wide World Photos.

THE FASHION INDUSTRY

The fashion industry in the United States grew rapidly after World War II, when Seventh Avenue apparel manufacturers began to visit European fashion centers to copy and mass-produce European couture. The "rag" business became the "fashion" business, paralleling the country's rapid growth. Today, fashion is an integral part of our economic system and so much a part of our culture that it is difficult to find a product that does not have some inherent element of fashion.[31]

Retailers communicate fashion to their customers through advertising, sales promotion, product presentation, and direct selling. Though fashion stimulates sales, fashion adds to the complexity of a retailer's job. When bed linens were white, buying decisions were often just reorders of the most popular selling sizes and fabrications. Today, a household-textile buying decision involves a vast number of purchase options that includes many merchandise resources, each offering myriad colors, patterns, and styles. A bed linen department is as fashionable as an apparel department, boasting

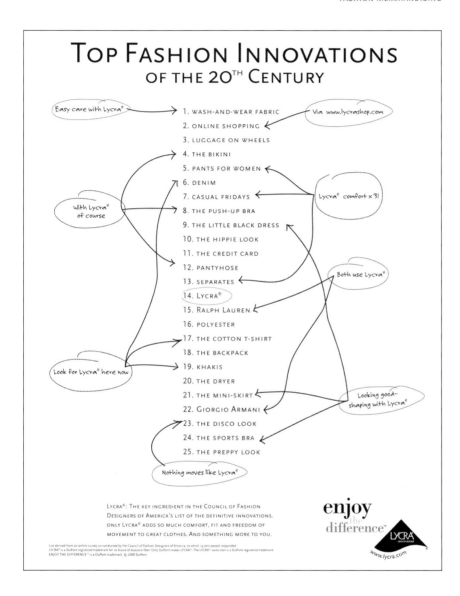

of designer names that include Calvin Klein and Ralph Lauren. Fashion adds risk to retail buying decisions. Large retailers commit to hundreds of thousands of dollars for a single fashion item or a group of related fashion items. Faulty fashion predictions impact sales and profit.

SUMMARY POINTS

- Fashion is a form of expression that is widely accepted by a group of people over time.
- A trend implies the direction or movement of a fashion. The word "trend" is often used synonymously with fashion.
- The fashion life cycle depicts the growth, culmination, and demise of a fashion.
- Fads are short-lived fashions. Classics are enduring fashions.
- Fashion goods have aesthetic qualities, change frequently, and are generally considered nonnecessities. Basic goods have functional qualities, change infrequently, and are generally considered necessities.
- Fashion acceptance can be explained by the trickle-down, trickle-across, and trickle-up theories.
- Sales are stimulated by the transformation of basic goods into fashion goods.
- Fashion is influenced by technological, economic, and societal change. Famous people and popular entertainment figures also influence fashion.

KEY TERMS AND CONCEPTS

basic goods	fashion goods	knockoff
classic	fashion laggard	trend
fad	fashion leader	trickle-across theory
fashion	fashion life cycle	trickle-down theory
fashion follower	high fashion	trickle-up theory

THINKING ABOUT IT

1. Trace the transformation of several products from basic to fashion.
2. Identify fashion trends that relate to demographics or lifestyles. What impact do the demographic or lifestyle trends have on the products or services that consumers buy or need?
3. In addition to those mentioned in the text, what stores or industries are beneficiaries of the cocooning trend?
4. Consider the fashion life cycle as it relates to a consumer electronics category, such as televisions or MP3 players. Identify the various life cycle phases. How do manufacturers stimulate sales when they see a plateau or decline coming?

5. Associate each trickle theory with a fashion. Trace the fashion's travel up, down, or across socioeconomic groups.

6. Identify instances in which pop culture, in the form of motion pictures, television shows, or other forms of entertainment, has influenced fashion.

7. Identify fashions from the past that have recently reappeared. How do the current interpretations of these fashions differ from their predecessors? Are the recent fashions as successful as the originals?

TEAMING UP

1. Each member of your team should identify fashion within a category of merchandise, such as apparel, home furnishings, or consumer electronics. Each team member should trace the fashion's evolution on the product life cycle and the basic–fashion continuum. Share your analyses as a group.

2. Each team member should identify and discuss a demographic or psychographic trend. From a merchandising perspective, do any of the trends reinforce one another? Have any of the trends evolved from other trends? Do any of the trends conflict? That is, would a retailer's response to one trend impede its response to another?

3. View an old movie as a team, then, each team member should identify fashions within a specific fashion category, such as men's apparel, women's apparel, home furnishing, music, and speech. As a group, discuss how fashions have changed. What were the societal factors that spurred the fashions to change? Which of the fashions would you like to see come back?

4. Each member of your team should analyze a consumer electronics category as it relates to the fashion life cycle. Have there been declines? Deaths? How have peaks been revived? How have declines been reversed? What is the category's future? Discuss your observations as a team.

5. Each team member should consider the impact of the economy, society, and technology on a specific category of merchandise. Do the three factors have equal impact? If not, why is one more influential than another? Discuss as a team.

SEARCHING THE NET

1. Search for a history of fads. Which fads do you remember? Estimate the duration of a dozen or so fads. What would you say is the average life expectancy of a fad?

2. Search for classic clothing items. What do you notice about availability? Price? Define the classics customer demographically and psychographically.

3. Search for examples of the impact of pop culture on recent fashion. Are you a fashion follower?

4. Search for examples of present-day fashions within any merchandise category. What were the influences that spurred the fashion's evolution?

CHAPTER SEVEN

Brands and Private Labels

After reading this chapter,
you will be able to discuss:

● The concept of branding.

● Licensing.

● Private labeling.

Most consumer products are identified in one of two ways: by a name associated with the product producer, such as Sony, or by a name associated with the store in which the product is sold, such as Macy's Charter Club. Consumers link certain characteristics, such as price, quality, styling, and reliability, to product names. Retailers make other associations, including sales and profit potential, with product identities. Chapter 7 deals with two types of products: national brands that bear an identity associated with their producer, and private labels that bear a name exclusive to the store in which they are sold.

BRANDED MERCHANDISE

Branded merchandise, or *brand-name merchandise*, is identified by a name and/or symbol associated with certain product characteristics. Lucky Brand, Wrangler, Louis Vuitton, Liz Claiborne, Ralph Lauren, and Escada are brands. Certain product characteristics are associated with each brand: Lucky Brand (high price), Wrangler (moderate price), Louis Vuitton (quality), Liz Claiborne (fit), Ralph Lauren (styling), and Escada (prestige). Most brand names imply multiple product characteristics. Louis Vuitton is known as much for high price and prestige as it is for quality. Packaging and labeling are important elements of brand identification. The clean, clinical-looking packaging of Clinique cosmetics is a symbol of the hypoallergenic nature of the product line.[1]

Brands are classified by their geographic range of distribution. A regional brand is distributed throughout a defined geographic section of the country, such as the Midwest; a national brand is distributed throughout the country; an international brand is distributed both throughout the United States and in other countries. Because of perishability, food products are more likely to be regional brands than durable goods. The consumer products discussed in this textbook generally are national brands, though many have become international brands through various forms of franchising and licensing.

Nike is a well-known international brand recognized worldwide by its famous "swoosh."

Brands are also defined by their customers. A mass market brand appeals to the masses by virtue of its "popular" price and middle-of-the-road product appeal. The brands carried by full-line discounters, and the lower-price brands at department stores generally are considered mass market brands. A niche brand is targeted to a very specific customer and thus has a much smaller distribution than a mass market brand. Some upscale department stores, such as Saks Fifth Avenue, distinguish themselves from other stores with niche brands. The fragrance assortment at Saks includes such brands as Chypre from Patyka, an organic fragrance from Hungary, and Spahnke & Groome, a men's fragrance targeted to affluent gays.[2] Brands are identified in other ways. A brand that bears the brand name of a designer or design company, such as Calvin Klein or Kate Spade, is called a designer brand, or *signature brand*.

The concept of branding is tied to many industries. Retail conglomerates market their various nameplates as brands. Federated Department Stores has two brands: Macy's, a moderate-price brand; and Bloomingdale's, a more upscale brand. Several years ago, Limited Stores, Inc. changed its corporate name to Limited Brands, Inc. to reflect the fact that its store names are brands. Today, the names of colleges and universities are often referred to as brands, symbolic of things like quality, prestige, and price.

FIGURE 7.1
Consumers associate characteristics such as styling with the identity of merchandise.
Calvin Klein courtesy Fairchild Publications, Inc.

Like fashions, brands have life cycles. Some brands survive for many years: Jockey International has been making underwear since 1900, Jantzen swimwear dates back to 1910, and Estée Lauder was founded in 1946. Other brands have gained prominence in a relatively short time. Reebok International was established in 1981; Juicy Couture in 1994.

A brand grows with increased sales through a greater number of distribution channels. Founded in 1976, the Liz Claiborne female apparel brand grew faster than any other line in Seventh Avenue history. By responding to the needs (and size!) of an increasing number of professional women, Liz quickly became the number-one female apparel brand in department stores.[3] Today, Liz Claiborne products are available at more than 30,000 retail locations worldwide.[4]

Like fashions, brands can plateau and then decline. Levi Strauss, a recognized jeanswear brand since the California Gold Rush, experienced a massive surge in popularity in the 1960s as baby boomers donned their Levis to distinguish themselves from the Establishment. Recently, however, Levi Strauss sales have faltered in a brutally competitive jeanswear market that releases multiple new brands each year.[5] Within a ten-year period from the early 1990s to the early 2000s, Levi Strauss sales slid from $7.1 billion to about $4 billion.[6]

Some brands eventually die. Gordon of Philadelphia and Bleyle were popular female apparel brands in the 1970s. Their market share diminished as new brands, such as Liz Claiborne and Jones New York, came into vogue. Sometimes a dead brand is relaunched with the hope of recapturing the success of its previous life. Wal-Mart revived White Stag, once an upscale female apparel brand. Target revived Fioruccci, a popular Italian brand from

FIGURE 7.2
Some brands, such as Jockey, have been around for decades. Image courtesy Advertising Archives.

the 1980s, with a line of retro-inspired pieces.[7] Several men's personal-care brands died in the 1960s and 1970s as men's grooming habits and hairstyles changed. A few have been relaunched with twenty-first-century adaptations, among them Vitalis, Brut, Brylcreem, and Aqua Velva, which was once described as the "toiletry of choice for used-car salesmen."[8]

A brand has value based on how well-known it is and the sales that it generates. The world's most valuable brand is Coca-Cola, worth $67 billion on the company's balance sheet.[9] Because brands have value, they can be bought and sold like any other organizational asset. Just as retail organizations grow into conglomerates with the acquisition of stores, consumer products companies grow into conglomerates with the acquisition of brands. With a stable of nearly 20 highly recognized brands like Speedo swimwear and Calvin Klein jeans, Warnaco has become one of the nation's largest apparel companies. The company's brands fall within three major categories: intimate apparel (Olga), swimwear (Speedo), and sportswear

(Calvin Klein Jeans).[10] Sara Lee is a consumer products company with an even more diversified brand portfolio. Its product categories include personal care, food and beverage, and branded apparel. Sara Lee's namesake bakery product line is within the food and beverage category. The company's branded apparel category includes intimate apparel and underwear brands, such as Bali, Hanes, and Playtex.[11]

Intense competition for market dominance leads to a continuous emergence of innovative branded products. Founded as the original swim performance brand in 1928, Speedo was the driving force behind swimwear's move from wool to silk, to cotton, and then to Lycra. Jockey invented the snug-fitting men's briefs that consumers now generically call "jockey shorts." Hanes developed the seamless stocking. Totes was the innovator of the pop-up umbrella. Timex developed Indiglo, a patented night-light technology that more than doubled the watchmaker's sales in two years.

FIGURE 7.4
Once a very popular denim brand, Levi Strauss is struggling in a brutally competitive jeanswear market. © Amy Etra/PhotoEdit.

Brand Positioning

Chapter 5 discussed positioning, referring to the marketplace position that a product holds relative to its competitors. Brands are positioned on factors such as price, product attributes, end use, intended customer, and channels of distribution. For a brand to be successful, it must be positioned differently than its competitors. While at first glance, two brands may seem alike, in theory, there is at least one distinction that sets them apart.

The female apparel industry is a good example of brand positioning by price. Apparel lines are classified by a price-and-quality hierarchy that has existed for many years with only occasional tweaking. The categories are as follows:

Designer lines are exclusive creations of a reputed designer houses, such as Donna Karan or Calvin Klein. Their distribution is limited, sometimes restricted to the designer's boutiques and very upscale stores.

A DESIGNER AND A BRAND

In 1976, a relatively unknown dress designer, her textile veteran husband, a merchant, and a production expert, founded a company that would revolutionize the fashion industry—from how women dress for work, to how apparel is sold in department stores. The partners, Liz Claiborne, Art Ortenberg, Leonard Boxer, and Jerome Chazen, each invested $50,000 in personal savings, and borrowed an additional $200,000 from friends and family to found what is today a nearly $5 billion public company.

Established at a time when women were entering the workforce in large numbers, Liz Claiborne and her partners saw the opportunity to provide versatile, fashionable wardrobes appropriate for work, but that still conveyed a sense of individuality and femininity. A working woman herself, Claiborne understood how liberating it would be to mix and match separates rather than to have to rely on the traditional dress or gray-flannel suit. The concept was simple: provide the ensemble-driven sportswear that had been available for many years at designer-level prices through the likes of Calvin Klein and Bill Blass, but make it affordable for the working woman. Thus, out of a small office on 40th street in Manhattan, Liz Claiborne the brand was born, transforming the way women dress and ultimately, how they shop.

There was a major stumbling block, however. Up until this point, department stores were classification oriented—pants were in one department, skirts in another, and tops in yet another. To put together a wardrobe, a customer had to go from department to department hoping for a match. Additionally, department store buyers were classification-focused, and accustomed to buying merchandise from one vendor across product lines. To overcome this, Liz Claiborne executives worked with retailers to test the concept of presenting all of the brand's related sportswear pieces in one department, thus streamlining the consumer's shopping experience. A revolutionary concept at the time, this is the basis for the brand and lifestyle boutiques that populate today's department stores.

Liz Claiborne Inc. became a large company in a small industry very quickly, and in 1981 went public to much fanfare. By 1986, Liz Claiborne Inc. was the first company founded by a woman to be listed in the Fortune 500. Now, with a portfolio of more than 40 brands, Liz Claiborne Inc. creates fashion for everyone—women and men, girls and boys, apparel and non-apparel, modern and classic, career and casual. From Main Street to the mall, department stores to specialty stores, and luxury retailers to discount retailers, Liz Claiborne, Inc. reaches consumers wherever they shop.

SOURCE
Liz Claiborne, Inc. (2006). Our Company. www.lizclaiborne inc.com/company/history.htm.

Bridge lines are lower-priced lines with limited distribution through prestigious stores, such as Saks Fifth Avenue, and fine specialty stores.

Better lines and moderate lines are broadly distributed, appearing at less prestigious department stores, including Macy's and Dillard's. Moderate lines have even broader distribution than better lines and may appear at stores such as J.C. Penney and Sears.

Mass market lines, formerly called *budget lines*, are carried in value-oriented stores, such as full-line discounters.

The system is consistently applied across the apparel industry. Ellen Tracy is a bridge line; Liz Claiborne a better line; Alfred Dunner a moderate line. VF Corporation, another apparel brand powerhouse, distributes Wrangler jeans to full-line discounters, including Kmart and Wal-Mart. Jones Apparel Group distributes more than 40 apparel and accessories brands, including bridge lines such as Anne Klein New York and Albert Nipon, better lines such as AK Anne Klein and Jones New York, and moderate lines such as Gloria Vanderbilt and Evan-Picone.

Other industries have less elaborate price-positioning systems. The jewelry industry has a three-level price/quality positioning system. At the high end is fine jewelry fashioned in 14k gold or better, with precious and semiprecious stones. At the low end is fashion jewelry, once called costume jewelry. Fashion jewelry is made of gold-plated metals and an array of glass and synthetic stones. As the name implies, bridge jewelry is the in-between price point. It includes sterling silver and some of the high-end costume lines.

A brand's positioning is tied to the type of retail store though which the brand is distributed. The cosmetics industry has a two-tier positioning system based on distribution. Prestige lines, such as Estée Lauder and Chanel, are distributed through department stores and are sold with the assistance of a beauty advisor trained by the cosmetics company. Mass market lines, such as Revlon and Maybelline, are sold in self-service environments at full-line discounters and chain drugstores. It is common for a company to own multiple brands within the same product line, each positioned differently based on retail channel. Warnaco distributes its high-end Lejaby intimate apparel brand to upscale department stores, such as Saks Fifth Avenue and Neiman Marcus. Another Warnaco brand, Body Nancy Ganz, is distributed through moderate department stores.[12]

Brands are also positioned based on product features and end use. The female apparel industry's sizing system uses fit as a brand-positioning tool.

Junior lines, such as Liz Claiborne's Juicy Couture, are cut for the youthful bodies of teens and young adults. Plus-size lines, such as Liz Claiborne's Elisabeth, are for full-figure women. Misses lines, which are the majority of apparel lines, are for average-size women. Petites are for women 5 feet, 4 inches and shorter. Many misses lines are available as petites.

Some apparel companies position their brands on styling, the standards for which are unique to each company. Liz Claiborne, Inc., classifies its female apparel brands as classic (Ellen Tracy), modern (Laundry by Shelli Segal), relaxed (Sigrid Olsen), denim/streetwear (Lucky Brand Jeans), and

SOURCE
Mitchell Gold + Bob Williams. (2006). About Us. www.mitchell gold. com/history.asp.

MITCHELL GOLD + BOB WILLIAMS: A BRAND THAT SAYS STYLE AND COMFORT

In 1989, Mitchell Gold and Bob Williams founded the Mitchell Gold Co. in Taylorsville, North Carolina. Gold's marketing experience coupled with Williams' creative talent were the seeds of the Mitchell Gold + Bob Williams brand. Their concept was simple. A furniture line called "Relaxed Design" drew from trends that the duo saw in the apparel industry: comfortable, classic, and affordable. Relaxed Design pieces were dressed in casual slipcovers of pre-washed fabrics like denim, khaki and velvet. Mitchell and Gold also created a less overwhelming shopping experience for customers by limiting choices.

Mitchell + Gold is sold through some of the country's trendiest furniture retailers, including Crate & Barrel, Restoration Hardware, Pottery Barn, and ABC Carpet & Home, as well as through leading catalog retailers, such as L.L. Bean, Neiman Marcus, and Chambers. The brand is so popular that fashionable hotel chains such as W Hotels tout the fact

their furnishings include the Mitchell Gold + Bob Williams brand. Mitchell Gold + Bob Williams advertisements are as progressive as their designs. By pushing the envelope in terms of style, content, and theme, the company's advertising campaigns are a strong departure from typical furniture ads. Who said furniture ads can't be as provocative as apparel or cosmetics ads?

Mitchell Gold is innovative in other ways. In 1998, the company built a 267,000 square-foot, state-of-the-art factory with a health-conscious café, employee gym, indoor walking track, and even an on-site daycare center for more than 550 children of employees. Along the way, the company has received numerous awards, including Design 100 awards from *Metropolitan Home* magazine. And today, the line, which started with dining chairs, offers both slipcovered and tailored upholstery with features such as down-blend cushions.

active (Prana).[13] Brands can be positioned on product features specific to the product category. Cosmetic lines are positioned as treatment, color, or fragrance. The intimate apparel industry positions brands on end use, with categories such as loungewear, sleepwear, shapewear, and daywear. To consumers the categories are robes, pajamas, slips, bras, and underwear.

Brands also are positioned on customer profile. Warnaco's swimwear lines are positioned on age: Anne Cole is a classic line for the 25- to 55-year-old customer; Ocean Pacific is for the 15- to 22-year-old customer.

Brand-Driven Purchases

Branding is especially important to the retailers of certain categories of merchandise. Purchases are brand-driven when clear distinctions differentiate brands. When brands are not clearly differentiated, consumers adopt a "one brand is as good as the next" attitude, basing their purchase on factors such as price or color. Fragrance purchases often are brand-driven because of each brand's distinctive scent. Purchases of denim blue jeans are brand-driven because of each brand's unique fit. The purchase of designer-label apparel, cosmetics, and toys are also brand-driven. Consumers are reluctant to accept substitutes for brand-driven purchases. Customers who consistently purchase the same brand are called *brand loyal.*

The concept of brand-driven purchases is best explained by example. Consider the customer who, when approached by a salesperson in a men's apparel store, states his needs as "a pair of Levi's 501s, and a tie to go with a navy-blue suit." The customer's jeans purchase is brand-driven. He likes the fit, easy care, and durability of the classic Levi Strauss 501 jeans style and will accept no substitute. The customer's necktie purchase is not brand-driven. Color and pattern are his major selection criteria. While price may have a role in his decision, and the hand of the fabric may come into play, brand is not a consideration. The customer may not even be familiar with any necktie brand.

Brands and Retail Stores

Producers of branded products use advertising and sales promotion to distinguish their brands from competitors'. Calvin Klein's strategy includes a mix of television and out-of-home advertising, as well as advertising in countless fashion-oriented consumer magazines. Advertising is

IT'S OKAY, THEY'RE WITH ME.

Keep your cool this summer, in the comfort of the White Satin   an entire range of styles, colours and fabrics: from lace through cotton

Wonderbra. Maximum uplift with minimum show, even under the   to satin. It even gives a choice of different shaped cleavages. Select

closest fitting clothing. (The only thing they'll notice is the boost in   your own style of flattery. At Debenhams, Top Shop, House of Fraser,

your self-confidence...) Wonderbra, however, is more than just a bra. It's   Contessa and other leading lingerie stockists and mail order catalogues.

THE ONE AND ONLY
wonderbra

THE WHITE SATIN WONDERBRA

FIGURE 7.5
Intense competition for
market dominance leads to
continuous emergence of
innovative branded
products, such as
Gossard's Wonderbra.
Image courtesy the
Advertising Archives.

an expensive proposition. Nike spends nearly a billion dollars a year on advertising, a figure that includes the cost of endorsements from celebrities like Tiger Woods.[14] A brand's advertising costs are inherent in the wholesale price of the merchandise. Thus, indirectly, retailers pay the marketing costs of heavily branded goods and feel that the cost is worth it because branded goods are "pre-sold" to customers eager to buy the brands they see advertised.

Producers of branded products often support the sale of their products in retail stores in ways besides advertising. Many provide product training, promotional aids, and funds for store-sponsored advertising. Others provide fixtures and signage especially designed for their product to enhance consistent and prominent presentation in all stores. Branded product producers sometimes share the risk of carrying a line by allowing retailers to return slow-selling goods for credit after an agreed-upon selling period.

Recall that the retail channels through which a brand is distributed are part of a brand's positioning. The symbiotic relationship between brands and retail stores is obvious. A customer's perception of a brand at Nordstrom or Bergdorf Goodman is different than her perception of a brand at Wal-Mart or Kmart. Many brands owe their success to an introduction by a reputed retailer. The men's designer label movement began in December 1965 when Lord & Taylor opened the first John Weitz shop at its Fifth Avenue store. Bloomingdale's was the first to carry Liz Claiborne, and to find space for a men's neckwear line designed by Ralph Lauren. Just as brands use retailers as a market-positioning tool, retailers use brands to define their market position and image. Wal-Mart enhanced its low fashion profile by buying labels such as White Stag and Puritan to use on private label merchandise made for its stores. The Bon-Ton upgraded its fashion image with a stronger presence of brands such as Liz Claiborne, Tommy Hilfiger, and Nautica.

Couristan...a work of art designed for living

Get ready for the Couristan Classics Summer Sale Period!
•Now is the time to "Sample Up", August 1st-August 15th for the Couristan Classics Summer Sale Period.

•Receive extra discounts off our lowest dealer pricing of the year, when you order new samples from the Classic Three: Gem, Kashimar and Mirage.

•We offer the largest assortment of sizes and shapes in the industry.

•The Classics are backed by a 25 year limited warranty.

•Let us be your warehouse. We guarantee shipping within 48 hours of processing your order for in stock items.

•Check inventory or track your order 24 hours a day, 7 days a week, 365 days a year with Direct-chek, Couristan's new Automated Voice Response System, Call 1-800-223-6186-7.

•Take advantage of our complete Co-op advertising packages and advertising allowance programs.

•Create a winning promotion, call 1-800-223-6186 ext.524 for the Couristan Sales Representative in your area.

COURISTAN
The foundation of any great room.
Two Executive Drive, Fort Lee, NJ 07024
1-800-223-6186 ext.524 • www.couristan.com
Featured rug: 9938/0004 Mirage, Sierra/Woodchip

FIGURE 7.6
Producers of branded products often support the sale of their product line at the retail level with inventory management services and cooperative advertising incentives. Couristan, Inc., creative elegance in fine area rugs and broadloom, Fort Lee, New Jersey.

To protect a brand's image, consumer product companies go to great lengths to ensure that their product does not get into unintended retail channels. In the aftermath of natural disasters such as hurricanes and tornadoes, Estée Lauder buys back its own product from the insurance companies that acquire damaged stock from department stores, fearing that the product will otherwise be bought by third-party wholesalers called diverters, who would then sell it to discount stores.[15]

Producers sometimes alter their distribution strategies when they see an opportunity elsewhere. Evan-Picone was a better misses sportswear line that was repositioned by new owners for a larger market as a moderate line.

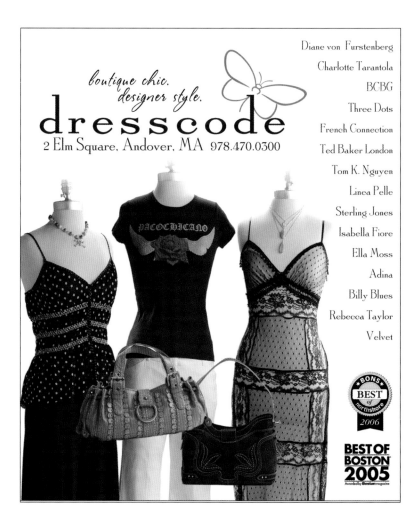

boutique chic.
designer style.
dresscode
2 Elm Square, Andover, MA   978.470.0300

Diane von Furstenberg
Charlotte Tarantola
BCBG
Three Dots
French Connection
Ted Baker London
Tom K. Nguyen
Linea Pelle
Sterling Jones
Isabella Fiore
Ella Moss
Adina
Billy Blues
Rebecca Taylor
Velvet

BONS BEST of northshore 2006

BEST OF BOSTON 2005
Awarded by Boston magazine

FIGURE 7.7
Retailers often position
themselves in the
marketplace by the brands
they carry. Image courtesy
Dress Code.

Such shifts become like a game of checkers. The VF Corporation rechanneled its Lee brand from full-line discounters to department and specialty stores. VF then created a line called Riders as a replacement for Lee at discount stores.

Sometimes producers attempt to increase market share by distributing their brands through multiple retail channels. Multiple-channel distribution is upsetting to higher-price retailers who feel that a brand's image is sullied when distributed through lower-price retailers. OshKosh B'Gosh, a producer of childrenswear, irked its upscale department store accounts, such

SUIT LINEAGE

While the man in the gray flannel suit could sum up his work wardrobe in one color, one cut, and one fabric, today suit manufacturers realize that dressing is also a reflection of one's multifaceted lifestyle. Now, as with cars or wine, there is a hierarchy in the fine suit lines. The same brand can take you from a casual business dinner or weekend conference to a boardroom presentation or formal dinner. With prices for entry-level suits starting under $600, one of these respected lines may well be within reach for many customers.

	Ermenegildo Zegna	
Napoli Couture	For those who delight in extraordinary quality, the tradition and extensive work-manship of a sartorial suit. Highly hand-tailored, optional button-through fly, exclusive fabrics.	$2,695*
Sartoriale	Quintessential Italian clothing built with finesse and flair. Renowned for Super 100's specialty fabrics.	$1,600*
Z Zegna	Well-priced and fashion-driven as characterized by ads featuring Oscar-winner Adrien Brody.	$875*
	Pal Zileri	
Sartoriale by Pal Zileri	Dressier, formal fabrics, impeccable finishing, highly hand-tailored.	$1,895*
Pal Zileri	A modern, sexy approach to classic Italian suits.	$1,295*
Pal by Pal Zileri	Younger, more cutting-edge line.	$895*
	Giorgio Armani	
Giorgio Armani Black Label	Old World handcraftsmanship for a sober business suit with the distinctive Armani drape. Sold exclusively in Giorgio Armani shops.	$2,025**
Giorgio Armani Collezioni	Still the most sought after label in Italian fashion, first popularized in 1980 when worn by Richard Gere in *American Gigolo*.	$1,495**
Emporio Armani	A younger collection that reflects Armani's more spirited, inventive ideas.	$898**
	Polo Ralph Lauren	
Ralph Lauren Purple Label	The fitted look of Savile Row designed to Ralph's personal style.	$2,995*
Polo by Ralph Lauren	Clothing that defines English-inspired American classicism.	$895*
Chaps	The Ralph Lauren look interpreted for the younger, style-conscious man.	$475*
	Joseph Abboud	
Black Label	Better side-vented American clothing expertly made from select Italian fabrics.	$895*
Joseph Abboud	Distinguished by monochromatic palettes that give a modern edge to traditional American design utilizing select European fabrics. A favorite of sports-casters including Bryant Gumbel and Bob Costas.	$650*
	Brooks Brothers	
Golden Fleece	A new line of high-end suits inspired by the Brooks Brothers archives.	$1,098*
Brooks Brothers 1818	The classic three-button, natural shoulder American suit, updated and improved.	$798*
Brooks Ease	Sold as separates, wrinkle resistant, good for travel, extremely comfortable, super 100 pure wool.	$598

* Starting price   ** Average price

SOURCE © *BusinessWeek*, The McGraw Hill Companies (September 8, 2003). Reprinted with permission.

as Bloomingdale's and Macy's, when it began to distribute through J.C. Penney and Sears. Upscale stores often discontinue brands when their producers begin distributing them through less prestigious stores. Federated Department Stores discontinued Revlon's Ultima II line because of broadened distribution through J.C. Penney.[16]

BRAND EXTENSION AND LICENSING

Brand extension involves adding related products to an existing product line or developing a new product line with the same brand identity. By extending a brand, a producer capitalizes on a brand's reputation, as well as the company's production expertise, and the channel relationships established with existing products. After more than 80 years as a men's underwear brand, Jockey International extended its brand to an underwear line for women called Jockey For Her. The line was an immediate success because of Jockey's stellar reputation as a men's underwear brand.[17] Brand extension is a common evolution. Today's most famous designers all started with a single product line that was eventually extended to other products. In 1969, Ralph Lauren extended the Polo brand of men's neckwear to an entire menswear line. As his reputation grew, he extended his brand to womenswear in 1971.[18]

Licensing is a form of brand extension involving the use of a merchandising property in the design of a product or a product line. Merchandising properties have many forms, including brand names (Totes), designer names (Calvin Klein), trademarks (Coca-Cola), designs (a polo player on a horse), characters (SpongeBob SquarePants), celebrity names (Jennifer Lopez), sports teams (Dallas Cowboys), and various forms of entertainment, such as movies (*High School Musical*), television shows (*The Simpsons*), and special events (the Olympics). In a licensing agreement, the owner of the merchandising property (the licensor) permits (licenses) a producer (the licensee) to use the property for a fee, or royalty, of about 5 to 6 percent of sales. The licensee is responsible for the design, production, and distribution of the product. Licensing is such an income-generating opportunity that some companies have created an organizational arm just for identifying licensing prospects. Disney Consumer Products is the licensing division of the Walt Disney Co. responsible for licensing Disney's many merchandising properties to the makers of apparel, toys, stationery, books, plush toys, and interactive games.

FIGURE 7.8
Totes extended its pop-up
umbrella brand to a host of
cold-weather accessories
products. Courtesy of Totes
Isotoner Corporation.

Licensing provides the licensor with an opportunity to extend a brand without having to develop, produce, or market a new product. A property becomes licensable after the brand's reputation for prestige, quality, style, or popularity has been established in the marketplace. The licensee reaps the marketing advantage of the established reputation or popularity of the

merchandising property. To protect the reputation of the merchandising property, licensors most often reserve the right to approve the material, color, quality, and design of the licensed product.

Licensees have expertise in the design, production, and distribution of the licensed product. Signature Eyewear is the eyewear licensee for Laura Ashley, bebe, Dakota Smith, Eddie Bauer, Hart Schaffner Marx, Nicole Miller, and Hummer.[19] As the world's largest shirtmaker, the Phillips-Van Heusen (PVH) Corporation has licenses for the Geoffrey Beene, Kenneth Cole New York, Kenneth Cole Reaction, BCBG Max Azria, BCBG Attitude, Michael Kors, Sean John, Chaps, and Donald J. Trump Signature Collection shirt brands. PVH markets its own shirt brands including Van Heusen, Calvin Klein, IZOD, Arrow, and G.H. Bass. Extending a brand by licensing to experts who understand the design, production, and distribution of a product is often a more prudent marketing strategy than developing brand extensions internally. Donna Karan is often criticized for keeping brand extensions in-house by industry observers who see greater growth opportunities in licensing. Conversely, today, Calvin Klein is essentially a licensing organization. The brand is owned by PVH, which licenses the design and production of most Calvin Klein products. The Calvin Klein collection is produced by Vestimenta Spa; the ck Calvin Klein bridge line is produced by GAV; the Calvin Klein better sportswear line is produced by the Kellwood Co.; Calvin Klein jeans and underwear are produced by the Warnaco Group. Calvin Klein fragrances are produced by Unilever Cosmetics International, which produces Elizabeth Arden cosmetics and other fragrances, such as White Diamonds and Passion; Calvin Klein hosiery is made by Kayser-Roth, the producer of No nonsense pantyhose; Calvin Klein watches are made by the Swatch Group AG, the world's largest producer of finished watches.

Extensive licensing can diminish the exclusivity of a brand's cachet. Halston's high-fashion image was severely tainted when the company licensed a line of female apparel called Halston III for distribution through J.C. Penney. The name eventually disappeared from the marketplace until an investment firm reintroduced the brand as a moderate line of men's, women's, and home lines for department store distribution. Tommy Hilfiger's standing has been diminished by overdistribution. To reestablish itself as an upscale brand, the company launched the H Hilfiger line, a high-end collection advertised in sleek black-and-white ads featuring David Bowie and Iman.[20] LVMH, the French consumer products company with more than 50 luxury brands, rescued Gucci from oversaturation by buying back hundreds of licenses from licensees who were damaging the brand's image by placing the Gucci logo on key chains and umbrellas.[21]

Licensing is lucrative. The Calvin Klein licensing empire began in 1974 with sales of $24,000. In ten years, the company's income from royalties grew to $7.3 million. Apparel and accessories represent the largest category of licensed products. Popular licensed apparel items include T-shirts, sweatshirts, and sleepwear. Other commonly licensed categories include novelties, toys, and stationery. Licensed products represent a significant amount of sales volume for many retailers. Some have assigned a buyer to be solely responsible for identifying hot properties and for merchandising shops and coordinating promotions tied to the licensed properties.

The licensing of designer names began in 1924 when the famous French designer Coco Chanel permitted the use of her name on a newly developed fragrance. The association was a controversial one at a time when designer names appeared only on high-fashion couture. Chanel No. 5 was an immediate success and remains so today.

Not every licensing effort is as successful, however. Some licensing debacles include Bill Blass chocolates, Ralph Lauren westernwear, and Yves Saint Laurent jeans. In general, licensing efforts fail when the brand extension strays too far from the core product line conceptually and/or when the core product line and the extension appeal to different groups of customers.

PRIVATE LABELS

Private label merchandise bears the name of the retail store in which it is sold, or a name used exclusively by the retailer. Products with a Brooks Brothers or Gap label are private labels, as are products with labels used exclusively by a store. Macy's private labels include Alfani, American Rag, First Impressions, Greendog, Hotel Collection, and Style & Co. Unlike branded goods that are "pre-sold" by producer-sponsored advertising, the retailer must rely on its own reputation to validate the quality, style, or value of private label merchandise. A Nordstrom label conveys an image of fashion, while a Wal-Mart label conveys an image of value. Private label merchandise is produced according to a retailer's specifications for color, styling, and fabrication. The goods are then packaged and labeled with the retailer's name or logo, or name unique to the retailer.

Private Brands

Macy's is recognized as a retail industry leader in developing private brand merchandise that differentiates the assortments in our stores and delivers exceptional value to the customer. In addition, selected Macy's private brand merchandise is sold through non-competitive department stores internationally.

Merchandise for each private brand, available "Only @ Macy's," is developed to appeal to a certain customer lifestyle and supported with marketing programs that create a precisely defined image.

ALFANI

For women, Alfani offers interchangeable separates and seasonless suits with a clean, modern sensibility and a refined fit. The collection features updated suiting and more relaxed "city" separates. Alfani for women includes sportswear, intimate apparel, jewelry, handbags and accessories.

Alfani offers men updated classics – clothing for the man who wants to look appropriate but up to date. Designed with an emphasis on fabric and detail, the collection brings newness to the wardrobe in a comfortable way. Alfani for men includes sportswear, clothing, pants, furnishings, shoes and accessories.

This brand aimed at the teen market consists of casual clothes with a strong denim base. Designed to offer clothing that is fresh, approachable and unique in spirit, American Rag appeals to young men and women who want a look that's original, authentic and relaxed.

Charter Club offers all-American style in a traditional and timeless collection of separates – for career, weekend wear and active leisure activities. It is designed for the woman who appreciates a clean, put-together look with the right balance of classic style and comfort. The brand includes sportswear, intimate apparel, jewelry, accessories, bedding and bath.

Club Room features men's classics for weekend or business casual occasions and tailored suiting for the career-oriented professional. Business casual clothing offers a more relaxed version of classic business wear. Weekend casual includes traditional sportswear. The brand includes sportswear, clothing, furnishings, pants, shoes and accessories.

first impressions

First Impressions classic clothing for newborns and infants is defined by fine fabrics and time-honored details. The collection's soft fabrications and sweet, traditional designs make First Impressions a favorite gift choice. The brand includes clothing and matching accessories for boys and girls with an emphasis on special occasion dressing.

greendog

A comprehensive brand of children's play and school clothes, greendog has an easygoing, natural style, a relaxed fit and an appealing price. Kids love the smart, fresh design and parents appreciate the great value and easy care. The brand includes mix and match pieces for school, casual or sport for infants, boys sizes 2 – 20 and girls sizes 2 – 16.

HOTEL COLLECTION

This luxury collection for the home evokes the cool, clean-lined style of a world-class hotel or spa, creating "an oasis in the modern world." Hotel offers high thread-count sheets and specialty fibers for the customer who appreciates quality and modern design. The sophisticated collection includes bedding, bath, tabletop and barware.

FIGURE 7.12
Federated Department Store's private labels. Courtesy of Federated Department Stores, Inc.

Some stores, such as Ann Taylor and Abercrombie & Fitch, offer only private labels. Other retailers, such as department stores and full-line discounters, balance a mix of both branded and private label merchandise. These retailers offer consumers brand and price alternatives by strategically locating private label goods adjacent to branded goods. Private labeling is not a new concept—it is the cornerstone of the merchandising strategies at J.C. Penney and Sears. Countless satisfied customers can attest to the quality and value of their Kenmore washing machines, Toughskins jeans, DieHard automotive batteries, and Craftsman tools purchased at Sears.

Retailers that conduct considerable private label business often have product development functions within their merchandising organizations responsible for designing private label goods and contracting their production. Macy's Merchandising Group (MMG) is the operating division of Federated Department Stores responsible for developing private label programs for Macy's and Bloomingdale's. MMG conceptualizes, designs, and sources Macy's private labels including Alfani, Charter Club, INC, Tassa Elba, and The Cellar. Though department stores are typically known for brands, Federated's growing private label business now represents about 20 percent of the company's annual sales volume.[22]

Some producers specialize in the design and production of private label goods. FesslerUSA, a private label contractor in Orwigsburg, Pennsylvania, specializes in knitwear for the contemporary and junior market.[23] Moretz Sports in Newton, North Carolina, makes private label socks for Wal-Mart, Kmart, and Target.[24] Other private label contractors are multi-faceted. The Kellwood Company in St. Louis produces private labels as well as its own branded product lines, including Sag Harbor and Koret sportswear. The company also has licenses for Nautica dress shirts and Ralph Lauren small leather goods.[25]

Brand/private label/licensor/licensee relationships often are intricately woven. For more than 30 years, No nonsense has been a highly regarded, value-priced brand of women's hosiery distributed through food, drug, and mass retailers. Over the years, the brand has been extended to include tights, socks, sleepwear, underwear, shoe-comfort products, and socks for men and children. As mentioned, No nonsense is owned by the Kayser-Roth Corporation of Greensboro, North Carolina. As the nation's major marketer and manufacturer of legwear, Kayser-Roth has licenses to market other well-known sock and hosiery brands, such as Timberland, Calvin Klein, and Burlington. The company also makes private label hosiery for major retailers. Kayser-Roth is owned by Golden Lady, a privately held legwear company headquartered in Mantova, Italy.

Positioning Private Labels

Traditionally, private labels were positioned at the opening, or lowest, price point in a basic category of merchandise. However, some department stores have upscaled their private labels in recent years by giving them a designer cachet. Macy's Tasso Elba menswear collection includes hand-stitched suits made of high-quality Italian wool for the urbane male.[26] Discount stores have also gotten onto the upscale bandwagon. Target hired world-renowned architect and designer Michael Graves to design everything from teakettles to dog houses. Target also hired the prestigious fashion designer Isaac Mizrahi to create apparel and home decor collections that bear his name. [27]

RANKING OF LICENSED PRODUCT CATEGORIES BY SALES	RANKING OF LICENSED PROPERTY TYPES BY SALES
Accessories	Art
Apparel	Celebrities
Domestics	Entertainment
Electronics	Fashion
Food/Beverage	Music
Footwear	Nonprofit
Furniture/Home furnishings	Publishing
Gifts/Novelties	Sports
Health and Beauty	Trademarks/Brands
Housewares	Toys/Games
Infant Products	
Music/Video	*United States and Canada only*
Publishing	
Sporting Goods	
Stationery/Paper	
Toys/Games	
Video games/Software	

FIGURE 7.13
Noted fashion designer
Isaac Mizrahi creates
private label products for
Target. © Frederick M.
Brown/Getty Images.

Note that an exclusive line is not quite the same as a private label. An exclusive line is a brand-name line created by the producer of the brand for exclusive distribution by a single retailer. Such arrangements have been common for many years between reputed design houses, such as Calvin Klein, and upscale department stores, such as Bloomingdale's. However, the concept is becoming common at the low end of the price spectrum. Noted upscale designers Michael Kors, Stella McCartney, and Karl Lagerfeld have all created value-priced, limited-edition lines for H&M.

Private labels sometimes are knockoffs of successful branded products or product lines. Macy's Charter Club and J.C. Penney's Hunt Club apparel lines bear a striking resemblance to Polo/Ralph Lauren. Tastefully designed in-store shops for private label collections further contribute to the designer illusion.

Sometimes the illusion is too close for comfort. Salvatore Ferragamo Italia once sued a department store conglomerate for violating Ferragamo's Gancini trademark with clasps on handbags that bore a design identical to the Gancini insignia, a design resembling omega in the Greek alphabet. Though the producers of branded goods are frustrated by the value-oriented imitations of their lines, consumers benefit from the rivalry. The competition between the innovators and the imitators ensures a continual flow of distinctive merchandise to the marketplace.

In recent years, private labels have invaded areas traditionally dominated by brands. At the "big five" toy chains, Wal-Mart, Toys "R" Us, Target, Kmart, and KB Toys, private labels now represent about 15 percent of sales, up from

SOURCE
FesslerUSA. (2006). History. www.fesslerusa.com/about _us/history.php.

TEE ANYONE?

FesslerUSA can trace its roots to January 1900, when Walter Meck, grandfather of the company's current CEO, left the family farm to begin knitting fabric and sewing garments in Schuylkill Haven, Pennsylvania. Since then, FesslerUSA has evolved from its humble beginnings as a cotton underwear manufacturer to a world-class producer of fashion T-shirts.

Though Walter Meck's son lost the business to the Fessler family in the 1950s, the Meck family regained control of what is now FesslerUSA in 1994. The Mecks restructured the company from the bottom up with a commitment to domestic production, private labeling, state-of-the-art knitting, design, and cutting equipment, and a first-class design support services

department. The results have been remarkable. Recognized as an industry leader in private label production to the fashion tee market, FesslerUSA serves a wide array of retailers. Some are department stores with in-house design teams. Others are retailers with ideas, but no design staff. The company caters to both with its garment dyed and dyeable products ranging from prepared-for-dye blanks to packaged products shipped retail ready. FesslerUSA also maintains an inventory of in-stock blanks in adult and children's sizes that can either be shipped PFD or dyed to custom colors. The blanks are often used for custom screen printing, embroidering, or embellishing.

5 percent just a few years ago, when private label toys were limited to plush toys and generic board games, such as checkers. The producers of branded toys don't like the competition. They warn that consumers will see less toy innovation in the future as toy research and development decreases because of declining sales.[28]

The Pros and Cons of Private Labels

Advantages   Private labels are advantageous to retailers for several reasons:

- Wholesale costs for private label goods are less than the wholesale cost of branded goods of comparable quality. Product development and marketing costs are inherent in the price of branded goods. Product development and marketing costs for private label goods are minimal.
- Because of lower wholesale costs, a retailer can price private label goods more competitively and more profitably than branded goods. Retailers often rely on private labels to boost their profits. Some say that the future of department stores is dependent on the success of their private labels, especially in women's apparel.
- Private label goods are exclusive to a store. This exclusivity allows the retailer considerable pricing latitude, since consumers have no basis for price comparison.
- Retailers can develop private label goods targeted specifically to their customers without being restricted to the offerings of the wholesale marketplace.

Disadvantages   Several disadvantages are associated with private label merchandise:

- There is no national advertising or any type of vendor support to promote the sale of private label goods.
- Consumers shun private labels as substitutes for brand-driven purchases. They sometimes associate a private label's low price with low quality.
- Private labeling often is a capital-intensive proposition. Goods contracted overseas are paid for months in advance of their arrival. This precludes many small or undercapitalized retailers from developing private labels.

Private Labels as Brands

Kurt Salmon Associates, an international management consulting organization, defines a brand as any recognizable name that adds value to a product because of consumers' perceptions of the name. A name that is meaningful to consumers is a brand. A name that is meaningless is not.

Some retailers promote their private labels with extensive advertising. Macy's has given a designer aura to some of its private labels by promoting them in *Vogue* magazine and by hiring celebrity spokespeople, like Heather Mills McCartney, to endorse the INC label in the same way that Louis Vuitton used actress Uma Thurman to promote handbags.[29] Some retailers extend their private labels as they would a brand. Through licensing, Eddie Bauer has extended the outdoor-inspired, classic American styling of its apparel lines to home products, such as bedding, decorative accessories, lighting, bath products, and window treatments.[30] According to the Kurt Salmon interpretation, these stores "brand" their private labels. Thus, Tasso Elba and Eddie Bauer are, in fact, brands, which is why private labels are often called *store brands* or *private brands*.

SUMMARY POINTS

- Branded merchandise is identified by a name and/or symbol that consumers associate with certain product characteristics such as price, quality, value, fit, styling, and prestige.
- Consumer purchases are brand-driven when clear distinctions exist among competing brands and when the distinctive characteristics are important to the consumer.
- Brands are extended by the addition of related products or product lines. Licensing is a form of brand extension requiring no capital investment on the part of the licensor.
- Private label merchandise is exclusive to a retailer's product mix and affords a retailer an opportunity for higher profit margins.

KEY TERMS AND CONCEPTS

better line	designer brand	mass market line
brand-driven purchase	designer line	moderate line
brand extension	diverter	niche brand
branded merchandise	exclusive line	private label
bridge line	licensing	
budget line	mass market brand	

THINKING ABOUT IT

1. Consider a well-known brand. How has the name been extended to other products or product lines? Has the brand's reputation helped sell the extensions?
2. Do you know of any brands that are dying? What is contributing to their demise?
3. What must product developers consider when extending the brand of a misses line to a plus-size line?
4. Make a list of product categories for which customer purchases are brand-driven. Consider the brand alternatives within each category. What makes the individual brands distinct?
5. Shop the cosmetics lines at a moderate department store and a full-line discounter. Compare the two product groups in terms of price, packaging, and sales promotion. How are the two positioned differently?
6. Research the licensed products of a well-known, upscale apparel line. Do you think that the brand is overextended?

TEAMING UP

1. Each member of your team should research information pertaining to a brand within a specific category of merchandise. As a team, discuss how each brand is positioned differently.
2. Each team member should shop a different category of merchandise in a department store. Compare the private labels and brands within the category relative to price, assortment, and quality. After sharing observations with one another, collectively determine the store's private label positioning strategy. Are the private labels positioned as opening price points? As non-fashion basics? As pseudo designer?

3. Each member of your team should shop the high-end brands and low-end brands within a category of merchandise, noting the product characteristics that distinguish the two brands. Is the price/quality range within some categories greater than in others?

SEARCHING THE NET

1. Search for the histories of several branded products. Compare the brands relative to innovative product development, brand extension, creative advertising and promotion, and licensing.
2. Search for the web sites of several branded products within a specific product category. Determine the market positioning of each brand based on the web site information.
3. Search for the web site of a consumer products company with a large stable of brands. What relationships do you see among the brands? The same customers? The same channels of distribution? The same production facilities? The same advertising vehicles?

CHAPTER EIGHT

Merchandise Resources

After reading this chapter, you will be able to discuss:

● The resources from which retail buyers obtain merchandise.

● The places at which retail buyers and their suppliers transact business.

● Imports as part of a merchandise mix.

● The functions of a resident buying office.

As marketing channel intermediaries, retailers play a critical role in linking producers and consumers. Understanding the role of retailers as channel intermediaries requires knowledge of the interactions that occur between retailers and their customers, as well as knowledge of the interactions that occur between retailers and their suppliers. The terms vendor, supplier, and resource are commonly used to refer to the sources from which retail buyers obtain merchandise to sell in their stores. Chapter 8 covers the various types of merchandise resources and the ways in which retailers interface with them.

MANUFACTURERS

A manufacturer uses labor and machinery to convert raw materials into finished products. The traditional concept of manufacturing encompasses a comprehensive range of functions, such as product design, materials procurement, and the complete production process. Today, the role of the manufacturer is often less inclusive. Many manufacturing organizations *assemble* finished products with component parts produced by other manufacturers. Some manufacturing organizations are actually design companies that develop product concepts and then contract other manufacturers to make the product according to clearly defined specifications. Many contract foreign producers because of the low labor costs in some countries. Manufacturers sometimes operate their own production facilities in foreign countries to reap this economic advantage.

Direct Sales Forces

Some manufacturers employ an internal staff of salespeople to sell their products to retailers. A direct sales force is responsible for meeting with prospective retail buyers, explaining the features of the organization's product line, and processing orders. As the liaison between the manufacturing organization and its retail accounts, a direct sales force often

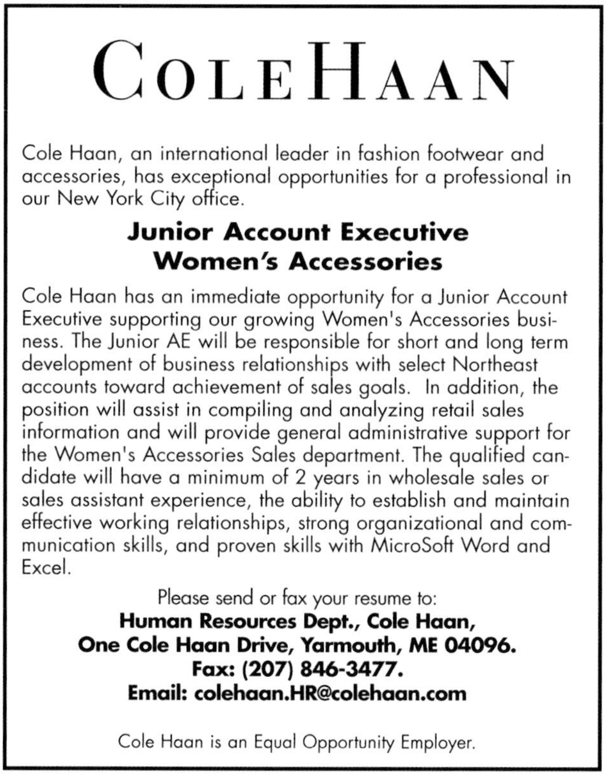

COLE HAAN

Cole Haan, an international leader in fashion footwear and accessories, has exceptional opportunities for a professional in our New York City office.

Junior Account Executive
Women's Accessories

Cole Haan has an immediate opportunity for a Junior Account Executive supporting our growing Women's Accessories business. The Junior AE will be responsible for short and long term development of business relationships with select Northeast accounts toward achievement of sales goals. In addition, the position will assist in compiling and analyzing retail sales information and will provide general administrative support for the Women's Accessories Sales department. The qualified candidate will have a minimum of 2 years in wholesale sales or sales assistant experience, the ability to establish and maintain effective working relationships, strong organizational and communication skills, and proven skills with MicroSoft Word and Excel.

Please send or fax your resume to:
**Human Resources Dept., Cole Haan,
One Cole Haan Drive, Yarmouth, ME 04096.
Fax: (207) 846-3477.
Email: colehaan.HR@colehaan.com**

Cole Haan is an Equal Opportunity Employer.

FIGURE 8.1
Some manufacturers employ a direct sales force to sell their product lines. Cole Haan is a trademark of Cole Haan and is used with permission.

troubleshoots problems with delivery, damaged goods, and credits for returned merchandise. The members of a direct sales force are regular, permanent employees of the manufacturing organization. Their sales responsibilities are often assigned by geographic territory. They are often paid a commission based on what they sell. Members of a direct sales force are often called *account representatives* or *account executives*.

Manufacturers' Sales Representatives

Some manufacturers contract the services of manufacturers' representatives as an alternative to employing a direct sales force. A manufacturer's sales representative, or *manufacturer's rep*, is an independent sales agent whose income is based on commissions earned by selling manufacturers' products within a defined geographic territory. Reps perform a brokerage function in that they bring buyers and sellers together without themselves assuming title, or ownership, of the goods that they sell. Manufacturers provide reps with product training, samples, and leads, as well as marketing communication tools, such as sales literature, catalogs, and other collateral material. Reps often maintain their own offices and showrooms, and absorb their own expenses for travel, support staff, and employee benefits. A rep firm may employ several reps, or a rep can work alone.

Many manufacturers' reps are multi-line reps, selling compatible but noncompetitive lines for more than one manufacturer or principal. Lines of belts, umbrellas, and cold-weather accessories (such as gloves, scarves, and hats) are noncompetitive in that a retail buyer's decision to purchase one line is independent of his or her decision to purchase another. The lines are compatible in that the responsibility for buying these lines is typically designated to the same buyer in most retail organizations. Showing multiple lines on a single sales call spreads the cost of sales over several lines.

Some companies employ both a direct sales force and manufacturers' reps, assigning reps to low-volume territories not large enough to warrant the expense of a direct sales-person. Though companies with a direct sales force exercise greater control over their sales function, there are several advantages to hiring manufacturers' reps:

- A rep has a developed sales territory with established retail accounts and can often penetrate a territory more effi-ciently than a direct salesperson.
- The compatibility of a rep's lines is often the basis for syner-gistic sales, where the sale of one line stimulates the sale of another.
- Unlike a direct sales force, a rep is paid only on what is sold with no additional employment expenses for travel or benefits.

Manufacturers and manufacturers' reps seek each other through the "reps wanted" and "lines wanted" classified sections of trade publications and on the Internet. The direct buying policies of many large retailers have threatened the livelihood of manufac-turers' reps. Power retailers such as Wal-Mart circumvent third-party inter-actions with reps by dealing directly with producers. By averting manufac-turers' reps' commissions, retailers can negotiate lower prices with producers.

FIGURE 8.2
Some manufacturers contract for the services of manufacturers' sales representatives as an alternative to a direct sales force. Courtesy of Pepe Jeans.

WHOLESALERS

Some manufacturers sell indirectly to retailers through an intermediary called a wholesaler. Unlike manufacturers' reps who do not assume title of the goods that they sell, wholesalers buy manufacturers' products and then resell them to retailers. These wholesalers facilitate the distribution of goods from producer to retailer. A producer minimizes its sales transac-tions by selling to a limited number of wholesalers instead of directly selling to many retailers. A retailer minimizes its purchase transactions by buying products from a few wholesalers, instead of directly from many producers. Wholesalers also sell products for industrial, commercial, and institutional use. *Distributor* and *jobber* are names commonly used to refer to wholesalers.

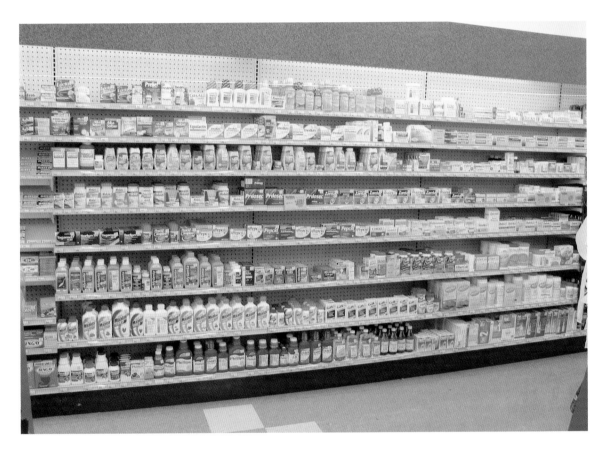

FIGURE 8.3
A rack jobber performs
a retailer's inventory
management function
for a product line. Image
courtesy Frank W. Kerr Co.

A wholesaler's selling price is most often higher than a producer's selling price in that the wholesaler's price must cover the wholesaler's operating costs and profit, though the volume discounts that wholesalers obtain from manufacturers cover a portion of these operating costs. In spite of higher prices, retailers sometimes elect to buy from wholesalers because of shorter lead time, the time lapse between the point at which an order is placed and the point at which an order is delivered. Small, independent retailers buy from wholesalers because wholesalers accept smaller orders than producers who often have minimum order requirements that exceed the inventory needs of many small retailers. Small, frequently delivered orders minimize a retailer's inventory investment, resulting in lower inventory carrying costs.

Many wholesalers offer financial, logistical, and marketing support to their customers. A *rack jobber* is a wholesaler that performs virtually all of a retailer's inventory management and promotional functions for a product line. The Frank W. Kerr Company, based in Novi, Michigan, is one of the nation's largest wholesalers for pharmaceuticals and health and beauty care products. The company tailors programs to meet the needs of a wide range of customers, from independent community pharmacies and specialty pharmacy providers to cooperatives, chain drugstores, chain drug warehouses, grocery stores, and mass merchandisers.[1] A computerized inventory management system replenishes stock as it is sold to ensure the constant availability of even the most popular products. Assortments are periodically adjusted based on rate of sale to maximize sales and to minimize inventory and space investments.

With the exception of imports, the typical channel of distribution for the retailers and the product categories discussed in this text does not include wholesalers. However, wholesalers are used extensively in food distribution and by small, independent retailers for certain categories of merchandise, such as toys, sporting goods, consumer electronics, hardware, prerecorded music, books, and office supplies. As in the case of other industries, there has been much consolidation within the wholesaling sector. The number of consumer magazine distributors has decreased from more than 300 to fewer than 20 within recent years.

Clearly there are economic advantages to buying directly from a source of production instead of a wholesaler. Christopher & Banks, a chain of nearly 90 value-price female apparel stores based Plymouth, Minnesota, attributes its emergence from Chapter 11 bankruptcy to a change in buying strategy, from buying Asian imports through wholesalers to buying directly from manufacturers.[2]

IMPORTS

Imports add variety and distinction to merchandise assortments with fabrications, designs, and workmanship unique to their country of origin and unavailable in the United States. Italian leathers, hand-loomed Indian rugs, and Belgian lace are all examples of distinctive imports. Wedgwood china from England, Louis Vuitton luggage and accessories from France, and Bally shoes from Switzerland have enhanced the exclusivity of the offerings of many U.S. retailers for decades.

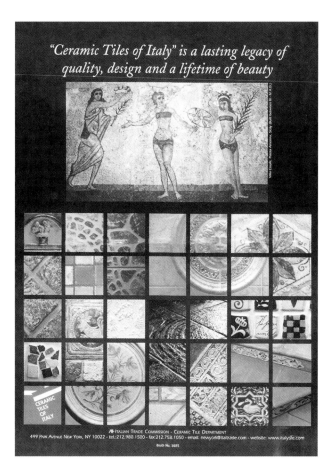

"Ceramic Tiles of Italy" is a lasting legacy of quality, design and a lifetime of beauty

ITALIAN TRADE COMMISSION - CERAMIC TILE DEPARTMENT
499 PARK AVENUE New York, NY 10022 - tel.:212.980.1500 - fax:212.758.1050 - email: newyork@italtrade.com - website: www.italytile.com
Booth No. 3685

FIGURE 8.4
Imports can add variety and distinction to merchandise assortments. Courtesy of the Italian Trade Commission.

Imports are often less expensive than goods of comparable quality made in the United States because of the lower wages paid to workers in less industrialized countries. Lower prices are especially true of labor-intensive products such as shoes, gloves, and men's shirts. Labor unions often are critical of retailers that sell imports, claiming that importing erodes the U.S. manufacturing base and exploits the underclasses of underdeveloped countries. Price-conscious consumers are unfazed by organized labor's position, however, and are more likely to make a purchase decision based on product appeal and value than on country of origin.

Manufacturers, wholesalers, and retailers import. As noted earlier in this chapter, many manufacturing organizations import domestically designed products produced by foreign contractors. Both domestic and foreign wholesalers import goods to the United States to sell directly to retailers or through manufacturers' reps. Large retailers bypass importers as channel intermediaries by directly importing goods. To avoid wholesalers' markups, Crate & Barrel directly imports its assortments from more than 300 overseas factories. Some retailers operate foreign buying offices that work in tandem with their domestic buying organization to source goods, place orders, and arrange shipment. Retailers that do not maintain foreign buying offices often contract the services of commissionaires familiar with a foreign market. A commissionaire is paid a commission to act as a retailer's agent in the market by screening resources, facilitating order placement, ensuring quality control, and making payment and shipping arrangements.

Imports are subject to tariffs, or *duties,* levied by the U.S. government to restrict foreign competition. Tariffs are based on import penetrations and the competitive price of domestic goods. Imports are restricted by quotas, quantitative limitations placed on the amount of merchandise that may be imported from a country within a time period. Quotas are established by country and by category of merchandise. The Generalized System of Preferences (GSP) allows certain products to be imported from developing countries without quotas. Importers often employ the services of customs brokers, agents licensed by the U.S. Treasury to represent importers in customs matters. Customs brokers expedite goods through customs by preparing the necessary customs forms, processing the payment of tariffs, and arranging for inland transportation.

The Downside of Imports

Though imports have many advantages, there are several factors that a retailer must consider when making a decision to buy imported goods:

- High procurement costs, involving overseas buying trips, packing, shipping, insurance, storage, tariffs, and commissionaires' and customs agents' fees, inflate the final actual, or landed cost of imports.
- Landed costs are sometimes uncertain because of fluctuations in currency rates of exchange.
- Imports require a longer lead time than domestic goods, sometimes as long as a year. Shipping delays can result in costly markdowns when merchandise arrives at the end of, or even after, the selling season for which it was purchased.
- Imports tie up a retailer's capital for considerable time in that imports are paid for prior to being shipped, long before the point at which they will generate sales.
- Retailers that import directly are responsible for compliance with the laws that govern tariffs and quotas, as well as those that govern product safety standards and labeling for textile fiber identification and care requirements.
- It is often difficult to collect on damaged or unacceptable goods, and it is costly to return them.

FIGURE 8.5
Some domestic wholesalers import goods to sell directly to retailers.

FIGURE 8.6
A commissionaire is paid a commission to act as a retailer's agent in a foreign market.

HONG KONG AGENT

OVER 10 yrs — Existing business exp & connections with Chinese National I/E Corp., looking for U.S. Importers of ladies apparel to manufactured in proc. For further info please contact Ms. Suiko Mabel Lee at fax (254).236. 85522 or G.P.O. Box 8750 Hong Kong

S O U R C I N G

By Israeli experienced agent in Israel and other countries. No duty or quota from Israel. Top quality. Contact NY office 212. 326.1120.

SOURCE
Encyclopedia of Chicago. (2006). www.encyclopedia. chicagohistory.org.

MARKETS

Retail buyers transact business with suppliers in several types of settings. Large retail organizations have *sample rooms* in which traveling vendors show their lines by appointment. Today, buyers are more likely to view lines in nonretail locations remote from their stores. The current offerings of manufacturers, manufacturers' reps, wholesalers, and importers are often

AN ARCHITECTURAL ICON

Conceived by the Marshall Field Company as a model of scientific efficiency in wholesale merchandising, Chicago's Merchandise Mart was designed to centralize the city's wholesale activities and the wholesale operations of Marshall Field's which were scattered throughout the city. The Mart opened in May 1930, six months into the Great Depression. At 4.0 million square feet, The Mart was the largest building in the world. The completion of the 4.3 million-square-foot Pentagon in 1943 changed the designation to the largest commercial building in the world.

In 1935, Marshall Field's wholesale division was liquidated, and in 1945, ownership of The Mart passed from Marshall Field's to Joseph P. Kennedy, former ambassador to Great Britain and father of John F. Kennedy, who would become the 35th president of the United States. Joseph Kennedy created office space on The Mart's lower floors, and marketed the upper floors as home furnishings and apparel showrooms.

In the 1950s and 1960s, The Merchandise Mart lost some of its wholesale market dominance as other marts began to sprout up throughout the country, including Dallas, Atlanta, and Los Angeles. Merchandise Mart Properties, Inc. (MMPI) expanded its property portfolio with the opening the Washington (D.C.) Design Center, and, in 1977, the Chicago Apparel Center adjacent to The Merchandise Mart. MMPI has become a specialist in marketing wholesale/retail complexes as both a property manager and tradeshow producer. In 1991, "Shops at The Mart" opened on The Mart's first and second floors, accommodating the retail needs of a daily crowd of 20,000 tenants and visitors, and enormous groups of market event and trade show attendees.

displayed in showrooms staffed by a sales force that presents the product line to prospective buyers. Showrooms for a particular merchandise category or group of related categories are often located in a major showroom building. In New York, 1411 and 1407 Broadway are major showroom buildings for moderate-to-better dresses and sportswear; 500 and 512 Seventh Avenue are moderate-to-bridge women's outerwear buildings. Forty One Madison is a major tabletop showroom building.

A market is a place where buyers and sellers come together to transact business. A market is often identified as a city, or a section of a city, in which a number of showrooms of related product categories are located. New York's fashion accessories market comprises approximately 20 buildings between Fifth and Eighth Avenues and 35th and 39th Streets. New York's legendary Garment District (now called the Fashion Center) is bordered by Fifth and Ninth Avenues and 35th and 41st Streets. Some markets are also major manufacturing centers. The offerings of more than 2,100 home furnishing manufacturers are permanently displayed in 150 showroom buildings in High Point and Thomasville, North Carolina, the production source of most of the furniture manufactured in the United States.

Though New York is still the nation's leading market for high-fashion apparel, its importance as an apparel market has diminished in recent years because of the growth of Atlanta, Chicago, Dallas, and Los Angeles as major markets. These regional markets sometimes specialize in specific categories of merchandise. Dallas is the ultimate roundup for westernwear including tack lines, western boots, hats, outerwear, and accessories. Smaller secondary markets are located in Boston, Charlotte, Denver, Kansas City, Miami, Minneapolis, Pittsburgh, San Francisco, and Seattle. Their draw is

FIGURE 8.7
Forty One Madison Avenue in New York City is a major showroom building for tabletop. Courtesy Stephen Sullivan.

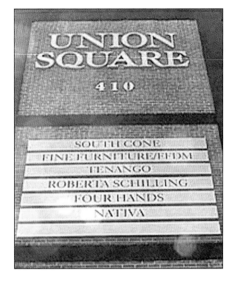

limited to the geographic areas in which they are located. A decline in the number of manufacturers' sales representatives and retail buyers has threatened the viability of many of these small markets.

Designed for "one-stop shopping" for buyers, a merchandise mart houses an entire market under one roof. Chicago's Merchandise Mart is the oldest mart in the United States, built by the preeminent merchant Marshall Field in 1930. The Atlanta Apparel Mart, the Denver Merchandise Mart, and The Fashion Center in San Francisco are other examples of merchandise marts.

A market center is a cluster of marts. An example is the Dallas Market Center (DMC), a complex covering 100 acres that includes four marts:

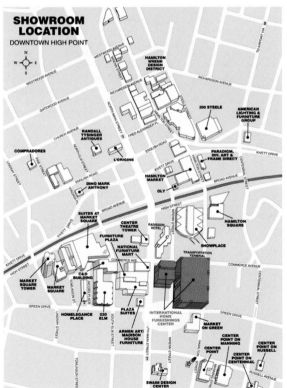

- The 15-story World Trade Center, which houses the DMC's Fashion Center, with more than 12,000 apparel and accessories lines, and the Gourmet Market, the largest permanent wholesale gourmet showroom in the world. The upper floors of the World Trade Center house showrooms of gifts, decorative accessories, lighting, furniture, rugs, bed and bath linens, fabric, jewelry, and toys.
- Market Hall, for temporary exhibits.
- The Trade Mart, 1 million square feet of showroom space housing more than 7,000 lines of gifts, decorative accessories, housewares, lighting, tabletop, and stationery.
- The International Floral & Gift Center, dedicated to the floral and holiday-trim industry.

FIGURE 8.8
High Point, North Carolina, is the nation's leading wholesale market for furniture. Union Square is a major showroom building in High Point. Source: www.unionsquarehp.com; www.ihfc.com.

The DMC is home to more than 2,200 permanent showrooms and hosts nearly 50 markets annually, drawing more than 200,000 retail buyers from the United States and abroad.[3]

TRADE SHOWS

A trade show is a group of temporary exhibits in a convention center, merchandise mart, or hotel, at which vendors of a single category of merchandise, or group of related categories, present goods to retail buyers. Trade-show exhibitors are often grouped together by product category or price level. Exhibits at the National Association of Men's Sportswear Buyers (NAMSB) show are grouped as contemporary, jeanswear, leather/outerwear, young men's and activewear, accessories, and footwear. Some trade shows cater to niche markets: BATMAN is the big and tall men's show. Other specialty shows include the Intimate Apparel Salon and the Bridal Expo.

The duration of a trade show ranges from a few days to a week. A trade show and its related events are often referred to as a *market* or *market week*. Some markets are annual events; others occur more frequently. Apparel markets are held as often as five times a year to coincide with the seasonal release of lines. The annual schedules for most apparel markets include:

- April—Fall I or Transition
- June—Fall II
- August—Resort/Holiday
- October/November—Spring
- January—Summer

10 TIPS FOR SHOPPING THE FASHION CENTER

1. Plan early. Not all showrooms require appointments but a 1 - 2 month lead time will ensure that you see all the resources on your list. Advance scheduling also helps when booking hotels and airlines. Call Carol Sommers at The Travel Services Program office at 800-776-1116 or 212-532-3400 for help with your travel plans.

2. Establish parameters. Determine your goals in terms of price points, sizes, delivery deadlines, quantities and fabrics.

3. Develop a resource target list. Contact The Fashion Center BID office a few weeks in advance of your trip and ask for category lists of manufacturers [Ph: 212-764-9600; Fx: 212-764-9697]. Read Women's Wear Daily to stay on top of trends, store merchandising concepts and merchandise range.

4. Try new vendors. New firms are constantly opening in The Fashion Center. Make sure you include a few of them on your agenda. You never know when you will discover a fashion diamond.

5. Reconfirm addresses. Firms often move location and addresses may have changed since your last visit. Be sure to double check addresses.

6. Ask questions in advance. Call manufacturers to determine if they will be able to meet your basic requirements in terms of delivery, payment schedules, etc. An hour of advance homework can save a half day of buying time!

7. Check trade show calendars. Consider tieing in your buying trip with a specific New York trade show. You'll enjoy an expanded market overview and see more resources.

8. Map out your schedule. Refer to The Fashion Center map on pages 18 - 19 when planning your appointments. A well-planned itinerary will make the most efficient use of your travel time.

9. Allow at least one hour per showroom visit. Your buying trip is critical to the success of your retail operation. Make sure you have ample time to devote to selection and negotiation.

10. Plan some play time. In addition to the world's best fashion, New York City offers world-class dining, theater, arts and entertainment. Make sure they're a part of your schedule, **too!**

FIGURE 8.9
The Fashion Center gives tips to buyers for shopping in New York City. Reprinted courtesy of Fashion Center Business Improvement District.

At markets, buyers get the opportunity to meet with major design and manufacturing executives and to network with buyers of the same merchandise category from other retail organizations. Trade shows offer educational opportunities in the form of seminars by industry experts. Topics at Atlanta's AmericasMart have included cross-merchandising apparel with giftware, visual merchandising, and technology. The Dallas Market Center publishes the New Buyer's Kit, an online primer that includes sections titled 8 Rules for a Market Trip, Surviving Market, and Quick Tips for Covering Market.[4]

A market's lure is enhanced by fashion shows, cocktail parties, and big-name entertainment. The large markets such as WWDMagic and Super-Show often will invite headline performers and sports celebrities to entice and entertain attendees.

SOURCE
George Little Management, LLC. (2006). About GLM. www.glmshows.com/review/final/about.html.

IT'S SHOWTIME!

George Little Management (GLM) was started in 1924 by George F. Little, the grandfather of the current principal owners. Since then, the company has become the largest producer and marketer of consumer product trade shows in North America, serving industries as diverse as giftware, social stationery, home textile, tabletop, gourmet housewares, contemporary furniture, and wellness. GLM produces more than 50 trade shows in some 20 cities across the United Sates and Canada. Together the events showcase nearly 30,000 exhibitors in almost six million square feet of exhibit space, attracting some 630,000 attendees. GLM is the single largest producer of trade shows in New York City with 19 wholesale events held annually at the Jacob K. Javits Convention Center, Passenger Ship Terminal Piers, and Penn Plaza Pavilion.

GLM is headquartered in White Plains, New York, with satellite offices in Los Angeles and Toronto. The company offers comprehensive trade show and con-ference management and marketing services that include exhibit sales and marketing; attendance promotion and buyer services; media relations; seminar and special event production; customer service and registration; database development and management; operations; display; financial services and accounting; and Internet development and marketing.

GLM is also actively involved in developing technology solutions for its buyer and supplier customers. In 2002, GLM entered into a marketing agreement with PointForce, Inc., the leading provider of outsourced IT software and services for gift and home suppliers across North America. To enhance its overseas presence, GLM has formed relationships with sales agencies in several countries including Japan, Korea, China, Hong Kong, Macao, Taiwan, the Philippines, Vietnam, Singapore, Malaysia, Indonesia, Nepal, Brunei, Thailand, India, Pakistan, Sri Lanka, Seychelles, Mauritius, and Bangladesh.

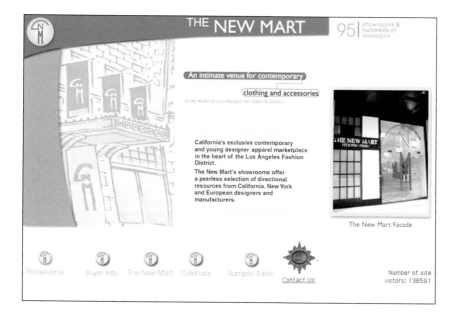

THE NEW MART

95 | showrooms & hundreds of resources

An intimate venue for contemporary

clothing and accessories

IN THE HEART OF LOS ANGELES THE FASHION DISTRICT

California's exclusive contemporary and young designer apparel marketplace in the heart of the Los Angeles Fashion District.

The New Mart's showrooms offer a peerless selection of directional resources from California, New York and European designers and manufacturers.

THE NEW MART
127 E 9TH STREET

The New Mart Facade

Showrooms   Buyer Info   The New Mart   Calendar   Sample Sales

Contact Us!

Number of site vistors: 138591

FIGURE 8.10
A trade show is a group of temporary exhibits for a single category of merchandise. Courtesy of The New Mart.

Trade Show Sponsors

A trade show is coordinated by a sponsor who secures the trade show facility and then rents space to exhibitors for a fee based on the size of the exhibit booth. The fee covers:

- *Drayage,* or the movement of goods from the facility's loading dock to the booth.
- Booth furniture such as tables, chairs, and risers.
- A listing in the trade-show directory of exhibitors by product category compiled for the convenience of the buyers.
- Publicity efforts designed to draw attendees to the event, such as advertisements in trade publications subscribed to by buyers.

Trade shows may be sponsored by trade associations, market centers, and/or management firms that specialize in trade-show production. George Little Management is the largest producer of trade shows for consumer goods. Some trade-show producers specialize in certain types of shows. ENK International is a New York–based company that produces high-end apparel and accessories shows including Accessorie Circuit, Intermezzo Collections, Fashion Coterie, and, for high-end menswear, the Collective.[5]

Some shows that are sponsored by trade associations are:

- The International Toy Fair sponsored annually in New York by the Toy Manufacturers of America featuring the products of nearly 2,000 toy manufacturers from around the world.
- The All Candy Expo sponsored annually in Chicago's McCormick Place by the National Confectioners Association featuring nearly 450 exhibitors.[6]
- The Fashion Footwear Association of New York (FFANY) and the School and Home Office Products Association (SHOPA) also sponsor trade shows.[7]

FIGURE 8.11
Merchandise marts, such as Atlanta Merchandise Mart, house an entire market under one roof. Image courtesy John Portman & Associates, Inc.

RESIDENT BUYING OFFICES

A resident buying office, or *buying office*, is a marketing and research consulting firm that serves as an adviser to a group of member, or client, stores. Located in major market centers, buying offices provide market information, merchandising guidance, and other services to their membership. New York City is home to the largest number of buying offices. Some have branches in other cities in the United States and around the world. Many buying offices specialize in certain categories of merchandise and/or types of stores, limiting their services to areas such as bridal, furs, or large sizes. The members of a buying office are often similar in terms of merchandise mix, size, and retailing format.

The original buying offices were buying services for the owners of apparel stores too distant to make frequent trips to New York, the major fashion market. For a fee, an office assumed the responsibility of selecting and ordering all or part of a client store's inventory. This allowed member stores to devote full-time attention to the task of operating their stores without the interruption of time-consuming and costly market trips.

The primary role of the present-day buying office is that of adviser, product developer, and importer for member stores. Buying offices forecast future market conditions by studying consumer behavior, demographics, and emerging trends. The information is channeled to client stores through a communication network of bulletins, surveys, and reports. Buying offices facilitate buyers' market trips by arranging travel and hotel accommodations, compiling lists of recommended resources to visit, and providing office space. Offices host buyers' meetings during major markets as a forum for exchanging ideas. Some offices respond to the needs of individual members by store visits and by researching solutions to problems peculiar to a store.

Market coverage responsibility in a buying office is assigned by merchandise category to *market specialists* sometimes called *market reps* or *resident buyers.* Market specialists communicate market conditions to client stores, such as fashion trends, new resources, hot items, opportunistic buys, and promotional opportunities. Their market expertise is based on daily market contact and information from various sources, such as vendors, member stores, mills, research firms, designers, and the trade media.

The wholesaling of private label merchandise has become an important buying office function. Buying offices source large quantities of goods for the collective needs of many member stores and then resell the goods to their clients, enabling even the smallest independent store to participate in private label programs. Another buying office function is group buying, the pooling of orders for merchandise, store fixtures, and services from many members to meet minimum order requirements or to negotiate quantity discounts.

FIGURE 8.12
Sometimes trade shows are sponsored by trade associations fro a product line. Provided by Fashion Footwear Association of New York (FFANY).

FIGURE 8.13
Some markets are annual, but apparel markets are more frequent. Courtesy Fairchild Publications, Inc.

The development of catalogs as regular-price or promotional direct-mail pieces is another important function of the buying office. The office produces a single catalog featuring goods common to the assortments of member stores at a fraction of the cost of each store producing its own piece. Production costs are minimized by negotiating cooperative advertising from the vendors whose merchandise is featured in the catalogs.

Types of Buying Offices

There are three major types of buying offices:

Salaried Office   A salaried, or *fee*, office is the most common type of buying office. A salaried office is owned and operated independently of its member stores, most of which are privately owned specialty stores that pay the buying office an annual fee for services. Collectively, salaried offices have more members than other types of buying offices. The Doneger Group has grown to be the largest independent office through the acquisition of several other offices, such as The Certified Fashion Guild, Burns Winkler, Jack Braustein, and Young Innovators. Though small retailers are more likely to rely on the services of buying offices than large retailers, large retailers sometimes rely on buying offices for services such as importing or off-price sourcing.

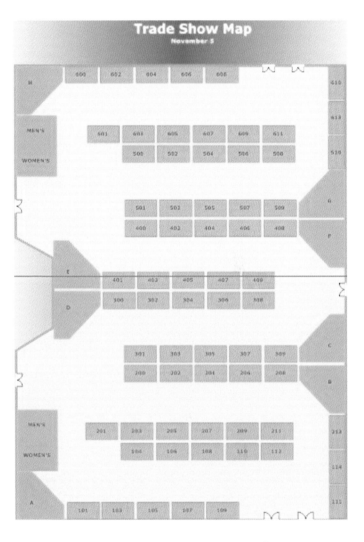

FIGURE 8.14
At a trade show, vendors present their lines to retail buyers in temporary exhibits. Source: www.smartdraw.com.

Syndicated Office   A syndicated office is owned and operated by a retail conglomerate. Macy's Merchandising Group (MMG) is a division of Federated Department Stores responsible for developing merchandising strategies for Macy's and Bloomingdale's. MMG coordinates Federated's innovative buying-team process whereby groups of buyers collectively determine the mix of suppliers for Federated stores. The buyers at division level then make assortment decisions on the offerings of each vendor. Federated's commitment to each of these key vendors is used as leverage to negotiate price, promotional support, delivery, and other concessions.

Private Office A private office is owned and operated by a single retail organization as an extension of its corporate merchandising function. Through a private office, a retailer maintains market presence even when its merchandising function is executed at a corporate office remote from a major market. Stein Mart, a chain of off-price better female apparel stores based in Jacksonville, Florida, and Ross Dress for Less, an off-pricer based in

FIGURE 8.15
A buying office is a marketing and research consulting firm that serves retail stores. Source: www.doneger.com.

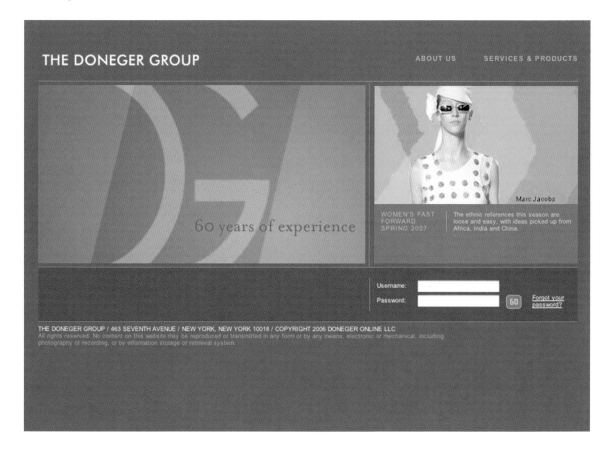

THE DONEGER GROUP

Located in the heart of the Fashion Center in New York, the Doneger Group is a salaried buying office founded in 1946 by Henry Doneger. Originally serving specialty retailers of women's apparel, the Doneger Group has expanded its client base and its merchandise categories through the acquisition of other offices, such as Estelle Shomer, Atlas Buying Corporation, and Independent Retailers Syndicate. The Doneger Group is a leading source of global market trends and customized merchandising strategies. Its market analysts shop, edit, and evaluate the marketplace to help companies make buying and merchandising decisions. Doneger serves domestic and international retail clients, advising on color, trends, key items, and market opportunities. Presently the Doneger Group's client list includes more that 850 stores representing more than 7,000 store locations.

The Doneger Group is organized into several divisions, each specializing in a particular product category. Those divisions include:

- **Henry Doneger Associates**, which offers market analysis and merchandising programs to womenswear, menswear, and childrenswear retailers in all classifications, sizes and price levels.
- **Carol Hoffman**, which represents women's specialty retailers in the contemporary, better, bridge, designer, and couture markets in all classifications of sportswear, dresses, outerwear, suits, accessories, and lingerie.
- **Price Point Buying**, which uncovers off-price deals in women's sportswear, outerwear, childrenswear, and menswear.
- **Tobe**, which provides trend forecasting, product development, and market news to a client base of department and specialty stores and discounters. Tobe publishes the *The Tobe Report*, the fashion industry's leading and most respected source of fashion industry information.

The Doneger Group offers a range of other services to its clients, including favorably priced group buys on hangers, packaging, mannequins, and store fixtures, as well as participation in various promotional and fashion catalogs.

SOURCE
The Doneger Group. (2006). About Us. www.doneger.com/web/231.htm.

Newark, California, have private offices in New York. Some retailers have moved their private offices out of New York in recent years. J.C. Penney transplanted its private buying offices from New York to Dallas, feeling it more important for the buying office to be close to the buyers than close to the market.

SUMMARY POINTS

- A manufacturer uses labor and machinery to convert raw materials into finished products. Manufacturers use either a direct sales force or manufacturers' reps to sell their products to retailers.
- Merchant wholesalers buy manufacturers' products and then resell them to retailers. Wholesalers facilitate the distribution of goods between a producer and a retailer.
- Imports add variety and distinction to a retailer's product mix and often afford a retailer an opportunity for higher profit margins.
- Showrooms, marts, markets, and trade shows are nonretail settings in which sellers and retail buyers come together to transact business.
- A buying office is a marketing and research consultant that serves as an adviser to its member or client stores by providing market information, merchandising guidance, and other services.

KEY TERMS AND CONCEPTS

commissionaire	manufacturer's sales	salaried buying office
custom broker	representative	showroom
direct sales force	market	syndicated buying
group buying	market center	office
landed cost	merchandise mart	tariff
major showroom	private buying office	trade show
building	quota	wholesaler
manufacturer	resident buying office	

THINKING ABOUT IT

1. What factors contribute to a buyer's decision to source imports instead of domestic goods?

2. The number of manufacturers' reps for certain categories of merchandise has been declining for many years. Why do you think this is happening?

3. The number and types of buying offices in the United States have diminished considerably in recent decades. What do you think is the cause?

TEAMING UP

1. Each member of your team should research trade shows for a specific category of merchandise within a department store or full-line discount store. As a group, compare the results of your searches. Is there overlap? That is, does one trade show cover multiple categories of merchandise? Do some categories have more trade shows than others? Which shows are more frequent than once a year? Why the need for multiple shows?

2. Each team member should assume the role of a manufacturers' rep for a category of merchandise within a department store or full-line discount store. Find opportunities to represent lines for the region of the country in which you live. Are the opportunities plentiful? Might you consider becoming a manufacturers' rep?

SEARCHING THE NET

1. Search for information on some of the trade shows mentioned in this chapter. Compare the shows in terms of size, attendees, and entertainment fanfare.

2. Search for information on salaried buying offices for a specific category of merchandise. How do the various buying offices compare in terms of the types of services offered?

3. Search for information pertaining to the various market centers across the United States. How do these market centers differ from New York as a market?

PART THREE

The Financial Aspects of Merchandising

○ MEASURES OF PRODUCTIVITY
○ MERCHANDISING ACCOUNTING
○ INVENTORY VALUATION

CHAPTER NINE

Measures of Productivity

After reading this chapter,
you will be able to discuss:

● Productivity as a mea-
sure of performance.

● The relationship
between turnover and
stock-to-sales ratios.

● Sales per square foot as
a measure of productivity.

Maximizing returns on an organization's assets is a universal business objective. Retailers maximize their return on inventory and selling space as organizational assets by using them in such a way that sales are optimal. In general, retailers want to maximize sales while minimizing investments of inventory and space. Chapter 9 deals with some of the measures that are used to monitor the performance of inventory and selling space as organizational assets.

PRODUCTIVITY

Productivity is a measure of the number of units of output produced per unit of input. Stated in mathematical terms:

$$productivity \ = \ \frac{output}{input}$$

Productivity measures performance. High productivity is a positive indication that output has been maximized with a minimum investment of input. Low productivity is an unsatisfactory indication of an ineffective use of input. Low productivity can be corrected by increasing output, decreasing input, or both increasing output and decreasing input.

Measures of productivity are common in the manufacturing sector, where input and output are often quantitatively defined. In an apparel manufacturing operation, the productivity of a pressing function can be measured by dividing the number of garments pressed by the amount of time it takes to press them.

$$productivity \ = \ \frac{units\ pressed\ (output)}{number\ of\ hours\ worked\ by\ presser\ (input)}$$

$$productivity \ = \ \frac{2,400\ garments}{8\ hours}$$

$$productivity \ = \ 300\ garments\ per\ hour$$

The concept of productivity is not as easily applied within service industries because of the difficulty in quantitatively defining output and input. Though sales are a numerically measured retail output, intangible output, such as customer satisfaction, is difficult to quantify. In spite of these limitations, retailers apply productivity measures whenever a relationship between input and output can be defined numerically.

TURNOVER

Turnover, or *stockturn*, is the number of times that an average inventory is sold within a time period. Turnover describes the movement of merchandise, or the velocity at which goods come in and out of a business unit, such as a department or store. Turnover reflects the amount of sales generated per dollar of inventory invested. Turnover is computed by dividing sales for a period by the average amount of inventory carried for the same period:

$$turnover = \frac{sales}{average\ inventory}$$

Turnover is generally computed to one decimal place.

An average inventory is the average amount of inventory on hand within a time period. Average inventory can be computed by dividing the sum of the beginning and ending inventories of a period by two. The average inventory for a month is computed by dividing the sum of the inventory on hand at the beginning of the month, called the beginning-of-month, or *BOM*, inventory, and the inventory on hand at the end of the month, called the end-of-month, or *EOM*, inventory, by two.

$$average\ inventory = \frac{BOM + EOM}{2}$$

Note that the EOM inventory of one month is equal to the BOM inventory of the succeeding month. It is logical to assume that if a store closes with a $2 million inventory on hand on the last day of a month, it will open the next day with a $2 million inventory on hand. Maintaining recorded

values of BOM and EOM inventories is a common inventory control practice in retail organizations.

An average inventory for a period longer than a month is based on the
average inventories of the months within the period.[1] The average inventory for a year is computed by dividing the sum of the average inventories
of each month in the year by 12.

$$average \ inventory = \frac{\dfrac{(BOM + EOM)_1}{2} + \dfrac{(BOM + EOM)_2}{2} \ \ldots \ + \ \dfrac{(BOM + EOM)_{12}}{2}}{12}$$

The formula can be simplified. Because each EOM is equal to the BOM of
the succeeding month, the EOMs can be eliminated from the formula
without affecting the value of the average. The EOM of the last month must
be retained in the computation, however, because it is not repeated as a
succeeding BOM.

$$average \ inventory = \frac{BOM_1 + BOM_2 + BOM_3 \ldots + BOM_{12} + EOM_{12}}{13}$$

The number 13 is used as the denominator because 13 figures are used
in the computation of the numerator: 12 BOMs and 1 EOM.

The formula can be adapted for other periods. The average inventory
for a six-month season beginning in February and ending in July is
computed as follows:

$$average \ inventory = \frac{BOM_{FEB} + BOM_{MAR} + BOM_{APR} + BOM_{MAY} + BOM_{JUN} + BOM_{JUL} + EOM_{JUL}}{7}$$

Computing Turnover

Consider the following example: The men's sweater department at Dolan's Department Store generated sales of $30,000 last year. The BOMs and EOMs for each month are listed in Table 9.1. Average inventory is computed as follows:

$$average\ inventory = \frac{BOM_1 + BOM_2 \ldots + BOM_{12} + EOM_{12}}{13}$$

$$average\ inventory = \frac{\begin{array}{c}\$2,500 + 2,500 + 2,500 + 5,000 + 2,500 + 7,500 + 2,500 \\ + 5,000 + 5,000 + 5,000 + 7,500 + 12,500 + 5,000\end{array}}{13}$$

$$average\ inventory = \frac{\$65,000}{13} = \$5,000$$

TABLE 9.1   BOM AND EOM INVENTORIES FOR MEN'S SWEATER DEPARTMENT, DOLAN'S DEPARTMENT STORE

Month	BOM	EOM
1	$ 2,500	$ 2,500
2	$ 2,500	$ 2,500
3	$ 2,500	$ 5,000
4	$ 5,000	$ 2,500
5	$ 2,500	$ 7,500
6	$ 7,500	$ 2,500
7	$ 2,500	$ 5,000
8	$ 5,000	$ 5,000
9	$ 5,000	$ 5,000
10	$ 5,000	$ 7,500
11	$ 7,500	$12,500
12	$12,500	$ 5,000

Each BOM is equal to the EOM of the preceding month.

Turnover is computed as follows:

$$turnover = \frac{sales}{average\ inventory}$$

$$turnover = \frac{\$30,000}{\$5,000} = 6.0$$

The turnover of the men's sweater department at Dolan's Department Store for last year was 6.0. In other words, an average inventory of $5,000 was sold six times.

The components of the turnover formula must agree in terms of time. To compute turnover for a year, sales for the year are divided by the average inventory for the same year. To compute turnover for a month, sales for the month are divided by the average inventory for the same month. Turnover can be computed for any period; however, annual turnover is the most commonly used. (See Table 9.2.) The remaining discussion of turnover presumes the period of a year unless otherwise specified.

Though turnover is typically calculated using the retail value of sales and inventory, turnover can also be calculated using units of sales and/or inventory, or the wholesale cost values of sales and/or inventory.

High versus Low Turnover

High turnover is generally more desirable than low turnover. The mathematical relationship between sales and average inventory in the turnover formula suggests that turnover can be increased by increasing sales, decreasing average inventory, or both increasing sales and decreasing average inventory. The latter strategy is an important merchandising objective for retailers: to generate more sales on less inventory.

To demonstrate the impact of average inventory on turnover, consider the following: A jeweler consistently sells 600 watches each year. Sales are highly predictable in that the jeweler sells exactly 50 watches each month. To prepare for the 2007 selling period, the jeweler wrote orders for 600 watches and arranged for their delivery just prior to the beginning of the year. As anticipated, the jeweler sold 50 watches during each month of 2007. The turnover (based on units) of the watches is calculated as follows:

TABLE 9.2   TURNOVER REPORT FOR FIVE CLASSIFICATIONS OF MERCHANDISE IN A TEN-UNIT CHAIN

CL.	TOTAL	SPFLD	PLAZA	LONG	WEST	EAST	BERK	ENFLD	HAMP	INGLE	MANCH
1 AV IN	35,267	4,382	1,724	2,962	2,655	5,271	3,118	4,853	2,753	3,306	4,265
SALES	44,603	3,475	1,527	2,390	2,979	7,332	4,766	5,416	3,339	7,908	5,467
TRNOVR	1.3	.8	.9	.8	1.1	1.4	1.5	1.1	1.2	2.4	1.3
2 AV IN	4,851	413	71	55	229	896	214	581	198	929	1,038
SALES	4,587	918	103	45	302	1,345	323	376	328	589	252
TRNOVR	.9	2.2	1.5	.8	1.3	1.5	1.5	.6	1.7	.6	.2
3 AV IN	16,015	1,964	52	1,010	—	2,738	3,276	1,338	64	2,888	2,588
SALES	10,309	1,232	22	890	—	1,607	1,194	539	10	3,150	1,661
TRNOVR	.6	.6	.4	.9	—	.6	.4	.4	.2	1.1	.6
4 AV IN	63,151	4,623	3,626	4,005	5,248	8,312	5,880	6,239	7,460	9,702	5,600
SALES	84,458	5,436	5,071	2,904	6,057	12,938	8,121	8,470	10,162	20,675	4,618
TRNOVR	1.3	1.2	1.4	.7	1.2	1.6	1.4	1.4	1.4	2.1	.8
5 AV IN	45,861	4,363	3,432	2,652	3,306	7,601	3,478	5,096	2,798	7,698	5,535
SALES	23,979	1,632	1,315	1,002	2,014	3,917	2,326	2,656	2,597	5,216	1,298
TRNOVR	.5	.4	.4	.4	.6	.5	.7	.5	.9	.7	.2

Period Ending 07/31/07

$$average\ inventory\ =\ \frac{BOM_1 + BOM_2 \ldots + BOM_{12} + EOM_{12}}{13}$$

$$average\ inventory\ 2007\ =$$

$$\frac{600 + 550 + 500 + 450 + 400 + 350 + 300 + 250 + 200 + 150 + 100 + 50 + 0}{13}$$

$$average\ inventory\ 2007\ =\ \frac{3900}{13}\ =\ 300$$

$$turnover\ =\ \frac{sales}{average\ inventory}$$

$$turnover\ =\ \frac{600}{300}\ =\ 2.0$$

Prior to the beginning of 2008, the jeweler sought inventory management advice from a retail consultant. The consultant suggested that the jeweler turn the watches faster by carrying less inventory throughout the year. The jeweler accomplished this objective by ordering 50 watches each month instead of 600 watches at the beginning of the year, thereby carrying an inventory of no more than a month's supply of watches at any point during the year. The turnover of the watches for 2008 is computed as follows:

$$average\ inventory\ =\ \frac{BOM_1 + BOM_2 \ldots + BOM_{12} + EOM_{12}}{13}$$

$$average\ inventory\ 2008\ =$$

$$\frac{50 + 50 + 50 + 50 + 50 + 50 + 50 + 50 + 50 + 50 + 50 + 50 + 0}{13}$$

$$average\ inventory\ 2008\ =\ \frac{600}{13}\ =\ 46$$

$$turnover\ =\ \frac{sales}{average\ inventory}$$

$$turnover\ =\ \frac{600}{46}\ =\ 13.0$$

Note that the sales for 2007 and 2008 are equal, but that the 2008 average inventory turned more than six times faster than the inventory of 2007. The consultant's suggestion to maintain smaller inventories was prudent advice that resulted in improved turnover.[2]

Why High Turnover Is More Desirable Than Low Turnover

There are several reasons high turnover is more desirable than low turnover:

- When inventories turn slowly, customers see the "same old thing" upon each return store visit. Customers who faithfully shopped the jeweler each month in 2007 saw the same selection of watches for an entire year. In 2008, customers saw a new selection each month.
- Slow-moving goods often become *shopworn*, that is, soiled or damaged because of exposure or customer handling.
- Finally, the money and space tied up in stagnant, slow-turning inventories inhibit investments in fresh new goods. Studies have shown that

---

TURNOVER

When two components of the turnover formula are known, the third can be computed by cross multiplying. Sales can be computed by multiplying both sides of the equation by average inventory when turnover and average inventory are known:

$$turnover = \frac{x}{average\ inventory}$$

$$x = turnover \times average\ inventory$$

When sales and turnover are known, average inventory can be computed by multiplying both sides of the equation by x and dividing by turnover:

$$turnover = \frac{sales}{x}$$

$$x = \frac{sales}{turnover}$$

the annual additional cost of holding excess inventory can be 25 to 32 percent of the value of the inventory.[3]

Though high turnover is generally a desirable goal, there are disadvantages associated with excessively high turnover.

- Just as low turnover can be indicative of too much inventory, high turnover can be indicative of too little inventory. Again consider the jeweler's scenario: Customers who shopped at the beginning of 2007 saw an extensive selection of 600 watches. The same customers who shopped at the beginning of 2008 saw a meager selection of only 50 watches. Imagine how disappointed customers were on their 2008 visit recalling the extensive assortment of the previous year. Thus, high turnover may be indicative of limited assortments of styles, colors, or sizes, an inventory condition that will result in lost sales.
- There are also disadvantages with placing many small orders instead of a few large orders. Again consider the jeweler: A single order was processed in 2007. Twelve orders were processed in 2008. This increased by twelvefold the cost of processing orders, tracking them, paying invoices, and so on.
- Buyers who purchase small quantities often forgo quantity discounts, which are price incentives based on quantities purchased. A buyer must decide whether these price concessions are worth the cost of carrying higher inventories.

A buyer's job involves making critical decisions relative to how much inventory to carry. These decisions are driven by multiple factors, including desired turnover, the availability of goods, the availability of cash to pay for them, and the amount of inventory needed to maintain adequate selections. Increasing turnover is an objective to which buyers dedicate considerable attention.

Turnover by Category of Merchandise

There is no universally good turnover rate. Acceptable turnover rates vary by category of merchandise relative to the characteristics of the goods. (See Table 9.3.) To illustrate this point, assume that the following three items in a department store sell and turn at the same rate as the watches in 2007:

Housewares Department: Toasters—Purchasing an inventory of 600 toasters for an entire year is an acceptable (though not ideal) buying decision. Changes in toaster styles are minimal over time, and toasters do not deteriorate by sitting on a stockroom shelf. The last 50 toasters on hand at the end of the year are as salable as the first 50 toasters sold at the beginning of the year.

Intimate Apparel Department: Robes—Purchasing an inventory of 600 robes for an entire year is not an acceptable buying decision. Seasonal changes in styles and fabrications require frequent inventory changes throughout the year. The lightweight spring robes in stock at the

TABLE 9.3   TURNOVER FOR SELECT RETAIL STORES

Department Stores	
Dillard's	2.8
Federated Department Stores	2.9
Kohl's	4.5
Nordstrom	4.3
Full-line Discounters	
Kmart	3.9
Wal-Mart	5.8
Category Killers	
Barnes & Noble	2.6
Best Buy	6.4
Circuit City	4.7
Home Accessories Stores	
Bed Bath & Beyond	2.7
Pier 1 Imports	2.8
Off-pricers	
Burlington Coat Factory	3.1
T.J. Maxx	5.0
Specialty Stores	
American Eagle	2.0
Ann Taylor	4.3
Gap	6.1
Nine West Group	2.0

beginning of the year are not salable at the end of the year when longer styles in flannels and velours are in demand.

Coffee Shop: Muffins—Purchasing an inventory of 600 muffins for an entire year is an unquestionably unacceptable buying decision. A muffin's limited shelf life renders the muffin unsalable the day after delivery, not to mention 12 months later.

The examples serve to demonstrate a fundamental principle related to turnover: that perishable goods need to turn more quickly than nonperishable goods. Perishable merchandise has a limited shelf life or selling period. In a broad interpretation, fashion goods are perishable. Fashion goods are less salable over time because of seasonal changes in color, style, and fabrication. The turnover of nonperishable goods should also be monitored. Nonperishables that remain on racks or shelves for extended periods can become shopworn while tying up valuable space and inventory dollars.

SPECIAL ORDERS

Retailers sell goods by special order when style, color, size, or fabric specifications are unique to each customer. Custom draperies and monogrammed stationery are examples of special order goods. Goods for which there is infrequent demand, such as extra-long men's suits, are often special ordered, as are big ticket items, such as furniture. Special orders minimize a retailer's inventory investment, since samples are often the only inventory carried in stock. Special order goods turn quickly, since special order sales are transacted as soon as the goods are received.

In spite of these inventory management advantages, special order sales are labor intensive in that each customer's purchase requires processing an order and arranging for subsequent pick-up or delivery. Problems occur when special order specifications are incorrect or incorrectly followed. The retailer must absorb the cost of errors attributable to the store. Perhaps the greatest difficulty with special orders is that customers have become accustomed to the immediate gratification of taking their purchases home with them, an opportunity that special orders do not afford them.

STOCK-TO-SALES RATIOS

A stock-to-sales ratio is the proportionate relationship between a BOM and sales for the corresponding month. The formula for computing a stock-to-sales ratio is:

$$stock\text{-}to\text{-}sales\ ratio = \frac{BOM}{sales}$$

When sales are $10,000 and BOM is $30,000, the stock-to-sales ratio is computed as follows:

$$stock\text{-}to\text{-}sales\ ratio = \frac{\$30,000}{\$10,000}$$

$$stock\text{-}to\text{-}sales\ ratio = 3.0$$

A 3.0 stock-to-sales ratio indicates that the BOM is three times sales. Stock-to-sales ratios are most often computed to one decimal place.

The breadth of an assortment is a determinant of its stock-to-sales ratio: the broader the assortment, the higher the stock-to-sales ratio. Consider the stock-to-sales ratios of men's dress shirts and men's sport shirts: Because dress shirts are buttoned at the neck, collar size must be rather precise. To accommodate this close fit, dress shirts are manufactured in collar sizes that usually range from 14½ inches to 17 inches, with half-inch increments between sizes.

TABLE 9.4   INVENTORY TURNOVER AND DAYS SALES IN ENDING INVENTORY
            U.S. NATIONAL AVERAGES

Type of Retailer	Turnover	Days Sales in Ending Inventory
Apparel and Accessories	3.5	109
Drug	5.3	71
Furniture and Accessories for the Home	4.1	93
General Merchandise	4.7	81
Grocery	12.7	30

Source: BizStats.com, 2003.

Because the sleeve length of a dress shirt must correspond to the sleeve length of a jacket, the sleeve-length sizing of a dress shirt must also be precise. Therefore, dress shirts are manufactured with sleeves that vary in lengths from 32 inches to 35 inches with 1-inch increments between sizes. A complete size assortment of one dress shirt style in one color is 24 shirts, six neck sizes times four sleeve lengths.

Men's sport shirts, on the other hand, are worn unbuttoned at the neck, and their fit is unrelated to any other garment. Thus, neither the collar nor

FIGURE 9.1
Retailers maximize sales per square foot by presenting as much merchandise as possible within a given area, a topic discussed later in this chapter. Courtesy FRCH Design Worldwide.

the sleeve of a sport shirt must be as exact a fit as the collar or sleeve of a dress shirt. Consequently, sport shirts are cut in four general sizes: small, medium, large, and extra-large, each size with average collar and sleeve-length combinations. A complete size assortment of one sport shirt style in one color is four shirts.

Therefore, a retailer who plans to sell an equal number of dress shirts and sport shirts will need more dress shirts than sport shirts. The amount of stock needed to sell a single style and color of dress shirt is 24 shirts, while the amount of stock needed to sell a *single* style and color of sport shirt is only four shirts. Thus, dress shirts will require a higher stock-to-sales ratio than sport shirts.[4]

In general, assortments with a broad range of sizes or styles require high stock-to-sales ratios. Women's shoes have a high stock-to-sales ratio because of an extensive assortment of numeric sizes and corresponding widths. Many department stores and full-line discounters have abandoned ready-made curtains and draperies as businesses because of high inventory requirements. Each style and color requires an assortment of lengths and several pairs of each to accommodate multi-pair purchases.

In essence, a stock-to-sales ratio is an inverse expression of turnover. A stock-to-sales ratio is computed by dividing an inventory figure (BOM) by sales. Turnover is computed by dividing sales by an inventory figure (average inventory). Thus, turnover and stock-to-sales ratios have an inverse relationship; that is, as one increases the other decreases. Consequently, a *high* turnover is indicative of a *low* stock-to-sales ratio, and a *low* turnover is indicative of a *high* stock-to-sales ratio.

As merchandising concepts, turnover and stock-to-sales ratios are often uttered in the same breath. Industry observers blame Gap's commitment to maintaining an in-stock position on waist sizes ranging from 28 inches to 46 inches and nine inseam lengths for the company's constant struggle to turn inventory quickly.

Buyers predicate buying decisions on turnover and stock-to-sales-ratios. Consider a slow-turning women's hosiery department. The buyer determines that the low turnover is a result of the high stock-to-sales ratios needed to ensure complete color and size assortments within each brand. To increase turnover, the buyer must choose between two strategies: carrying the same number of brands with reduced assortments of size and color, or carrying fewer brands with full assortments of size and color.

The latter is the preferable alternative. Carrying the same number of brands with reduced assortments of sizes and colors will frustrate customers looking for a particular size or color within a brand. It is less frustrating to a customer to find a brand unavailable than to find many brands represented by poor assortments. A shrewd buyer would edit the number of brands carried, eliminating those that closely duplicate each other in terms of price, quality, color, and style assortment.

In theory, a stock-to-sales ratio cannot be less than 1.0. A stock-to-sales ratio is 1.0 when BOM and sales are equal, implying that all of the merchandise on hand at the beginning of the month is sold during the month. This is an infrequent circumstance except in the case of very fast-turning goods continuously replenished throughout the month, or seasonal merchandise, such as Christmas decorations where it is hoped that all of December's BOM will be sold by the end the month.

Stock-to-Sales Ratio Variations

Busy selling periods require lower stock-to-sales ratios than slower periods. To demonstrate this principle, consider an assortment of cotton sweaters available in five colors and four sizes (S/M/L/XL). Assume that the buyer plans to sell only one sweater during the first month of the season. A BOM of 20 sweaters is required, representing a complete assortment of five colors and four sizes. Assume that the buyer increases the sales plan to two sweaters. Because planned sales have doubled, should the buyer double the BOM to include two of each size and color? Hardly. A BOM of 20 sweaters is still an adequate assortment to support the sale of two sweaters, since the chance of a second customer wanting the same size and color as the first customer is only 1 in 20, assuming that one size and color combination is as desirable as another. Nineteen sweaters represents a 95 percent in-stock rate ($19/20 = 0.95 = 95\%$), a very acceptable inventory position for most categories of merchandise.

When planned sales are one sweater, the stock-to-sales ratio is 20.0 (20:1). When planned sales are two sweaters, the stock-to-sales ratio is only 10.0 (20:2), substantiating the claim (though rather simplistically) that "peak" selling months require lower stock-to-sales ratios than "slow" months. At some point during the season, planned sweater sales will reach a point that will necessitate increasing the inventory of each size and color as the chance of two customers wanting the same size and color increases.

However, at no point will a full assortment of sweaters be required for each customer.

Table 9.5 lists monthly stock-to-sales ratios for a department. Note that the range of ratios falls between 1.5 and 5.0. The months with the highest sales have the lowest stock-to-sales ratios, while the months with the lowest sales have the highest stock-to-sales ratios. Since periods of high sales require lower stock-to-sales ratios than periods of low sales, it is reasonable to conclude that merchandise turns faster during periods of high sales than periods of low sales. During peak selling periods, merchandise flows in and out of stores rapidly, while during slow selling periods goods turn at much slower rates. (See Table 9.6.)

SALES PER SQUARE FOOT

Sales per square foot is a measure of productivity that reflects the amount of sales generated relative to the amount of space dedicated to selling the goods. As input in the productivity ratio, square footage represents the

TABLE 9.5   MONTHLY STOCK-TO-SALES RATIOS
FOR A DEPARTMENT

Month	Sales	BOM	Stock-to-Sales Ratio
1	$ 20,000	$ 40,000	2.0
2	$ 20,000	$ 40,000	2.0
3	$ 25,000	$ 45,000	1.8
4	$ 10,000	$ 30,000	3.0
5	$ 10,000	$ 30,000	3.0
6	$ 5,000	$ 25,000	5.0
7	$ 5,000	$ 25,000	5.0
8	$ 5,000	$ 25,000	5.0
9	$ 40,000	$ 60,000	1.5
10	$ 30,000	$ 50,000	1.7
11	$ 40,000	$ 60,000	1.5
12	$ 30,000	$ 50,000	1.7
TOTAL	$240,000	$480,000	2.0

The aggregate stock-to-sales ratio for the year is 2.0 based on total BOMs divided by total sales.

TABLE 9.6   MONTHLY STOCK-TO-SALES RATIOS
             FOR MEN'S SPECIALTY STORES

Month	Stock-to-Sales Ratio
February	8.6
March	8.3
April	8.3
May	8.4
June	7.3
July	8.5
August	8.8
September	8.8
October	8.7
November	8.5
December	4.4
January	7.9

capital outlay for constructing the retail space, and the operational expenses associated with renting, heating, lighting, cleaning, and staffing the space. Square footage is based on the physical dimensions of a selling area and often includes stockrooms, fitting rooms, service areas, and adjacent aisles. The formula for computing sales per square foot is:

$$sales\ per\ square\ foot = \frac{sales}{square\ footage}$$

Sales per square foot can be calculated for any time period; however, annual computation is the most common. Though sales-per-square-foot productivity is most often computed for spaces occupied by entire categories of merchandise, it may also be computed for a spatial entity as small as a fixture. In advertising to retailers, Eastman Kodak claimed that a touch-screen digital-imaging system could generate $4,000 per square foot annually based on sales projections of $70 a day.[5]

The following demonstrates the calculation of sales per square foot: Assume that a department store allocates 1,000 square feet within its misses sportswear area to an Alfred Dunner shop. Last year the shop generated sales of $400,000. Sales per square foot for the shop are computed as follows:

$$sales\ per\ square\ foot\ =\ \frac{sales}{square\ footage}$$

$$sales\ per\ square\ foot\ =\ \frac{\$400,000}{1,000\ square\ feet}$$

$$sales\ per\ square\ foot\ =\ \$400$$

Each square foot of space dedicated to the Alfred Dunner line generated sales of $400.

As a measure of productivity, high sales-per-square-foot values are generally more desirable than low values. The mathematical relationship between sales and square footage suggests that sales-per-square-foot productivity can be increased by increasing sales, decreasing square footage, or both increasing sales and decreasing square footage. Generating more sales in less space is a universal objective for every retailer.

Though high sales per square foot are desirable, excessively high sales per square foot can be an indication that a selling area is too crowded and is generating too much sales volume from a limited amount of space. A crowded shopping environment can inhibit sales and the effective presentation of goods while creating an uncomfortable shopping environment.

Space productivity expectations differ by category of merchandise. The physical size of merchandise is a factor. If a department store's fashion jewelry counter and furniture department generate the same annual sales volume, the sales per square foot of the fashion jewelry department will be higher than the sales per square foot of the furniture department because of the lesser amount of space required to present the jewelry. Sales-per-square-foot expectations vary by type of store. (See Table 9.7.) A department store's wide aisles and comfortable shopping environment yield lower sales per square foot than space-challenged off-pricers.

TABLE 9.7   SALES PER SQUARE FOOT FOR SELECT RETAIL STORES

Apparel and Accessories Stores

Hot Topic	$619
Gymboree	$511
Aeropostale	$471
Cache Stores	$438
Ann Taylor	$434
Abercrombie & Fitch	$379
American Eagle Outfitters	$372
J. Crew	$365
Gap	$349
Claire's	$339
Pacific Sunwear	$330
Nordstrom	$319
Wet Seal	$267
Children's Place	$263
Lane Bryant	$223
Catherines	$168
Dress Barn	$140
Burlington Coat Factory	$114

Warehouse Clubs

Costco	$771
Sam's Club	$497

Home Furnishings Stores

Williams-Sonoma (includes Pottery Barn)	$410
Bombay Company	$296
Bed Bath & Beyond	$229
Pier 1 Imports	$182
Linens 'n Things	$171

Jewelry Stores

Tiffany	$2,109
Zales	$839
Bailey Banks & Biddle	$728

Source: BizStats.com, 2006.

Turnover is another factor relevant to sales-per-square-foot expectations. If men's sport shirts and men's dress shirts generate the same annual volume, but sport shirts turn twice as fast as dress shirts, then the average inventory of dress shirts is twice the average inventory of sport shirts. Because sport shirts require only half the space of dress shirts, sport shirts are more productive in terms of sales per square foot. Gap once reduced its inventory from $73 per square foot one year to $51 four years later, a move that made Wall Street happy in that lower inventory is indicative of higher turnover.[6]

Though sales per square foot is the most commonly used measure of space productivity, productivity can be measured for any unit of space. Cubic feet can be used when height or vertical dimension is a factor in presenting goods for sale, as in the case of stacked goods. Linear inches can be used to measure the space productivity of linear configurations of space, such as shelving. In the catalog industry, space is defined as pages, and sales per page are the industry's standard measure of productivity. Numerators other than sales can be used as an output relative to spatial input. Some stores compute gross margin per square foot. Gross margin is a gross-profit figure from which net profit is derived and a topic that is discussed in Chapter 10.

Retail industry pundits pay close attention to sales-per-square-foot productivity. The retail expansion binge that has spanned the last two decades has caused considerable concern among those who follow the industry closely. During that time, retailers opened five times as many stores as they closed, an expansion rate unwarranted by commensurate growth in consumer spending. The disproportionate increase in retail space caused sales per square foot to plummet from a high of $197 in the 1970s, to $181 in the 1980s, and to $160 in the 1990s.[7]

Space Allocation

Retail selling space is strategically allocated to various merchandise categories to maximize sales per square foot. Consider the following: A 10,000-square-foot specialty store generates annual sales of $3 million. The space is divided among four categories of merchandise. The square footage, annual sales, and sales per square foot for each category appear in Table 9.8. The figures in the Industry Standard column are hypothetical sales-per-square-foot industry standards. Standards such as these are often provided by retail trade organizations as benchmarks to which retailers can compare their performance.

TABLE 9.8   SALES PER SQUARE FOOT FOR WOMEN'S SPECIALTY STORE

Category	Square Footage	Annual Sales	Sales/Square Foot	Industry Standard
Sportswear	4,000	$1,600,000	$400	$400
Dresses	3,000	$ 300,000	$100	$250
Outerwear	2,000	$ 400,000	$200	$320
Accessories	1,000	$ 700,000	$700	$400
TOTAL	10,000	$3,000,000	$300	$339

Note that the store's sales per square foot of $300 are behind the industry standard of $339. In other words, the store is not generating enough sales relative to its size. Further analysis reveals the problem areas: Dresses at $100 per square foot and outerwear at $200 per square foot are performing behind the industry standards of $250 per square foot and $320 per square foot, respectively. Sportswear and accessories are not problems. The sales per square foot of the sportswear area match the industry standard. At $700 per foot, the sales per square foot of the accessories area far exceed the industry standard of $400 per foot.

The problem has frustrated the owner, who has tried to build dress and outerwear sales with direct-mail advertising, new merchandise resources, and promotional pricing. However, none of the tactics have been successful. It is apparent that both businesses have reached a plateau with little promise of future growth.

The owner decides that the best strategy for bringing the store's sales per square foot closer to industry standards is to reallocate space. The retailer determines that:

- The ideal amount of space for a $300,000 dress area is 1,200 square feet ($300,000 divided by the industry standard of $250 equals 1,200).
- The ideal amount of space for a $400,000 outerwear area is 1,250 square feet ($400,000 divided by the industry standard of $320 equals 1,250).
- Reducing the dress area by 1,800 square feet (the present 3,000 square feet less 1,200 square feet) and the outerwear area by 750 square feet (the

present 2,000 square feet less 1,250 square feet) will permit the expansion of the accessories area by 2,550 square feet (1,800 square feet plus 750 square feet). This will more than double the size of the accessories area (2,550 square feet plus 1,000 square feet equals 3,550 square feet).

The wisdom of expanding the accessories area so dramatically may be questioned. At the current annual volume of $700,000, the addition of 2,550 square feet will drop the area's productivity from $700 per square foot to $197 per square foot ($700,000 divided by 3,550 square feet), $203 below the industry standard. However, at $700 per square foot, the area's productivity was nearly twice the industry standard, an indication of over-crowding and unrealized sales potential. Expanding the area will create a more comfortable shopping environment, facilitate more attractive presentations of goods, and allow for expanding selections of the popular items and resources. The retailer can expect to generate considerably higher sales that will bring the resulting sales-per-square-foot productivity for the store closer to industry standards.

SPACE MANAGEMENT

Space management is the strategic arrangement of products to maximize sales with a minimum investment of space and fixtures. Space management involves the development of visual models of product arrangements called planograms. Planograms incorporate an organization's standards for merchandise presentation, product adjacencies, and customer convenience. Planograms ensure the consistent arrangement of goods within stores in multi-unit organizations. A planogram can represent an entire store, a store section, or a single fixture or wall section. Planograms can be general, indicating the approximate location of merchandise categories, or specific, indicating the precise location of individual items on fixtures. Planograms are periodically reset to reflect seasonal changes in product assortments. Planograms of fashion goods are reset more often than planograms of basic goods.

Electronic space management software builds predictive models of optimum inventory levels and assortments based on the wholesale cost, retail price, and turnover of each product in an assortment. "What if" capabilities allow the software user to observe the fiscal impact of adding or deleting items from an assortment. Most space management software produces color planograms with product images in scaled dimensions that

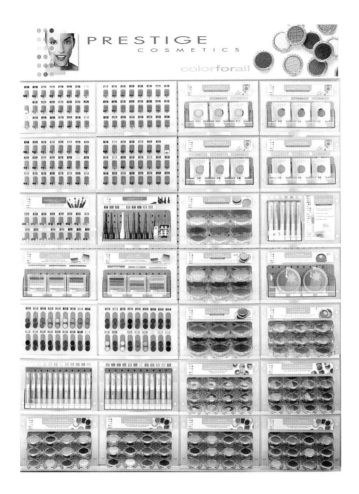

FIGURE 9.2
A planogram is an optimum
product arrangement.
Courtesy Fairchild
Publications, Inc.

can be electronically transmitted to stores. The planograms are automatically adjusted by store based on sales data scanned at point of sale. Quantities of slow-turning items are reduced (or deleted) from the assortment,
while quantities of fast-turning items are increased. One retailer added
three dozen new, high-ticket, high-margin items to a 200-item assortment
in existing space by freeing space occupied by overstocked items and dropping slow-moving items. Movement information is also shared with
suppliers to ensure timely replenishment of stock. (See Table 9.9.)

Electronic space management is closely allied to category management,
a micromerchandising concept of managing individual brands or cate-

TABLE 9.9   SPACE PRODUCTIVITY REPORT COMPARING PERCENT
OF TURNOVER TO PERCENT OF SPACE OCCUPIED

Style #	% Movemt	% Space	Style #	% Movemt	% Space
3305	0.8	1.5	4147	3.4	1.8
3113	0.7	1.6	3853	1.6	1.5
6616	0.7	1.7	4918	3.5	1.6
1808	0.5	1.6	6921	2.5	1.5
2000	1.9	1.7	2426	2.4	1.7
4343	1.7	1.6	5783	2.1	1.4
9015	0.8	1.6	9687	3.7	1.8
3864	2.0	1.6	4688	3.4	1.6
7401	3.9	1.7	2498	3.0	1.5
3673	1.7	1.9	6957	3.6	1.6
8848	1.2	1.8	0289	1.9	1.6
7074	1.4	1.6	3278	3.0	1.6
3066	0.7	1.6	4489	1.1	1.4
0089	1.3	1.8	6895	0.6	1.2
7085	0.2	1.7	8980	0.9	1.5
2242	1.0	1.5	4880	1.3	1.6
2757	2.1	1.6	0890	1.2	1.8
7004	0.5	1.7	2134	0.7	3.1
5309	1.6	1.6	2778	0.7	1.4
1016	2.1	1.7	3095	1.4	1.4
1226	0.7	1.5	9800	0.5	1.4
0704	1.3	1.6	7783	0.3	1.4
1004	1.1	1.7	4348	1.8	1.8
3997	1.4	1.5	2390	2.5	1.9
5937	1.2	1.5	0063	1.5	2.8
2618	1.5	1.6	3373	0.7	1.6
9972	1.4	1.7	5218	2.6	1.8
5740	1.1	1.6	1001	2.1	1.7
5611	0.7	1.9	4979	2.5	1.5
1089	3.9	2.2	100.0	100.0	
6668	2.4	1.6			

gories of merchandise as units of business. Electronic space management
was first used in the food industry; however, applications to durable goods
and apparel are becoming common. Sears uses electronic space management for home softlines, such as bed and bath linens and ready-made
draperies, and for basic apparel, such as jeans, underwear, and hosiery.

SUMMARY POINTS

- Productivity is a measure of the number of units of output produced per unit of input.
- Turnover is the number of times that an average inventory is sold over a time period. Turnover can be increased by increasing sales, decreasing average inventory, or both. Turnover expectations differ by category of merchandise.
- A stock-to-sales ratio indicates the proportionate relationship between a beginning-of-month inventory and the sales for a month. Goods requiring extensive assortments have high stock-to-sales ratios. Goods requiring limited assortments have low stock-to-sales ratios.
- Peak selling periods require lower stock-to-sales ratios than slower selling periods.
- Sales per square foot is a measure of productivity that reflects the amount of sales generated relative to the amount of retail space dedicated to sale of the goods.

KEY TERMS AND CONCEPTS

average inventory	end-of-month inventory	sales per square foot
beginning-of-month inventory	perishable goods	space management
	planogram	stock-to-sales ratio
category management	productivity	turnover

THINKING ABOUT IT

1. Productivity is a concept with many retailing applications. How would you compute sales staff productivity in a retail store? How would you define output? Input? How would you determine the productivity of the selling staff as a whole? Of an individual salesperson?

2. Rank the turnover of the following categories of merchandise from lowest to highest. Base your turnover assumptions on perishability or shelf life:

   In a candy store:
   Chocolates
   Fudge
   Hard candy

In a department store:
   Athletic footwear (e.g., sneakers)
   Bedding (e.g., blankets, sheets, coverlets)
   Fine china and glassware
   Swimwear (i.e., bathing suits)
In a men's store:
   Basic underwear (e.g., white T-shirts and briefs)
   Fashion underwear (e.g., colored/patterned boxers and briefs)
   Sweaters
In a stationery and greeting card store:
   Desk accessories (e.g., letter openers, mouse pads, pen sets)
   Holiday greeting cards (e.g., Christmas, Passover, Valentine's Day)
   Everyday greeting cards (e.g., birthday, anniversary, get well)
In a supermarket:
   Frozen foods
   Household cleaning products
   Produce (e.g., fruits and vegetables)
   Scratch bakery (i.e., made on premises)

3. Consider the following categories of merchandise. What assortment characteristics influence the stock-to-sales ratios of each? To answer this question, think about how much inventory a retailer needs to carry to be in business for just one customer.

   Dinnerware—boxed sets
   Dinnerware—open stock
   Dress shoes—men's
   Dress shoes—women's
   Greeting cards—birthday
   Greeting cards—get well
   Window treatments—custom
   Window treatments—ready-made

4. Review a store's in-stock position of a product line with multiple product characteristics such as style, size, and color. Have some styles, sizes, or colors sold out? Are there styles, sizes, or colors that seem to

sell more quickly than others? Which do you think turn fastest? Slowest? Do any seem to be turning "too fast"?

5. A shoe retailer carries a large assortment of casual, dress, and athletic shoes for men, women, and children in 4,000-square-foot locations. The retailer plans to open several new stores, most of which will be considerably smaller than existing locations. Based on your knowledge of turnover and stock-to-sales ratios, what advice can you give the retailer relative to determining a merchandise mix for the new stores?

TEAMING UP

1. As a team, visit the cosmetics department at a local department store. Each team member should: examine a single cosmetics line relative to its breadth of assortment by looking at the number of unique items within the assortment. Share your observations with one another and then collectively determine the cosmetics lines with the highest and lowest stock-to-sales ratios. Note: The amount of counter space dedicated to a particular line is an indication of the sales that the line generates. Though sales have an impact on a stock-to-sales ratio, it is the proportionate amount of inventory needed to support sales that drives the stock-to-sales-ratio.

2. As a team, visit a local shopping center in search of a crowded store— that is, a store with little aisle space or space between fixtures. Act as shoppers searching for a particular item. Upon completion of the shopping exercise, discuss the impact of the crowded conditions on your ability to find the item for which you were looking, and the store's overall "shopability." How much do you think that the store loses in sales in a day because of crowded shopping conditions? In a year? Expressed as a percent, how much additional space would the store need to present its merchandise aesthetically in a comfortable shopping environment?

SEARCHING THE NET

1. Do a keyword search for "inventory turnover" to find the turnover of various categories of merchandise and types of stores. Compare the turnover of the various categories and stores. Explain the differences. What inferences can you make concerning perishability and assortment?

2. Do a keyword search of "sales per square foot" to find the sales per square foot of various categories of merchandise and types of stores. Compare the sales per square foot of the various categories and stores. Explain the differences.

3. Look for a trade publication article on inventory turnover in a retail organization using your library's business databases. Is poor turnover mentioned? If so, what are the causes? Is improved turnover mentioned? To what factors is the improvement attributed?

4. Using your library's business databases, look for a trade publication article on sales per square foot in a retail organization. Is poor sales per square foot mentioned? If so, what are the causes? Is improved sales per square foot mentioned? To what factors is the improvement attributed?

5. Search for planogram software. Research the many commercial products available. Compare product characteristics. Which would you recommend to the owner of a kitchen store carrying cookware, tableware, gadgets, and gourmet food items?

SOLVING PROBLEMS

1. Refer to the figures in Table 9.1 to compute the following:
   - Average inventory for the last quarter of the year
   - Average inventory for the first six months of the year
   - Turnover for the last six months of the year assuming sales of $20,000 for the period

2. A divisional merchandise manager is comparing last year's turnover results for his five departments to industry standards from a trade association. The results are as follows:

Department	Sales	Turnover	Standard
A	1.5 million	6.3	6.7
B	5.0 million	5.2	8.1
C	3.2 million	7.8	6.3
D	7.0 million	9.1	7.2
E	4.3 million	6.2	6.5

What was the division's average inventory for last year? What was turnover for the division? To meet industry standard, what should the division's average inventory be for next year assuming that sales will be planned up by 10 percent? What should average inventory be by department?

3. The following list refers to the number of stock-keeping units that need to be carried to maintain a full assortment of sizes, styles, and colors for each of five lines. Assume that the average unit price is $3.50 and that the average monthly sales for each line is $100. Compute the stock-to-sales ratio for each.

Line	Units
Line A	100
Line B	120
Line C	80
Line D	200
Line E	140

What inferences can you make relative to the turnover of each line?

4. The following is a list of sales-per-square-foot figures for the merchandise divisions of a department store slated for expansion. Corporate sales-per-square-foot standards for each division are also included.

Division	Square feet	Sales/Square feet	Standard
A	20,000	800	500
B	10,000	600	450
C	50,000	550	600
D	20,000	500	550
E	30,000	500	450

How many additional square feet are required to match corporate productivity standards, assuming sales remain unchanged? Which divisions need additional space? How much space does each need?

5. A storeowner wants to expand her women's accessories business by opening two new stores. Presently she generates about $1,250 a square foot on $1 million in annual sales, and is pleased with this productivity. The storeowner hopes to generate about the same amount of volume in her new locations. A realtor wants to show the storeowner several possible sites, all at shopping centers with stores that complement her accessories store. The square feet of the locations are:

Location	Square Feet
A	600
B	750
C	850
D	1,000
E	1,200
F	1,500

The storeowner would like to rule out locations that are either too small or too large to suit her needs. Which locations do you think are not worth it for her to visit?

CHAPTER TEN

Merchandising Accounting

After reading this chapter, you will be able to discuss:

● Fundamental accounting concepts from a merchandising perspective.

● The interpretation of retail financial statements.

● Gross margin return on investment as a measure of inventory performance.

Because merchandising outcomes have considerable impact on a retail organization's fiscal objectives, an understanding of financial statements is important to the organization's merchants. Chapter 10 covers the analysis and interpretation of some of the financial statements studied in accounting courses with an emphasis on merchandising applications and retail inventories.

CASH FLOW

Cash flow is the balance of cash coming into and going out of an organization. A positive cash flow means that more cash is coming into the organization than going out. A negative cash flow means that more cash is going out of the organization than coming in. A positive cash flow is preferable to a negative cash flow; however, even the most successful retailers experience negative cash flow periodically.

Consider the following: A men's shop conducts approximately 20 percent of its annual business between Thanksgiving and Christmas. The owner arranges for the delivery of goods bought for the holiday season by October 31. The retailer pays most invoices within 10 days to take advantage of early-payment discounts, and the remaining balances within 30 days. Thus, most holiday merchandise is paid for by mid-November, even though the goods will not begin to yield an appreciable amount of cash from sales until late November. About half of the retailer's customers charge their purchases to store-sponsored charge accounts. These sales do not begin to generate cash until about 30 days after the purchases are made. Full payment for holiday purchases averages 90 days.

Figure 10.1 depicts the retailer's cash flow from October through March. A negative cash flow is any point on the graph where the "cash-out" line is higher than the "cash-in" line. Periods of negative cash flow occur from mid-October through the beginning of December, and again from the end of February through March. The latter negative cash flow is a result of the arrival and payment of spring merchandise in a period of limited cash generation due to low sales volume.

A positive cash flow is any point on the graph where the cash-in line is higher than the cash-out line, such as the period between the beginning of December and early February. A balanced cash flow is represented by points where the cash-in and cash-out lines coincide, for example, throughout much of the latter part of February.

Retailers resolve negative cash flow with short-term borrowing from lending institutions. The borrowed funds enable retailers to meet their financial obligations to suppliers to ensure the continued shipment of orders. Short-term borrowing allows retailers to take advantage of prompt-payment discounts that help offset the interest expense incurred by borrowing. Many retailers have an open line of credit with lending institutions that allows the retailer to borrow and pay back money in a manner similar to that of a revolving charge account with an established limit and regular payments with interest.

Cash flow is important to a retail organization's buyers in that payments to suppliers account for significant outlays of money within most retail accounting periods. Buyers can enhance a positive cash flow in two ways:

1. By scheduling the delivery of goods as close as possible to their point of sale
2. By negotiating payment terms that delay payments to suppliers as long as possible

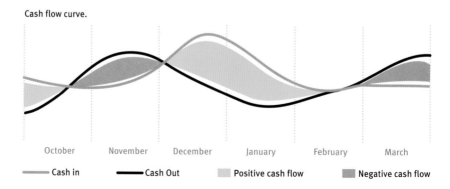

Cash flow curve.

FIGURE 10.1
A cash flow curve.

Shipments that arrive and are paid for far in advance of their selling season hinder cash flow.

BALANCE SHEETS

A balance sheet is a statement of an organization's assets, liabilities, and owners' equity at a particular point in time. (See Figure 10.2.) Assets are *owned* by an organization. Cash, inventory, and store fixtures are among a retailer's assets. Assets are classified according to their liquidity, or the like-

CONSOLIDATED BALANCE SHEETS

Dollars and shares in thousands, except per share amounts	Jan. 29, 2006	Jan. 30, 2005
ASSETS		
Current assets		
Cash and cash equivalents	$ 360,982	$ 239,210
Accounts receivable (less allowance for doubtful accounts of $168 and $217)	51,020	42,520
Merchandise inventories – net	520,292	452,421
Prepaid catalog expenses	53,925	53,520
Prepaid expenses	31,847	38,018
Deferred income taxes	57,267	39,015
Other assets	7,831	9,061
Total current assets	1,083,164	873,765
Property and equipment – net	880,305	852,412
Other assets (less accumulated amortization of $679 and $2,066)	18,151	19,368
Total assets	$1,981,620	$1,745,545
LIABILITIES AND SHAREHOLDERS' EQUITY		
Current liabilities		
Accounts payable	$ 196,074	$ 173,781
Accrued salaries, benefits and other	93,434	86,767
Customer deposits	172,775	148,535
Income taxes payable	83,589	72,052
Current portion of long-term debt	18,864	23,435
Other liabilities	25,656	17,587
Total current liabilities	590,392	522,157
Deferred rent and lease incentives	218,254	212,193
Long-term debt	14,490	19,154
Deferred income tax liabilities	18,455	21,057
Other long-term obligations	14,711	13,322
Total liabilities	856,302	787,883
Commitments and contingencies – See Note L		
Shareholders' equity		
Preferred stock, $.01 par value, 7,500 shares authorized, none issued	—	—
Common stock, $.01 par value, 253,125 shares authorized, 114,779 shares issued and outstanding at January 29, 2006; 115,372 shares issued and outstanding at January 30, 2005	1,148	1,154
Additional paid-in capital	325,146	286,720
Retained earnings	791,329	664,619
Accumulated other comprehensive income	7,695	5,169
Total shareholders' equity	1,125,318	957,662
Total liabilities and shareholders' equity	$1,981,620	$1,745,545

See Notes to Consolidated Financial Statements.

FIGURE 10.2
A balance sheet is a statement of assets, liabilities, and owners' equity.

lihood of their conversion to cash. A *short-term*, or *current*, *asset* will be converted to cash within a year in the normal operation of business. Cash is a retailer's most liquid asset. A *long-term*, or *noncurrent*, *asset* will not be converted to cash within a year in the normal operation of business. A retailer's long-term assets include store facilities and fixtures.

Inventory is a current asset that receives considerable attention in this text. Inventory is converted to cash as it is sold. The more quickly that inventory is converted to cash, the more quickly the cash can be again invested into new inventory, which in turn, will generate more sales. Inventory not quickly converted to cash often decreases in value as an asset, especially if it is perishable and becomes unsalable over time.

Liabilities are *debts owed* by an organization. Liabilities are classified according to the time in which they are due to be paid. Payment on a *short-term* liability is due within one year. Payment on a *long-term* liability is due in one year or longer. A retailer's short-term liabilities include payables to suppliers, and short-term debts to lending institutions for money borrowed to balance cash flow. Long-term liabilities include mortgages on land and buildings, and long-term financing for extensive expansion and renovation projects.

Owners' equity is the difference between assets and liabilities. Owners' equity is also called *shareowners' equity* and *shareholders' equity*. The relationship between assets, liabilities, and owners' equity is such that:

$$assets = liabilities + owners'\ equity$$

Balance sheet components are in a constant state of flux and subject to momentary change. For instance, inventory increases and cash decreases whenever a shipment from a supplier is received and paid for. A balance sheet reflects neither sales nor profit performance. Two retailers with similar balance sheets can produce vastly different sales and profit results.

FINANCIAL RATIOS

Financial ratios are analytical tools based on the proportionate relationship between two balance sheet components. Financial ratios are used to assess an organization's level of solvency or financial stability. A current ratio is the relationship between current assets and current liabilities. A current ratio measures an organization's short-term debt-paying ability, or ability to pay off current debts with current assets. The formula for the current ratio is:

$$current\ ratio\ =\ \frac{current\ assets}{current\ liabilities}$$

A current ratio less than 1.0 indicates that current liabilities are greater than current assets and that current assets are insufficient to pay off current liabilities, a highly undesirable financial position. A 2.0 current ratio indicates that current assets are twice current liabilities. (See Table 10.1.) Generally, 2.0 is considered an acceptable current ratio, though this standard

TABLE 10.1   CURRENT RATIOS FOR SELECT RETAIL STORES

Department Stores	
Dillard's	2.01
Federated Department Stores	1.62
Kohl's	2.44
Nordstrom	2.06
Full-line Discounters	
Kmart	1.67
Wal-Mart	1.69
Category Killers	
Barnes & Noble	1.50
Best Buy	1.37
Toys "R" Us	2.27
Home Accessories Stores	
Bed Bath & Beyond	2.81
Pier 1 Imports	2.51
Off-pricers	
Burlington Coat Factory	2.46
T.J. Maxx	1.81
Specialty Stores	
American Eagle	1.46
Ann Taylor	2.68
Gap	1.90
Nine West Group	1.46

varies by type of industry. Credit rating services use financial ratios to determine an organization's credit worthiness. Compiled by Dun & Bradstreet, the nation's largest credit-rating service, the *D&B Comprehensive Report* compares organizations' financial ratios and other credit rating indicators to industry benchmarks. Suppliers use the *D&B Comprehensive Report* to determine the risk associated with extending credit to retailers.

Financial ratios are also important to factors. A factor is a financial intermediary peculiar to the apparel industry that assumes responsibility for collecting manufacturers' receivables from retailers. Factors buy receivables at discounted rates from manufacturers to cover the cost and financial risk associated with collecting them. Factors keep a watchful eye on the fiscal status of retailers and refuse to approve shipments to stores whose financial statements send signals of an inability to pay promptly.

FIGURE 10.3
A factor is a financial intermediary that collects manufacturers' receivables from retailers.

Though factoring is typically associated with the apparel industry, the service is becoming more and more prevalent in nonapparel industries such as furniture, floor coverings, and consumer electronics. The bankruptcies of many major retailers have caused factors to raise their credit-approval standards to protect themselves against the possibility of unpaid claims in recent years. Major factoring firms include Capital Business Credit, LLC, and America's Factors, Inc.[1]

INCOME STATEMENTS

An income statement is a statement of an organization's profit performance for a specific period of time. (See Figure 10.4 on page 256.) The fundamental components of an income statement are revenue, expenses, and net income. The relationship among the components is expressed by the equation:

$$revenue - expenses = net\ income$$

The income statement is sometimes called a *statement of earnings*, or a *profit and loss (P&L) statement*. A profit results when expenses are less than revenue and net income is positive. A loss results when expenses are greater than revenue and net income is negative.

Unlike a balance sheet that represents a particular *point in time*, an income statement represents a specific *span of time*, such as a year, a six-month season, a quarter, or a month. Income statements can be computed for an entire organization or for a unit of business within an organization, such as an individual store, a group of stores, or a department. Profit or loss is based on the revenue and expenses directly associated with each unit of business.

TABLE 10.2   CURRENT RATIOS FOR FIVE TYPES OF RETAILERS DEFINED
             BY PRODUCT CATEGORY

Type of Retailer	Current Ratio
Apparel and Accessories	2.1
Home Furnishings and Accessories	1.9
General Merchandise	1.4
Grocery	1.2
Other Retail	1.9

Source: BizStats.com.

Consolidated Statements of Earnings			
		Fiscal Year Ended	
Dollars and shares in thousands, except per share amounts	Jan. 29, 2006	Jan. 30, 2005	Feb. 1, 2004
Net revenues	$3,538,947	$3,136,931	$2,754,368
Cost of goods sold	2,103,465	1,865,786	1,643,791
Gross margin	1,435,482	1,271,145	1,110,577
Selling, general and administrative expenses	1,090,392	961,176	855,790
Interest income	(5,683)	(1,939)	(873)
Interest expense	1,975	1,703	22
Earnings before income taxes	348,798	310,205	255,638
Income taxes	133,932	118,971	98,427
Net earnings	$ 214,866	$ 191,234	$ 157,211
Basic earnings per share	$ 1.86	$ 1.65	$ 1.36
Diluted earnings per share	$ 1.81	$ 1.60	$ 1.32
Shares used in calculation of earnings per share:			
Basic	115,616	116,159	115,583
Diluted	118,427	119,347	119,016

FIGURE 10.4
An income statement is a statement of revenue, expenses, and net income.

Income Statement Components

Retail income statements have five major components: net revenue, cost of goods sold, gross margin, expenses, and net income. The relationship among the components is such that:

$$\begin{array}{r} net\ revenue \\ -\ \underline{cost\ of\ goods\ sold} \\ gross\ margin \end{array}$$

$$\begin{array}{r} -\ \underline{expenses} \\ net\ income\ (loss) \end{array}$$

Because sales are typically a retailer's major source of revenue, the term *net sales* often appears on retailers' income statements. Other sources of revenue may include rent from leasing or renting property, or interest on accounts receivable. Net sales are the "top line" of the income statement from which all other income statement components are derived. High net sales attest to the ability of an organization's buyers to select assortments of goods that are appealing to the store's target customers.

Net sales are equal to gross sales minus customer returns:

$$net\ sales\ =\ gross\ sales\ -\ customer\ returns$$

Though never appearing on an income statement, records of gross sales are maintained for other reasons, such as determining customer return rates:

$$customer\ return\ rate\ =\ \frac{customer\ returns}{gross\ sales}\ \times\ 100$$

Customer returns of $4,000 on gross sales of $100,000 represents a return of 4 percent on gross sales:

$$customer\ return\ rate\ =\ \frac{\$4,000}{\$100,000}\ \times\ 100$$

$$customer\ return\ rate\ =\ 4\%$$

Customer return rates are computed for stores, categories of merchandise, and brands. A high customer return rate can be indicative of poor customer service, poor product quality, or poor fit.

The cost of goods sold, also called the *cost of merchandise sold* or the *cost of sales,* includes the billed cost of merchandise plus shipping and workroom costs, less cash discounts for early payment and returns to vendors.

$$
\begin{aligned}
&\ \ \ \ billed\ cost\ of\ merchandise\\
&+\ shipping\ costs\\
&+\ workroom\ costs\\
&-\ cash\ discounts\\
&\underline{-\ returns\ to\ vendors}\\
&\ \ \ \ cost\ of\ goods\ sold
\end{aligned}
$$

Shipping costs are the inbound delivery costs for transporting goods from suppliers. Workroom costs represent activities that prepare merchandise for sale, such as steaming and pressing apparel, and repairing merchandise damaged during shipment. Workroom activities change the merchandise in some way. Expenses for ticketing, hanging, or presenting merchandise on fixtures are not workroom costs. Returns to vendors (RTVs) are chargebacks to vendors for defective or slow-selling goods returned for credit. Cash discounts are invoice concessions from suppliers for prompt payment, a topic that receives considerable attention in Chapter 14.

Expenses are incurred in the day-to-day operation of an organization. Expense categories include payroll, rent, utilities, advertising, and interest on debt. Expenses are classified as either direct or indirect. A direct expense is attributable to a specific unit of business; an indirect expense is not. Direct expenses cease to exist when the unit of business is eliminated. A store's rent is a direct expense that would no longer exist if the store were closed. Newspaper advertising for a region of stores is an indirect expense for each store that would continue to exist if one of the stores in the region were closed.

Most retailers make every effort to allocate expenses directly. For instance, the advertising expense for a region of stores might be allocated to the stores in the region based on the sales volume of each store. Most of a retail organization's expenses are operational in nature, their control falling within the realm of the finance division or store administration.

Gross margin, or *gross profit*, is the difference between sales and the cost of goods sold. Retailers rely on gross margin to cover operating expenses, and ultimately profit. Gross margin expectations vary by retailing format and type of merchandise. A discount store's "no-frills" strategy yields lower operating expenses than those of a department store, and a discount store's gross margins are typically lower than those of a department store. (See Table 10.3.) A men's shop expects higher gross margins from its sportswear category than its suit category in that gross margins for suits are often eroded by alteration-workroom costs. Generating gross margin is fundamental to a buyer's mission in a retail organization. Buyers maximize gross margin in two ways:

1. Negotiating favorable prices with vendors thus maintaining a low cost of goods sold
2. Managing retail prices in a way that will maximize net sales

Many retailers include buying and occupancy costs in the cost of goods sold that appears in their annual reports. The practice inflates the cost of goods sold and reduces gross margin, a tactic that camouflages the *real* cost of goods sold, which is a carefully guarded secret in retail organizations.

TABLE 10.3   GROSS MARGIN PERCENTAGES FOR SELECT RETAIL STORES

Department Stores	
Dillard's	31.8
Federated Department Stores	40.3
Kohl's	31.2
Nordstrom	33.5
Full-line Discounters	
Kmart	21.8
Wal-Mart	20.8
Category Killers	
Barnes & Noble	25.0
Best Buy	15.9
Toys "R" Us	28.0
Home Accessories Stores	
Bed Bath & Beyond	41.3
Lands' End	46.6
Pier 1 Imports	41.4
Off-pricers	
Burlington Coat Factory	34.1
T.J. Maxx	23.2
Specialty Stores	
Ann Taylor	42.5
American Eagle	38.2
Gap	46.4
Nine West Group	42.5

Though buying and occupancy costs are included in the cost of goods sold in public financial statements, most retailers follow the traditional format for internal management reports.

Net income, sometimes called *net earnings*, or *net profit, earnings before taxes*, or *bottom line*, is equal to gross margin minus expenses. Because generating net income is fundamental to a company's existence, all of the activities of a retail organization are directly or indirectly pointed to this goal. From an income statement perspective, net income can be increased by:

- Increasing sales
- Increasing gross margin
- Decreasing cost of goods sold
- Decreasing expenses
- Any combination of the above

Component Percentages

A component percentage is a ratio of an income statement component, such as gross margin, expenses, or net income, to net sales expressed as a percentage. The following are formulas for computing four component percentages:

$$cost\ of\ goods\ sold\ \% = \frac{cost\ of\ goods\ sold}{net\ sales} \times 100$$

$$gross\ margin\ \% = \frac{gross\ margin}{net\ sales} \times 100$$

$$expenses\ \% = \frac{expenses}{net\ sales} \times 100$$

$$net\ income\ \% = \frac{net\ income}{net\ sales} \times 100$$

Component percentages are often used to evaluate performance between two time periods, a comparison called a time-series comparison. To demonstrate, refer to the information in Table 10.4, which was derived from two successive annual income statements from a chain of stores. The figures in the percent columns are based on the above formulas. Note that sales increased from year one to year two by $637,298,000, representing a gain of 11.5 percent. In spite of this sizable gain in sales, the company's net income as a percentage of sales slipped by 1.1 percent because of two factors: lower gross margin (−0.4 percent) and an increase in expenses (+0.7 percent). Though the percentages are seemingly minuscule, the drop in net income from 11.8 percent to 10.7 percent represents $67,768,877.

Note that the component percentages converted multidigit dollar figures into more comprehensible numbers. Component percentages also facilitate comparing stores or organizations of vastly different volume. A meaningful

TABLE 10.4   A TIME-SERIES COMPARISON OF THE LIMITED'S INCOME
               STATEMENT COMPONENTS

	Year 2	% Sales	Year 1	% Sales
Net Sales	$6,160,807	100.0%	$5,523,509	100.0%
Cost of Goods Sold	$4,367,264	70.9%	$3,893,070	70.5%
Gross Margin	$1,793,543	29.1%	$1,630,439	29.5%
Expenses	$1,133,241	18.4%	$ 977,001	17.7%
Net Income	$ 660,302	10.7%	$ 653,438	11.8%

Dollar figures are expressed in thousands

SOURCE
Holmes, S. and Zellner,
W. (April 12, 2004).
The Costco Way.
BusinessWeek, pp.
76–77.

HIGH WAGES AND HIGH PROFIT: A FISCAL ANOMALY

Though Wal-Mart is a favorite of Wall Street, Costco consistently beats Wall Street's profit expectations. What is strange about this is that Costco pays its workers higher wages than Wal-Mart, which leads analysts to fear that Costco's operating expenses will get out of hand and erode the company's profit. "At Costco, it's better to be an employee or a customer than a shareholder," says Deutsche Bank analyst Bill Dreher.

Wal-Mart, like many other companies, believes that shareholders are best served if employers hold down expenses, including the cost of labor. But surprisingly, Costco's high-wage approach actually beats Wal-Mart, and its warehouse club subsidiary, Sam's Club, at its own game. According to an analysis by *BusinessWeek*, Costco has lower employee turnover and higher productivity than Sam's Club because Costco compensates its employees more generously than Sam's Club,

thus motivating and retaining good workers, one-fifth of whom are unionized. Combined with a smart business strategy that sells a mix of higher-margin products to more affluent customers, Costco actually keeps its labor costs lower than Sam's Club as a percentage of sales, and its 68,000 hourly workers in the United States sell more merchandise per square foot. Put another way, the 102,000 Sam's Club employees in the U.S. recently generated some $35 billion in sales in one year, while Costco sold $34 billion with one-third fewer employees.

Bottom line: Over the past five years, Costco's operating income grew faster than Sam's Club. Most of Wall Street doesn't see the broader picture, however, and focuses on the up-front savings Costco would gain if it paid workers less. But a few analysts concede that Costco suffers from the Street's bias toward the low-wage model.

comparison can be made between the performance of a $6 *million* retailer and a $6 *billion* retailer, because percentage ratios onvert income statement components to an easy-to-compare scale of 0 to ± 100 percent, regardless of the dollar magnitude of the components. Naturally, other factors must be considered when comparing the two retailers. A multibillion-dollar organization reaps economic advantages unattainable by small retailers.

GROSS MARGIN RETURN ON INVESTMENT

Prudent merchandising decisions are often based on multiple pieces of information. For example, assume that a retailer must eliminate one of two

TABLE 10.5A   COST OF GOODS SOLD AND NET INCOME PERCENTAGES FOR SEVEN
TYPES OF RETAILERS DEFINED BY PRODUCT CATEGORY

Type of Retailer	Cost of Goods Sold	Net Income
Apparel and Accessories	59.1%	5.7%
Electronics	70.7%	4.8%
Home Furnishings and Accessories	61.7%	4.8%
Health, Beauty, and Drug	66.5%	5.3%
Non-Store	58.7%	6.7%
Sporting Goods, Books, Music, and Hobby	62.7%	4.8%
General Merchandise	64.5%	4.9%

Source: BizRate.com.

TABLE 10.5B   2005 INCOME STATEMENT COMPONENT PERCENTAGES
FOR SIX RETAILERS[2]

	Gap	Home Depot	Limited Brands	Target	TJX Companies	Williams-Sonoma
COGS	36.6%	66.5%	64.1%	68.1%	76.2%	40.5%
Gross Margin	63.9%	33.5%	35.9%	31.9%	23.8%	59.5%
Expenses	52.2%	22.1%	29.0%	22.9%	16.6%	49.6%
Net Income	11.2%	11.4%	6.9%	8.2%	7.2%	9.9%

Source: BizRate.com.

categories of merchandise from a store's assortment because of space constraints. Basing the decision solely on sales performance is an information-
poor decision; the lower sales producer might be generating more gross
margin than the higher sales producer. Table 10.6 compares the sales and
gross margin of the two categories. Note that Category A sales exceed category B sales by $50,000. However, Category B generates $30,000 more gross
margin than Category A, and it is thus a larger contributor to the store's net
income. The analysis suggests that Category B, the lower sales producer,
should be retained in the assortment, not Category A. Naturally, factors
other than sales and gross margin should be considered as well. Even high-
gross-margin producers fall under scrutiny if they have high selling expenses
or poor space productivity.

Gross margin return on investment (GMROI) integrates two performance measures, gross margin and turnover, to create a single measure of
performance. The formula for GMROI (pronounced *jim-roy*) is:

$$GMROI = \frac{gross\ margin\ dollars}{net\ sales} \times \frac{net\ sales}{average\ inventory}$$

Note that gross margin divided by net sales is the component percentage
formula for gross margin (without the × 100), while net sales divided by
average inventory is the formula for turnover.[3] The formula can be simplified by canceling net sales.

$$GMROI = \frac{gross\ margin\ dollars}{average\ inventory}$$

The derived formula measures the amount of gross margin dollars generated per dollar of average inventory invested.

TABLE 10.6   GROSS MARGIN COMPARISON OF TWO CATEGORIES

	Category A	Category B
Sales	$300,000	$250,000
Cost of Goods Sold	$180,000	$100,000
Gross Margin $	$120,000	$150,000
Gross Margin %	40%	60%

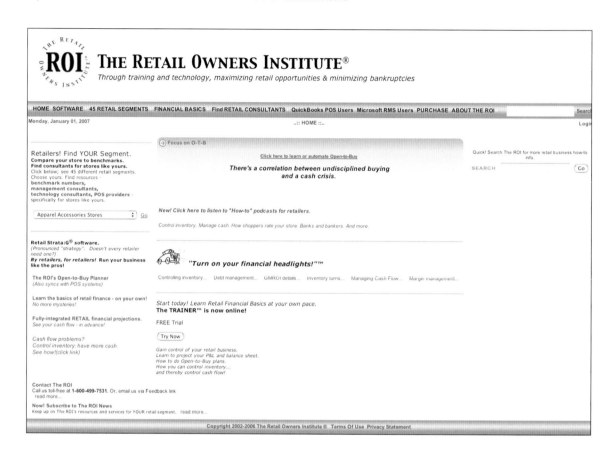

FIGURE 10.5
The Retail Owners Institute
stresses the imporatnce of
improving GMROI to
increase profit. Source:
www.retailowner.com.

The following example demonstrates the use of GMROI. As a result of a store renovation, a gourmet cooking shop will gain enough additional selling space to expand a single category of merchandise. The choice has been narrowed to three categories: specialty foods, countertop appliances, and open-stock glassware. The shop's annual volume is $2 million. Each category represents about 20 percent of the shop's business. The remaining business is generated by categories, such as cookbooks, cookware, and table and kitchen linens. Countertop appliances yield a 20 percent gross margin ($80,000), specialty foods a 30 percent gross margin ($120,000), and glassware a 50 percent gross margin ($200,000). Specialty foods turn fastest at 10.0 times a year with an average inventory of $40,000 at cost. Countertop appliances turn 4.0 times a year with an average inventory of $100,000 at

TABLE 10.7   GMROI FOR THREE MERCHANDISE CATEGORIES

	Gross Margin	Average Inventory	GMROI
Specialty Foods	$120,000	$ 40,000	3.0
Countertop Appliances	$ 80,000	$100,000	0.8
Glassware	$200,000	$160,000	1.25

cost. Glassware is the slowest-turning category at 2.5 times a year with an average inventory of $160,000 at cost. The GMROI for each category is computed by dividing gross margin dollars by average inventory. The results appear in Table 10.7.

Note that specialty foods yield the highest GMROI (3.0) and that countertop appliances yield the lowest GMROI (0.8). If the decision to expand a category of merchandise were based solely on the gross margin, glassware would be the chosen category. However, when turnover is considered,

SOURCE
Are Target's falling margins a problem in its battle with Wal-Mart? © The Economist Newspaper Limited, London (May 20, 2006).

WHO'S THE TARGET?

The competition between Target and Wal-Mart is keen. The result? Both companies try to mirror image each other. Wal-Mart has tried to make itself more appealing to middle-class shoppers, a market niche that Target has made for itself. Wal-Mart already lures plenty of customers with rock-bottom prices for groceries, but wants them to toss more high-margin items, such as clothing and household goods, into their shopping carts before heading for the till. Wal-Mart is also adding more expensive versions of these products to its shelves to attract middle-class customers.

To counter, Target revamped its stores to entice customers to buy more food and other consumables like paper goods. The outcome? Target boosted its sales by selling more to each customer, but the company's margins fell because the additional sales were on low-margin goods. In other words, the average customer purchase increased, but the company's profit margin decreased.

In essence, the product offerings of the two companies are converging. The two chains will still maintain their distinction: Wal-Mart will remain the relentless cost cutter, and Target the trendier place to shop and save. What really makes them alike is that both are adding stores and making money.

specialty foods fall under a favorable light. Though specialty foods generate fewer gross margin dollars than countertop appliances or glassware, inventory investments for specialty foods are considerably less than inventory investments for the other two categories. In other words, specialty foods yield more gross margin dollars per dollar of inventory carried than countertop appliances or glassware.

In general, *high* turnover and *high* gross margins yield *high* GMROI, while *low* turnover and *low* gross margins yield *low* GMROI. In the example, specialty foods' high turnover compensates for its low gross margin. Conversely, a high gross margin can also compensate for low turnover. Because high turnover and high gross margin are very desirable merchandising objectives, maximizing GMROI is a major objective for most buyers. (See Table 10.8.)

TABLE 10.8   GMROI FOR SELECT RETAIL STORES

Department Stores	
Federated Department Stores	1.1
Kohl's	1.4
Nordstrom	1.4
Full-line Discounters	
Kmart	2.1
Wal-Mart	2.0
Home Accessories Stores	
Bed Bath & Beyond	1.1
Pier 1 Imports	1.1
Off-pricers	
Burlington Coat Factory	1.0
T.J. Maxx	1.1
Specialty Stores	
American Eagle	2.7
Ann Taylor	1.9
Gap	2.3
Nine West Group	0.8

SUMMARY POINTS

- Cash flow is the balance of cash coming into and going out of an organization.
- A balance sheet is a statement of a retailer's assets, liabilities, and owners' equity. Assets are *owned* by a retailer. Liabilities are *owed*. Net worth is the difference between the two.
- Financial ratios combine two balance sheet components to assess financial stability. The current ratio is a measure of an organization's short-term debt-paying ability used by credit-rating organizations to determine credit worthiness.
- An income statement reflects a retailer's profit performance for a specific period. Its components include net sales, cost of goods sold, gross margin, and profit.
- Gross margin return on investment (GMROI) combines gross margin and turnover in a single measure of performance, measuring the amount of gross margin generated per dollar of average inventory invested.

KEY TERMS AND CONCEPTS

assets	financial ratio	loss
balance sheet	gross margin	net income
cash discount	gross margin return on	net sales
cash flow	investment (GMROI)	owners' equity
component percentage	gross sales	profit
cost of goods sold	income statement	return to vendor
current ratio	indirect expense	time-series comparison
direct expense	liabilities	workroom cost
factor	liquidity	

THINKING ABOUT IT

1. How might a specialty store owner speed up cash flow—that is, decrease the time between the point at which he or she pays vendors and the point at which customers buy?

2. GMROI combines two measures of performance to create a single comprehensive measure. Are there other measures of performance that can be combined to create a single measure? Could three measures be combined? What two measures will not create a valid measure when combined?

3. The current ratio uses two balance sheet components to create a measure of a retailer's ability to pay its short-term debt. What other balance sheet components can be used to create other ratios? What would the ratios measure?

4. How might the GMROI of an apparel department compare to the GMROI of a furniture department in the same store? Explain.

5. How does the cash flow of a warehouse club compare to the cash flow of a department store? Why?

TEAMING UP

1. Each member of your team should find the most recent annual reports for two retailers within a specific retailing format or category of merchandise. Using the consolidated income statements within the annual reports, compute component percentages for gross margin, expenses, and net income. (Multiple expenses may have to be combined to come up with a single expense figure.) Compare the component percentages for the two retailers. Are they close? Can you explain the variances? As a group, compare component percentages within different retailing formats and explain the variances.

2. Each team member should find the most recent annual reports for poor performers within a specific retailing format or category of merchandise. (Your instructor will help you to identify the poor performers. The list changes often.) Review the company's income statements for the past three years. (Most annual reports include multiple-year income statement comparisons.) Do you see any year-to-year improvement in sales, gross margin, or net income? What does the retailer need to do to become a stellar performer? Share your analysis with the team.

SEARCHING THE NET

1. Search for the most recent annual reports from several of your favorite retail stores. Besides financial information, what other worthwhile information is included in the annual reports? Would you buy stock in the companies based on what you have read?

2. Search for lists of retail performance measures, such as current ratio, gross margin, net income, and GMROI, reported by store, retailing format, or category of merchandise. Compare performance among the

reporting entities. Can you account for variances? What advice would you give to the poor performers?

SOLVING PROBLEMS

1. A retailer's current assets are $7.4 million. Presently, his current ratio is 1.5. The retailer wants to borrow money to fund an expansion; however, a lender tells him that, to borrow money, the retailer must bring his current ratio up to 2.0. What are the retailer's current liabilities? By how much must he reduce his current liabilities to obtain a loan, assuming that current assets remain constant?

2. Complete the following grid:

	Store 1	Store 2	Store 3	Store 4	Store 5	Store 6
Net sales	$12.0		$155.0			$4,056.7
Cost of goods sold		$42.6		$951.2	$90.0	
Gross margin—dollars	$5.9	$38.1		$487.6		$2,387.2
Gross margin—percent						
Expenses—dollars	$4.2		$88.2		$41.1	
Expenses—percent						
Net income—dollars		$6.2	$7.6	$22.7	$.5	$128.5
Net income—percent						

Dollars are expressed in millions.

3. Review the component percentages for each store in problem 2 above. Which store is the best performer? The poorest performer? What advice would you give to the poorest performer relative to improving performance? Suggest how to increase net income by increasing gross margin and/or decreasing expenses by specific dollar amounts.

4. Complete the following grid:

	Department A	Department B	Department C	Department D	Department E	Department F
Sales	$1.5		$78.0		$32.5	$45.2
Turnover	7.2	3.5	4.5	12.0		
Average inventory		$.4		$15.0	$4.5	$7.1
COGS		$.6	$52.3	$41.3		
Gross margin—dollars	$.7				$12.9	$15.8
Gross margin—percent						
GMROI						

Dollars are expressed in millions.

USING EXCEL

1. Create a spreadsheet to track a store's current ratio by month for a year.
2. Create a spreadsheet to track a store's balance sheet components by month for a year.
3. Create a spreadsheet to track a store's income statement components by month for a year. Accrue the monthly figures so that at any point, the spreadsheet will show year-to-date performance.
4. Create a spreadsheet to track a store's income statement components comparing each component to a plan. Compute deviations from plans by dollar and percentage. That is, if plan sales for a month are $10,000 and actual sales are $11,000, then the deviation is +$1,000 ($11,000 − $10,000 = $1,000), which is +10 percent of the plan ($1,000 ÷ $10,000 = 0.1 = 10 percent).
5. Create a spreadsheet for a five-store chain to compute GMROI for each store and for the total chain.

CHAPTER ELEVEN

Inventory Valuation

After reading this chapter, you will be able to discuss:

● Perpetual inventory systems.

● The fiscal impact of shortage.

● Last in, first out (LIFO) and first in, first out (FIFO) as methods of inventory valuation.

Inventory values have considerable impact on a retail organization's financial statements. On a balance sheet, inventory is an asset that impacts a company's net worth. On an income statement, gross margin and net income are both derived from the cost of goods sold. The maintenance of inventory records and the assessment of inventory value are important merchandising functions and the subject of Chapter 11.

INVENTORY VALUES

Retailers periodically determine the value of their inventories to prepare financial statements. Preparing an income statement requires computing the cost of goods sold. Cost of goods sold is equal to the value of the inventory on hand at the beginning of the fiscal period, plus the value of the inventory purchased during the period, minus the value of the inventory on hand at the end of the period:

$$
\begin{array}{ll}
& \textit{inventory on hand at the beginning of the fiscal period} \\
+ & \textit{purchases} \\
- & \underline{\textit{inventory on hand at the end of the fiscal period}} \\
& \textit{cost of goods sold}
\end{array}
$$

Retailers also determine inventory values to prepare balance sheets.

The most reliable method of determining the value of an inventory is to count it. A physical inventory involves counting and valuating an inventory item by item. Retailers conduct physical inventories at least once a year to determine the cost of goods sold and gross margin for annual financial statements. Most retailers conduct physical inventories twice a year.

To prepare interim monthly and quarterly financial statements, most retailers need to establish the value of their inventory more often than annually or semi-annually. To avoid having to physically count an inventory more than twice a year, retailers maintain a perpetual inventory. A perpetual inventory system is an inventory accounting system whereby the value of an inventory is maintained on a continual basis by adjusting a beginning physical inventory by purchases, sales, and price changes. The resulting figure is called the book inventory. The nomenclature dates back to the days when inventory records were maintained in books or ledgers. Today, the "book" value of an inventory is likely to be maintained electronically on a computer system.

In theory, a book inventory should always equal a physical inventory. The balance between a book and physical inventory is maintained by adjusting the book inventory by any changes in inventory status. When new goods are received, the book is adjusted upward by the value of the goods received. When goods are sold, the book is adjusted downward by the value of the goods sold. The book is also adjusted by price changes, such as markdowns, and any other factors that affect the value of a store's inventory, such as returns to vendors and customer returns.

OVERAGE AND SHORTAGE

Though in theory a book inventory should always equal a physical inventory, the two seldom match. The discrepancy between the two is called an overage when the book inventory is *less* than the physical inventory. The discrepancy is called a shortage when the book inventory is greater than the physical inventory. A shortage is sometimes called *shrinkage*. Most retailers track shortages and overages by department, store, and category of merchandise.

External theft by customers and internal theft by employees are frequent causes of shortage. Shoplifted items remain on the book, causing the book value to exceed the physical value when a physical inventory is taken. Shoplifting accounts for only a portion of shortage and does not explain overage. Virtually all overages as well as many shortages are rooted in paper or clerical errors, as the following scenarios demonstrate:

- A vase is received into a gift shop's inventory and booked at a $28 retail. The item is ticketed at $28, but the "8" looks like a "6." When the vase is sold, the sale is transacted at $26. The book inventory is adjusted downward by $26, resulting in an overstatement of $2, which will emerge as a $2 shortage at the next physical inventory.

• At the end of the selling season, a buyer marks down the remaining pieces of a swimwear group from current clearance prices to 75 percent off the original retail. Fifty pieces of swimwear were each marked down $15, from $44.99 to $29.99. The information was accurately recorded on a change-of-price form; however, the person responsible for entering price-change transactions into the inventory management system entered just "5" on the keyboard instead of "50" when inputting the number of units marked down. The book inventory was adjusted downward by $75 (5 units at $15) instead of $750 (50 units at $15). This resulted in a $675 overstatement of the book inventory that will emerge as a $675 shortage at the next physical inventory.

• A furniture store used optical scanning sheets in conducting a physical inventory. A sheet recording a $150 lamp and a $350 table was mislaid and never optically scanned as part of the store's inventory. This resulted in a $500 understatement of the physical inventory and a $500 shortage.

The examples are just three of the innumerable scenarios that cause paper shortage in retail stores. Though shortages resulted in the examples, overages would have been the outcome if circumstances had been changed slightly: if the vase had been sold at a price *higher* than booked, if a figure *greater* than the number of pieces that were marked down were input, or if the lamp and table were recorded twice on inventory sheets.

Shortage and overage are expressed as a percentage of net sales of the period between the current and previous physical inventories. Assume that a department has a book inventory of $92,525, a semi-annual physical inventory of $87,375, and net sales of $500,000 for the six-month period. The difference between the book and physical inventories is $5,150. Since the book inventory is greater than the physical inventory, the result is a shortage. The shortage percentage is calculated by dividing the shortage by the net sales for the period and multiplying by 100:

$$shortage\ \% \ = \ \frac{shortage\ \$}{net\ sales} \ \times \ 100$$

$$shortage\ \% \ = \ \frac{\$5,150}{\$500,000} \ \times \ 100$$

$$shortage\ \% \ = \ 0.0103 \ \times \ 100$$

$$shortage\ \% \ = \ 1\%$$

Shortage varies by category of merchandise relative to factors such as the size and desirability of the merchandise, and the number of units handled in inventory transactions. Fashion jewelry displayed on top of a counter has a high shortage risk because of its pilferable size. Polo/Ralph Lauren menswear is vulnerable to shoplifting because of its desirability as a product and high street value. Transactional errors are more likely to occur in a greeting card store where *hundreds* of sales transactions are typical of each day than in a furniture store where *a hundred* sales transactions would represent a very busy day. Shortage also varies by retailing format.

PHYSICAL INVENTORY

A physical inventory involves identifying each unit of merchandise by price and compiling this information by category and store location. Additional information such as vendor, age, or style number is sometimes required to update management reports that track inventories at these levels. A physical inventory is a tedious function, requiring weeks of preparation that involves tasks such as reticketing merchandise and grouping goods together by price to expedite counting. Rigid controls, such as numbered inventory sheets and detailed floor plans, are used to guarantee the accuracy of a physical inventory.

Stores are often closed during a physical inventory to avoid distraction by the public. Closing stores adds to the cost of taking a physical inventory because of the loss of business during the store's closing. To minimize the loss of business, physical inventories are scheduled on the least productive days of the week and at the least productive time of day. To minimize counting, physical inventories are conducted at times when inventories are at their lowest point. Physical inventory data is compiled either internally by the store's finance division or externally by a contracted service. The results are compared to book inventories to determine shortages and overages.

Some retailers inventory selected departments or stores more often than semi-annually. A retailer may inventory a high shortage department, such as fashion jewelry, quarterly, or highly pilferable items, such as digital cameras, weekly. A change in department or category structure may necessitate an interim inventory. If Liz Claiborne handbags are transferred from the moderate-handbag category to the better-handbag category, a physical inventory of the line is taken so that the better category can be charged for the merchandise and the moderate category credited.

Inventory reconciliation involves scrutinizing the discrepancies between book and physical inventories in search of possible resolutions. Consider an $11,347 shortage in one category in one store and an overage of the same amount in the same category in another store. The discrepancy may be attributed to the incorrect processing of (or failure to process) paperwork representing the transfer of goods from the overage store to the shortage store. Thus the problem can be resolved by charging the overage store $11,347 and likewise crediting the shortage store. When inventory reconciliation is complete, the remaining discrepancies between book and physical inventories are wiped away by adjusting the book inventories to match the reconciled physical inventories. For one brief moment in time, the book and physical inventories match.

Technological advancements have enhanced the accuracy and speed of physical inventories. Many retailers scan bar codes into computers that compile inventory information down to the stock-keeping unit, or *SKU*, level. Some inventory management systems generate lists of booked items identified by SKU. The lists can then be compared to the inventory on hand, enabling the retailer to identify shortages, not only by a dollar amount within a category or store but by individual item.

THE FISCAL IMPACT OF SHORTAGE

Inventory shortages and overages affect net profit because of their impact on the cost of goods sold. Shortages *increase* the cost of goods sold and *reduce* gross margin and net income. Overages *decrease* the cost of goods sold and *increase* gross margin and net income. The following scenario demonstrates this principle: Assume that a gift shop's end-of-the-year physical inventory of $50,000 is equal to the book inventory. The cost of goods sold for the period is computed as follows:

beginning-of-year physical inventory	$ 75,000
merchandise receipts during the year	+ $575,000
merchandise available for sale	$650,000
end-of-year physical inventory	− $ 50,000
cost of goods sold	$600,000

The shop's income statement for the period is as follows:

net sales	$1,000,000	
cost of goods sold	600,000	60%
gross margin	400,000	40%
expenses	350,000	35%
net income	$50,000	5%

Assume that end-of-the-year physical inventory was $30,000, indicating a $20,000 shortage. The cost of goods sold is computed as follows:

beginning-of-year physical inventory	$ 75,000
merchandise receipts during the year	+ $575,000
merchandise available for sale	$650,000
end-of-year physical inventory	− $ 30,000
cost of goods sold	$620,000

The income statement reflecting this change is as follows:

net sales	$1,000,000	
cost of goods sold	620,000	62%
gross margin	380,000	38%
expenses	350,000	35%
net income	$ 30,000	3%

Note that the cost of goods sold increased from 60 percent to 62 percent of net sales and that net income decreased from 5 percent of net sales to 3 percent. A $20,000 overage would have the reverse effect on the cost of goods sold and net income. The cost of goods sold would drop to $580,000 and 58 percent of net sales, while net income would increase to $70,000 and 7 percent of net sales.

The example demonstrates the effect of shortage in eroding net income. Though overage produces "paper profit," overage is destined to return as a shortage in subsequent accounting periods. Assume that a $1,000 gold chain is listed at $1,500 by an inventory-taker, creating a $500 inventory overage. Because book and physical inventory discrepancies are corrected by adjusting the book inventory to match the physical, the chain will be carried on the book at $1,500 until the next physical inventory. If the chain is sold at the correct price of $1,000, the book will be adjusted downward by that amount, leaving $500 of unaccounted-for inventory—in other words, a shortage of $500. If the chain is not sold during the subsequent inventory period, a $500 shortage will appear at the next physical inventory if the chain is correctly listed at $1,000.

Buyers prefer inventory overages to inventory shortages because of their positive impact on gross margin and net income. However, neither overages nor shortages are desirable in that both reflect inaccurate record keeping and/or poor inventory management. Shortages receive more attention than overages because a shortage is the more likely occurrence. In essence, the types of errors that create shortages are often the same mistakes that create overages.

Shortage Control

Though retailers employ exhaustive efforts to curb theft and the paper errors that cause overage and shortage, inequities between book and physical inventories are inevitable. When retailers open their doors to the public, they become vulnerable to shoplifting. By relying on people to order merchandise, receive and ticket goods, effect price changes, and ring sales on registers, retailers become susceptible to the consequences of human error.

Buyers are accountable for shortage even though many have little control over the stores or distribution centers where many shortages originate. Buyers control shortage by monitoring the position and value of inventory through reports of inventory position, price change, and receipts. They foster good inventory management through clear communication regarding ticketing of merchandise, inventory counts, price changes, and returns to vendors.

Point-of-Sale Systems

Computerized inventory management systems that track thousands of inventory items by store, merchandise category, style number, or brand

FIGURE 11.2
A point-of-sale system is a network of computerized cash registers linked to a centralized location that facilitates the management of retail inventories. Retail Pro is a registered trademark of Retail Technologies International.

across hundreds of locations, from the point at which they are ordered to the point at which they are sold, have facilitated the maintenance of perpetual inventory systems. A point-of-sale (POS) system is a network of computerized cash registers linked to a central processing point, often referred to as a *back office*. A POS system processes sales transactions and related functions, such as credit verification and sales tax computation. As goods are sold, product information, such as style, size, and vendor, is transmitted to the back office by a multidigit number keyed into the register or an electronically scanned bar code. The information is stored in a database and used to adjust book inventories and to compile reports of inventory status that are used to plan assortments, make reorder and markdown decisions, and balance inventories among stores.

At store level, POS information is used to track salespeople's productivity and customer transactions by hour of the day and day of the week for use in scheduling the sales staff. Some POS systems have an e-mail feature for

SOURCE
About.com (2006). Historical Inventions, Bar Code. www.inventors.about.com/library/bl/bl12.htm.

A HISTORY OF THE BAR CODE

Bar coding is a method of automatic identification and data collection. The first patent for a bar code product was issued in 1952 to inventors Joseph Woodland and Bernard Silver.

In 1948, Bernard Silver was a graduate student at Drexel Institute of Technology in Philadelphia. A local food-chain storeowner made an inquiry to Drexel concerning the possibility of developing a method of automatically reading product information at checkout. Silver joined with fellow graduate student Joseph Woodland to work on a solution. Woodland and Silver filed their patent application for the "classifying apparatus and method" describing their invention as an "article classification through the medium of identifying patterns."

Bar coding was first used commercially in 1966, and the need for industry standards was soon realized. By 1970, the Universal Grocery Products Identification Code (UGPIC) was written by a company called Logicon, Inc. The first company to produce equipment using UGPIC was the American Company Monarch Marking. UGPIC evolved into the UPC symbol set or Universal Product Code, which is still used in the United States. George J. Laurer is considered the inventor of UPC, which was introduced in 1973. In 1974, the first UPC scanner was installed at a Marsh's supermarket in Troy, Ohio. The first product to have a bar code was Wrigley's gum.

communicating announcements of promotions and price changes from a central office to stores. As noted in Chapter 5, POS information also has marketing applications. Customers identified by store-issued shoppers' cards or credit cards can be profiled by their purchases and targeted for catalog mailings or other niche marketing strategies. Individual stores can be profiled by their best sellers so that store-specific assortments can be developed. Athlete's Foot, a group of more than 400 athletic-footwear stores, can identify a city's favorite sport by the most popular styles of athletic shoes: Detroit prefers basketball, Boston running, and Atlanta tennis.[1] Once appropriate for only large volume, high-transaction retailers, POS systems are now available to small retailers at an affordable cost.

LIFO AND FIFO

Determining the cost of goods sold at the end of a fiscal period is complicated by variations in the cost of merchandise bought during the period. Goods acquired at the beginning of a fiscal period are likely to have been purchased at lower prices than goods acquired at the end of a fiscal period. Two assumptions can be made relative to the cost of goods acquired and sold during the fiscal period:

- The goods acquired at the end of a fiscal period are sold before the goods purchased earlier in the fiscal period. This describes an inventory concept called *last in, first out,* or LIFO.
- The goods acquired at the beginning of a fiscal period are sold before goods purchased later in a fiscal period. This describes an inventory valuation concept called *first in, first out,* or FIFO.

Consider the following: A pro shop sells knit shirts in basic colors. The inventory is carried from one season to the next and is periodically replenished with new receipts. The shop began a fiscal year with an opening inventory of 1,000 shirts at a unit cost of $25. The shirts retailed at $50. When the shop reordered 2,000 units of the same shirt later in the year, the unit cost had increased to $26. These shirts were retailed at $52. The remaining original inventory was marked up $2 per unit to $52 to maintain price consistency. Assume that 2,800 shirts were sold throughout the fiscal year: 900 at a $50 retail and 1,900 at a $52 retail.

The following is a computation for the cost of goods available for sale during the year:

beginning inventory at cost (1,000 units at $25)	$25,000
additional receipts (2,000 units at $26)	$52,000
total cost of goods available for sale	$77,000

The following is a computation for annual sales:

900 units at $50	$45,000
1,900 units at $52	$98,800
2,800 units representing retail sales of	$143,800

LIFO assumes that the receipts that arrived later in the year were sold prior to the beginning inventory. The following is a computation of the cost of goods sold based on LIFO:

2,000 shirts at $26 each	$52,000
800 shirts at $25 each	$20,000
2,800 shirts at total cost of goods sold	$72,000

LIFO assumes an ending inventory value of $5,000 (200 shirts at $25 each).

FIFO assumes that the beginning inventory was sold prior to the receipts that arrived later in the year. The following is a computation of cost of goods sold based on FIFO:

1,000 shirts at $25 each	$25,000
1,800 shirts at $26 each	$46,800
2,800 shirts at total cost of goods sold	$71,800

FIFO assumes an ending inventory value of $5,200 (200 shirts at $26 each).

The following is a computation of gross margin based on LIFO:

sales	$143,800
cost of goods sold	$ 72,000
gross margin	$ 71,800

The following is a computation of gross margin based on FIFO:

sales	$143,800
cost of goods sold	$ 71,800
gross margin	$ 72,000

Note that FIFO generates a gross margin that is $200 higher than LIFO. The higher FIFO gross margin will ultimately yield higher net income. FIFO will consistently generate higher gross margin and net income than LIFO in periods of inflation when the cost of inventory rises from the beginning of the period to the end. In cases of price decreases, FIFO will yield lower gross margin and net income. Table 11.1 summarizes the effect of LIFO and FIFO during periods of inflation.

The effects of LIFO and FIFO are proportionate to the amount of inflation that occurs during an accounting period. In a period of *very high* inflation, FIFO will yield a *very low* cost of goods sold and *very high* gross margin and net income. LIFO will yield a *very high* cost of goods sold and a *very low* gross margin and net income. LIFO and FIFO are not intended to reflect the way in which merchandise is actually sold. Stores typically rotate inventories to ensure that older stock sells before becoming shopworn.

LIFO is adopted as an accounting strategy to improve cash flow through the deferral of income tax. Because corporate taxes are paid on net income, a LIFO-induced net income reduction results in the deferral of tax payment, which results in improved cash flow. The domino effect continues: Recall that a negative cash flow is balanced by borrowing money and that the related interest expense reduces net income. By improving cash flow, LIFO results in less borrowing, lower interest payments, and improved earnings. The adoption of LIFO in a period of relatively low inflation will have little

TABLE 11.1   COMPARISON OF LIFO AND FIFO

LIFO	*FIFO*
yields higher cost of goods sold	yields lower cost of goods sold
yields lower ending inventory values	yields higher ending inventory values
yields lower gross margin	yields higher gross margin
yields lower net income	yields higher net income

impact on net income; however, LIFO's impact on net income during a period of high inflation is significant. This is why many retailers adopted LIFO during the early 1970s, a period of double-digit inflation.

LIFO is a theoretical accounting assumption contrary to the actual physical flow of merchandise. LIFO retailers often maintain two sets of inventory figures: one for external financial reports that reflects inventory value using LIFO and another for nonfinancial internal management reports using FIFO that more accurately reflects the actual movement of goods. Federal tax law revisions have encouraged retailers to adopt LIFO. Previously, the Internal Revenue Service required conformity between the statement of inventory on the balance sheet, the computation of cost of goods sold, and the preparation of tax statements. However, income-tax laws have been relaxed to allow LIFO calculations for the preparation of tax statements, and FIFO inventory calculations for financial statements. Thus, a retailer can *minimize* the amount of taxes paid by using LIFO for tax purposes and *maximize* the statement of earnings on financial statements by using FIFO. Today more than 50 percent of all major retailers use LIFO as an inventory method. Some elect to use a combination of both LIFO and FIFO. Kmart, for instance, uses LIFO for domestic goods and FIFO for imports.

To assist retailers in determining cost of goods sold, the U.S. Department of Labor issues a semi-annual (January and July) *Department Store Price Index*, or *BLS*, that reflects price inflation on various categories of merchandise. Many companies develop their own indices to measure inflation within the fiscal year, finding internally derived data more accurate.

SUMMARY POINTS

- A physical inventory is the actual value of inventory determined by a physical count. An inventory's book value is its recorded value. In theory, the book value of inventory should equal the physical value.
- Overage occurs when the book inventory is less than the physical inventory. Shortage occurs when the book inventory is greater than the physical inventory. A physical inventory is conducted periodically to determine overage or shortage.
- Shortages and overages affect net income because of their impact on cost of goods sold.

- A POS system is a network of computerized registers linked to a central processing point.
- LIFO and FIFO are concepts used to determine inventory values for accounting purposes.

KEY TERMS AND CONCEPTS

book inventory	LIFO	point-of-sale system
external theft	overage	shortage
FIFO	perpetual inventory	
internal theft	system	
inventory reconciliation	physical inventory	

THINKING ABOUT IT

1. Besides the errors described in the "Overage and Shortage" section of this chapter, what other errors might occur in a retailer's day-to-day operation that would create an inventory shortage or overage?
2. Why are some retailers reluctant to use technologically sophisticated shoplifting prevention devices, such as those offered by Sensormatic?
3. Discuss the value of a POS system to a "mom and pop" retailer relative to accuracy and cost effectiveness.
4. Compare LIFO and FIFO as accounting theories to the actual movement of inventory in a retail store.

TEAMING UP

1. As a team, research industry standards for shortage for various categories of merchandise and/or types of stores. Discuss the shortage differences between categories and/or types of stores. Do the high-shortage categories and stores have common characteristics?
2. Each member of your team should shop a department in a full-line discount store, looking for shortage potential either from shoplifting or from charging customers incorrect prices. As a group, compare shopping experiences and determine which departments/merchandise categories are most vulnerable to shortage.

SEARCHING THE NET

1. Search for information on companies that conduct physical inventories for retail stores. Compare the companies. Which would you hire if you were a retailer with many SKUs, such as a greeting card store?
2. Find a trade publication article on inventory shortage (or shrinkage) in retail organizations. What are its causes? Remedies?
3. Search for information on the many anti-shoplifting devices available. Compare product characteristics. Which would you recommend to the owner of an off-price children's apparel store? Which categories of merchandise would you recommend tagging?

SOLVING PROBLEMS

1. Determine the overage/shortage in each of the following scenarios:
   - A $100 dress is stolen from a store.
   - A markdown from $20 to $16.99 is recorded as 10 units instead of 50.
   - A sale of $100 is incorrectly recorded as $120.
   - Goods received on the books at $2 per unit are incorrectly ticketed as $3 per unit; there are 100 units.
   - The return of a $50 blouse by a customer is recorded as $60.
   - The return of a $50 blouse by a customer is recorded as a sale of $80.
   - A broken $60 vase is thrown into the trash. No transaction is recorded to remove the vase from the books.
   - A markup is taken on 200 items from $80 to $90; the data entry person enters 20 items.
   - Goods transferred from Store 1 to Store 2 were miscounted; 50 items at $20 each were recorded as 60 items.
   - A salesperson guessed at the selling price of an $80 item and recorded the transaction at $85.
2. Determine the overage/shortage for a men's store when the following occurred:
   - A sweater markdown from $45 to $35.99 is entered as 100 units instead of 500.
   - A $12 sale of underwear is incorrectly transacted as $120.
   - The return of a $65.99 jacket by a customer is transacted as a credit of $75.99.

- A hundred wallets received on the books at $40 per unit are incorrectly ticketed as $44 per unit.
- A $60 shirt is stolen.
- A markup is taken on 300 pairs of trousers from $80 to $85; the price tickets are never changed.
- A salesperson guessed at a selling price of a $285 unticketed sport coat and transacted the sale at $265.

3. What is the store's overage/shortage percent in problem 2 above when the store's annual sales are $515,786?
4. In the LIFO/FIFO example given in the "LIFO and FIFO" section on page 280, assume all of the shirts were sold at $50. What is the effect on cost of goods sold? Gross margin?

USING EXCEL

1. Create a spreadsheet to compute a store's cost of goods for every month of the year using the formula on page 271.
2. Create a spreadsheet to compute overage/shortage percent for a store's five departments using the formula on page 274. Accrue the figures to compute overage/shortage for the store.
3. Create a spreadsheet for number 2 in the "Solving Problems" section of this chapter. Suggestions: Create a "book" column to show the impact of each scenario on book inventory, a "physical" column to show the impact on the physical inventory, a column to reflect the difference between the two, and a column to indicate whether the situation resulted in an overage or shortage. Remember that three things reduce inventory (sales, markdowns, and returns to vendors) and that three things increase inventory (customer returns, markups, and new merchandise receipts). Remember that shortage is an absolute value that has no positive or negative sign.

PART FOUR

Pricing, Planning, and Purchasing Retail Inventories

CHAPTER 12

Retail Pricing

After reading this chapter, you will be able to discuss:

● The intricacies of retail pricing.

● The interrelationship of retail pricing components.

● Promotional pricing.

● The impact of pricing on an organization's sales and profitability.

What constitutes the "right" retail price? The simple answer to this complex question is that a retail price should be high enough to cover an organization's profit objectives, but low enough to entice customers to buy. The retail prices at which goods are sold become the net sales component of an income statement. Thus, the higher the retail price the higher the gross margin and net profit. However, when merchandise is priced too high, it doesn't sell. Today's savvy consumers are always on the lookout for low prices and will quickly switch their patronage to the retailer with the best values. Setting retail prices is an important merchandising function and the topic of Chapter 12.

MARKUP

A retail price has two components: cost and markup. Cost is the portion of a retail price that is paid to the supplier. The terms *wholesale cost* and *wholesale price* are used synonymously with cost to refer to a supplier's price. Markup, or *markon*, is the amount added to cost to establish a retail price. The relationship between cost, markup, and retail price is such that:

$$retail\ price\ =\ cost\ +\ markup$$

When a retailer adds a $2 markup to an item purchased at a wholesale cost of $6, the retail price is $8.

$$retail\ price\ =\ cost\ +\ markup$$
$$\$8\ =\ \$6\ +\ \$2$$

When any two elements of a formula are known, the third can be derived. When retail price and cost are known, markup can be determined:

$$retail\ price\ =\ cost\ +\ markup$$
$$retail\ price\ =\ cost\ +\ x$$

Then:

$$x\ =\ retail\ -\ cost$$
$$x\ =\ \$8\ -\ \$6$$
$$markup\ =\ \$2$$

When retail price and markup are known, cost can be determined:

$$retail\ price\ =\ cost\ +\ markup$$
$$retail\ price\ =\ x\ +\ markup$$

Then:

$$x\ =\ retail\ price\ -\ markup$$
$$x\ =\ \$8\ -\ \$2$$
$$cost\ =\ \$6$$

Markup can be expressed as a percentage of cost or retail. The formula for expressing markup as a percentage of retail is:

$$markup\ percent\ =\ \frac{markup}{retail\ price}\ \times\ 100$$

$$markup\ percent\ =\ \frac{\$2}{\$8}\ \times\ 100$$

$$markup\ percent\ =\ 25\%$$

The formula for expressing markup as a percentage of cost is:

$$markup\ percent\ = \ \frac{markup}{cost} \times 100$$

$$markup\ percent\ = \ \frac{\$2}{\$6} \times 100$$

$$markup\ percent\ = \ 33\%$$

Thus, a $2 markup on an item priced at $8 can be expressed either as 25 percent or 33 percent.

Consumers and nonretailers in general are likely to refer to markup as a percentage of cost. They often speak of doubling an item's cost to establish a retail price, called *keystoning*, as a 100 percent markup. An item with a $5 cost that is retailed at $10 has a 100 percent markup when markup is expressed as a percentage of cost:

$$markup\ percent\ = \ \frac{markup}{cost} \times 100$$

$$markup\ percent\ = \ \frac{\$5}{\$5} \times 100$$

$$markup\ percent\ = \ 100\%$$

However, retailers refer to markup as a percentage of retail. The item with a $5 cost and that is retailed at $10 has a 50 percent markup when markup is expressed as a percentage of retail:

$$markup\ percent\ = \ \frac{markup}{retail\ price} \times 100$$

$$markup\ percent\ = \ \frac{\$5}{\$10} \times 100$$

$$markup\ percent\ = \ 50\%$$

In retailing vernacular, markup as percentage of retail is always assumed unless otherwise specified. Subsequent references to markup in this textbook will assume markup as a percentage of retail.

When any two components of the markup percent formula are known, the third can be derived. When markup percent and retail price are known, markup can be determined:

$$markup\ percent = \frac{x}{retail\ price} \times 100$$

$$x = \frac{markup\ percent \times retail\ price}{100}$$

$$x = \frac{50 \times 10}{100}$$

$$x = \$5$$

When markup percent and markup dollars are known, the formula can be solved for retail price:

$$markup\ percent = \frac{markup}{x} \times 100$$

$$x = \frac{markup}{markup\ percent} \times 100$$

$$x = \frac{5}{50} \times 100$$

$$x = \$10$$

Types of Markup

Markups fall into several descriptive categories. The most common markup categories are:

Initial Markup   An initial markup is the markup added to cost to establish the first price at which an item will be offered for sale, often called the regular, or *original,* price.

Additional Markup   An additional markup is the markup added to raise an existing retail price. Additional markups are often used to equate the retail prices of goods purchased at different costs. The following scenario demonstrates this application.

A men's store sells packaged underwear at a 50 percent markup. Presently, packaged T-shirts purchased at a $5 cost are retailing at $10 per package. A new shipment of T-shirts has just arrived with an invoice price of $5.25 per package reflecting a manufacturer's price increase of 25 cents per unit. To maintain the store's standard 50 percent markup, the new shipment of T-shirts will be retailed at $10.50 per package. To equate the retail prices of the old goods with the retail prices of the new goods, the store adds a $0.50 per package *additional markup* to the T-shirts that were in stock prior to the manufacturer's price increase.

An additional markup is expressed as a percentage of the retail onto which the markup is added:

$$additional\ markup\ percent\ = \frac{markup}{present\ retail} \times 100$$

In the case of the T-shirts, the $0.50 added to the existing $10.00 retail represents a 5 percent additional markup.

$$additional\ markup\ percent\ = \frac{\$0.50}{\$10.00} \times 100$$

$$additional\ markup\ percent\ = \ 5\%$$

Cumulative Markup   A cumulative markup is the aggregate markup percent on a group of goods with varying markups. The cumulative markup percent is equal to the total markup dollars on all of the goods divided by the sum of the retail prices of all of the goods, multiplied by 100.

$$cumulative\ markup\ percent\ = \frac{total\ markup}{total\ retail\ dollars} \times 100$$

Assume that a menswear buyer purchases 500 silk neckties from three vendors at three different wholesale prices:

100 ties at $9.25
200 ties at $9.50
200 ties at $9.75

To facilitate presentation and signing, the buyer retails all of the ties at a single unit price of $20. The cumulative markup for the ties is computed as follows:

$$cumulative\ markup\ percent = \frac{total\ markup}{total\ retail\ dollars} \times 100$$

$$cumulative\ markup\ percent = \frac{100(\$10.75) + 200(\$10.50) + 200(\$10.25)}{500(\$20)} \times 100$$

$$cumulative\ markup\ percent = \frac{\$5,225}{\$10,000} \times 100$$

$$cumulative\ markup\ percent = 52.3\%$$

Note that a cumulative markup cannot be determined by averaging multiple markup percentages. This calculation is valid only if equal units are associated with each markup. Such an erroneous calculation would have resulted in a cumulative markup of 52.5 percent not 52.3 percent.[1]

MARKDOWNS

A markdown, or *price reduction*, is a downward adjustment in a retail price. A markdown is often expressed as a percentage of the retail price on which the markdown is taken. The markdown percent formula is:

$$markdown\ percent = \frac{markdown\ dollars}{current\ retail\ price} \times 100$$

The markdown percent of a $10 markdown taken on a $50 sweater is computed as follows:

$$markdown\ percent \ = \ \frac{\$10}{\$50} \times 100$$

$$markdown\ percent \ = \ 20\%$$

Sometimes an additional markdown is applied to an item already marked down. The additional markdown is often stated as a percentage of the already marked down price. The markdown percent of an additional markdown of $10 on the $50 sweater already marked down to $40 is calculated as follows:

$$markdown\ percent \ = \ \frac{\$10}{\$40} \times 100$$

$$markdown\ percent \ = \ 25\%$$

Sometimes the total of all the markdowns on an item is expressed as a markdown percentage of the original retail price. Thus the total markdown of $20 ($10 + $10) in the example may be advertised as a 40 percent markdown:

$$markdown\ percent \ = \ \frac{total\ markdown\ dollars}{original\ retail\ price} \times 100$$

$$markdown\ percent \ = \ \frac{\$20}{\$50} \times 100$$

$$markdown\ percent \ = \ 40\%$$

Markdown dollars can be computed when a markdown percent and original retail price are known:

$$markdown\ dollars \ = \ \frac{original\ retail\ price \ \times \ markdown\ percent}{100}$$

A 30 percent markdown on a dress currently retailing at $80 is computed as follows:

$$markdown\ dollars\ =\ \frac{\$80\ \times\ 30}{100}$$

$$markdown\ dollars\ =\ \$24$$

A new marked down retail price is computed by subtracting the markdown dollars from the original retail.

$$marked\ down\ retail\ price\ =\ original\ retail\ price\ -\ markdown\ dollars$$

$$marked\ down\ retail\ price\ =\ \$80\ -\ \$24$$

$$marked\ down\ retail\ price\ =\ \$56$$

Because markdown goods are sold at lower-than-intended retail prices, markdowns have a negative impact on a company's gross margin and net profit. Therefore, retail organizations monitor markdowns very carefully with the hope of minimizing them by keeping them under control. Companies often track markdowns by department, category, and/or vendor. As an evaluative tool, the total markdown dollars taken for a period is compared to the net sales for the same period. For instance, if the total markdowns taken during August in a junior dress department are $50,000, and net sales for the month are $500,000, markdowns for August are computed as follows:

$$markdown\ rate\ for\ a\ period\ =\ \frac{total\ markdown\ dollars\ for\ the\ period}{net\ sales\ for\ the\ period}\ \times\ 100$$

$$markdown\ rate\ =\ \frac{\$50,000}{\$500,000}\ \times\ 100$$

$$markdown\ rate\ =\ 10\%$$

Because markdowns should be minimized, a markdown figure less than 10 percent is more desirable than a markdown figure greater than 10 percent. Markdown expectations vary by category of merchandise and time of year. For instance, markdowns on cold-weather outerwear are high toward the end of the winter when goods are being marked down to clear the way for spring merchandise.

Types of Markdowns

Markdowns fall into several descriptive categories. The most common markdown categories are discussed below.

Damage A damage markdown is a price reduction on goods damaged after delivery from a vendor.[2] Some retailers sell damaged goods to customers "as is." A $100 dress with broken buttons reduced to $75 is a good buy for a customer willing to spend a few dollars and a little time sewing on a new set of buttons. Selling the dress at a markdown price may be also be advantageous to the retailer in that $25 markdown may be less costly in terms of time and effort than sending the garment out for repair. Damaged merchandise that is not salable, such as broken glassware, must be "marked out of stock" by a markdown to zero retail. When damaged goods are disposed of without being marked out of stock, their retail value remains on the book resulting in a shortage at the next physical inventory.

Employee Discount An employee discount is a price reduction on employee purchases, an employment benefit characteristic of the retail industry. Employee discounts usually range between 5 and 50 percent. The amount varies according to the markup on the goods being discounted which is why department stores typically offer higher employee discounts than discounters, and why stores are more generous with discounts on high-markup goods, such as apparel, than low-markup goods such as sale merchandise or consumer electronics.[3] Hefty employee discounts are typical of apparel retailers who hope to induce their employees to buy their merchandise and wear it to work as a way of promoting it.

Promotional A promotional markdown is a price reduction on merchandise featured in a promotional event, commonly called a sale. Promotional markdowns are called temporary markdowns because the promotional goods are marked back up to regular price after the promotional event has ended. The duration of a promotion can range from a few hours, such as a Midnight Madness Sale, to several weeks, such as a semi-annual Home Sale. To ensure the credibility of an event, it is important that promoted merchandise is not offered at promotional prices during nonpromotional periods.

FIGURE 12.1
A promotional markdown is a
temporary price reduction on
merchandise featured in a
promotional event. Courtesy
of Bloomingdale's.

Clearance   A clearance markdown is a price reduction that induces the sale of residual or slow-selling merchandise. Clearance markdowns are called permanent markdowns because clearance goods do not return to a regular price, or any higher price, at a later date. Prices on clearance goods are reduced by subsequent additional markdowns until all of the merchandise has sold. A buyer of cold-weather accessories may take a 20 percent clearance markdown on gloves at the end of December. If the gloves do not sell out within a few weeks, the buyer will likely take additional markdowns of 35 percent, 50 percent, and eventually 75 percent off original prices until all of the gloves are sold.

TABLE 12.1   REPORT OF TEMPORARY AND PERMANENT MARKDOWNS

DEPT 149	CLASS	WTD POS MKDNS	WTD PERM/TEMP	WTD TOTALS	MTD POS MKDNS	MTD PERM/TEMP	MTD TOTALS
	1	1177.2	.0	1177.2	3577.5	224.3	3801.8
	2	259.4	.0	259.4	1241.3	395.2	1636.5
	3	107.1	.0	107.1	416.9	286.7	703.6
	4	351.7	.0	351.7	968.5	.0	968.5
	5	619.3	60.0	679.3	2051.4	464.4	2515.8
	6	306.9	.0	306.9	720.2	36.0	756.2
	7	824.8	.0	824.8	2001.1	415.1	2416.1
	8	.0	.0	.0	.0	30.0	30.0
	ALL	3646.5	60.0	3706.5	10,976.8	1851.6	12,828.4

Clearance Merchandise

Clearance markdowns are taken on various types of residual or "leftover" merchandise including the types of goods below.

Discontinued Goods   Goods that will not be part of future assortments are discontinued goods. Discontinued goods can include a category, a product line, or a single style, pattern, or color. A department store may discontinue a slow-selling cosmetics line. A women's specialty store may discontinue dresses to devote more space to sportswear. A manufacturer may discontinue unpopular colors in an assortment of bath towels, which, in turn, are discontinued by the retailers that carry them.

Seasonal Merchandise   Merchandise that is salable for a limited period of time, often defined by a season or holiday, is seasonal merchandise. Seasonal goods are marked down for clearance as their period of salability comes to a close. Velour shirts are marked down as the winter passes and customers begin to seek apparel for warmer weather. Examples of seasonal merchandise include swimwear, gloves, and Christmas-motif sweaters.

Broken Assortments   Broken assortments are residual items within a group or set of related or coordinated merchandise. Items within sets or

groups become candidates for clearance markdowns when assortments become "piecy." The remaining pieces of a Jones New York jacket/blouse/skirt coordinate group are marked down when so few pieces of the group remain that it is no longer possible to coordinate an ensemble in any one size or color.

Slow Sellers

Clearance markdowns are also taken on goods that sell at slower than anticipated rates of sale. There are innumerable factors that can cause slow selling. Some of the more common problems include:

Weather   Weather atypical of a season affects the sale of seasonal goods such as boots, wool sweaters, patio furniture, and shorts. Buyers are often quick to blame poor sales on the weather, since weather is a variable beyond their control.

Poor Assortment   Buyers are diligent in their efforts to choose assortments that will appeal to their target customers. The process is far from foolproof, however, and even the most carefully chosen assortments of items, brands,

TABLE 12.2   MARKDOWN REPORT FOR A SLEEPWEAR DEPARTMENT

RUN DATE: 05/22/07
WEEK ENDING: 05/21/07
PAGE 89
INTIMATE APPAREL
CCN: 540 SLEEPWEAR

VENDOR NAME	SALES				PUR MU%	STOCK		MARKDOWNS	
	TY	LY	%CHG	%TOTL	STD	$	%TOTL	$	%SLS
PRIVATE LABEL	577.3	285.4	102.3	30.7	51.8	474.1	26.8	75.2	13.0
MISS ELAINE	271.8	133.6	103.5	14.5	53.2	233.3	13.2	54.9	20.2
CAROLE HOCHMAN	116.4	37.3	212.2	6.2	54.4	69.2	3.9	15.7	13.5
DAMEA	129.5	54.9	136.0	6.9	57.3	101.0	5.7	15.8	12.2
KOMAR	145.8	81.6	78.7	7.8	52.3	119.8	6.8	24.5	16.8
VAL MODE	155.8	138.4	12.5	8.3	53.9	223.8	12.6	48.1	30.9
AUGUST SILK	85.8	50.8	69.1	4.6	53.8	100.9	5.7	19.4	22.6
LANZ	74.5	75.3	−1.1	4.0	51.9	97.4	5.5	31.7	42.6
EILEEN WEST	78.6	60.0	31.0	4.2	53.8	74.3	4.2	23.2	29.5
NICOLE	26.3	47.3	−44.4	1.4	54.4	67.4	3.8	5.8	22.2
LORRAINE	19.9	15.2	30.9	1.1	56.1	72.2	4.1	6.1	30.4
NATORI	32.0	35.1	−8.9	1.7	53.9	40.6	2.3	10.9	34.0
CINEMA	48.0	66.5	−27.9	2.6	48.2	24.6	1.4	7.0	14.6
DONNKENNY	32.1	.0	.0	1.7	53.0	25.4	1.4	18.4	57.4
VANITY FAIR	15.9	62.3	−74.4	.9	41.2	8.0	.5	5.5	34.4
SARA BETH	12.3	35.9	−65.8	.7	60.0	15.9	.9	5.9	48.0
RELIABLE MILWAUKEE	1.4	.5	193.9	.1	−1.4	−.1	.1	3.9	
KATHERINE	16.4	9.0	81.4	.9	48.9	16.3	.9	9.8	59.8
BODY DRAMA	10.8	58.6	−81.5	.6		6.6	.4	7.7	71.5
JENNIFER SMITH	1.2	53.5	−97.8	.1		.8	.1	.7	56.6
HOST	7.2	.0	.0	.4		3.1	.2	6.7	92.8
CAL DYNASTY	2.2	60.5	−96.3	.1		2.9	.2	1.4	62.8
EVE STILLMAN	3.3	5.0	−33.5	.2		2.6	.2	1.6	47.7
DIOR	6.8	12.5	−45.6	.4	103.2	7.2	.4	3.7	54.4
ALL BREED & HARTLAN	1.4	15.7	−90.8	.1		2.4	.1	.5	35.9
GILLIGAN	.0	116.8	.0	.0		1.4	.1	.5	.0
UNIDENTIFIED OTHER	.0	3.3	.0	.0		−22.1	−1.3	.4	.0
P.M. STORIES	.0	1.7	.0	.0		.0	.0	.1	.0
EVA DALE	1.9	.0	.0	.1	79.3	3.6	.2	1.9	100.5
N A P	1.9	24.8	−92.4	.1	56.7	.6	.0	2.1	109.8
CHARACTER	.0	3.6	.0	.0		.0	.0	.0	.0
TOSCA	.0	21.5	.0	.0		.2	.0	.1	.0
GROUND CONTROL	.0	3.9	.0	.0		.0	.0	.0	.0
ROBERT KLEIN	.0	4.2	.0	.0		.0	.0	.0	.0
INTIMATES	.0	7.2	.0	.0		.0	.0	.0	.0
ME AND MY PALS	.0	2.2	.0	.0		.0	.0	.0	.0
VALERIE JONES	.0	16.5	.0	.0		.0	.0	.1	.0
MISS DIOR	.0	13.4	.0	.0		.1	.0	.0	.0
OTHERS	2.3	1.3	73.4	.1		−1.1	−.1	.8	36.6
TOTAL	1878.7	1615.5	16.3	100.0	53.1	1772.4	100.0	406.4	21.6

price points, sizes, styles, fabrics, and colors become slow sellers when customers determine that the hemlines are too short, the colors are garish, or the prices are too high.

Poor Presentation   A sportswear group placed on a main aisle in one store may sell out in a week, while the same group remotely placed in the rear of a selling area in another store may not sell a single piece in two weeks. The way in which goods are fixtured, faced, folded, hung, sized, or colorized can greatly enhance their rate of sale. Unfortunately, not all of the merchandise in a store can be presented in prime locations.

Late Delivery   Seasonal and trend-sensitive goods that arrive after their selling peak become slow sellers. Velvet special occasion dresses are salable for New Year's Eve celebrations. They are useless if they arrive on December 30. To avoid this dilemma, purchase orders include a "do not ship later than" date as a caution to vendors not to ship too late in the selling season.

Clearance markdowns induce the sale of even the slowest selling merchandise. The dress that a customer perceived as a "dog" at $200 becomes ever so attractive at $149.99. Though clearance markdowns are heaviest at the ends of selling seasons, most buyers regularly review inventories to edit slow sellers and broken assortments, which is why clearance racks or clearance sections have become ubiquitous in many retail stores. Clearance prices traditionally have a "9" ending, such as $29.99, indicated in red. It is wise to show the original price of clearance markdowns so that customers can appreciate the value of the markdown.

In spite of their negative impact on gross margin, clearance markdowns are an important element in a buyer's effort to maintain clean assortments and to free up inventory dollars and fixtures for new goods. Clearance markdowns have a positive impact on turnover in that they decrease the value of inventory and induce sales. A buyer can be subject to as much criticism for taking too few clearance markdowns as for taking too many.

MAINTAINED MARKUP

Maintained markup is the difference between the cost of merchandise and the actual retail selling price. It is the net markup that remains after markdowns and additional markups have been subtracted or added to an initial markup. The formula for maintained markup is:

maintained markup = initial markup + additional markups − markdowns

Because reductions are more likely to exceed additional markups, the formula is often stated:

maintained markup = initial markup − net markdowns

Gross margin can be derived from maintained markup by subtracting transportation and workroom costs and adding cash discounts:

$$\textit{gross margin} = \textit{maintained markup} - \textit{transportation costs}$$
$$- \textit{workroom costs} + \textit{cash discounts}$$

Therefore, maintained markup is equal to gross margin before transportation and workroom costs and cash discounts are considered:

$$\textit{maintained markup} = \textit{gross margin} + \textit{transportation costs}$$
$$+ \textit{workroom costs} - \textit{cash discounts}$$

Maintained markup and initial markup are equal when goods are sold at original price. Maintained markup and gross margin are equal when:

- There are no transportation costs, workroom costs, or discounts, or the net value of all three is zero.

Maintained markup is an indicator of how well merchandise sustains markup. The following scenario demonstrates the use of maintained markup as an evaluative tool.

A sportswear buyer purchased cotton sweaters from two resources. Group A was purchased at $20 per unit and initially retailed at $40. Of the 2,000 sweaters in this group, 1,500 sold at regular price. At the end of the season, the remaining 500 sweaters were marked down: 300 sold at a first markdown price of $30, 150 sold at a further marked down price of $20, and the remaining 50 sold at a final markdown price of $10. Group B was purchased at a $17 per unit and initially retailed at $40. Of the 3,000 sweaters in this group, 1,200 sold at regular price. At the end of the season, the remaining 1,800 sweaters were marked down; 800 sold at a first markdown price of $30; 500 at a further marked down price of $20; and the remaining 500 sold at a final markdown price of $10.

After all of the sweaters sold out the buyer computed the maintained markup *dollars* for each group of sweaters as reflected in Table 12.3. Table 12.4 reflects the computation of the maintained markup *percentage* for each group of sweaters. Note the following relative to the data in Tables 12.3 and 12.4:

- The initial markup of Group A was 50 percent and that the initial markup of Group B was 57.5 percent. However, subsequent markdowns eroded the initial markup of each group resulting in an average maintained markup of 44.8 percent for Group A and 41.4 percent for Group B.

TABLE 12.3   MAINTAINED MARKUP DOLLARS FOR TWO GROUPS OF SWEATERS

Price	Group A Cost 5 $20/unit				Group B Cost 5 $17/unit			
	# Sold	Sales $	MU$/Unit	Total MU$	# Sold	Sales $	MU$/Unit	Total MU$
$40	1500	$60,000	$ 20	$30,000	1200	$48,000	$23	$27,600
$30	300	$ 9,000	$ 10	$ 3,000	800	$24,000	$13	$10,400
$20	150	$ 3,000	0	0	500	$10,000	$ 3	$ 1,500
$10	50	$ 500	−$ 10	−$ 500	500	$ 5,000	−$ 7	−$ 3,500
TOTAL	2000	$72,500	$16.25	$32,500	3000	$87,000	$12	$36,000

TABLE 12.4   MAINTAINED MARKUP PERCENTAGES
FOR TWO GROUPS OF SWEATERS

	Group A	Group B
Total initial markup dollars	$40,000	$ 69,000
Total original retail dollars	$80,000	$120,000
Initial markup percent	50%	57.5%
Total maintained markup dollars	$32,500	$ 36,000
Total actual retail dollars	$72,500	$ 87,000
Maintained markup percent	44.8%	41.4%

- Though the initial markup of Group A was lower than the initial markup of Group B, the maintained markup of Group A was higher than the maintained markup of Group B.
- Though 75 percent of Group A (1,500 of 2,000 units) sold at the original $40 retail, only 40 percent of Group B (1,200 of 3,000 units) sold at the original price of $40.
- Only 2.5 percent of Group A sold at a below-cost retail (50 of 2,000 units), whereas more than 16 percent of Group B (500 of 3,000 units) were sold below cost.

The buyer priced the Group B sweaters at a higher initial markup than the Group A sweaters, hoping to yield a higher maintained markup. However, it was the Group A sweaters that sustained higher markup over time. Customers seemingly resisted the $40 original price on the Group B sweaters, but they perceived the same price for the Group A sweaters as a good value. Perhaps Group B would have sold better at an original price based on a more modest initial markup.

Tactical Price Changes

A tactical price change is a strategic markup or markdown that falls within a retail price zone defined at one end by a retail price with a standard markup and at the other end by a retail price with an inflated markup. A markup within the zone is called a markdown cancellation. A markdown within the zone is called a markup cancellation.

The concept of tactical price changes is best explained by an example: A sales representative has offered a retail buyer a closeout price of $15 per pair on a popular pant style. The original wholesale price was $20. The buyer identifies this as a great promotional opportunity in that, at $15 a pair, the pants can be retailed at $29.99 and still yield the department's standard initial markup of 50 percent. The buyer wrote an order for the pants with instructions to the store's distribution center to book and ticket the goods at a $40 retail. The buyer plans to offer the pants at the $40 retail for a few weeks before reducing them to $29.99. By so doing, he hopes to validate the comparative price and to enhance customer perception of the promotional price as a real bargain.

The tactical retail price zone in this scenario is $29.99 at the low end, a point of normal markup, and $40 at the high end, an inflated retail price.

Price changes within this zone are called markup cancellations and mark-down cancellations. A price reduction from $40 to $29.99 is a markup cancellation, not a markdown, because the new price of $29.99 falls within the tactical price zone. A price increase from $29.99 to $40 is a markdown cancellation, not a markup. Price changes to points lower than $29.99 are classified as markdowns.

Markup cancellations are unlike typical markdowns in that markdowns taken within the tactical zone are a reflection of a buyer's pricing strategy and not a result of poorly chosen assortments. Tracking markup cancellations and markdowns separately ensures that a buyer's ability to control markdowns isn't tainted by strategic planning.

Not all retailers make a distinction between markdowns and markup cancellations and markup and markdown cancellations, feeling that the effort to track them outweighs its worth. Also, there is difficulty in defining "normal" and "inflated" markup in many retail organizations.

Managing Markdowns

Like sales and inventory, markdowns are planned and tracked over time by department and/or category of merchandise and markdown type. Last year's markdowns for the same time period are used to project this year's markdowns, since, like sales, markdowns fall into cyclical patterns. Markdown projections are also validated against industry standards for comparable types of stores and categories of merchandise. Markdowns are monitored throughout the season to ensure that actual markdowns do not exceed projections. Excessive markdowns may yield high sales due to the attractive prices of the reduced merchandise; however, gross margin and net income will be negatively affected.

ESTABLISHING AN INITIAL MARKUP

Buyers must price goods at an initial markup that will ensure final selling prices consistent with the organization's profit objectives. In essence, an initial markup must be high enough to cover:

- Transportation and workroom costs (less cash discounts)
- Expenses and net profit
- Markdowns

The formula for establishing an initial markup percentage reflects the notion that a markup percentage is equal to markup divided by retail. For the case in point, initial markup is the numerator. Its computation reflects the fact that an initial markup must cover the aforementioned:

$$transportation \ + \ workroom \ costs \ - \ cash \ discounts \ + \ expenses \\ + \ net \ profit \ + \ markdowns$$

The numerator can be simplified by recalling from Chapter 10 that:

$$gross \ margin \ = \ expenses \ + \ net \ profit$$

Therefore, gross margin can be substituted for expenses and profit in the numerator:

$$gross \ margin \ + \ transportation \ + \ workroom \ costs \\ - \ cash \ discounts \ + \ markdowns$$

Recall also that:

$$maintained \ markup \ = \ gross \ margin \ + \ transportation \\ + \ workroom \ costs \ - \ cash \ discounts.$$

Therefore, the numerator can be further simplified by substituting maintained markup for transportation costs, workroom costs, cash discounts, and gross margin:

$$maintained \ markup \ + \ markdowns$$

The denominator of the formula reflects the fact that initial retail prices will be eroded by markdowns before becoming net sales:

$$net \ sales \ + \ markdowns$$

Thus, the formula for computing an initial markup percent is:

$$initial \ markup \ \% \ = \ \frac{maintained \ markup \ + \ markdowns}{net \ sales \ + \ markdowns} \ \times \ 100$$

Factors That Drive Initial Markup

In general, high figures in the numerator of the initial markup formula will yield a high initial markup percentage, while low figures will yield a low percentage. The following factors have an impact on how high or low an initial markup will be:

- *Markdowns.* An apparel department requires a higher initial markup to achieve the same maintained markup as the cosmetics department because of the apparel department's high clearance markdown rate. Reductions are virtually nonexistent in the cosmetics department, where damages and residual merchandise, such as unsold holiday gift sets, are returned to vendors for credit.
- *Transportation costs.* Bulky items, such as furniture, necessitate a high initial markup to cover high transportation costs.
- *Workroom costs.* A bridal shop that offers free alterations requires a higher initial markup to achieve the same maintained markup as a dress shop. The workroom costs for turning a hem on very full, multitiered wedding dresses are considerably greater than the workroom costs for turning hems on straight skirts.
- *Direct expenses.* Direct expenses can include commissions or specialized supplies, such as velvet jewelry boxes. Wal-Mart abandoned its small pet business because of high direct expenses. Though birds, hamsters, and gerbils had the same initial markup as tropical fish, the cost of feeding and caring for a small animal completely erodes its markup if the animal isn't sold within two weeks.

Calculating an Initial Markup Percentage

The following scenario demonstrates the calculation of an initial markup percentage.

A shoe buyer's maintained markup objective for a season is 40 percent. The buyer anticipates seasonal markdowns of 20 percent. An initial markup for the season is calculated as follows:

$$\text{initial markup \%} = \frac{\text{maintained markup } + \text{ markdowns}}{\text{net sales } + \text{ markdowns}} \times 100$$

$$\text{initial markup \%} = \frac{40\% + 20\%}{100\% + 20\%} \times 100$$

$$\text{initial markup \%} = \frac{0.40 + 0.20}{1.00 + 0.20} \times 100$$

$$\text{initial markup \%} = \frac{0.6}{1.2} \times 100$$

$$\text{initial markup \%} = 50\%$$

TABLE 12.5   MARKDOWN PERCENTAGES FOR MEN'S SPECIALTY STORES BY
             CATEGORY OF MERCHANDISE

Category	% Markdown
Men's Clothing	
Men's Suits	18.9
Men's Coats	24.3
Sport Coats	22.5
Dress Slacks	13.3
Total Men's Clothing	19.2
Men's Sportswear	
Sport Shirts	20.9
Sweaters	24.2
Activewear	25.2
Casual Slacks	19.5
Jeans	8.4
Jackets & Heavy Outerwear	25.6
Coordinated Leisurewear	20.4
Total Men's Sportswear	21.7
Men's Furnishings	
Dress Shirts	12.8
Neckwear	11.9
Hosiery	6.0
Men's Belts	5.4
Men's Accessories	8.7
Underwear	5.3
Sleepwear	8.7
Men's Headwear	15.1
Total Men's Furnishings	10.8

Thus, a buyer who anticipates a 20 percent markdown rate for the season must price goods at an initial markup of 50 percent to maintain a 40 percent markup. Though the above formula is preferable because of its simplicity, any of the formulas from which it was derived may be used to calculate an initial markup. Either dollars or percentages can be used in the computation. Note that net sales is always 100 percent when using percentages in the computation.

Computing an Initial Retail Price

Converting an initial markup percentage to a retail price requires the use of a simple formula based on a cost complement, the difference between the initial markup percentage and 100 percent, and the wholesale cost of the item being priced:

$$retail\ price = \frac{cost}{100\% - initial\ markup\ \%}$$

Assume that a buyer sees an interesting item at a trade show priced at $12.50. The buyer needs to retail goods at a 55 percent initial markup to achieve a desired maintained markup for the department. The buyer calculates the retail price of the $12.50 item at a 55 percent markup as follows:

$$retail\ price = \frac{cost}{100\% - initial\ markup\ \%}$$

$$retail\ price = \frac{\$12.50}{1.0 - 0.55}$$

$$retail\ price = \frac{\$12.50}{0.45}$$

$$retail\ price = \$27.78$$

The retail price of a $12.50 item at a 55 percent markup is $27.78. For the sake of simplicity and a little extra markup, odd-ending prices are typically rounded up to the nearest zero-ending price ($27.80) or whole dollar price ($28.00).

PROMOTIONAL PRICING

A promotional price is a discounted price that is less than a conventional or regular price. Once the hallmark of discounters, promotional pricing has become an important element in the merchandising strategies of many department and specialty stores. Promotional pricing is often linked to one of the advertised events discussed in Chapter 5.

Retailers conduct price promotions to:

- Generate customer traffic.
- Stimulate sales during a slow selling period.
- Induce the sale of related nonpromotional merchandise.
- Engage in competitive pricing with other retailers.
- Establish an image as a value-oriented retailer.

Price changes require book inventory adjustments to maintain the balance between book and physical inventory values. Because promotional prices are temporary, they require two adjustments: markdowns at the beginning of a promotion, and markups at the end of a promotion.

SOURCE
Teceschi, B. (September 2, 2002). Scientifically priced retail goods. *New York Times.*

SCIENTIFIC PRICING

Like all retailers, Saks Fifth Avenue faces the problem of deciding when to mark down, and how much without discounting so early that the company sells out of the merchandise too soon, or so late that the stores look like museums for unwanted merchandise. There is a high-tech solution to this age-old dilemma. Price optimization software helps merchants to make pricing decisions more scientifically and less by gut instinct. Spotlight Solutions is a Cincinnati software vendor that developed the price optimization software that Saks uses to set different prices in different stores or regions. The software analyzes sales data from past years as well as the current selling season, then determines which goods to mark down to what price at which stores and then delivers its recommendations to merchandising managers over the Internet. The software system also suggests the timing of the markdowns. It works on the assumption that Saks can achieve a better average sale price across all of its stores with discounts at different times in different places. The software system has been partly responsible for improving Saks' gross margins and inventory position. It is estimated that price optimization technology has the potential to improve gross margin by 10 percent. The technology is also used by companies that do not mark down goods, such as supermarkets. By tweaking prices and adjusting for demand, merchants use the software to anticipate profits and plan sales and inventory accordingly.

Computerized price lookup (PLU) technology has facilitated this process. PLU involves maintaining a system file of every stock-keeping unit (SKU) in inventory and a corresponding retail price. When the SKU is identified at point of sale by a number or bar code, the system "looks up" the price and transmits it to a cash register display or monitor while processing the transaction at the looked-up price. The prices in the file can be changed to promotional prices for promotional events, eliminating the need for a physical count of inventory before or after the promotion. Preparing for a promotional event merely involves identifying promoted merchandise with the appropriate signage indicating that the reduction will be taken at the register. This permits retailers to increase the frequency of promotions by reducing the stock handling costs associated with event preparation and recovery. A PLU system also allows more rigid price control by preventing salespeople from discounting nonpromotional items.

Everyday Low Pricing

Though promotional events produce immediate sales results, their long-term effect is questionable. Frequent promotions encourage customers to wait for sales and to buy only at promotional prices. Because promotional goods carry lower markup, this can be devastating to gross margin and net income. An intense promotional schedule also may cause customers to question the "real" price of goods, assuming that retailers cover promotional markdowns with inflated markups. One study showed that three-quarters of consumers believed that department stores intentionally inflated prices so that their promotional markdowns appear to be more significant.

Everyday low pricing (EDLP) is a value-oriented pricing strategy involving continuous promotional pricing without the support of advertised events. Everyday low prices are either a retailer's lowest promotional price, or a price between the retailer's highest regular price and lowest promotional price. EDLP facilitates inventory management since product demand is more stable when not driven by sporadic sales. The lower gross margins associated with EDLP strategy are often offset by reduced advertising expenses, as well as reduced labor expenses, since fewer floor moves are required for sale setup and recovery. EDLP is a shopping advantage for customers too busy to chase promotions.

EDLP is fundamental to the warehouse club concept and to the success of discounters such as Wal-Mart and Toys "R" Us, both of which have employed an EDLP strategy since their inception. However, EDLP has not been successful for every retailer. Sears once closed its stores for two days to retag every piece of merchandise with permanently reduced prices. A year later, Sears abandoned EDLP because sales increases were not significant enough to offset the decreases in gross margin. Feeling that their customers enjoy the excitement of promotional events, Target combines its EDLP program with advertised promotions.

FIGURE 12.3
Wal-Mart's claim of "Always Low Prices" avoids the use of the superlative "lowest."

DECEPTIVE PRICING

The Federal Trade Commission (FTC) is a regulatory agency that prevents unfair competition in the marketplace by protecting consumers from abuses such as constraint of trade and deceptive advertising. The FTC issues guidelines that prescribe standards of conduct for various industry segments, including retailers. In addition to FTC guidelines, each state has specific statutes that govern retail trade practices. Because laws vary by state, retailers that conduct business in several states often ensure compliance to the statutes in all states by conforming to the guidelines of the most stringent state. To avoid embarrassment and/or penalty, retailers should be familiar with topics governed by various forms of protective legislation.

Regular Price Comparisons   A stated reduction from an original or regular price is a common form of price promotion. However, the strategy is legitimate only if the promoted items are offered at regular price for a sufficient period of time. That "sufficient period of time" varies by state. One state attorney general's office offers the following guidelines for determining the legitimacy of a regular price comparison:

- At least 25 percent of the goods were sold at the regular price during the previous six months, or
- The goods were offered at the regular price for at least 70 percent of the time during the previous six months. This allows approximately 55 promotional days in a six-month period, or ten promotional days a month.

A nonpromotional price should be effected within a reasonable amount of time after a promotion has ended, and it should be maintained for a sufficient amount of time thereafter. One state attorney general's office recommends effecting the regular price within 60 days after the end of a promotion and maintaining the regular price for a minimum of 90 days.

If criteria such as these are not met, it may be determined that a promotional price is, in fact, the regular price and that promoting the goods as a "sale" is a deceptive practice. A Colorado appeals court upheld the state attorney general's allegations that advertising by one department store chain was deceptive and that the company had no intention of selling some of its advertised goods at regular price.

In general, regular price comparisons should be genuine and not based on exaggerated prices. A retailer should not cushion high promotional markdowns with an excessively high initial markup that exceeds the initial markup customarily taken on the item or merchandise category.

Comparisons to Competitors' Prices   Price comparisons to competitors' offerings must be for identical merchandise. Comparing one style or grade of merchandise to another style or grade is deceptive.

Lowest Price A retailer must validate a lowest price claim with proof of the customary prices of competitors, a difficult substantiation when competitors have frequent price promotions. Wal-Mart's claim of "Always low prices" avoids the use of the superlative "lowest" for this reason.

Free Merchandise   Retailers sometimes offer customers free merchandise, frequently on condition of a purchase. Advertising for this type of promotion often reads:

- "Buy one, get one free"
- "One-cent sale"
- "Two-for-one sale"
- "Gift with purchase"

In general, the offer of free merchandise must be temporary; otherwise, the "gift" becomes part of the retailer's everyday offerings. Also, raising the regular price of the required purchase to cover the cost of the free merchandise is a deceptive practice.

Going Out of Business   A company should not be established with the intent of going out of business to have a liquidation sale. Many states ensure adherence to this principle by requiring that a business operate for a minimum time period, such as a year, before conducting a going-out-of-business sale (GOB).

A GOB must be validated by a planned cessation of business. The sale inventory should not be salted with lower-quality goods at higher than normal markup that appear to be part of the regular inventory. States ensure adherence to this guideline by requiring a complete list of inventory on hand at the point at which a going-out-of-business notice is filed.

Bait and Switch   Promoting an item as *bait* to lure customers into a store to sell them a higher-margin item is illegal. Retailers guilty of bait and switch have even penalized salespeople who sold the advertised merchandise instead of a substitute. To avoid bait-and-switch implications, retailers should have a sufficient quantity of advertised promotional merchandise on hand to meet anticipated demand, unless the advertisement discloses the number of items available or states "while supply lasts." A key factor in determining the existence of bait and switch is the number of times that an item was advertised compared to the number of times it was actually sold.

The Raincheck Rule   The Federal Trade Commission's *Unavailability Rule* or *Raincheck Rule* is a guide for handling cases of out-of-stock advertised merchandise. The guide suggests that retailers:

- Issue a raincheck that will allow customers to buy the advertised merchandise at a later date at the sale price.
- Offer substitute merchandise of comparable value to the promoted item.
- Offer a compensation that is at least equal in value to the reduction on the promoted merchandise.

FIGURE 12.4
Retailers sometimes offer customers free merchandise on condition of purchase. Courtesy of Bloomingdale's.

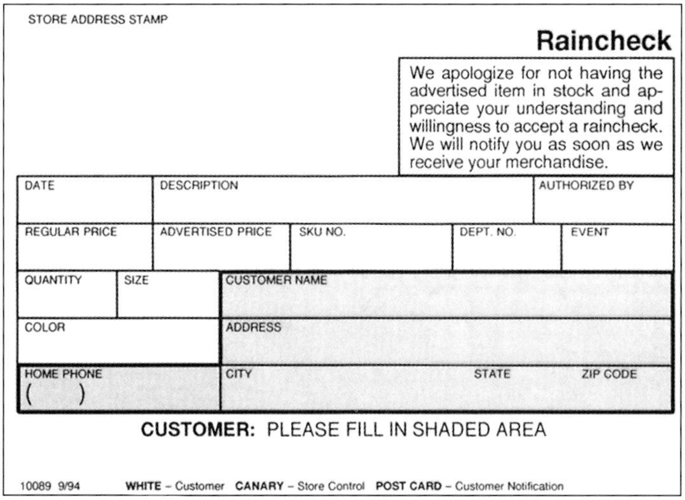

FIGURE 12.5
A raincheck allows a
customer to buy out-of-
stock advertised
merchandise at sale price
at a later date.

Predatory Pricing   Some states have antitrust laws that prohibit predatory pricing, a low-price strategy designed to put competitors out of business. Small independent retailers claim that large retailers engage in predatory pricing when they sell loss leaders, goods priced below cost. Volume discounts enable large retailers to sell an item at a price that is often lower than the wholesale price charged the small retailer. Wal-Mart was found guilty of violating the Arkansas Unfair Practice Act and was ordered to pay nearly $300,000 in punitive damages to three Arkansas pharmacies for selling some 200 items ranging from prescription drugs to cosmetics below cost.

RESALE PRICE MAINTENANCE

Resale price maintenance (RPM), or vertical price fixing, is the practice whereby producers enforce the sale of their products at a prescribed manufacturer's suggested retail price (MSRP). The Miller Tidings Act (1936) permitted the practice of fair trade to insulate small independent retailers from price competition with large chains that paid lower wholesale prices because of quantity discounts. Fair trade allegedly sheltered the image of a product in that a consumer's perception of a product's quality is often tied to its retail price. Fair trade was highly criticized by discounters and consumer advocacy groups as a form of price fixing and a violation of the Sherman Antitrust Act of 1890, which prohibits constraint of trade. In 1975, the Consumer Goods Pricing Act made RPM and fair trade illegal.

The definition of *price fixing* is ambiguous, leading some to conclude that certain industry practices constitute illegal acts. A manufacturer can choose to channel its products to retailers on the basis of service, training, warranties, and repair and thus refuse to sell to discounters that offer limited service. Upon the complaint of a retailer that a competitor is failing to maintain suggested price levels, a supplier can cut shipment to the price cutter, as long as the supplier does not coerce the discounter to sell

at a suggested price. Producers can also structure their cooperative advertisement agreements around a minimum advertised price (MAP) to make
retailers that sell below the MAP ineligible for cooperative advertising
dollars.

The most aggressive opponents of RPM are discount retailers who claim
that RPM is contrary to the free market system and that consumers have
the right to buy products at competitive prices through multiple retail channels. Manufacturers of prestige products support RPM because they fear
that their products will lose their cachet in consumers' eyes if discounted
by mass merchandisers. These suppliers fear that the conventional retail

SOURCE
Mohl, B. (May 14, 2006).
For BJ's, ignoring item
pricing is a bargain. *The
Boston Globe*.

WHEN IGNORING A PRICING LAW IS A BARGAIN

BJ's Wholesale Club finds it cheaper to ignore an item-pricing law in Massachusetts than comply with it. The law, enacted under the Consumer Protection Act in the 1970s, requires prices to be on all items offered for sale to the public. For failing to comply, the Massachusetts-based BJ's paid $49,000 in fines one year. But for a retailer that reported a profit of $128 million that same year, $49,000 was insignifi-cant, and much less than the cost of complying with the item-pricing law, which could cost each store $150,000 to $300,000 a year. BJ's operates 18 stores in Massachusetts, so its item-pricing costs would far exceed $49,000.

Advocates of the item-pricing law say that con-sumers value item pricing because it makes it easier to check a price, comparison shop, and verify a register receipt. Retailers say putting the price on the shelf next to the item is sufficient, that item pricing drives up prices, and thus the benefits to consumers are not worth the cost. In 1986, supermarkets grum-bled that the item-pricing regulation was onerous and

sought a number of exemptions. The result was a separate item-pricing law for food stores that exempted milk, eggs, and several other types of prod-ucts. The Massachusetts Division of Standards was given the power to enforce the law with fines.

In 2002, Home Depot settled a class-action lawsuit over item pricing by paying a $3.8 million fine, with half of the money going to lawyers, and half going to nonprofit groups. The settlement spurred many more lawsuits, including one against BJ's. The lawsuits got the attention of retailers. The retailers pressured the state's attorney general to revise the original item-pricing regulation so that nonfood retailers could avoid marking prices on individual items in their stores as long as they installed scan-ners every 5000 square feet, allowing consumers to check prices themselves. The amended regulation dropped the provision about offering prices on items for sale, so BJ's found itself covered by two item-pricing laws: one for its food items, and one for its nonfood items.

channels will discontinue their product lines sooner than engage in price competition with discounters.

Supreme Court rulings and the prevailing political climates have influenced the enforcement of price-fixing legislation by the Justice Department's Antitrust Division and the Federal Trade Commission's Bureau of Competition. The Stride Rite Corporation once paid $7.2 million in

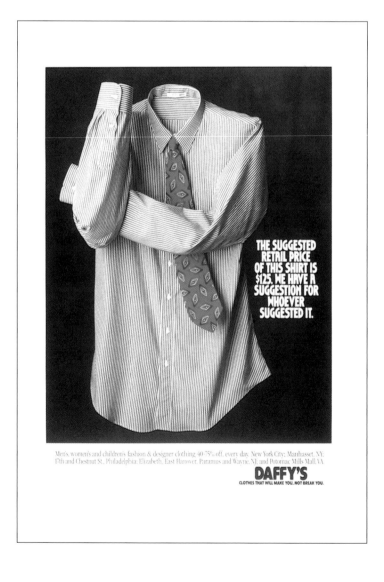

FIGURE 12.6
Daffy's is positioned as a price leader in the greater New York metropolitan area. Devito/Verdi.

damages to settle a price-fixing suit brought by the attorneys general of 50 states and the Federal Trade Commission. Stride Rite had threatened to stop supplying its most popular Keds sneaker styles to retailers that discounted prices. The company was found guilty of price conspiracy when it encouraged retailers to report competitors' price cutting. In a similar situation, Reebok International once paid a $9.5 million settlement for threatening to terminate shipment to retailers that violated Reebok's pricing policy.

PRICING: A SCIENCE AND AN ART

Pricing has been called a science and an art. As a science, price is a quantitative decision based on the numeric relationships among various pricing components. As an art, price is a qualitative decision based on intuition and creativity. The following two scenarios demonstrate the nonquantitative considerations that surround pricing decisions.

Right Price, Wrong Customer A menswear buyer came across a well-styled and constructed, nicely fabricated dress shirt during a market visit. The buyer perceived the shirt as an exceptionally good value at a $20 wholesale cost but realized that the shirt needed to be priced at $45 retail to meet the department's maintained markup objective. Because the store's customers have historically resisted shirts priced higher than $35, the buyer is faced with a dilemma. If the shirts are retailed at $45, they are not likely to sell. If the shirts are retailed at $35, they are likely to sell, but the department's maintained markup expectations will not be met. The decision is clear. The buyer must pass up the shirts and continue the quest for goods that will allow a retail price consistent with customers' price expectations and the store's profit objectives.

No Easy Answer A buyer has computed an initial markup percentage objective for the handbag department but realizes that the figure is not an immediate answer to every pricing decision. Factors relative to the type of goods, accepted pricing standards, and competition bear considerable weight on the pricing of individual classes or items as the following considerations for pricing four groups of handbags demonstrates. The four groups are Coach, a seasonal straw and canvas group, a private label group, and an assortment of handcrafted novelty evening bags.

- The pricing of Coach is restricted by the fact that the prestigious line is heavily branded and sold by other stores in the shopping center.
- The prices for the seasonal bags must include a generous provision for seasonal markdowns.
- The private label goods afford considerable pricing flexibility and healthy markup opportunity, since customers have no basis for price comparisons.
- Similarly, handcrafted evening bags afford considerable pricing latitude as blind items, goods for which consumers have no frame of reference, because of the absence of brand identity and/or infrequent purchase.

SUMMARY POINTS

- Retail prices must be high enough to cover profit objectives but low enough to stimulate customer purchase.
- A retail price has two components: cost and markup. Markup is expressed as a percentage of the retail price.
- The various types of markup include initial markup, additional markup, and cumulative markup.
- Markdowns are downward adjustments in retail prices. Four categories of reductions include damaged merchandise, employee discounts, clearance markdowns, and promotional markdowns.
- Clearance markdowns are permanent reductions used to liquidate residual merchandise and slow sellers.
- Maintained markup is the difference between the cost of merchandise and the actual selling price.
- Tactical price changes involve a strategy for manipulating markup and markdown within a tactical price zone.
- A retail price can be computed when a desired markup and cost are known.
- Promotional markdowns are temporary reductions for sale events.
- Everyday low pricing is a value-oriented pricing strategy that eliminates the need for extensive promotional advertising.
- Each state has guidelines for valid price referencing to avoid deceptive pricing.
- Resale price maintenance (RPM) is the control of retail prices by a supplier. RPM is illegal under certain circumstances.

KEY TERMS AND CONCEPTS

additional mark-down	everyday low pricing (EDLP)	permanent mark-down
additional markup	fair trade	predatory pricing
bait and switch	initial markup	price lookup (PLU)
blind item	loss leader	promotional mark-down
broken assortments	maintained markup	
clearance mark-down	manufacturer's suggested retail price	raincheck
cost	markdown	regular price
cost complement	markdown cancellation	resale price maintenance (RPM)
cumulative markup	markup	retail price
damage markdown	markup cancellation	seasonal merchandise
discontinued goods	minimum advertised price	tactical price change
employee discount		temporary markdown

THINKING ABOUT IT

1. What goods have the potential to become "residual" or "slow selling"? Fashion? Basic? Seasonal? Nonseasonal? What can be done to minimize the clearance markdowns taken on these goods?

2. A hosiery buyer is writing orders for two groups of cotton socks. One group is an assortment of basic colors. The other group is a holiday assortment with Christmas tree and snowman motifs. The buyer wants to generate the same maintained markup percentage from each group. Which group will require a higher initial markup and why?

3. A furniture retailer operates stores in California, Maine, and Georgia. Most of the retailer's resources ship from High Point, North Carolina. Which stores will require the highest markup if the retailer wants to generate equal maintained markup from all stores? What workroom costs might have to be considered in the computation of initial markup?

4. Compare the promotional pricing strategies of several retailers within different retail formats. What differences and similarities do you note in terms of promotion frequency, advertising vehicles, and the types of merchandise promoted? Compare the promotional pricing strategies of several retailers within the same format. What differences and similarities do you note?

TEAMING UP

1. As a team, search for industry standards for markdowns for various categories of merchandise and/or types of stores. Discuss the differences among the categories/types of stores. To what do you attribute the differences?

2. Each member of a team should shop the markdowns within a selling area in a department store to determine the ratio of promotional markdowns to clearance markdowns, and the likely reasons for the latter. As a team, compare shopping experiences and determine which departments/merchandise categories are most vulnerable to nonpromotional markdowns and the reasons why.

SEARCHING THE NET

1. Search online for recent news coverage of a retailer found guilty of illegal pricing practices. What was the offense? What were the consequences? Do you agree with the judgment?

2. Find a trade publication article on managing markdowns in a retail store. What are the recommendations?

3. Search online for mention of EDLP in any publication. Does this strategy work for some retailers? When does it seem not to work?

SOLVING PROBLEMS

1. Complete the following grid:

Cost	Markup	Retail	Percentage of Retail Markup	Percentage of Cost Markup
$88.00		$108.00		
	$1.29	$3.87		
$2,386.27		$3,800.00		
$4.78				48.2%
		$4.00	48.2%	
	$3.29		64.5%	
	$4.62			158%
		$0.39	78.2%	
		$5.00		100%

Round percentages to one decimal place, and dollars to two decimal places.

2. What is the cumulative markup percent on three groups of towels when 100 towels are bought at $10.00; 200 towels are bought at $11.50; and 300 towels are bought at $12.00? Each towel retails at $20.00.

3. What is the markdown price of a $20 item that has been marked down 35 percent? What is the price when a 20 percent markdown is taken on the markdown price? What is the price when a 20 percent markdown is taken on the second markdown price? What is the price when the item is marked 50 percent off the original price? Seventy-five percent off?

4. Complete the following grid:

Original Retail	Markdown Percent	Marked Down Retail	Units Marked Down	Total Markdown Dollars
$20.00	25%		645	
	35%	$17.55	249	
$22.50		$16.88	98	
$3,999.00	20%		5	
$0.49		$0.44	1,649	
	50%	$9.99	20	

Round percentages to one decimal place; round dollars to two decimal places. Markdown percent is a percentage of retail.

5. Compute maintained markup when:

- Gross margin is $50,000
- Workroom costs are $2,000
- Cash discounts are $3,000

6. Compute a maintained markup percent when a $35 (cost) item originally retails at $80.00 and:

- 50 sell at regular price.
- 29 sell at 25 percent off regular price.
- 15 sell at 50 percent off regular price.
- 5 sell at 75 percent off regular price.
- 1 is stolen.

7. Complete the following grid:

Cost	Maintained Markup Objective	Anticipated Markdowns	Initial Markup Percent	Initial Retail Price
$5.00	55%	20%		
$0.43	63.2%	0%		
$347	28%	5%		
$3.39	42%	48.2%		
$7.50	47.5%	2%		

USING EXCEL

1. Create a spreadsheet to compute markup as a percentage of cost and markup as a percentage of retail for ten items when cost and retail are known. Compute total markup figures for all ten items.

2. Create a spreadsheet to compute a cumulative markup for varying quantities of ten items when the cost of each item is known, and when the retail price for each item is the same.

3. Create a spreadsheet to compute markdown dollars for ten items when retail and markdown percent are known. Compute total markdown dollars and a total markdown percent.

4. Create a spreadsheet to compute the maintained markup percent on an item when cost and initial markup dollars are known, and varying quantities of the item are sold at the original price, and at various markdown prices.

5. Create a spreadsheet to compute a retail price when a maintained markup objective, anticipated markdowns, and cost are known.

CHAPTER THIRTEEN

Planning Sales and Inventory

After reading this chapter, you will be able to discuss:

● The importance of planning in a retail organization.

● Sales planning and the relevance of sales plans to other organizational plans.

● Inventory planning methods.

● Assortment planning.

● Resources of information for planning decisions.

Planning involves establishing an organization's goals or objectives and strategies to achieve them. The planning process often includes forecasting, the attempt to predict trends or outcomes. Planning occurs at all organizational levels and is critical to a company's success. The absence of planning has been likened to taking a trip without a road map. Chapter 13 covers sales planning and inventory planning, two forecasting functions that are germane to the merchandising function of a retail organization.

TYPES OF PLANS

Plans are categorized by the time period that they cover. A long-range plan covers a three- to five-year period or longer. Developed by top management, long-range plans have significant impact on an organization and include strategies for expansion, market position, and major capital expenditures. A short-term plan covers periods shorter than a year. Developed by lower-level managers, short-term plans are narrower in scope than long-range plans. Schedules and budgets are two common forms of short-term plans.

Plans are categorized by their point of origin and the direction that they travel within a table of organization. A top-down plan originates at the upper levels of an organization and affects planning at lower levels. For instance, the top management of a retail organization may project a corporate sales objective for the forthcoming year. The sales plan is then broken down by merchandise division. Sales are then planned for each department within the division. Buyers and planners then determine the categories, vendors, and items that will best support departmental sales plans and, ultimately, the organization's sales goal.

A bottom-up plan is developed at lower levels of the organization as a building block of an organization-wide plan. An organizational sales objective based on the sum total of plans developed at departmental level would reflect bottom-up planning. Most organizations combine top-down and bottom-up planning, recognizing that planning is a two-way street that requires input at every managerial level.

THE 4–5–4 PLANNING CALENDAR

The 4–5–4 calendar is an accounting calendar universally adopted by retailers. The calendar is called 4–5–4 because each month has exactly four weeks (28 days) or five weeks (35 days). Months are chronologically arranged in a 4-week month, 5-week month, 4-week month sequence. Within the 4–5–4 calendar, four months have five weeks: March, June, September, and December. The remaining eight months have four weeks. The beginning and end of a month on the 4–5–4 calendar do not necessarily coincide with the beginning and end of the same month on a conventional Gregorian calendar. Note that in Figure 13.1, June begins on May 31and ends on July 4.

The 4–5–4 calendar has two six-month seasons: spring, which runs from February through July, and fall, which runs from August through January. The weeks of a month on the 4–5–4 calendar are referred to ordinally. In Figure 13.1, April 5 through April 11 is the first week of April, or Week 1 of April. A year on the 4–5–4 calendar has 364 days and exactly 52 weeks. The

FIGURE 13.1
The 4-5-4 calendar is an accounting calendar used by retailers to structure their fiscal year.

Gregorian calendar has 365 days and 52 weeks and a day. Thus, an additional week is added to January in the 4–5–4 calendar every five or six years to account for this extra day and for the 366th day of leap years. The nearly universal adoption of the 4–5–4 calendar has ensured that everyone is "on the same page" when referring to time periods such as "the last week of December." The one-calendar concept enhances communication within the retailing industry and between retailers and their suppliers.

PLANNING STRUCTURES

Retailers structure their merchandising organizations by product line. Divisions, departments, classifications, and subclasses are the building blocks that retailers use to create pyramid-like hierarchies to define units of business and organizational responsibilities. Divisions, departments, classifications, and subclasses are defined by product line. Divisions are the most broadly defined unit. Subclasses are the most narrowly defined unit. In Figure 13.2, the men's division of Dolan's Department Store is organized into five departments: basics, furnishings, sportswear, collections, and clothing. The men's basics department is grouped into four classifications: underwear, hosiery, pajamas, and robes. Though not indicated in Figure 13.2, the men's underwear classification might be further divided into subclasses such as briefs, boxers, and T-shirts.

Item (shirts) and vendor (Perry Ellis) are the most common designations for departments, classifications, and subclasses. Brand-driven business units, such as fashion apparel and cosmetics, are typically identified by vendor. Other designations are based on:

- Price range (moderate)
- Size range (junior)
- End use (sportswear)
- Lifestyle (active)
- Selling season (holiday)
- Product composition/fabrication (brass/silk)
- Customer (female)

Multiple designations are often combined to create a single business unit identity such as "misses better sportswear." Designations need not be consistent from one business unit to another. A store may identify high-fashion

FIGURE 13.2
A system of departments
and classes for the men's
division in a retail store.

handbags by vendor (Coach and Dooney & Bourke) and less fashion-oriented handbags by fabrication (leather, vinyl, fabric, straw) or style (evening, shoulder, clutch, briefcase, satchel). Business unit identities within a retail organization often parallel those of the wholesale market. A *housewares* buyer buys for a *housewares* department at a *housewares* market.

There are no universal standards for structuring a merchandise hierarchy. Knit shirts may be a department in the men's sportswear division in one retail organization and a subclass of the men's sportswear classification in another retail organization. In general, merchandise hierarchies in large retail organizations have a greater number of precisely defined business units than the merchandise hierarchies of small retail organizations. A large organization's knit shirt volume is high enough to stand alone as a department, whereas a small organization's knit shirt volume is not. Assortment diversity affects the number of units within a hierarchy. A department with a few homogeneous products has fewer classifications than a department with many heterogeneous products.

Business unit hierarchies are used as a basis for planning and tracking sales and inventory. Each defined unit must represent enough sales volume to warrant being planned and tracked separately. Defining merchandising hierarchies by division, department, classification, and subclass is a common but not universal practice within the retail industry. Some retailers use closely related terms such as *category* or *product group*. One major retailer groups merchandise into fine departments and major departments.

PLANNING SALES

Sales planning is a critically important function in a retail organization in that expense plans, inventory purchases, and profit objectives are all predicated upon plan sales. A store's seasonal selling payroll budget is based on projected sales. Planning sales too low will result in an understaffed store, while planning sales too high will result in an overstaffed store. Sales plans also drive inventory purchases. Sales plans that are too high will yield an overstocked condition and poor turnover; sales plans that are too low will yield an understocked condition and lost sales. Sales plans often include growth strategies for cultivating additional business through new items, vendors, and categories.

Retailers look to the past and present to predict future sales. Last year's sales are often used as a base for planning this year's sales, anticipating that recurring conditions and events that drove sales last year will drive them again this year. Examples include seasonal weather conditions that stimulate the sale of swimwear, lawn furniture, wool coats, and boots, and annual gift-giving occasions, such as Valentine's Day, Father's Day, and Christmas, that drive sales of chocolates, shirts and ties, and toys.

The past sales upon which future sales are projected must be comparable. Easter may fall as early as late March or as late as the end of April. Sales for the week prior to Easter last year are comparable to sales for the week prior to Easter this year, even though the weeks may fall in different months. Changes in back-to-school dates (based on when Labor Day falls), a store's promotional calendar, and the number of days between Thanksgiving and Christmas are other factors that must be considered when determining comparable, or "comp," sales. Business units must also be comparable. A "12 percent sales increase over last year for comparable stores" implies that a comparison is being made between stores that were open for business this year and last year, and that new stores opened since last year and/or stores closed since last year are not included in the comparison.

Historical sales used as a planning base should be typical of the period. Last year's cold-weather accessories sales for November are an invalid reference for projecting this November's sales if last November was atypically warm. Using last year's sales to project this year's sales will yield an understocked condition if this November's weather is typical of the season. When there is no historical reference point on which to project sales, as in the case of a new store or a new category of merchandise or vendor, the sales history of a similar business unit is often used until a history is developed.

Current trends are valid predictors of future sales in that recent trends are chronologically closer to the future than the distant past. Assume that it is fall and that a planner is using information from a trailing nine months sales report to project sales for a sportswear line for the forthcoming spring season (see Table 13.1). The planner's immediate reaction is to base this spring's plan on last spring's sales with a modest increase to reflect higher wholesale prices. However, the planner notices that last spring's sales were relatively flat, but that impressive gains have been posted since the beginning of the current season. The planner decides to plan more aggressively, interpreting the current sales trends as an indicator that the line is garnering a loyal following.

Innumerable internal and external factors influence an organization's sales plans. A store's decision to become more upscale will be supported by aggressive sales plans for better goods and modest sales plans for moderate goods. Economic conditions, such as inflation, interest rates, and the general state of the economy, are also evaluated for their potential impact on sales. Slumps in housing construction reduce demand for window treatments. The impact of economic factors varies by type of goods and customer profile. Sales of trendy fashion goods are affected more dramatically by negative economic conditions than sales of functional items, such as refrigerators. The spending patterns of lower-income groups are more sensitive to economic shifts than those of upper-income groups.

TABLE 13.1   TRAILING NINE MONTHS SALES REPORT

Month	Plan	Actual	Percent +/−
February	$ 18,000	$ 18,218	+1%
March	$ 24,000	$ 24,676	+3%
April	$ 28,000	$ 28,795	+3%
May	$ 40,000	$ 41,446	+4%
June	$ 20,000	$ 21,267	+6%
July	$ 15,000	$ 15,311	+2%
August	$ 25,000	$ 27,428	+10%
September	$ 30,000	$ 34,654	+16%
October	$ 35,000	$ 42,659	+21%
TOTAL	$235,000	$254,454	+8%

Demographic shifts, fashion trends, and changes in competition impact a retail organization's sales plans. A decline in the teenage population during the 1980s led to downsized junior departments. However, a blossoming teenage population in the 1990s caused many retailers to recapture the junior business with aggressive sales plans and larger inventory commitments. Fashion trends impact sales. A shift toward casual dress in the workplace will have a negative effect on the sale of men's ties and women's hosiery, but a positive impact on the sale of men's twill pants and female sportswear. Changes in competition affect sales plans. The addition of complementary stores in a shopping area may increase customer traffic and positively impact sales, while new direct competition will have a negative impact on sales.

Unpredictable and uncontrollable factors make sales planning an inexact process. When Sunglass Hut International executives chided the company's managers for lackluster sales and profit in their more than 1,500 stores, the only retort was cloudy skies.[1] Though objective indicators such as current sales trends and inflation are used to project sales, determining the impact of these indicators as well their interaction is often a best guess. Will a manufacturer's price increase induce customers to explore substitute brands? How much will new competition impact sales? For how long? The best plans are the flexible ones that allow for the unforeseen circumstances that might affect them.

PLANNING INVENTORY

Attaining a sales objective is contingent upon having sufficient inventory to support the plan. However, having too much inventory poses problems such as slow turnover and high clearance markdowns. Inventories must be strategically planned so that sales objectives are met with minimum inventory investments.

A buyer's purchase and delivery decisions are predicated on inventory projections based on the interaction of two factors: plan sales and desired turnover. To understand the relationship of plan sales and turnover to purchase and delivery decisions, recall the jeweler from Chapter 9 who sold 600 watches a year. The jeweler found that purchasing 600 watches at the beginning of the year resulted in an annual turnover of 2.0. The jeweler determined limiting purchases to 50 watches each month would increase turnover to 13.0.

Buyer	DIV MGR	GEN MGR	DEPT

6-MONTH MERCHANDISING PLAN FOR PERIOD FROM .... TO .... YEAR ....

STORE NO.

ACT LY	PLANNED THIS YEAR	ACT TY	NET SALES		FEB/AUG	MAR/SEP	APR/OCT	MAY/NOV	JUN/DEC	JUL/JAN
	NET SALES		LAST YEAR							
	AV MO STOCK		PLAN							
	STOCK TURN		THIS YEAR							
	MARK DN %		EOM STOCK	JAN/JUL	FEB/AUG	MAR/SEP	APR/OCT	MAY/NOV	JUN/DEC	JUL/JAN
	GROSS MARG		ACT LY							
	MAINT M/U		PLAN TY							
			ACT TY							
			MD LY							
			MD TY							

STORE NO.

ACT LY	PLANNED THIS YEAR	ACT TY	NET SALES		FEB/AUG	MAR/SEP	APR/OCT	MAY/NOV	JUN/DEC	JUL/JAN
	NET SALES		LAST YEAR							
	AV MO STOCK		PLAN							
	STOCK TURN		THIS YEAR							
	MARK DN %		EOM STOCK	JAN/JUL	FEB/AUG	MAR/SEP	APR/OCT	MAY/NOV	JUN/DEC	JUL/JAN
	GROSS MARG		ACT LY							
	MAINT M/U		PLAN TY							
			ACT TY							
			MD LY							
			MD TY							

STORE NO.

ACT LY	PLANNED THIS YEAR	ACT TY	NET SALES		FEB/AUG	MAR/SEP	APR/OCT	MAY/NOV	JUN/DEC	JUL/JAN
	NET SALES		LAST YEAR							
	AV MO STOCK		PLAN							
	STOCK TURN		THIS YEAR							
	MARK DN %		EOM STOCK	JAN/JUL	FEB/AUG	MAR/SEP	APR/OCT	MAY/NOV	JUN/DEC	JUL/JAN
	GROSS MARG		ACT LY							
	MAINT M/U		PLAN TY							
			ACT TY							
			MD LY							
			MD TY							

STORE NO.

ACT LY	PLANNED THIS YEAR	ACT TY	NET SALES		FEB/AUG	MAR/SEP	APR/OCT	MAY/NOV	JUN/DEC	JUL/JAN
	NET SALES		LAST YEAR							
	AV MO STOCK		PLAN							
	STOCK TURN		THIS YEAR							
	MARK DN %		EOM STOCK	JAN/JUL	FEB/AUG	MAR/SEP	APR/OCT	MAY/NOV	JUN/DEC	JUL/JAN
	GROSS MARG		ACT LY							
	MAINT M/U		PLAN TY							
			ACT TY							
			MD LY							
			MD TY							

STORE NO.

ACT LY	PLANNED THIS YEAR	ACT TY	NET SALES		FEB/AUG	MAR/SEP	APR/OCT	MAY/NOV	JUN/DEC	JUL/JAN
	NET SALES		LAST YEAR							
	AV MO STOCK		PLAN							
	STOCK TURN		THIS YEAR							
	MARK DN %		EOM STOCK	JAN/JUL	FEB/AUG	MAR/SEP	APR/OCT	MAY/NOV	JUN/DEC	JUL/JAN
	GROSS MARG		ACT LY							
	MAINT M/U		PLAN TY							
			ACT TY							
			MD LY							
			MD TY							

FIGURE 13.3
A six-month merchandising plan.

Five methods of planning inventory are presented in this chapter:

- Basic stock method
- Percentage variation method
- Stock-to-sales ratio method
- Weeks-of-supply method
- Formula for replenishment of staple merchandise

All five formulas combine sales projections and some variation of turnover to determine the amount of inventory needed to achieve a desired sales goal for a certain time period.

Basic Stock Method The basic stock method asserts that a beginning-of-month (BOM) inventory should be equal to the plan sales for the month plus a basic inventory. The basic stock method formula is:

$$BOM \ = \ plan \ monthly \ sales \ + \ (average \ inventory \ - \ average \ monthly \ sales)$$

The following example demonstrates using the basic stock method to plan the BOMs for a year for a store with a monthly sales plan as indicated in Table 13.2 and a desired turnover of 4.0.

Average inventory is computed by dividing annual sales by turnover.

$$turnover \ = \ \frac{sales}{average \ inventory}$$

$$4.0 \ = \ \frac{\$720,000}{average \ inventory}$$

$$average \ inventory \ = \ \$180,000$$

Average monthly sales is computed by dividing annual sales by 12:

$$average \ monthly \ sales \ = \ \frac{annual \ sales}{12}$$

$$average \ monthly \ sales \ = \ \frac{\$720,000}{12}$$

$$average \ monthly \ sales \ = \ \$60,000$$

The difference between average inventory and average monthly sales is the basic inventory.

basic inventory = *average inventory* − *average monthly sales*
basic inventory = $180,000 − $60,000
basic inventory = $120,000

The basic inventory is added to each month's planned sales to compute BOM. The results are tabulated in Table 13.3.

When turnover is 12.0 the average monthly sales and the average inventory will be equal in the basic stock method. The basic stock will be zero, and BOM will always equal plan sales. When turnover is greater than 12.0, the average monthly sales will be greater than the average inventory. The basic stock will be a negative number, and BOM will be less than plan sales. Thus, the basic stock method can only be used when turnover is less than 12.0. The method can be adapted to a six-month or three-month planning period by using the desired turnover for the period and computing average monthly sales based on either three or six months.

TABLE 13.2 PLAN SALES FOR A YEAR

Month	Plan Sales
February	$ 30,000
March	$ 60,000
April	$ 90,000
May	$ 60,000
June	$ 60,000
July	$ 30,000
August	$ 30,000
September	$ 60,000
October	$ 60,000
November	$ 90,000
December	$120,000
January	$ 30,000
TOTAL	$720,000

TABLE 13.3   PLAN SALES AND BOMS FOR A YEAR USING
THE BASIC STOCK METHOD

Month	Plan Sales	Plan BOM Inventory
February	$ 30,000	$150,000
March	$ 60,000	$180,000
April	$ 90,000	$210,000
May	$ 60,000	$180,000
June	$ 60,000	$180,000
July	$ 30,000	$150,000
August	$ 30,000	$150,000
September	$ 60,000	$180,000
October	$ 60,000	$180,000
November	$ 90,000	$210,000
December	$120,000	$240,000
January	$ 30,000	$150,000

Percentage Variation Method   The percentage variation method asserts that a BOM should be a percentage of average inventory. The percentage will vary each month based on plan sales. The percentage variation method formula is:

$$BOM = average\ inventory \times 0.5 \left(1 + \frac{plan\ sales\ for\ the\ month}{average\ monthly\ sales} \right)$$

The following applies the percentage variation method to the data in Table 13.2. The calculation of the BOM for February is:

$$BOM = \$180,000 \times 0.5 \left(1 + \frac{\$30,000}{\$60,000} \right)$$

$$BOM = \$180,000 \times 0.5\ (1 + 0.5)$$

$$BOM = \$180,000 \times 0.75$$

$$BOM = \$135,000$$

Table 13.4 lists BOMs for a year computed by the percentage variation method. Note that when plan sales are equal to average monthly sales, the BOM is equal to the average inventory. When plan sales are less than average

TABLE 13.4   PLAN SALES AND BOMs FOR A YEAR USING THE
PERCENTAGE VARIATION METHOD

Month	Plan Sales	Plan BOM Inventory
February	$ 30,000	$135,000
March	$ 60,000	$180,000
April	$ 90,000	$225,000
May	$ 60,000	$180,000
June	$ 60,000	$180,000
July	$ 30,000	$135,000
August	$ 30,000	$135,000
September	$ 60,000	$180,000
October	$ 60,000	$180,000
November	$ 90,000	$225,000
December	$120,000	$270,000
January	$ 30,000	$135,000

monthly sales, the BOM is less than the average inventory. When plan sales are greater than average monthly sales, the BOM is greater than average inventory. Thus, an average sales plan will require an average inventory as a BOM. A lower than average sales plan will require a BOM less than average inventory. A higher than average sales plan will require a BOM greater than average inventory.

Though the basic stock method is simpler than the percentage variation method the latter is more sensitive to fluctuations in plan sales. Table 13.5 compares the BOMs generated from both methods. Note that the range between the highest and lowest BOM in the percentage variation method ($135,000) is greater than the range between the highest and lowest BOM in the basic stock method ($90,000). The percentage variation method yields higher BOMs than the basic stock method when sales plans are high and lower BOMs than the basic stock method when sales plans are low.

Stock-to-Sales-Ratio Method The BOMs generated by the stock-to-sales-ratio method are based on a desired stock-to-sales ratio for a month. The stock-to-sales-ratio method formula is:

TABLE 13.5   A COMPARISON OF BOMS USING THE BASIC STOCK
             METHOD AND THE PERCENTAGE VARIATION METHOD

Month	Plan Sales	BOM-Basic Stock Method	BOM-Percentage Variation Method
March	$ 60,000	$ 180,000	$ 180,000
April	$ 90,000	$ 210,000	$ 225,000
May	$ 60,000	$ 180,000	$ 180,000
June	$ 60,000	$ 180,000	$ 180,000
July	$ 30,000	$ 150,000	$ 135,000
August	$ 30,000	$ 150,000	$ 135,000
September	$ 60,000	$ 180,000	$ 180,000
October	$ 60,000	$ 180,000	$ 180,000
November	$ 90,000	$ 210,000	$ 225,000
December	$120,000	$ 240,000	$ 270,000
January	$ 30,000	$ 150,000	$ 135,000
February	$ 30,000	$ 150,000	$ 135,000
TOTAL	$720,000	$2,160,000	$2,160,000

$$BOM = plan\ sales \times desired\ stock\text{-}to\text{-}sales\ ratio$$

If a desired stock-to-sales ratio is 3.0 and plan sales are $8,000, the BOM is computed as follows:

$$BOM = \$8,000 \times 3.0$$
$$BOM = \$24,000$$

Recall from Chapter 9 that peak selling periods require lower stock-to-sales ratios than slow selling periods. To demonstrate this principle, the BOMs generated by the percentage variation method were divided by plan sales to calculate the stock-to-sales ratios for each month. The results are tabulated in Table 13.6.

Note that months with high sales plans have low stock-to-sales ratios, while months with low sales plans have high stock-to-sales ratios. Therefore, the stock-to-sales ratios used in the stock-to-sales-ratio method should vary relative to the sales volume each month. The stock-to-sales-ratio method is inappropriately applied when an annualized stock-to-sales ratio is used to

TABLE 13.6   PLAN SALES AND BOMS USING THE STOCK-TO-SALES RATIO METHOD

Month	Plan Sales	S/S Ratio	BOM
January	$ 30,000	4.5	$ 135,000
February	$ 30,000	4.5	$ 135,000
March	$ 60,000	3.0	$ 180,000
April	$ 90,000	2.5	$ 225,000
May	$ 60,000	3.0	$ 180,000
June	$ 60,000	3.0	$ 180,000
July	$ 30,000	4.5	$ 135,000
August	$ 30,000	4.5	$ 135,000
September	$ 60,000	3.0	$ 180,000
October	$ 60,000	3.0	$ 180,000
November	$ 90,000	2.5	$ 225,000
December	$120,000	2.3	$ 270,000
TOTAL	$720,000	3.0	$2,160,000

plan each month's BOM. A range of stock-to-sales ratios should be used unless there is little sales fluctuation from month to month.

Weeks-of-Supply Method   The three inventory planning methods covered thus far assume that inventories are planned by month. However, fast-turning inventories are planned for shorter periods because fast-turning goods require more frequent replenishment than slow-turning goods.

The weeks-of-supply method asserts that the amount of inventory required to support plan sales for a week is driven by the number of weeks that the inventory will last based on a projected turnover. The weeks-of-supply formula is:

$$weeks\ of\ supply\ =\ \frac{52}{turnover}$$

If the desired turnover is 6.0, then weeks of supply is calculated as follows:

$$weeks\ of\ supply\ =\ \frac{52}{6.0}$$

$$weeks\ of\ supply\ =\ 8.7$$

An implication of the formula is that at any point throughout the year a buyer must have enough inventory on hand to support 8.7 weeks of sales if he or she intends to achieve an annual turnover of 6.0. A further implication is that to achieve a certain sales objective, a buyer needs enough inventory to last 8.7 weeks. Therefore, the formula for projecting an inventory based on the weeks-of-supply method is:

$$plan\ inventory\ =\ plan\ sales \times\ weeks\ of\ supply$$

If plan sales for a week are $5,000 and weeks of supply is 8.7, then:

$$plan\ inventory\ =\ plan\ sales \times\ weeks\ of\ supply$$
$$plan\ inventory\ =\ \$5,000 \times\ 8.7$$
$$plan\ inventory\ =\ \$43,500$$

Based on a 6.0 turnover, the amount of inventory required to support a sales plan of $5,000 is $43,500. Note that as turnover increases, weeks of supply decreases and that as turnover decreases, weeks of supply increases. The weeks-of-supply numerator is adjusted accordingly when turnover for a period other than a year is used in the computation. The numerator would be 26 if turnover were for a half year. The weeks' supply method is best applied when sales are relatively stable.

Weeks of supply, or *weeks' supply*, is frequently used to evaluate inventory levels. In this case, weeks' supply is an indicator of the number of days an inventory will last if sold at a current rate of sale. The higher the weeks' supply, the longer the inventory will last and the slower it will turn. Thus, weeks' supply can be used as an indicator of too much or too little inventory.

The weeks-of-supply concept has many derivations. Days of supply, or *days' supply*, is a close cousin of weeks' supply. Days' supply is the number of days an inventory will last if sold at a current rate of sale. Some stores use a *weekly percent sell* as a weeks-of-supply indicator. The weekly percent sell is the percent of stock on hand that will sell in one week at a current rate of sale. The higher the percentage, the faster the inventory will turn. (See Table 13.7.)

TABLE 13.7　WEEKS OF SUPPLY AND WEEKLY PERCENT
SELL FOR VARIOUS TURNOVER RATES

Annual Turnover	Six-Month Turnover	Weeks of Supply	Weekly % Sell
12.0	6.0	4	23
11.0	5.5	5	21
10.0	5.0	5	19
9.0	4.5	6	17
8.0	4.0	7	15
7.0	3.5	7	13
6.0	3.0	9	12
5.5	2.75	9	11
5.0	2.5	10	10
4.5	2.25	12	9
4.0	2.0	13	8
3.5	1.75	15	7
3.0	1.5	17	6
2.5	1.25	21	5
2.0	1.0	26	4

Formula for Periodic Replenishment of Staple Merchandise　The formula for periodic replenishment of staple merchandise asserts that staples should be replenished based on the amount of units sold during a typical selling period, the time lapse between the arrival of reorders, and a safety, or reserve, stock. The formula for the periodic replenishment of staples is:

$$M = (RP + DP)\,S + R$$

- M (maximum) is the amount of inventory needed for the period.
- RP (reorder period) is the time period that defines the frequency with which orders are placed.
- DP (delivery period) is the time period between the point at which an order is placed and the point at which the goods are available for sale.
- S (rate of sale) is the number of units that are typically sold during the reorder period.
- R (reserve stock) is additional stock to avoid stockouts if sales exceed plan. The formula for reserve stock is $2.3\sqrt{(LT)S}$, where LT (lead time) is the sum of RP and DP.

The following demonstrates using the formula to replenish goods ordered biweekly and delivered in a week, in a store that sells 100 items per week.

$$M = (RP + DP)S + R$$

$$M = (2\ weeks + 1\ week) \times 100\ units\ per\ week + R$$

$$R = 2.3\sqrt{(2\ weeks + 1\ week) \times 100\ units\ per\ week}$$

$$R = 40$$

$$M = 300 + 40$$

$$M = 340$$

OPEN TO BUY

Open to buy is the amount of merchandise that a buyer needs to order to support plan sales for a period. Open to buy is derived from plan purchases. Plan purchases are based on the:

- Amount of inventory brought forward from the previous period (BOM)
- Plan sales for the period
- Amount of inventory that must be rolled over to the next period (EOM)
- Plan markdowns for the period[2]

The formula for plan purchases is:

$$\begin{array}{r} plan\ sales\ for\ month \\ +\ \ plan\ markdowns \\ +\ \ plan\ EOM \\ -\ \ plan\ BOM \\ \hline plan\ purchases \end{array}$$

Open to buy is the difference between plan purchases and merchandise on-order. The formula for open to buy is:

$$\begin{array}{r} plan\ purchases \\ -\ \ on\ order \\ \hline open\ to\ buy \end{array}$$

			(a.) SALES	-SALES	-SALES	-SALES	-SALES	-SALES	-SALES	-SALES	-SALES
(a1.)	APR		PERIOD PLN	13.9	10.6	21.6	27.9	12.2	11.5	17.9	2.7
(a2.)	MAR		PTD TY	17.4	13.0	32.3	27.3	18.9	14.6	19.8	3.0
(a3.)			LY	19.4	14.9	25.3	29.0	15.0	14.0	21.6	3.1
(a4.)	MAR TY-LY		%CHG	-7.7	-12.8	58.6	-5.9	26.0	4.3	-8.3	-3.2
(a5.)	YR TD BOP		MAR TY	12.3	12.0	23.1	19.1	10.2	9.8	13.9	2.3
(a6.)			LY	12.4	9.5	8.5	15.0	8.1	6.5	9.9	1.6
(a7.)	YR TY-LY		%CHG	-0.5	26.3	171.8	27.3	25.9	50.8	40.4	43.8
(b.)			STOCK	STK	STK	STK	STK	STK	STK	STK	STK
(b1.)	MAR AUDIT		OH BOP	62.6	65.0	74.8	80.2	58.4	47.6	71.0	23.5
(b2.)	MAR -MEMO-BNJ		BOP	23.1	5.9	17.0	14.9	4.9	7.2	10.0	1.1
(b3.)	MAR NET RCPTS		PTD	37.5	34.2	60.0	76.8	50.1	36.3	53.1	14.3
(b4.)	MAR TRANSFERS		IN	0.2	0.8	12.1	2.4	0.3	1.0	3.1	0.2
(b5.)			OUT	-3.2	-5.4	-0.7	-2.4	-5.8	-2.6	-5.6	-0.2
(b6.)	LAST WK ON HND		TY	81.8	82.4	105.1	126.3	72.1	64.8	92.4	32.9
(b7.)	APR BOP STOCK		PLN	95.3	49.4	86.0	77.0	47.9	59.8	67.8	15.2
(b8.)	THIS WK ON HND		TY	88.0	81.6	114.0	129.7	84.1	67.7	101.8	34.8
(b9.)			LY	108.7	57.8	104.3	89.2	54.9	67.5	79.8	17.3
(b10.)	TY-LY		%CHG	-20.7	23.8	9.7	40.5	29.2	0.2	22.0	17.5
(b11.)	MAY BOP STOCK		PLN	105.5	51.4	91.2	77.2	51.7	56.4	70.0	18.0
(c.)	OUTSTANDING		OTB	OUTST	OUTST	OUTST	OUTST	OUTST	OUTST	OUTST	OUTST
	MAR		OUTST	1.6	6.3	19.3	12.1	4.8	11.7	15.8	8.6
	APR		OUTST	34.9	16.8	22.7	21.3	5.1	17.1	20.0	9.4
	MAY		OUTST	14.0	11.5	17.5	17.5	13.0	10.1	14.7	7.0
(c1.)	JUN		OUTST								
(c2.)	AFTER JUN		OUTST								
(d.)	APR OP-TO-BUY		BAL	-3.6	-42.1	-41.5	-54.7	-28.4	-27.4	-43.9	-32.1
(e.)			MARKUP								
(e1.)	FEB		ACT %	47.2	47.1	48.4	51.1	47.1	46.9	47.1	47.3
(e2.)	FEB		PLAN %								
(e3.)	MMU—SEAS TD		TY								
(e4.)	BOP MAR		LY								
(f.)			MARKDOWNS	MKD	MKD	MKD	MKD	MKD	MKD	MKD	MKD
(f1.)	MAR		PTD								
(f2.)	MAR		PLN	0.9	0.8	1.3	1.0	0.9	1.2	1.0	0.4
(f3.)	YR TD BOP MAR		TY$	0.2	0.2	1.0	0.4	0.4	0.5	0.4	0.1
			TY%	1.6	1.7	4.3	2.1	3.9	5.1	2.9	4.3
				DEPT	DEPT	DEPT	DEPT	DEPT	DEPT	DEPT	DEPT
				04-02-	04-02-	04-02-	04-02-	04-02-	04-02-	04-02-	04-02-

━ JARROD & YOUNG ━

FIGURE 13.4
An open-to-buy report.

Open to buy can be likened to a checkbook balance. Plan purchases are like a beginning checkbook balance. Placing an order is like writing a check. The buyer begins each month with a new balance. The balance decreases as the buyer writes orders. A buyer with "no open to buy" has a zero open to buy balance. A buyer who has exhausted one month's open to buy can write orders against the next month's open to buy. A buyer "bought up through March" can place orders against April's open to buy.

cathy®   **by Cathy Guisewite**

A buyer is "overbought" when on-order exceeds plan purchases, a condition comparable to an overdrawn checking account. Some buyers overbuy anticipating that some orders will be short shipped or not shipped at all. Order cancellation is the most common remedy for an overbought condition. Like sales, open to buy is planned at various organizational levels such as department and classification.

Discrepancies between plan and actual sales necessitate frequent open to buy adjustments. Poor sales for a month will increase the EOM carried into the subsequent month (BOM), necessitating a reduction in open to buy. Favorable sales will decrease the EOM carried into the subsequent month, necessitating an increase in open to buy. Failure to adjust open to buy as needed will result in overinventoried or underinventoried conditions. Open to buy can be expressed as dollars or units.

Like open to buy, open to ship is a figure that defines inventory needs. Merchandise allocators use open to ship to determine the type and amount of merchandise to ship to stores from a distribution center. Open to ship is the difference between a store's projected inventory needs and inventory on hand.

ASSORTMENT PLANNING

Plan purchases is the amount of inventory that needs to be bought to support a sales goal. However, this *right amount* of inventory is only the first step in determining the *right* inventory. Plan purchases must be translated into an assortment plan that defines the goods by product characteristics. The characteristics most used to plan assortments include the following.

BRAND	CLASS.	Pre-Pack	Make Up	Open Stock	RETAIL PRICE RANGE	ORDER MINIMUM	UPC CODE	E.D.I. READY	Narrow	Medium	Wide	Extra Widths
A'MANO	D	•	•	•	$35-600	12	•	•	4-12	4-12	4-12	
Accessoire Diffusion	D, C, B, HB		•		$145-300	60				4-12		
Accessory Group Inc.,Clip-Ons	AC		•	•	$4-12	4						
Acme	B			•	$80-150	None	•	•	6-9	5-10		
Adirondack Collection	C, S, AC		•		$40-75	12	•	•		5-11 full sizes		
Aerosoles - Women	C, B, S	•	•	•	$30-60	None	•	•	7.5-9	5-12		
Alfie's Original Souliers	D, C, B		•		$49-79	12				5-12		
Allure	D, C, B	•	•	•	$60-120	72	•	•	5-10	4-12	6-10	
Amalfi	D, C	•	•	•	$79-150	12	•	•	5-12	4-12	4-10	4A-C
Amante	D, C		•		$60-125	500			4-12	4-12	4-12	
American Eagle	D, C, B	•		•	$20-70	12	•	•		5-11		
Amiana (For Women)	D, S		•		$100-200	36		•	5-10	4-11		
Amour By Pepe Jimenez	D	•	•	•	$60-125	None			6-11	3.5-12		S
André Assous	C, B	•	•		$22-200	12			7-9	4-11		
Andrea Cecconi	D, C		•		$115-250	12				5-11		
Andrea Pfister S.R.L.	D, B, AC, HB		•		$200-450	100				36-40		
Ann-Marino	D, C	•		•	$38-90	12	•	•	7-9	5.5-11		
Anne Jordan	D, C	•			$40-80	12				5-12	7-10	
Anne Klein	D, C, B	•	•		$120-240	108		•	7-10	4-10		
Anne Klein II	D, C, B	•	•	•	$80-145	108		•	7-10	4-10		
Aqua-Talia By Bootlegger	B		•		$80-120	36				5-11		
Arche	C, B, HB		•		$145-210	100				5-12		
Atsco/Private Labels	D, C, B, AC,S	•	•	•	$20-150	None			4-12	4-12	4-12	XW
Auditions	D, C, B			•	$40-100	None	•		5-11,12,13	5-12,13	5-12,13	SS-WW

Abbreviations & Symbols: Classifications: **D** - Dress Shoes / **C** - Casuals / **B** - Boots / **AT** - Athletics / **S** - Slippers / **SV** - Service Footwear
AC - Accessories / **HB** - Handbags / **LG** - Leather Goods / **AP** - Apparel / **SC** - Shoe Care Products
• – Available

FIGURE 13.6
Buyers use vendor profiles such as this to plan shoe assortments by style, price, and size. Provided by Fashion Footwear Association of New York (FFANY).

Price   The price range of an assortment is defined by its opening, or lowest, price-point and its ending, or highest, price point. An assortment can be planned with multiple price ranges. For instance, a gift shop might define its assortments within three price categories:

· Gifts under $10
· Gifts between $10 and $100
· Gifts over $100

Assortments are sometimes characterized by more general pricing terms, such as *moderate* or *better*. An assortment's price range must be consistent with a store's image and target customer. Thousand-dollar dresses at Sears and washable polyester suits at Brooks Brothers are inconsistent with each store's image and customer. There is no consistent

JARROD & YOUNG

A. SUB-CLASSIFICATION	Sub-Classification	% to Stock	Open-to-Buy in $
	Straight line	20	20,000
	Side pleat	20	20,000
	A-line	15	15,000
	Wrap	15	15,000
	Trouser	15	15,000
	Full	5	5,000
	Dirndl	10	10,000
		100%	$100,000 (OTB share)

B. PRICES	Price Range	% to Stock
	$130.00	5
	120.00	10
	100.00	30
	80.00	30
	75.00	15
	65.00	10
		100%

C. COLORS	Colors	% to Stock
	Gray heather	10
	Navy	10
	Black	25
	Brown	10
	Red	10
	Taupe	15
	Novelty	20
		100%

D. SIZES	Sizes	% to Stock
	4	8
	6	16
	8	25
	10	25
	12	18
	14	8
	16	–
	18	–
	20	–
		100%

E. FABRICS	Fabrics	% to Stock
	Wool/gabardine and/or crepe	25
	Wool/flannel	40
	Wool/silk	10
	Poly/wool	20
	Acrylic/rayon	5
		100%

FIGURE 13.7
Assortments can be planned as percentages of total inventory by factors such as price, color, size, and fabric.

method for defining assortment by price. One store may consider leather handbags as better and vinyl handbags as moderate. Another store may include low-end leathers in its moderate assortment, and high-end vinyls in its better assortment.

Brand   Sometimes assortments are planned by brand. A department store may define its cosmetics assortment as Estée Lauder, Clinique, Chanel, Lancôme, Origins, and so on. Like price, the brands within an assortment must be consistent with a store's image. Within the context of planning an assortment by brand, buyers also consider private labels. Buyers often seek private label substitutes for basic items with weak brand identity, since private label goods generate more gross margin than branded goods. However, the mix of private labels and brands must be carefully balanced. An extensive choice of brands is often an assortment feature that draws many customers to a store, especially for brand-driven purchases.

Size   Because sized merchandise seldom sells in equal quantities, buyers must be careful to plan assortments according to the sizes in greatest demand. An end-of-season clearance rack with a disproportionate number of *smalls* often is indicative of an overabundance of one size and lost sales to customers seeking other sizes. Suppliers often recommend size distributions based on historical sales records. Shoe manufacturers pack individual shoe styles in case lots, called size runs, that include specific size assortments.

Color   Though assortments are not often planned by specific colors such as "blue," color categories, such as basic, fashion, or neutral, often are used as a basis for planning assortments. A men's dress-shirt assortment may be planned as solids and fancies.

Fabrication   Sometimes fabric is an important assortment distinction. Silk is an important assortment characteristic in women's dresses and men's neckties. A men's dress-shirt assortment may be planned as cottons and blends (of polyester and cotton). A sweater assortment might be planned as wool, cotton, and acrylic.

Style   The style or look of product may determine its significance in an assortment. A sweater assortment may be defined as:

- Crew neck
- Cardigan
- Vest

A dress assortment may be planned as casual and special occasion. Some assortments are planned by item. Assortments of small leather goods include key chains, wallets, checkbooks, and change purses. Items are sometimes identified as classifications or subclasses within department/class structures.

Assortment plans vary by month and season. Cotton sweaters give way to wool sweaters as seasons change. Lacy teddies become an important women's sleepwear item in February for Valentine's Day. The demand for table linens surges just before Thanksgiving. A full-line discounter reports of planning large inventories of cup hooks in November to respond to a demand by customers who use them to hang holiday lights. Assortment plans are also linked to a store's promotional calendar. A storewide Anniversary Sale requires extensive quantities of goods with broad appeal that can be promotionally priced.

Buyers constantly review their assortment to ensure that they are satisfying customers' needs and, in turn, the store's sales objectives. For instance, buyers replace lackluster brands with brands that show promise of being better investments of inventory and space. Naturally, profit objectives must also be considered. The brands that generate the most sales are not necessarily the most productive in terms of gross margin. Some of the best-selling brands sell only at promotional prices. These brands are good volume generators but poor gross margin producers.

Factors external to the organization, such as fashion and economic trends, impact assortment plans. Strapless dresses becoming fashionable

ASSORTMENT PLAN			
	Store A	Store B	Store C
Bath & Body	360	720	720
Gift Sets	240	300	336
Accessories	72	114	216
Candles	72	96	96
Soaps	72	144	216
Total Units	816	1374	1584

FIGURE 13.8
A unit assortment plan for body care products provided by a vendor.

will encourage an innerwear buyer to maintain a selection of strapless bras. During trying economic times, buyers will slant assortments toward basic practical items at the expense of trendy frivolous items. One fabric mill reports that black velvet special occasion dresses become very popular during poor economic times because of their fashion durability. Assortment plans are driven by a store's merchandising objectives. A desire to upgrade a store's image will affect the selection of price and brand. A desire for exclusivity will influence the selection of brands and styles.

Recall from Chapter 2 that assortments are characterized by depth and breadth and that there is often a trade-off between the two. A store with a wide assortment of cosmetics brands limits the amount of space that can be dedicated to the selection within each line. By discontinuing brands, the store will free up space for greater depth within the lines that are retained. In general, narrow and deep assortments are more desirable than broad and shallow assortments. It is better to carry full assortments of a few product lines than piecy assortments of many product lines. A selection is *overassorted* when it has too much breadth and too little depth. Exclusive specialty shops are an exception to this generalization where uniqueness is a fundamental assortment characteristic.

Assortment plans can be quantified by units, dollars, or percentages. An assortment of small, medium, large, and extra-large knits may be planned in a unit ratio of 2:3:2:1. A misses sportswear assortment may be planned as 40 percent better and 60 percent moderate. The assortment of a men's collections department may be 50 percent Polo, 25 percent Tommy Hilfiger, and 25 percent Claiborne.

Trends in Planning

Because planning involves the interaction of so many inexact variables, efforts have been made to computerize functions with the hope of making the process more precise. Computerized planning systems have facilitated the planning of assortments by individual SKU and store. "What if" capabilities allow planners to observe instantly the effect of adjusting various planning variables. Because tedious calculations are eliminated, planners devote more time to analytical functions, and less time to computational functions. Computerized planning also integrates plans from various organizational levels to ensure a match between financial and merchandise plans, bottom-up and top-down plans, and unit and dollar plans.

Category management involves managing a product category as if it were a separate business entity, such as a store or department. Category management is a customer-driven concept that uses planning technology and historical sales data to develop ideal space allocation and assortments by store. Some observers warn of the dangers of category management in that only the highest turning and highest margin goods are retained in assortments at the expense of core products that may not be profitable but are popular with consumers. Critics also fear that running a store as a collection of disjointed businesses will disrupt the store's cohesiveness and sales synergy.

Though computerized planning systems have become common, even in small retail organizations, an understanding of manual systems is fundamental to understanding automated systems, since computerized systems are based on the same theoretical constructs as manual systems.

FIGURE 13.9
Consumer magazines are sources of information on current fashion trends.

PLANNING INFORMATION

Planning involves integrating information from a diverse group of sources. Information on a store's sales history, current sales trends, and inventory status is obtained from internal organizational sources. However, information pertaining to fashion trends, market conditions, and the status of competitors must be obtained from sources external to the organization. The following is a discussion of several external information sources often tapped by retailers, including consumer publications, trade publications, trade associations, forecasting services, and reporting services.

Consumer publications are magazines and newspapers available to the public at newsstands. Targeted to clearly defined market niches, the editorial content of consumer publications provides retailers with insight into the lifestyles, tastes, and needs of specific market segments. Fashion magazines such as *Vogue, Mademoiselle,* and *GQ* are sources of information on current fashion trends for women and men. Newspapers such as the *Wall Street Journal,* and magazines such as *BusinessWeek, Fortune,* and *Forbes,* offer timely information on the general business climate.

Trade publications are targeted to members of a specific industry segment. They feature editorials, business analyses, and information on the current status of major industry players, new products, and governmental legislation relative to the industry. Trade publication advertising provides retailers with information on merchandise resources, trade shows, and trade services. Trade publications often conduct studies of interest to their readership.

Fairchild Publications is the leading source of apparel industry publications including *Women's Wear Daily* (*WWD*), for the women's apparel industry; *Daily News Record* (*DNR*), for the textile and men's apparel industries; and *Home Furnishings Network* (*HFN*) for the home furnishings and accessories industries. Buyer's guides are supplements to *HFN* that cover specific merchandise categories. A typical buyer's guide includes sections such as:

- *State of the Market*: Statistics on a category's growth potential, major resources, and market share by retail channel of distribution
- *Products Inside and Out*: Information on materials and production processes, and glossaries of terms related to the product
- *Merchandising the Category*: Suggestions for pricing, promoting, and presenting the category

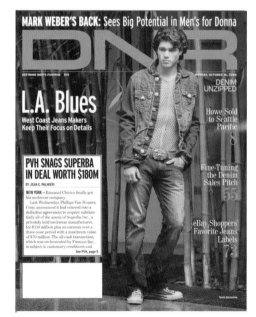

Other timely sources of information on retailers and their suppliers include *Retailing Today* and *Chain Store Age*, both put out by Lebhar-Friedman, a publisher of retailing periodicals, newsletters, and directories. Trade publications are often targeted to specific product categories. *Gifts & Decorative Accessories* is a monthly publication for gifts, tabletop, gourmet, home accessories, greeting cards, and stationery published by Reed Business Information, a publisher of more than 80 business-to-business publications. All of the aforementioned consumer and trade publications are available online, some without charge.

Trade associations represent the interests of a particular industry segment. Supported by dues-paying members, trade associations promote goodwill, lobby before legislatures, conduct research, produce trade shows, sponsor conferences, and publish newsletters. The largest trade associations for retailers include the National Retail Federation (NRF), the Retail Industry Leaders Association (RILA), and the International Council of Shopping Centers (ICSC). Some trade associations represent narrow segments of the retail industry such as the National Association of Men's Sportswear Buyers (NAMSB) and the Apparel Retailers Association.

Trade associations for manufacturers are authoritative sources of information on the product lines marketed by their members. The American Apparel and Footwear Association represents the interests of apparel, footwear, and other sewn-products companies. The 600-member Cosmetics, Toiletry, and Fragrance Association (CTFA) has two membership levels. Active members are the manufacturers and distributors of personal care products. Associate members are suppliers of ingredients, raw materials, packaging, and services used in the production and marketing of personal care products, and the publishers of consumer and trade publications.

Forecasting services study history and prevailing socioeconomic and market conditions to predict trends in advance of a selling season. The Color Association of the United States (CAUS) and Intercolor are color forecasting services subscribed to by fiber, textile, and apparel producers, and retailers that develop their own private label merchandise. Reporting services survey and analyze specific industry segments, reporting their findings to service subscribers. The *Tobe Report* is a heavily illustrated fashion report that dates back to 1927. The report is a merchandising guide for apparel retailers used to identify the hottest fashion trends and merchandise resources. Johnson's

FIGURE 13.11
Consultants are professional advisors who offer their expertise to retailers on a contractual fee basis. Source: www.doyleandassociates. com.

Redbook Service is a reporting service that tracks trends in retail sales and the economy to predict changes in consumer spending.

Other Information Sources

Suppliers often provide retailers product information and market studies designed to support the sale of their product. Though the information is biased, it is free and readily available. Consultants are advisers who offer expertise, analyze issues, or resolve problems on a contractual fee basis. Barnard's Consulting Group is a retail forecasting and consulting firm that performs market analyses, develops marketing strategies, and conducts seminars for retailers in the United States and Europe. Local, state, and federal governments are reli-

able sources of information on population, consumer spending, and economic conditions. The *Census of Retail Trade: Area Statistics* is a document prepared by the federal government that is very useful to retailers.

Academic institutions are other sources of information. The Center for Retailing Studies (CRS) at Texas A&M University is a corporately sponsored organization, which sponsors an annual symposium for retailing executives and professors who teach and conduct research in retailing. In conjunction with the Zale Corporation, the CRS co-publishes the *Retailing Issues Letter*, a bimonthly essay on critical issues facing retailers. Academic publications available at college and university libraries, such as the *Journal of Retailing* and *Journal of Marketing*, are other sources of helpful information. The American Collegiate Retailing Association and the International Textiles and Apparel Association are professional associations of college professors, many of whom conduct and publish scholarly research on merchandising topics.

FIGURE 13.12
The Center for Retailing Studies at Texas A&M University sponsors symposiums for retailing executives and professors who teach and conduct research in retailing. Reprinted with permission. Copyright © 2006 Center for Retailing Studies, Department of Marketing, Texas A&M University, College Station, Texas. All rights reserved.

SUMMARY POINTS

- Planning involves establishing an organization's goals or objectives and the strategies to achieve them.
- The 4–5–4 calendar is an accounting calendar used by retailers to structure their fiscal year.
- Divisions, departments, classifications, and subclasses define related groups of merchandise as manageable units of businesses.
- Sales plans are based on history and the current trends that may impact future sales.
- The attainment of sales objectives is contingent upon having a sufficient amount of inventory to support plan sales. Inventory planning methods are based on plan sales and a desired turnover objective.
- Open to buy is the amount of inventory that needs to be purchased for a specific selling period.

- Merchandise assortments are planned by brand, size, price, color, style, lifestyle, and various other factors.
- External information sources include consumer publications, trade publications, trade associations, forecasting services, and reporting services.

KEY TERMS AND CONCEPTS

basic stock method	forecasting	reporting service
bottom-up plan	forecasting service	short-term plan
category management	4–5–4 calendar	spring
classification	method	stock-to-sales-ratio
comparable	long-range plan	method
consultant	opening price point	subclass
consumer publication	open to buy	top-down plan
days-of-supply method	open to ship	trade association
department	percentage variation	trade publication
division	method	weeks-of-supply
ending price point	planning	method
fall	plan purchases	

THINKING ABOUT IT

1. Develop a structure of departments, classes, and subclasses for the following merchandise. Justify each segmentation as a unit of business:

   - Intimate apparel
   - Ready-to-wear
   - Home division
   - Accessories
   - Children's

2. Make a list of cyclical factors that affect the sale of apparel. Classify each relative to their reliability as a predictor. Explain how the impact of these factors will vary by category of merchandise.

3. Make a list of current economic, demographic, lifestyle, and fashion trends that should be considered when planning sales for a forthcoming season for the following departments:

- Cosmetics
- Activewear
- Infants and toddlers
- China and crystal

4. What problems do you perceive in a sales planning method that is exclusively top down? Exclusively bottom up?

5. Structure an assortment plan for the following:

- An assortment by vendor of prestige cosmetics lines for a department store by percent
- An assortment by vendor of mass market cosmetics lines for a full-line discounter by percent
- A size-and-color assortment for 2,500 wool, crew-neck sweaters available in S/M/L/XL, in ecru, navy, burgundy, black, and gray
- An item assortment for a fine jewelry case featuring onyx
- A knit/woven, size assortment of 5,000 junior tops in S/M/L
- A style, color, and size assortment of a major brand of blue jeans

TEAMING UP 1.   Each member of your team should pick an annual holiday, such as Independence Day or Halloween, and determine the categories of merchandise in either a department store or full-line discount store for which the holiday provides potential for business. For instance, at a full-line discount store, Valentine's Day generates business in greeting cards, candy, crafts, intimate apparel, men's underwear, plush toys, and so on. Share the lists with one another to determine which departments are holiday dependent and which have unrealized holiday potential.

2. Each team member should shop a department within a department store or full-line discount store to determine the product characteristics by which the departments' assortments are planned. Compare lists to determine the product characteristics most likely to drive assortments.

SEARCHING THE NET

1. Search for information on sales planning systems for retail stores. What are the highlights of the various systems? What environmental variables are factored into the systems to generate sales plans?

2. Search online for informational sources, such as consumer publications, trade publications, and trade associations, for a specific category of merchandise. Create a list that a buyer for the category might use to plan assortments.

3. Search for information pertaining to planning as an organizational function. What are the various types of plans? Who does them?

SOLVING PROBLEMS

1. Complete the following grid assuming a 4.0 annual turnover:

Month	Plan Sales	BOM by the Basic Stock Method	Stock-to-Sales Ratio (Based on the BOMs generated by the Basic Stock Method)	BOM by the Percentage Variation Method	Stock-to-Sales Ratio (Based on the BOMs generated by the Percentage Variation Method)
February	$9,000				
March	$15,000				
April	$18,000				
May	$15,000				
June	$12,000				
July	$9,000				
Total Spring	$78,000				
August	$9,000				
September	$15,000				
October	$18,000				
November	$20,000				
December	$30,000				
January	$10,000				
Total Fall	$102,000				
Total Year	$180,000				

2. Complete the following grid using the weeks-of-supply method:

Plan Sales for a Week	Annual Turnover	Weeks of Supply	Inventory
$5,000	2.0		
$8,000	4.0		
$9,100	8.0		
$500	10.0		
$21,000	16.0		

3. Complete the following grid solving for R and M using the formula for the periodic replenishment of staple merchandise:

RP	DP	S	R	M
1	1	$100		
2	.5	$250		
1	2	$50		
2	3	$3,000		
4	8	$5		

4. Complete the following grid solving for open to buy using a set of BOMs from problem number 1 above (either the ones generated by basic stock method or the percentage variation method):

Month	Plan Markdowns	Plan Purchases
February	$7,000	
March	$5,000	
April	$500	
May	$1,000	
June	$2,000	
July	$6,000	
August	$5,000	
September	$1,000	
October	$500	
November	$500	
December	$1,000	
January	$3,000	

Note: Use the BOM of February as the EOM of January. A negative plan purchase figure means that the inventory brought forward from the previous month will be adequate to cover sales for the month.

USING EXCEL

1. Create a spreadsheet to compute BOMs for a six-month season using the basic stock method.
2. Create a spreadsheet to compute BOMs for a six-month season using the percentage variation method.
3. Create a spreadsheet to compute BOMs for a six-month season using the stock-to-sales ratio method.
4. Create a spreadsheet to compute weekly inventories for a month using the weeks-of-supply method.
5. Create a spreadsheet to compute M using the formula for periodic replenishment of staple merchandise.

DOLAN'S DEPARTMENT STORE

Dolan's Department Store is a simulation in which as many as 43 students can assume the role of buyer within a hypothetical department store chain. As a buyer, each is student is responsible for planning the sales, inventory, markdowns, and open to buy for a single department in a new store. Students must become intimately familiar with the merchandise in their assigned department, gathering information on categories of merchandise, brands, target customer, peak selling periods, and so on. Much of this knowledge can be derived by scrutinizing the offerings of a local department store, such as Bloomingdale's, Macy's, or Lord & Taylor. Dolan's is much like Lord & Taylor relative to store size and pricing strategy. As a regional department store, Dolan's is much like Bon-Ton and Boscov's organizationally.

A History of Dolan's Department Store

The first Dolan's Department Store opened in Providence, Rhode Island, in 1885 as Dolan's Dry Goods. By the early years of the Great Depression, the founder, John M. Dolan, had opened downtown stores in Hartford, Connecticut; Poughkeepsie, New York; and Portland, Maine. Upon Mr. Dolan's death in 1940, the stores were sold to four members of Dolan's management. To provide capital for an expansion program into strip shopping centers in the 1950s, Dolan's issued several thousand shares of stock to three other investors, giving each of the now seven owners equal ownership. In 2001, the descendents of the seven owners sold Dolan's to a venture-capitalist organization. In the past few years, Dolan's steady growth and solid performance has caught the attention of Wall Street investors. The hope is that Dolan's will go public with an IPO sometime in the next few years.

Dolan's growth has been steadily paced. In the 1950s, the company's entree into the suburbs was through strip centers in fast-growing, middle-income communities throughout New England, upstate New York, and southern New Jersey. In the 1960s, Dolan's became an anchor for some of the earliest enclosed centers in the Northeast. The company grew conservatively throughout the 1970s, haunted by double-digit inflation, an energy crisis, and a generally bad economy. During the heydays of the 1980s and 1990s, Dolan's built more new stores, this time venturing into Pennsylvania and Ohio, often moving into locations of department stores that had gone out of business. Dolan's biggest growth spurt occurred just before and immediately after 2000. This time, expansion was through the acquisition of smaller, less successful department store chains at bargain-basement prices. Presently, the Dolan's store count is at 92.

Dolan's annual sales volume is approximately $3 billion. Dolan's stores range in size from 20,000 to 120,000 square feet. Smaller stores tend to be apparel-only. Some stores generate as little as $20 million in annual sales (a 0.7 percent penetration of the company's total business), while others attain sales volume upward of $80 million (a 2.7 percent penetration). About 25 percent of Dolan's stores are in revived strip centers, some having been there since the 1950s. The remaining 75 percent are in enclosed centers, mostly regional. Dolan's has a clearly defined market niche. Knowing better than to compete with department store behemoths, the company has strategically chosen secondary market locations not served by Federated Department Stores, or former May Department Stores. Dolan's diversity of size and location has made it adaptable to almost any market. This has been a key element in the company's success.

Dolan's merchandise mix is 75 percent upper-moderate and 25 percent better, a mix that varies by store depending on the market. Dolan's six merchandise divisions include:

Accessories	20%
Children's	10%
Home	20%
Men's	20%
Ready-to-wear	30%

Dolan's is planning to open a new store in the Crystal Mall in the shoreline community of Waterford, Connecticut. Opened in 1984, the 800,000-square-foot, two-level center is anchored by Macy's, Sears, and J.C. Penney. Dolan's will occupy a 90,000-square-foot location that opens into the mall at both levels. The store has entrances from each of the mall's two parking levels. The site is ideally located in the middle of the center in close proximity to escalators and scenic elevators. Dolan's hopes to target the upscale customer in this center by offering a mix that is 50 percent moderate and 50 percent better.

THE DOLAN'S PROJECT

The Dolan's project is a forecasting exercise in which sales, inventories, markdowns, and open to buy are planned for the new Crystal Mall store. The departments in the Crystal Mall store are listed in Dolan's Appendix A on pages 368 and 369. Dolan's divisional merchandise managers have planned annual sales for each new store department for the first year of operation. As a new store, there is no history on which to base the plans. Thus, the divisionals used last year's sales from similar-size Dolan's stores in comparable markets as a planning base. The sales plans in Dolan's Appendix A are stated in millions. Thus, $4.0 is $4 million, $.4 is $400,000, and so on. High-volume departments should not be intimidating. It takes as much effort to plan the lowest-volume department as the highest. The project has six parts. Each part builds upon the previous, so it is necessary to complete the parts in succession.

Part 1. *Develop a department/classification/subclass hierarchy.*   Recall from the beginning of this chapter that retailers create hierarchies of divisions, departments, classifications, and subclasses to define units of business, and that these business units are identified at various levels by brand, category, price, size, end use, lifestyle, selling season, product composition/fabrication, and customer. Thus, a men's sportswear department might be defined at class level by brand (Tommy Hilfiger) and at subclass level by item (sweaters).

The purpose of creating the hierarchy is to break the department down into meaningful and manageable units of business that can be planned and tracked. Business units should not be defined too minutely. For instance, it is not prudent to track every countertop appliance in the housewares department. Better to track countertop appliances by brand (Cuisinart) and general categories, such as food processors. As a rule, having five to ten classes per department and five to ten subclasses per class is about right for most departments. A department with a diverse group of products needs to be structured with more classes and subclasses than a department with a less diverse group of products. Subclasses may be repeated for multiple classes. If a misses sportswear department is broken down by brand (class) and then by item (subclass), the subclasses of sweaters, blouses, pants, jackets, and skirts can be repeated for every brand. Remember that every item in a department must fit into a class and subclass. Thus, it is wise to create a "miscellaneous" class for each department as a catchall for insignificant, low-volume generating items, as well as a "miscellaneous" subclass for each class.

Part 2. *Develop an events/promotions calendar.* Dolan's Appendix B on page 370 is a list of divisional and storewide promotional events supported corporately with newspaper advertising and direct mail. All departments participate in storewide events. All departments within a division participate in divisional events. The task involved in Dolan's Part 2 is to create departmental events calendars that incorporate all of the required storewide and divisional events, as well as department-specific events conceived of by the buyer. Examples of department-specific events include a prom dress promotion in junior dresses and a bra-fitting clinic in intimate apparel. Events can be vendor-driven, such as a gift-with-purchase Elizabeth Arden event in cosmetics, or a Liz Claiborne trunk show in better sportswear. Events can be holiday-driven, such as a table-linen promotion just before Thanksgiving, or a holiday party dress promotion at the end of December in social occasion dresses. Events should be regular price, though an occasional "25 percent off" promotion for a specific brand or category is acceptable. Plan on approximately 20 events for each department for the year, including the divisional and storewide events. Pattern the departmental events calendar after Dolan's Appendix B, listing each event, and the week(s) during which the event will run. Use the 4–5–4 planning calendar on page 326 or find the current year's 4–5–4 calendar online. Part 2 is the most creative aspect of the Dolan's project. Be daring. Think earnestly about ways to stimulate your business.

Part 3. *Plan annual sales by week.* The object of Dolan's Part 3 is to break down each department's annual sales plan into weekly sales plans. This is a multi-step process that first involves breaking the annual sales plan down by month. As a first step, consider penetration of business for all departments in all Dolan's stores by month:

February	4%	August	6%
March	7%	September	8%
April	10%	October	10%
May	6%	November	13%
June	7%	December	18%
July	6%	January	5%
Total Spring	40%	Total Fall	60%

Part 3A. *Adjust the above percentages to reflect your department's sales in all Dolan's stores.*　To do this, consider your department's peaks and valleys, both of which vary from one department to another. For instance, the china and glass department does big business during prime wedding months: May, June, September, and October. A lot of fragrances are sold for holiday gift-giving in December, and again at Valentine's Day. Dads receive an incredible number of shirts as Father's Day gifts in June. Valleys also vary by department. Swimwear sales are down during the winter months, especially in northern stores. Outerwear sales are down during summer months.

Your task is to massage the above figures to reflect sales in your department in all Dolan's stores. Rearrange the figures as you see fit. The only "right answer" is that the total of the 12 percentages equals 100. Remember to tie in the events calendar from Dolan's Part 2. Heavy promotion months will generate more business than months in which promotions are sparse.

Part 3B. *Adjust the percentages just derived for your department in all Dolan's stores to become percentages for your department in the new Dolan's store.*　To do this, consider the location of the new store. For most Dolan's stores, the customer base remains pretty static throughout the year. However, the customer base for the new Waterford store will shift dramatically by season. Because of its shoreline location, the new Dolan's store will be what is known as a resort store, patronized by a relatively small year-round customer base and also patronized by a large group of vacationing seasonal customers who tend to be big spenders. This means that percentages of business for the summer months will be higher at the Crystal Mall Dolan's than at other Dolan's stores.

To create a set of percentages for your department in the new Dolan's store, massage the Part 3A percentages with the resort-store location in mind. Many departments in the Crystal Mall Dolan's will have a higher penetration of summer business than Dolan's stores as a whole. Likewise, departments that yield a high percentage of business in all Dolan's stores in months like December will likely yield lower percentages of December business at the Crystal Mall store in that the customers are just not there. Once again, there is no precise science for determining these figures. As in Dolan's 3A, the 12 percentages in 3B must total 100.

Part 3C. *To finally break your department's sales down by week, multiply the percentages in Part 3B by your department's annual sales to come up with monthly sales for your department in the new store.* Break these monthly sales down into weekly sales using the 4–5–4 calendar, and the events calendar from Dolan's Part 2. Use Excel. The result should be 52 weekly sales figures that total back to monthly sales, which in turn total to the annual sales figure in Dolan's Appendix A.

The following is an example of how sales might be planned for a $4 million department in the Crystal Mall store:

	Week 1	Week 2	Week 3	Week 4	Week 5	Percent of Annual Plan Sales	Total Plan Sales
February	$40,000	$100,000	$10,000	$10,000		4%	$160,000
March	$25,000	$25,000	$180,000	$25,000	$25,000	7%	$280,000
April	$150,000	$150,000	$50,000	$50,000		10%	$400,000
May	$50,000	$50,000	$100,000	$40,000		6%	$240,000
June	$40,000	$40,000	$50,000	$50,000	$100,000	7%	$280,000
July	$60,000	$60,000	$60,000	$60,000		6%	$240,000
Spring Total						40%	$1,600,000
August	$80,000	$50,000	$50,000	$60,000		6%	$240,000
September	$40,000	$100,000	$100,000	$40,000	$40,000	8%	$320,000
October	$25,000	$75,000	$150,000	$150,000		10%	$400,000
November	$75,000	$95,000	$150,000	$200,000		13%	$520,000
December	$100,000	$140,000	$200,000	$250,000	$30,000	18%	$720,000
January	$50,000	$50,000	$60,000	$40,000		5%	$200,000
Fall Total						60%	$2,400,00
Annual Total						100%	$4,000,000

Part 4. *Plan markdowns for the year.*   The objective of Dolan's Part 4 is to allocate the markdowns for the new store to four categories: damages, employee discounts, clearance, and promotional. Refer to the markdown percentages listed in Dolan's Appendix C on pages 371 and 372. . Note that markdown rates vary dramatically by department. For instance, cosmetics markdowns are negligible in that the vendors provide the department's promotional items (hence no promotional markdowns), and seasonal items, such as holiday gift sets, are returned to the vendor for credit instead of being marked down and cleared (hence no clearance markdowns). Swimwear, on the other hand, has a high markdown rate because of end-of-season clearance markdowns. To complete Dolan's Part 4, figure your department's markdown dollars by multiplying the plan sales from Dolan's Appendix A by the appropriate markdown percent in Dolan's Appendix C.

Next, allocate the markdown dollars as a percent of total markdowns to the four markdown categories, detailed in Parts 4A to 4D.

Part 4A. *Damages.*   The percentage of total markdown dollars allocated to damages will vary from one department to another based on the susceptibility of the merchandise to damage. Because of breakage, china and glassware will need a higher percentage of total markdown dollars to cover damages than an apparel department. For the purposes of this exercise, allocate 2 percent of the department's markdown dollars to damages if the merchandise is highly vulnerable to damage and 1 percent to less vulnerable departments. Allocate the damage markdown dollars evenly by month, since predicting when damages are going to occur is anybody's best guess.

Part 4B. *Employee discounts.* Employee discounts represent a high percentage of total markdowns (maybe 40 percent) in low-clearance-markdown departments where only a small percentage of total markdown dollars is needed to cover clearance markdowns. Employee discounts represent a low percentage of total markdowns (maybe 10 percent) in high-clearance-markdown departments where a large percentage of total markdown dollars is needed to cover clearance markdowns. Allocate employee discounts by month according to the figures derived in Part 3A, because Dolan's employees shop pretty much like Dolan's customers in all stores.

Part 4C. *Clearance markdown.*   A high percentage of total markdowns should be allocated to clearance markdowns for seasonal fashion goods (maybe 40 percent), and a smaller percentage to basic goods, or any merchandise carried from one season to another (maybe 10 percent). In the case of seasonal fashion departments, distribute clearance markdown dollars generously to high-clearance months, such as January, February, June, July, and August.

Part 4D. *Promotional markdowns.*   Promotional markdowns should represent the largest percentage of total markdowns. However, in high-clearance departments, clearance markdowns will come close to equaling promotional markdowns as a percentage of total markdowns. Promotional markdown dollars should be distributed by month in accordance with the events calendar in Dolan's Part 2.

The following is an example of how markdowns might be distributed in a $4 million department with a 6.2 percent annualized markdown rate.

Annual Markdowns = 6.2% Annual Sales = $4,000,000	Damages	Employee Discounts	Clearance	Promotional	Total
February	$207	$992	$16,000	$6,200	$23,399
March	$207	$1,736	$16,000	$12,400	$30,343
April	$207	$2,480	$4,000	$12,400	$19,087
May	$207	$1,488	$2,000	$6,200	$9,895
June	$207	$1,736	$16,000	$12,400	$30,343
July	$207	$1,488	$16,000	$6,200	$23,895
August	$207	$1,488	$8,000	$6,200	$15,895
September	$207	$1,984	$5,000	$6,200	$13,391
October	$206	$2,480	$2,000	$12,400	$17,086
November	$206	$3,224	$2,000	$12,400	$17,830
December	$206	$4,464	$7,000	$12,400	$24,070
January	$206	$1,240	$15,120	$6,200	$22,766
Total	$2,480	$24,800	$109,120	$111,600	$248,000
% of Markdown to Total Markdowns $	1%	10%	44%	45%	100%

Part 5. *Plan BOM inventories.*   Use the plan sales from Dolan's Part 3, the turnover figure from Dolan's Appendix C, and either the basic stock method or the percentage variation method.

Part 6. *Plan purchases by month.*   Use the plan sales from Dolan's Part 3, the markdowns from Dolan's Part 4, and the BOMs (EOMs) from Dolan's Part 5. (Use the BOM of February as the EOM of January.)

DOLAN'S APPENDIX A
Annual Plan Sales
(in millions)
Dolan's at the Crystal Mall
Waterford, Connecticut

Accessories Division

Cosmetics	2.0
Fragrances	1.0
Handbags (includes small leather goods)	1.8
Shoes (includes athletic, men's)	2.0
Hosiery (includes sheer hosiery and socks)	0.6
Jewelry—fine	2.0
Jewelry—costume and bridge (includes watches)	1.6
Fashion accessories (scarves, sunglasses, cold weather)	0.4
Intimate apparel—bras	1.0
Intimate apparel—daywear (slips and pants)	0.6
Intimate apparel—robes/sleepwear	1.6
Total division	14.6

Children's Division

Boys—4–7	0.5
Boys—8–20	0.9
Girls—4–6x	0.5
Girls—7–14	0.9
Infants (includes layette and toddlers)	0.4
Total division	3.2

Home Division

Candy and gourmet	0.4
China and glassware	1.6
Luggage (Joe and Joe)	0.8
Housewares—cookware and small appliances	0.7
Housewares—tabletop	0.5
Linens—bed and bath (includes bath accessories)	1.4
Linens—table and kitchen	0.6
Stationery (includes greeting cards and gifts)	0.4
Total division	6.4

Men's Division

Clothing (includes suits, sport coats, and outerwear)	1.6
Furnishings (includes shirts and ties)	1.2
Basics (underwear, pajamas, and robes)	0.8
Accessories (belts, small leather goods, and jewelry)	0.3
Shoes	1.0
Sportswear (includes sweaters, active and weekend)	2.0
Young men's (sportswear)	1.6
Collections (includes Tommy Hilfiger, Calvin Klein, etc.)	1.0
Total division	9.5

Ready-to-Wear Division

Dresses—career and casual	1.2
Dresses—junior	0.4
Dresses—social occasion	0.4
Sportswear—active (includes swimwear and fleece)	1.0
Sportswear—better (Jones, Liz Claiborne, etc.)	1.0
Sportswear—bridge and designer (Ellen Tracy, Anne Klein II, etc.)	0.4
Sportswear—junior	1.6
Sportswear—moderate (includes Alfred Dunner, McNaughton, etc.)	2.4
Sportswear special size—Women's	0.6
Sportswear special size—Petites	0.6
Coats and suits (includes juniors)	1.0
Total division	10.6
Total store	44.3

DOLAN'S APPENDIX B
Storewide and Divisional Promotional Calendar

Month	Week(s)	Event
February	2	Valentine's Day Mailer
March	2	March Home Sale
	3	One-Day Sale
April	1,2	Anniversary Sale
May	1	Mother's Day Mailer
June	1	One-Day Sale
	2	Father's Day Mailer
	5	Pre-Inventory Clearance
July	4	Summer Clearance
August	4	Back-to-School Sale
September	2	One-Day Sale
	3	Home Sale
October	2	Harvest of Values (Fall Sale)
November	2	One-Day Sale
December	1	Coupon Sale
January	3	Pre-Inventory Clearance
	4	Winter Clearance

DOLAN'S APPENDIX C
　　Turnover and Markdowns
　　Dolan's at the Crystal Mall
　　Waterford, Connecticut

	Turnover	*Markdowns*
Accessories Division		
Cosmetics	3.3	0.7
Fragrances	2.6	0.6
Handbags	4.1	6.2
Shoes	4.9	19.5
Hosiery	3.3	5.7
Jewelry—fine	2.5	4.2
Jewelry—costume and bridge	2.8	8.0
Fashion accessories	4.2	9.3
Intimate apparel—bras	3.9	5.0
Intimate apparel—daywear	3.8	5.0
Intimate apparel—robes/sleepwear	4.8	9.7
Children's Division		
Boys—4–7	4.6	9.4
Boys—8–20	4.6	9.4
Girls—4–6x	4.7	8.6
Girls—7–14	4.7	8.6
Infants	4.2	0.8
Home Division		
Candy and gourmet	10.6	3.2
China and glassware	2.9	7.0
Housewares—cookware and small appliances	3.1	5.1
Housewares—tabletop	3.2	5.2
Linens—bed and bath	2.7	6.2
Linens—table and kitchen	2.9	6.3
Stationery	4.2	1.5

Men's Division

Clothing	3.9	14.7
Furnishings	4.1	12.0
Basics	4.8	9.3
Accessories	3.9	9.5
Shoes	4.2	12.8
Sportswear	4.4	18.4
Young men's	5.1	19.8
Collections	4.9	20.1

Ready-to-Wear Division

Dresses—career and casual	3.8	23.1
Dresses—junior	3.1	24.2
Dresses—social occasion	3.7	21.2
Sportswear—active	5.0	17.1
Sportswear—better	5.2	21.1
Sportswear—bridge and designer	4.8	22.1
Sportswear—junior	5.3	24.3
Sportswear—Moderate	5.1	19.5
Sportswear special size—Women's	3.0	18.4
Sportswear special size—Petites	3.3	15.9
Coats and Suits	4.1	15.4

CHAPTER FOURTEEN

Purchase Terms

After reading this chapter, you will be able to discuss:

● The retail buyer's role as a negotiator.

● The impact of vendor payment terms on cash flow and gross margin.

● Basic transportation terms.

● The importance of strategic partnerships between retailers and their vendors.

A retail buyer's task of seeking quality products at favorable prices is not unlike a consumer's quest for the best values in the retail marketplace. Though consumers have considerable product options, price is rarely negotiable. A greater degree of pricing flexibility exists in the wholesale marketplace, where price and other purchase agreements are often negotiable. Retailers who negotiate favorable wholesale prices can pass their savings on to consumers in the form of lower retail prices and thus compete more effectively with other retailers. Favorable nonprice vendor agreements can increase gross margin, decrease processing expenses, and improve cash flow. Chapter 14 covers the negotiable points of wholesale purchase agreements and their effect on a retailer's pricing and profitability.

PURCHASE ORDERS

A purchase order is a contractual sales agreement between a retailer and a vendor in which items of merchandise, prices, delivery dates, and payment terms are specified. Purchase orders are often categorized by factors such as the type of goods ordered and order status.

Advance Order   An advance order is a commitment to buy merchandise that may not be available for delivery until the distant future. Producers use advance orders as a barometer to gauge production.

Back Order   A back order is for merchandise that was ordered but never shipped. Vendors "short ship" orders when they run out of the styles, colors, or sizes ordered by the retailer. Some vendors substitute out-of-stock goods with other styles, colors, or sizes, much to the dismay of retailers.

Complete Order   A complete, or filled, order has been totally shipped by the vendor.

JARROD & YOUNG PURCHASE ORDER

Buyer .... DMM .... Date .... Page .... Of ....

| SPECIAL INSTRUCTIONS | DEPT. NO. | MARK ALL PACKAGES & INVOICES WITH OUR ORDER NO. AND CONTINUATION NO. | ORDER NO. 5858075 | CONTINUATION NO. | CHARGE MONTH | DELIVERY DATE | CANCEL IF NOT REC'D BY | MFR NO. | ORDER DATE |

☐
☐
☐
☐ OTHER

☐ CONFIRMATION OF ORDER-DO NOT DUPLICATE

NAME

ADDRESS

CITY   STATE   ZIP CODE

TICKETING INSTRUCTIONS

SHIP TO: ☐ (Drop Ship) Individual Stores ☐ J&Y Warehs. Route 89E DM, Iowa

VENDOR DUNS NUMBER

DISCOUNT

FOB

SHIPPED FROM

FOR ACCOUNTS PAYABLE USE ONLY

FREIGHT TERMS
☐ Vendor Pays   ☐ .... Pays
☐ Special ....

TERMS All terms begin on date of receipt of goods and invoice by Jarrod & Young. Under EOM terms merchandise received on or after the 25th of any month will be paid for as though received on the first of the following month. This order is 1) subject to all of the terms and conditions stated on both sides of this order, please note particularly conditions appearing on reverse side, 2) not valid unless counter signed by a divisional merchandise manager or an officer. (over)

BILLING & SHIPPING INSTRUCTIONS

BILLING
To assure prompt payment
1. Prepare a separate invoice for each department and location within a shipment.
2. Enclose each location's invoice with shipment in a clearly marked "lead" carton. If this is not possible, send your invoices, no later than the shipment date to Jarrod & Young.
3. The invoice must cover only the merchandise shipped, and show:
   a) Vendor name
   b) Vendor DUNS number
   c) J & Y Purchase Order number
   d) J & Y Department number
   e) Location name and number
   f) Complete description of merchandise by style, color, size and unit cost, with line extensions.
Address all inquiries about invoices to the Box 741 address, above.

PACKING & SHIPPING
4. Shipment must be packed, labeled and segregated by Store, Department, and Order number.
5. The Packing List must be enclosed in a clearly marked "lead" carton and must show, by location:
   a) Vendor name
   b) Purchase Order number
   c) Invoice number, when feasible
   d) Department number
   e) Location name and number
6. Merchandise quantities should not differ from the original order.
7. Partial shipments are not permitted unless stipulated on the face of this Purchase Order.
8. The label on each carton must show:
   a) Vendor name
   b) Purchase Order number
   c) Department number
   d) Location name and number
Failure to comply with the above instructions may subject you to a charge to offset the additional costs incurred in processing your invoice and merchandise.

ROUTING
9. Based upon the freight terms on the face of this order, J & Y is responsible for freight.
   a) Route shipments according to our "STANDARD ROUTING LETTER"
   b) Multi-store shipments consigned to the same bill of lading destination on one day must be combined and shipped on a single bill of lading. The piece count and weight by store should be shown on that bill of lading.
   c) When air freight is authorized, an air freight authorization number (supplied by buyer) must be shown on all shipping documents
Failure to follow our routing instructions, with or without incurring higher transportation charges, shall be considered as your agreement to PAY ALL TRANSPORTATION CHARGES. Authority to deviate must be obtained from the J & Y Traffic Manager or his authorized representative prior to shipment.
If you have any questions on the above labeling, packing or shipping instructions and/or require a routing letter address your inquiries to J & Y traffic manager, Des Moines, Iowa.

LINE	MANUFAC-TURER'S STYLE NO.	STYLE NO.	CLASS	DESCRIPTION	COLOR NAME	COLOR NO.	SIZE	TOTAL QUANTITY	UNIT COST	UNIT RETAIL	DM	CR	Am	CB	IC	SC	Dv	Wh	TOTAL COST	TOTAL RETAIL
1																				
2																				
3																				
4																				
5																				
6																				
7																				
8																				
9																				
10																				
11																				
12																				
13																				
14																				
15																				
16																				
17																				
18																				
19																				
20																				
21																				
22																				
23																				
24																				
25																				
26																				
27																				

RETAIL

COST

REPRODUCTION

MU%

RETAIL

COST

FIGURE 14.1
A sample purchase order.

Fill-In Order A fill-in order replenishes sold-out sizes/styles/colors of a basic inventory assortment.

No-Order A no-order refers to merchandise that arrives at a retailer's distribution center without a supporting purchase order.

Past-Due Order A past-due order is not yet received by the specified delivery date on the purchase order.

Reorder A reorder is for previously ordered goods. Reorders are typical of fast-selling items. Not all merchandise may be reordered. Because fashion goods change so quickly, basic goods are more likely to be reordered than fashion goods.

```
PM278(16.00)          PO WITHIN VENDOR INQUIRY              02/25/03   15:15:23
                                    VENDOR DUNS NUMBER:   51318665   USER: T01
  VENDOR NAME: SAHARA
    PO                  SHIP                      PO                  SHIP
  NUMBER  DEPT POM     DATE   PO STATUS         NUMBER  DEPT POM     DATE   PO STATUS
  01002476 0390  Y  12/03/02 OPEN ORDER        01017326 0390  Y  03/05/03 OPEN ORDER
  01022375 0390  Y  04/01/03 OPEN ORDER        01022607 0390  Y  03/20/03 OPEN ORDER
  01025071 0390  Y  04/10/03 PEND W/ERR        01025766 0390  Y  03/20/03 PEND W/ERR
  01026012 0390  Y  04/12/03 OPEN ORDER        01026400 0390  Y  04/10/03 CANCELED
  09008307 0390  Y  03/25/03 PEND MGMT         39005262 0390  Y  02/01/02 CANCELED
  39005353 0390  Y  02/15/02 CANCELED          39005767 0390  Y  10/01/02 CANCELED
  39005791 0390  Y  11/20/02 CANCELED          39005809 0390  Y  04/01/03 OPEN ORDER
  39005825 0390  Y  02/20/03 OPEN ORDER        39005833 0390  Y  02/10/03 OPEN ORDER
  39005841 0390  Y  01/15/03 OPEN ORDER        39005858 0390  Y  03/01/03 OPEN ORDER
  39005866 0390  Y  01/25/03 OPEN ORDER        39005874 0390  Y  02/20/03 OPEN ORDER
  39005882 0390  Y  12/15/02 OPEN ORDER        39005916 0390  Y  11/13/02 CANCELED
  39005932 0390  Y  03/01/03 OPEN ORDER        71025766 0390  Y  03/20/03 CANCELED
  76138226 0390  Y  04/01/03 OPEN ORDER        76138234 0390  Y  03/10/03 OPEN ORDER
  76138242 0390  Y  02/04/03 OPEN ORDER        76138259 0390  Y  11/25/02 OPEN ORDER
  76138267 0390  Y  11/25/02 OPEN ORDER        76138275 0390  Y  01/29/03 OPEN ORDER
  76216790 0390  Y  11/25/02 OPEN ORDER        76216808 0390  Y  11/25/02 PEND W/ERR
          PF1=MENU        PF2=HELP      PF3=RECOVER      ENTER=CONTINUE
** 968 ** PRESS ENTER FOR MORE POS
```

FIGURE 14.2
POM systems track purchase orders by number, ship date, and status.

Rush Order   A rush, or priority, order is expedited by the vendor and the retail distribution center, often to replenish a low assortment of fast-selling merchandise, to cover a breaking advertisement, or for the grand opening of a new store.

Special Order   A special order is for an individual customer. Special orders are often restricted by a vendor's minimum-order specifications. Some retailers wait until enough special orders have accrued to satisfy the minimum. However, this delay can lead to customer frustration.

Standing Order   A standing, or open, order is an outstanding order to which additional items can be added without generating new paper.

Purchase order management (POM) systems have transformed purchase order processing from an inefficient superintensive procedure involving hand-written documents into a computerized system for preparing and transmitting orders electronically. POM systems also track purchase orders by factors such as order number, delivery date, vendor, and category of merchandise.

DISCOUNTS

Buyers often receive special price reductions in the price of merchandise called discounts. A quantity discount is a reduction in price based on the

Phone: 773.890.1466
Fax: 773.890.1467
E mail: sales@hoohobbers.com

2847 West 47th Place   Chicago, IL   60632

Innovations for children ᴛᴛᴛ

Price List, Specifications and Conditions

- *Opening Order Minimum: $350.00 (with account approval)*

- *Reorder Minimum: $150.00*

- *Freight is F.O.B. Factory. All orders ship UPS, unless specified otherwise. Actual shipping charges are added to your invoice. Truck orders ship freight collect.*

- *Payment for initial orders may be by credit card (MC, VISA, Discover), COD or cash in advance.*

- *Open account status (net 30) is available upon completion and approval of Credit Application.*

- *All returns must have prior approval from our Customer Service Department. An authorization number will be issued. The authorization number must appear on all cartons. No merchandise will be accepted without authorization.*

- *We will replace any defective item or part. Feel free to have your customer call us with any problem.*

- *Case weight & cube information is not available on softgoods. These items are boxed at time of shipment. Actual case weight and size varies dependent upon the particular mix of softgoods ordered.*

made in the
USA

FIGURE 14.3
One vendor's purchase
terms and conditions.

amount of merchandise purchased. A *noncumulative discount* applies to each order placed. A *cumulative discount* applies to orders placed over time. The discount increases as the accumulated value of the orders increases. Noncumulative discounts encourage large individual orders, while cumulative discounts encourage a steady flow of repeat orders. A quantity discount can be stated as a percentage applied to a total invoice or as a reduction in unit cost. The unit cost of an item may be $1; however, if more than 500 units are purchased, the unit price becomes $0.98; if 1,000 units are purchased, the unit price becomes $0.95, and so on.

Vendors offer quantity discounts as sales inducements and to encourage the placement of large orders, since it is less costly to pick, pack, ship, and invoice a few large orders than many small orders. Most vendors have a minimum order requirement, a dollar or unit amount that defines the smallest order that the vendor is willing to accept. Quantity discounts give large retailers a competitive pricing advantage over small independent retailers. Wal-Mart profitably retails some items at prices lower than the wholesale price paid by small independents. However, retailers should avoid the temptation to buy excessive amounts of merchandise for the sake of obtaining quantity discounts. Markdowns on excessive inventory can more than negate the advantage of the discounts.

A seasonal discount is a reduction in price for orders placed in advance of the normal ordering period. Seasonal discounts are sometimes stated as price schedules of discounted unit costs for orders placed before specified dates. Pricing programs such as these are often dubbed "Early Bird Specials" or "Preseason Incentive Programs." Seasonal discounts often involve long-term purchase commitments. A retailer that commits to seasonal orders of

$2 million may receive a discount after orders of $1 million have been placed. Long-term purchase commitments allow producers to plan production strategically and to balance the peaks and valleys of the production cycles of seasonal goods. However, retailers assume risk by committing to goods far in advance of a selling season, especially fashion goods. To minimize this risk, some producers offer seasonal discounts based on dollar commitments, allowing buyers to select specific styles closer to the selling season.

Just as the retailer offers slow-selling, end-of-season merchandise at markdown prices to consumers, vendors offer retailers their slow sellers, closeouts, and overruns at off-price at the end of a season. These opportunistic buys are often referred to as end-of-season discounts.

DATING

Part of the buying process involves negotiating arrangements for payment. Payment terms are stated on the vendor's invoice, an itemized statement that lists the goods shipped, the unit and extended cost, and any additional charges for transportation and/or insurance.[1] The term dating refers to the period allowed for the payment of an invoice. "Net 30" is a common dating expression meaning that full payment of the invoice is due within 30 days of the date of invoice (DOI), the date that the invoice was issued.

A cash discount is a reduction in the amount due on an invoice when payment is made on or before a specified date. Unless otherwise specified, the cash discount period begins on the DOI and expires on the designated cash discount date. The net payment period begins on the cash discount date and ends on the specified net payment date. A cash discount is not applied until all other discounts have been deducted. Cash discounts are applied to merchandise charges only. Shipping and insurance charges are not discountable.

A common expression of cash discount terms is "2/10 net 30," read "two ten net thirty." This means that a 2 percent discount may be deducted from an invoice paid within ten days of the DOI. Once the cash-discount period has expired, the full amount of the invoice is due within 30 days of the DOI. The expression "2/10, 1/15, net 30" means that a 2 percent discount may be deducted from an invoice paid within ten days of the DOI, or a 1 percent discount if paid between 11 and 15 days. Once both discount periods have expired, the full amount of the invoice is due within 30 days of the date of invoice. The expression 2/10 net 30 may also be written as "2/10, n/30." When terms are not stated, it is assumed that full payment is due in 30 days.

Regular, or *ordinary*, dating assumes the DOI as the first day of the payment period. Discount and payment periods can be extended by beginning the period later than the DOI. An EOM notation means that the periods begin at the end of the month in which the invoice is dated. If the terms of an August 15 invoice are 2/10 net 30 EOM, the discount period begins August 31 and a 2 percent discount may be deducted until September 10. Full payment is due by September 30.

Some vendors consider invoices dated the 25th of a month or after as if they were dated the first of the following month. In the case of an August 25 invoice dated 2/10 EOM, a 2 percent discount may be deducted through October 10. Full payment is due by October 31. These are highly favorable terms for the retailer, who has approximately six weeks to generate cash from the sale of the merchandise and still take advantage of the discount.

There are a number of special types of dating:

- Proximo, or *prox*, dating specifies the day of the following month by which the cash discount must be taken; *2% 15th prox. net 30* means that a 2 percent discount may be deducted through the 15th of the following month. Full payment is due within 30 days of the DOI.
- Advance dating delays the beginning of discount and payment periods until a future date noted "as of." If the terms of an August 15 invoice are *2/10 net 30, as of December 1*, a 2 percent discount may be deducted through December 11. Full payment is due by December 31. Advance dating is also called *post* or *seasonal* dating and is common in the menswear industry.
- Extra dating adds additional days to the discount and payment periods. If the terms of an August 15 invoice are *2/10, 60X* or *2/10, 60 ex.*, a 2 percent discount may be deducted until October 25. Full payment is due November 15. Vendors use advance and extra dating to induce retailers to accept early shipments of merchandise, preferring to show high receivables on their balance sheets rather than high inventories. A vendor may use these forms of dating to test merchandise in certain stores as early predictors of a season's selling trends.
- ROG, or receipt-of-goods, dating delays the beginning of the discount and payment periods until the goods are received by the retailer. If the

terms of a shipment invoiced August 15 are *2/10 net 30 ROG*, and the goods arrive on September 1, a 2 percent discount may be deducted through September 11. Full payment is due by October 1. ROG dating compensates for extended shipping time due to slow transportation modes or the transportation of goods over a considerable distance. ROG dating is not used frequently.

- Cash, or *immediate*, dating are payment arrangements with no provision for discount or payment periods. COD, or cash on delivery, means that cash payment is due upon the delivery of the goods. Vendors ship COD to new retailers with no established credit, or to retailers with poor credit histories. *Cash in advance* (CIA) and *cash before delivery* (CBD) are other forms of cash dating.

Goods sold on consignment are not paid for until they are sold. Consignment arrangements are not common but are sometimes used to sell big-ticket items with a slow or unpredictable rate of sale, such as works of art, to minimize the retailer's risk:

- A positive cash flow is ensured since goods are not paid for until after they are sold.
- The retailer's capital is not tied up in inventory.
- Goods are returned to the vendor if not sold within an agreed upon time period.

Though arrangements are similar, there is a distinction between goods sold on consignment and goods sold on memorandum. The title of consignment goods passes from the vendor to the consumer but never passes to the retailer. The title of memorandum goods passes from the vendor to the retailer, usually when the goods are shipped, and then passes to the consumer at the point of sale.

Dating is a frequent point of negotiation between retailers and their vendors. Lengthy payment periods allow a retailer to generate a considerable amount of cash from the sale of goods before having to pay for them, thus enhancing a positive cash flow. Vendors, on the other hand, prefer shorter payment periods, wishing to balance their own cash flow and to meet financial obligations, such as payroll and payments to their vendors. Some vendors offer incentive programs that combine both discount and dating terms. One footwear resource offers multiple-discount and extended-payment-period programs for replenishment orders based on quantities purchased. The program qualifies retailers for:

- A 1 percent discount and 30-day credit terms with a minimum purchase of 3,600 pairs per year.
- A 2 percent discount and 60-day credit terms with a minimum purchase of 9,600 pairs per year.
- A 3 percent discount and 60-day credit terms with a minimum purchase of 12,500 pairs per year.

COMPUTING DISCOUNTS

Cash discounts are computed by multiplying the discount rate by the cost of the goods as billed on the invoice:

cash discount = discount rate × billed cost

A 2 percent discount on a $100,000 shipment is computed as follows:

cash discount = 2% × $100,000
cash discount = 0.02 × $100,000
cash discount = $2,000

The cash discount is then subtracted from billed cost to determine balance due:

balance due = billed cost − cash discount
balance due = $100,000 − $2,000
balance due = $98,000

Balance due can be computed with a single-step formula:

balance due = (100% − discount rate) × billed cost
balance due = (100% − 2%) × $100,000
balance due = 0.98 × $100,000
balance due = $98,000

NINE TECHNIQUES OF SUCCESSFUL VENDOR NEGOTIATIONS

1. **Act Collaboratively, Not Competitively.** Negotiation is not "me against you." Recognize that the other party has to come away with a benefit, too. Show them how giving you what you want will help them get what they want.

2. **Prepare.** Do your homework about the other party; gather as much information about them as possible. Even rehearse and outline your remarks.

3. **Know What You Want.** Being able to state specific proposals or plans gives you strength. Don't wait to "see what they offer us." Know in advance what you must have, and what you can afford to give up. Each time you make a concession, get something in return.

4. **Don't Let Your Ego Get in the Way.** When you think of the negotiating process as winning or losing, you have too much ego involved. Don't get sidetracked by personalities or emotions. Stick to the issues.

5. **Learn to Make Time Your Ally.** Time is at the heart of every negotiation. Learn to make it work for you. Try to learn the other party's deadline without giving away yours. Most concessions occur at somebody's deadline.

6. **If You Can't Agree on Point One, Go to Point Two.** Agree even in small increments. Don't get hung up on one issue. It is easier to come back to an issue after you have reached some agreement, and the other person has invested time and energy in working with you.

7. **Be a Creative Risk-Taker.** If you are known to not take risks, you are predictable and can be easily manipulated. Create your own solutions; there is usually more than one way to get the results you want.

8. **Closing the Negotiation: Wrap it Up.** Don't stay around and chat after you have reached an agreement. If you have what you want, close the negotiation. Don't linger too long, or it may unravel.

9. **Develop Long-term Relationships.** Focusing on long-term goals will keep both parties from being sidetracked by short-term frustrations. Knowing you are both in for the long haul means you can solve any problem that arises.

SOURCE:
Prepared by Elizabeth Tahir, president of Liz Tahir Consulting, a retail marketing and management consulting and training firm in New Orleans, Louisiana.

Anticipation is an additional discount for paying an invoice prior to a cash discount date. The discount is based on the prevailing prime rate of business interest, the number of days that the payment is made prior to the cash-discount date, and the balance of the invoice after discount. The formula for computing the additional discount is:[2]

$$additional\ discount\ =\ invoice\ balance\ \times\ interest\ rate\ \times\ time$$

Assume that the DOI on the above invoice was August 15, and that payment was made on August 20, five days in advance of the August 25 cash discount date. If the prevailing interest rate is 3 percent, the additional discount is computed as follows:

$$
\begin{aligned}
additional\ discount\ &=\ invoice\ balance\ \times\ interest\ rate\ \times\ time \\
additional\ discount\ &=\ \$98{,}000\ \times\ 0.03\ \times\ 5/360 \\
additional\ discount\ &=\ \$40.83
\end{aligned}
$$

The additional discount is deducted from the $98,000 invoice balance, leaving a new balance due of $97,959.17. Anticipation is not a common discounting practice. Many vendors stipulate "no anticipation" as part of their dating terms.

The Long-Term Impact of Discounts

Discounts can dramatically impact a retailer's profitability over time. Consider the retailer who forfeits a $2,000 discount on a $100,000 shipment invoiced *2/10 net 30*. The retailer has effectively paid an annual interest rate of 35.7 percent to use $100,000 for the 20 days between the cash discount date and the net payment date, as the following calculation demonstrates:

$$
\begin{aligned}
interest\ &=\ principal\ \times\ rate\ \times\ time \\
\$2{,}000\ &=\ \$100{,}000\ \times\ rate\ \times\ 20/360 \\
\$2{,}000\ &=\ \$100{,}000\ \times\ rate\ \times\ 0.056 \\
\$2{,}000\ &=\ \$5{,}600\ \times\ rate \\
\$2{,}000/5600\ &=\ rate \\
0.35714\ &=\ rate \\
35.7\%\ &=\ rate
\end{aligned}
$$

When a negative cash flow prevents a retailer from taking advantage of a cash discount, it is often wise to borrow the money to pay the invoice within the cash discount period. The cash discount savings will exceed the interest on the loan, because annual borrowing rates are lower than annualized cash discount rates. Borrowing for short periods to take advantage of cash discounts is a common retailing practice. Favorable dating arrangements yield another important fiscal advantage: because cash discounts decrease the cost of goods sold, they increase gross margin and ultimately net profit.

TRANSPORTATION

Arrangements for transporting goods from a vendor to a retail distribution center is a function of the retailer's traffic department. Cost-effective transportation arrangements minimize the cost of goods sold, and maximize gross margin and net profit. Transportation costs are a function of the weight and bulk of the merchandise shipped, the distance between the vendor's and retailer's distribution centers, and the mode of transportation used.

The rates charged by the transportation industry were once regulated by federal agencies, such as the Interstate Commerce Commission and the Civil Aeronautics Board. However, legislation, such as the Motor Carrier Act and the Staggers Rail Act, has significantly deregulated the transportation industry. Deregulation has fostered intense competition among transporters of goods, or carriers, who can now tailor rates and services to match the needs of individual shippers. The complexities of a deregulated transportation environment have increased the importance of the traffic function in retail organizations. Traffic managers now have the ability to increase service and decrease costs by favorable negotiations with carriers just as buyers negotiate favorable terms with their vendors.

Transportation Terms

Transportation terms identify the bearer of the cost of shipping goods from the vendor to the retailer, as well as the point at which the title of the goods passes from one to the other. Though transportation arrangements are the responsibility of a store's traffic department, transportation terms are the responsibility of the buyer. The cost of transporting goods from vendors is typically absorbed by the retailer. However, transportation terms are sometimes negotiated whereby the vendor absorbs all or part of the transportation costs. Because transportation costs increase the cost of goods sold, favorable transportation terms maximize gross margin and net profit.

FOB stands for *free on board*. Words such as *origin, factory, destination,* or the name of a city that follow FOB refer to the point to which a vendor pays transportation charges and the point at which the title of the goods passes from the vendor to the retailer. *FOB factory* means that the retailer pays the transportation charges from the vendor's factory and assumes title to the goods at that point. *FOB destination* means that the vendor pays the transportation charges to the retail destination without relinquishing title until that point.

The point at which title transfers from the vendor to the retailer is important when determining the responsibility for lost or damaged goods. When title is transferred to the retailer at the point at which the goods are shipped, the retailer must pay for all of the goods shipped and obtain compensation from the freight carrier for lost or damaged goods. When title is not transferred to the retailer until the goods reach the store, the vendor is responsible for replacing lost or damaged goods and for recovering the loss from the carrier.

Sometimes vendors establish an FOB point that equates the cost of transporting their goods to the cost of transporting competitors' goods. A Los Angeles–based vendor competing with a Chicago-based vendor for a Philadelphia retailer's business may ship goods *FOB Chicago*. Shared shipping responsibility can also be expressed as:

FOB factory (or store), charges shared: _____ % factory, _____ % store

The following is a list of agreements between retailers and their vendors that indicate payment responsibility for transportation costs and the point at which the title of goods is transferred from the vendor to the retailer:

- *FOB origin, freight collect.* The retailer pays the freight charges and owns the goods while in transit.
- *FOB origin, freight prepaid.* The vendor pays the freight charges, but the retailer owns the goods while in transit.
- *FOB origin, freight prepaid and charged back.* The vendor pays the freight charges but is reimbursed for them by invoicing the retailer for the

freight charges along with the merchandise. The retailer owns the goods while in transit.

- *FOB destination, freight collect.* The retailer pays the freight charges, but the vendor owns the goods while in transit.
- *FOB destination, freight prepaid.* The vendor pays the freight charges and owns the goods while in transit.
- *FOB destination, freight collect and allowed.* The retailer pays the freight charges but is reimbursed for them by a chargeback deducted from the vendor's invoice. The vendor owns the goods while in transit.

Timing the shipment of goods is an important part of a merchandising strategy. Because orders are placed against an open to buy planned for a specific period, the timely arrival of merchandise ensures that inventory levels are appropriate to planned sales. Most purchase orders specify two dates to define the delivery parameters: *a do not ship before* date and a *do not ship after* date. Early arrival of goods can be as devastating as late arrival. Unless extra dating has been arranged, early shipments can lead to imbalanced cash flow. Storage is also an issue related to early shipments.

Transportation Arrangements

Transportation terms are a function of the retail buyer. Four transportation modes are used to transport goods from vendors to retailers:

- *Motor carriers*, or truckers, are the most common form of transportation used to transport domestic goods from vendors to retailers. Motor carriers provide door-to-door service by picking up shipments from a vendor and delivering them directly to a retailer's distribution center. Motor carriers are also used to supplement other forms of transportation that do not offer door-to-door service. Roadway Express is the nation's largest motor carrier for freight.
- *Railroad*s are an economical transportation mode used for long hauls of heavy, bulky commodities. Retailers transport goods by rail in conjunction with other transportation modes, such as trucks, reaping the economic advantages of rail and the door-to-door efficiencies of truck. The combination of two or more modes of transportation is called intermodal transportation.
- *Airlines* are the most rapid and most expensive transportation mode.

Airlines expose shipments to the least potential for damage, pilferage, or obsolescence. They are only used to transport valuable or highly perishable goods.

• *Water carriers* are a slow but economic transportation mode used by retailers to import goods directly from foreign sources.

Several services are also available for shipping small packages, including the parcel-post service of the U.S. Postal Service and United Parcel Service, a private door-to-door service for transporting packages under 70 pounds. Federal Express and Emery Air Freight also provide expedient delivery of very small packages and documents, as do intercity bus lines such as Greyhound.

Transportation firms are categorized as common, contract, and private:

• **Common carrier**   A common carrier establishes uniform rates and schedules for all shippers.
• **Contract carrier**   A contract carrier negotiates individual agreements with shippers or small groups of shippers.
• **Private carrier**   Some organizations operate as private carriers, shipping goods with their own transportation equipment.

Retailers sometimes contract the services of transportation intermediaries called consolidators, or *freight forwarders*. Consolidators combine less-than-truckload (ltl) shipments from multiple vendors into truckload (tl) shipments, and then contract carriers to deliver the tl shipments to

FIGURE 14.4
Retailers use water carriers to directly import goods from foreign resources. Courtesy Seaboard Marine.

their retail destinations. Because ltl rates are higher than the tl rates, a consolidator makes a profit by charging shippers rates that are lower than the ltl rates, but higher than tl rates.

Time and cost are the two major factors considered when determining a transportation mode. In general, slower modes of transportation are more economical than more expeditious modes and are appropriate for transporting goods shipped in advance of their selling season. However, retailers often pay premium transportation rates to expedite the delivery of perishable goods or goods with immediate consumer demand. A retailer that desperately needs goods for an ad breaking in 48 hours will pay premium transportation rates to ensure delivery to cover the ad. Rapid transportation also decreases the amount of time that goods remain in the merchandise pipeline.

FIGURE 14.5
Wal-Mart operates as a private carrier, shipping goods from Wal-Mart distribution centers to Wal-Mart stores with its own transportation fleet. © Davis Barber/PhotoEdit.

DISTRIBUTION CENTERS

Single-unit retail operations ship goods from vendors directly to their stores at which point they are unpacked, ticketed, and prepared for the selling floor. Most multiunit retailers ship goods to a central distribution point where they are processed and then distributed to stores. The distribution center (DC) performs critical inventory management functions by expediting processing to ensure the timely arrival of goods in stores, and by working closely with buyers to resolve issues related to damaged receipts, short shipments, and vendor substitutions. The following is a list of the major functions performed by retail distribution centers:

- *Receiving*—Unloading shipments at the dock.
- *Checking*—Matching the contents of shipments against a packing slip. Quality assurance is often a part of this function.
- *Marking*—Price labeling or ticketing the merchandise.
- *Putaway*—Warehousing basic merchandise for future replenishment of stores, or bulk items, such as furniture, for direct shipment to customers.

- *Picking*—Distributing putaway goods to stores or customers.
- *Distribution*—Allocating shipments to stores.
- *Shipping*—Routing merchandise to stores.
- *Vendor Return*—Processing returns of damaged or slow-selling goods to vendors for credit.
- *Traffic*—Coordinating the inbound delivery from vendors and outbound shipments to stores.

VENDOR PARTNERSHIPS

Vendor partnerships are collaborations between retailers and their vendors that go beyond the traditional interactions between the two. These partnerships often involve strategies for pumping goods through the distribution channel more rapidly and efficiently than in nonpartnered interactions. The net results are often reduced distribution costs, better inventory control, increased sales, and improved gross margin and GMROI.

Floor-Ready Merchandise

Floor-ready merchandise (FRM) involves a negotiated agreement whereby the vendor agrees to package, case, fold, hang, and /or ticket merchandise in a such a way that it is ready for the selling floor upon its arrival at the store's distribution center. FRM eliminates redundancies. For instance, hanging goods are sometime shipped to retailers on flimsy shipping hangers that are then replaced with higher-quality selling-floor hangers at the retailer's distribution center. FRM is shipped on selling-floor hangers, thus eliminating the labor-intensive hanger-changing process at the distribution center.

FRM also involves source tagging of goods with antitheft tags or price tags. Tagging is a function that a vendor can perform more cost effectively than a retailer as part of its own ticketing or packaging process. Source tagging expedites the processing of goods at the retail distribution center. Radio frequency identification (RFID) is the state-of-the-art tagging system. RFID tags have silicon chips embedded with bar code information, such as vendor, style, and color. The tags are attached to or incorporated into products and read with radio waves, thus expediting processing, distribution, and tracking. Wal-Mart requires its major vendors to place RFID tags on all shipments. In time, other retailers likely will follow suit, especially as the system becomes more refined.[3]

FRM can also extend to the manner in which goods are packed for shipment to the retailer. Though some vendors case pack, or *prepack*, shipments with a standard assortment of sizes, colors, and styles, FRM assortments are packed specific to the replenishment needs of individual stores. These shipments can be sent directly to stores without being sorted at retail distribution centers. This facilitates cross docking whereby the distribution center functions like a trucking terminal with merchandise arriving in a truck in one bay and going out in another truck in another bay with virtually no processing in between.

The benefits of FRM are far-reaching. Distribution center operating costs can be reduced by as much as 80 percent, and the average amount of time that goods remain in a DC can decrease from a few days to a few hours. The long-term result is an increase in turnover and GMROI.[4]

Markdown Allowances

Though buyers hope that goods will sell at prices consistent with their gross-margin objectives, each order is a gamble in that some goods may eventually require drastic markdowns. Vendors can share this risk in two ways:

- Return agreements whereby the retailer is allowed to return unsold goods after a specified period.
- Markdown allowances, or markdown money, whereby the vendor compensates the retailer for markdowns. The compensation often is based on the difference between a guaranteed gross margin and the actual gross margin with an allowance against future purchases.

MOOTSIES TOOTSIES

Shoes to Die For

SIZE RUN AND BREAKDOWN INFORMATION:

RUN	WIDTH	SIZE RUN	BREAKDOWN
			5 - 6 - 7 - 8 - 9 - 10
D	M	6/10 × 12	1 1 1 2 2 2 2 1
R	M	6/10 × 18	1 2 2 3 3 3 2 2
G	M	5/10 × 18	1 2 5 5 3 2
CD	M	6/10 × 18	2 5 5 4 2
KT	M	6/10 × 12	1 3 3 3 2
AA	N	7/10 × 6	1 1 1 1 1 1

FIGURE 14.6
Shoe vendors case pack shipments with standard assortments of sizes.

In essence, markdown allowances are a strategy through which a retailer negotiates favorable wholesale prices. Markdown allowances are a sensitive issue between retailers and their vendors. New vendors feel that the only way that they will ever conduct business with some retailers is with the promise of markdown dollars. Retailers claim that they need the insurance of markdown dollars until a new vendor proves its worth. Vendors resent sharing markdown expenses, feeling that markdowns are often attributable to factors controllable by the retailer, such as poor merchandise presentation and inadequate selling floor coverage.

Promotional Support

Many vendors offer retailers promotional opportunities to enhance the recognition and sale of their products in stores. Cooperative advertising is an agreement between a retailer and a vendor to share advertising expense. The level of a vendor's participation in a cooperative advertising program is based on a retailer's purchases over a specified time period, usually a year. Most cooperative advertising programs place restrictions on the items advertised and the advertising medium and schedule. Some vendors prepare generic advertising for their products that retailers can adapt for their own use with tag lines, such as "Available at all Boscov stores," dubbed onto electronic ads, or store logos integrated into print ads. Retailers save considerable production costs by using vendor-prepared advertising.

Other forms of promotional support by vendors include:

- **Product demonstrations** Some vendors provide demonstrators to show the effective use of their product or product line in stores. Cosmetic makeovers and countertop-appliance demonstrations are common vendor-sponsored demonstrations in department stores.
- **Premiums**   A premium is a product offered without charge or at a very low retail price to customers who have made a minimum purchase within a product line. Advertising for premiums often reads: "Yours free with any $__ purchase of__" or "Yours for $__ with any $___ purchase of__." Premiums are common in the prestige cosmetics industry where a free premium is called a gift with purchase (GWP), and a paid-for premium is called a purchase with purchase (PWP). Pioneered by Estée Lauder, the gift-with-purchase has become an industry standard.[5]

- **Samples**   Samples are small quantities of a product offered without charge to customers independent of a purchase within a line. Samples are common in the prestige fragrance industry.
- **Contest and drawings**   Contests are promotional activities that require the demonstration of a skill. Drawings, or *sweepstakes*, are games of chance. Contests are popular for children's products.
- **Displays and exhibits**   Some vendors loan retailers museum-like exhibits for use in displays or in conjunction with a vendor promotion.

Some vendors provide point-of-purchase signage and fixtures to enhance the sale of their product line in stores, a topic discussed in Chapter 16. Other vendors sponsor training schools for salespeople to highlight new products and provide selling tips. Some vendors pay commissions or other incentives to the retail salespeople who sell their product line.

FIGURE 14.7
A premium is a product offered to customers without charge or at a very low price. Courtesy The BON TON Stores Inc.

FIGURE 14.8
Tagging is a function that vendors can perform more effectively than retailers.
Source: www.beallsinc.com.

Electronic Data Interchange

Electronic data interchange (EDI) is a partnership between a retailer and a vendor that involves a backward flow of customer purchase information through the distribution pipeline beginning at the retailer's point of sale. The partners use the information to execute their functions more efficiently. EDI is sometimes extended to include vendors' vendors, such as fabric mills.

EDI involves developing model assortments of product styles, sizes, and colors by store based on sales histories, sales projections, desired turnover, and lead time for delivery. Product information is captured electronically at point of sale and is periodically transmitted to vendors who then replenish the depleted inventory. EDI is most often used for basic, reorderable goods with broad assortments of styles, sizes, or colors, such as cosmetics and hosiery.

There are several positive outcomes associated with EDI:

- **Improved in-stock position** The in-stock position of EDI merchandise is 95 percent or better, since assortments are rapidly replenished as merchandise is sold.[6] The in-stock position of non-EDI merchandise is often as low as 50 percent. Fewer stockouts result in increased sales, since customers are likely to find their choice of size, color, and style.
- **Better inventory management** EDI improves turnover, since fast-selling goods are reordered, while slow-turning goods are not. EDI also enhances space productivity, since slow sellers are edited from assortments, freeing up valuable shelf and floor space for more productive goods. Frequent small orders also reduce the amount of inventory carried.

- Shortened lead time   Because time-consuming manual ordering tasks are eliminated, some retailers experience as much as a 50 percent reduction in lead time by implementing EDI. At one department store, EDI accelerated delivery to the selling floor by ten days. Sales increased by 11 percent with 19 percent less inventory on hand.[7]
- Greater efficiency   EDI eliminates errors due to manual counts, data entry, and illegible orders. By reducing administrative tasks, EDI permits buyers to concentrate on selecting merchandise and developing merchandising programs.
- Increased profitability   A higher markup is maintained on EDI merchandise, since only merchandise that is selling is reordered. One department store chain estimates that the maintained markup on EDI merchandise is 3 to 4 percent higher than on non-EDI merchandise, and that every dollar invested in EDI-replenished goods is 16.3 percent more profitable than non-EDI goods.[8]

Advance shipping notices (ASN) and *shippers container marking* (SCM) are two technologically advanced concepts that have enhanced EDI's success. An ASN is a vendor's electronic notification to a retailer that an order has been

SOURCE
Zellner, W. and Berner, R. (February 16, 2004). Wal-Mart eases its grip. *BusinessWeek*. p. 40.

WAL-MART EASES ITS GRIP

Wal-Mart, known for squeezing suppliers for low prices, has become more flexible in dealing with its vendors. The reason? Driving down wholesale prices was driving down Wal-Mart's retail prices, thus making it hard for Wal-Mart to show healthy same-store sales gains. Moreover, the chain's lower prices didn't always create enough new volume to cover rising costs. Weaker-than-expected sales and profits left the retail giant's stock lagging.

Vendors are relieved. Often faced with price increases on raw materials, vendors are now not as fearful of raising their prices and losing Wal-Mart to a cheaper rival. Some analysts believe that the gains aren't likely to be big. They say that Wal-Mart will still push suppliers to cut costs, but may be willing to let them keep more of the savings from any efficiencies. The situation will occur mostly with branded goods. In such cases, Wal-Mart will simply pass on price increases to consumers, holding its own margins steady. But where Wal-Mart oversees the sourcing of its own private label products, it will keep any savings. This will lead to better gross margins, while still reducing prices for consumers.

FIGURE 14.9
Electronic data interchange is a backward flow of customer purchase information through the distribution pipeline that begins when bar codes are scanned at point of sale. © David Young-Wolff/PhotoEdit.

shipped. SCM involves identifying the contents of cartons by bar codes that are scanned into a retailer's inventory upon receipt. The cartons are then sent directly to stores without further distribution and processing. This paperless transaction speeds up the flow of merchandise while significantly reducing processing expenses.

Vendors also benefit from EDI. EDI provides them with sales information that can be used to manage inventories and plan production. To complete the trading linkage, some vendors develop similar partnerships with their own vendors, matching consumer demand at one end of the merchandise pipeline to the availability of raw materials at the other. The standardization of EDI forms and procedures has facilitated the widespread application of EDI. Once the property of large retailers and vendors, EDI is now technologically and fiscally feasible for small retailers and vendors.

EDI requires a bond of trust between the retailer and vendor. The retailer must feel confident that a vendor will not share its sales information with competitive retailers and that the actual carton content matches what is indicated on the SCM. EDI has become a condition of transacting business with many retailers. One retailer encourages EDI partnerships by charging vendors a handling fee for every purchase order not generated through EDI.

The Vendor Matrix

A vendor matrix is a list of preferred vendors selected at conglomerate level. The decision to include a vendor in a matrix is based on the product line's compatibility with the organization's merchandising objectives, favorable price negotiations, and various forms of vendor support, in exchange for a retailer's commitment to space and established inventory levels. Some organizations limit their buyers to conducting business only with matrix vendors. Retailers have reduced the number of vendors with whom they conduct business by as much as 50 percent as a result of adopting a matrix.

These streamlined vendor structures are criticized as unholy alliances between large retailers and large vendors that limit business opportunities for small vendors. Some feel that a matrix transforms a buying function into an order-filling function by limiting a buyer's autonomy.

Vendor Relations

Maximizing consumer sales is an objective that is common to both retailers and their vendors. Though retailers and their vendors share common sales goals, their individual profit objectives are sometimes a source of conflict. A vendor's profit is derived from selling goods to retailers at the *highest*

SOURCE
Rozhon, T. (February 25, 2005). First the markdown, then the showdown. *New York Times*.

FROM MARKDOWNS TO SHOWDOWNS

For years, markdown allowances were inherent in the relationships between large retailers and their vendors. As originally conceived, markdown money compensated retailers when a specific style or product grouping turned out to be an unexpectedly weak seller. The retailer and the vendor shared the expense of liquidating the inventory. But over time, things have changed. Retailers aren't just asking for markdown help on troubled merchandise, they're asking for markdown help on everything. Markdown money has become a revenue stream.

Twenty years ago, when the retail industry was far more fragmented, vendors had the leverage to insist that retailers assume the financial risk of their purchases. If a retailer bought it, and it didn't sell, the retailer took the markdown hit. Through mergers and acquisitions, retailers have become large. Large retailers have the market leverage to force the financial risk of carrying inventory onto their vendors.

Underlying this battle over markdown money is one inescapable conclusion: retailers buy too much merchandise. Without any markdown risk of their own, retailers have no reason to prudently manage their inventory. Buy a big number, sell what you can at your planned margins, and then slash away as deeply as you need to sell it all through. Their vendors went along because of the size of the purchase orders. For a long time, the vendors understood how to play this game; they simply built the markdown money into their prices upfront, and everybody was happy. But because retailers treat markdown money like revenue, they expect increases every year.

Excess inventory is excess inventory. It doesn't matter whether the cost of marking it down later has been buried in the purchase price. All that does is inflate the retail price, shrink the gross margin, or both. And the carrying cost of retail inventory, which includes costs of storage, financing, insurance, handling, shrink, damage, and obsolescence, is typically 2 to 2.5 percent a month.

TJX
THE TJX COMPANIES, INC.
Framingham, Massachusetts

T·J·MAXX   *Marshalls·*   HomeGoods·   WINNERS   TK·MAXX   A.J.Wright·

To Our Manufacturers And Suppliers: Statement of Policy Concerning Gifts

We are taking this opportunity to restate our policy concerning gift-giving, not only during the forthcoming holiday season, but at all times of the year, on any occasion. Gifts, no matter how well intentioned by the donor, tend to shake the moral structure of the firmest business foundations by substituting subjective emotions and motives for objective judgment based on service, quality and price.

Accordingly, for the mutual protection of our suppliers, our associates and the Company, we prohibit our associates from accepting gifts, gratuities, payments or favors of any kind. Any gifts received by our associates will be returned to the donor or donated to charitable organizations. Our associates are advised that violation of this policy is considered to be a grievous matter.

We call upon you to assist us and our associates by refraining from giving or offering such gifts. Your awareness of and cooperation with this policy will foster the continuation of fair business practices that favor our close association.

Best wishes for a happy holiday season and a prosperous New Year.

Bernard Cammarata
Chairman of the Board

Edmond J. English
President and Chief Executive Officer

The Marmaxx Group/T.J. Maxx/Marshalls
HG Buying, Inc./HomeGoods, Inc.
Winners Apparel, Ltd.   T.K. Maxx
Concord Buying Group Inc./A. J. Wright

FIGURE 14.10
To avoid conflicts of interest, most retailers prohibit buyers from accepting gifts from vendors. © 2000 The TJX Companies, Inc.

possible prices, while a retailer's profit is derived from purchasing goods from vendors at the *lowest* possible prices. To circumvent conflict, some retailers publish vendor-relations guidelines that establish parameters for professional interactions. To avoid conflicts of interest, many retailers prohibit buyers from accepting gifts or any form of hospitality from vendors, other than an occasional lunch.

In spite of these provisions, interactions between retailers and their vendors are sometimes adversarial. Vendors provoke retailers by shipping short, shipping late, or making random substitutes for out-of-stock goods. Retailers often retaliate by levying chargeback penalties for incomplete orders or damaged or mislabeled goods. A vendor once reported a $50.50 chargeback on an item with an upside down label: $0.50 was for the error and $50 was for a minimum penalty charge. Another vendor reported a $10,000 chargeback on a $20,000 order for goods that arrived two weeks late. The vendor disputed the chargeback because the goods eventually sold out at regular price, even though they arrived late. In 2003, Saks, Inc. paid $21.5 million back to suppliers for chargebacks that the company was unable to substantiate with documentation. Onward Kashiyama was one of the suppliers. When the licensee for Michael Kors threatened to sue Saks, the company received a refund check for $716,000 from Saks with no itemized breakdown.[9]

Other transgressions can be traced to the retailer. Common abuses to vendors include taking cash discounts on invoices after cash discount periods have expired, returning as flawed merchandise that was damaged on the selling floor, and canceling ready-to-be-shipped orders with little notice. A New York State Supreme Court judge found Wal-Mart's cancellation clause in its purchase order "unconscionable" due to the financial ramifications to the vendor. The clause gave Wal-Mart the right to cancel an order any time prior to shipment, regardless of the stage of production.[10]

SUMMARY POINTS

- Quantity and seasonal discounts are reductions in the cost of merchandise that are mutually advantageous to the vendor and the retailer.
- Dating is the time period allowed for the payment of an invoice. Favorable dating terms reduce the cost of goods sold and improve a retailer's cash flow.
- Transportation terms identify the bearer of the cost of shipping goods from the vendor to the retailer, as well as the point at which the title of the goods passes from one to the other. Time and cost are the two factors that are considered when determining a transportation mode.
- Vendor partnerships are collaborations between retailers and their vendors to reduce distribution costs, control inventory, increase sales, and improve gross margin and GMROI.
- Electronic data interchange is a trading partnership among marketing channel members whereby each member can access customer purchase information to execute more efficiently their function in the supply pipeline.

- A vendor matrix is a list of a retailer's preferred merchandise resources.
- Retailers and vendors should work together cooperatively to achieve their goals.

KEY TERMS AND CONCEPTS

advance dating	discount	net payment date
anticipation	distribution center	net payment period
case-packed goods	drawing	premium
cash dating	electronic data	private carrier
cash discount	interchange (EDI)	proximo dating
cash discount date	EOM dating	purchase order
cash discount period	extra dating	purchase with purchase
cash on delivery (COD)	floor-ready	(PWP)
common carrier	merchandise (FRM)	quantity discount
consignment goods	free on board (FOB)	receipt-of-goods (ROG)
consolidator	gift with purchase	dating
contest	(GWP)	regular dating
contract carrier	intermodal	seasonal discount
cooperative advertising	transportation	source tagging
cross docking	invoice	vendor matrix
date of invoice (DOI)	memorandum goods	vendor partnership
dating	minimum order	

THINKING ABOUT IT

1. Quantity discounts are very tempting as a means of increasing gross margin by reducing cost of goods sold. When is it best to forego quantity discounts? On what type of merchandise can quantity discounts be especially dangerous?
2. Seasonal discounts are also tempting. When is it best to forego seasonal discounts? On what type of merchandise can seasonal discounts be especially dangerous?
3. Though dating varies significantly by category of merchandise, it is relatively consistent within a category. Can you think of reasons for discrepancies among product categories?
4. What are the long-term disadvantages of poor vendor relationships?
5. List some categories of merchandise for which you think EDI is a perfect

application. List other categories where you don't think EDI would work. Compare the two lists. How are they alike? Different?

6. Why are vendor matrixes becoming more and more common? What would life be like without them?

TEAMING UP

1. Each member of your team should consider a category of merchandise sold at a department store or full-line discounter. What are the characteristics of the merchandise that determine how it should be shipped from a vendor? Share your observations as a team, and then collectively determine which categories are most vulnerable to bad shipping decisions and which are the least vulnerable.

2. Each team member should research examples of vendor support to retailers as discussed in the "Vendor Partnerships" section of this chapter. Share findings with the group to determine the type of vendor support that seems to be most common today. The least common? Does vendor support seem to differ by category of merchandise? Are there categories for which there seems to be a lot of support? Little support?

SEARCHING THE NET

1. Search for recent trade publication coverage of RFID. What are the pros? The cons?

2. Search for news coverage of current issues facing the trucking industry.

3. Do a key word search for the term "vendor partnership." Where does the term pop up? What do you see as some of the latest vendor-partnership trends?

SOLVING PROBLEMS

1. What is the billed cost for 3,000 sweaters when the unit cost is $30.00 for the first 100, $29.75 for more than 100 units, and $29.00 for than 500 units? What is the billed cost for 300 units?

2. A $3,000 shipment to a retailer is invoiced on August 1 and received on August 5. Complete the following grid, determining the last day for taking the discount and the amount due after the discount when payment terms are stated as follows:

Terms	Last day to take discount	Date when full payment is due
2/10 net 30		
2/10 net 30 ROG		
2/10 net 30 EOM		
2% 15th prox. net 30		
2/10 net 30, as of October 1		
2/10, 60X		

3. What additional discount would be taken in problem 2 above if payment were made on August 6 and the prevailing interest rate were 5 percent?
4. A retailer asks a vendor in Los Angeles to ship goods to a consolidator in Secaucus, New Jersey. What part of the shipping does the retailer pay for when the goods are shipped:

- FOB origin
- FOB origin, freight prepaid
- FOB origin, freight prepaid and charged back
- FOB destination, freight collect
- FOB destination, freight prepaid
- FOB destination, freight collect and allowed

USING EXCEL
1. Create a spreadsheet to compute a cumulative discount.
2. Create a spreadsheet to compute cash discount.
3. Create a spreadsheet to compute the long-term impact of forfeiting discounts (see pages 382 through 383).

PART FIVE

Merchandise Control and Presentation

○ MERCHANDISING CONTROLS AND REPORT ANALYSIS
○ STORE LAYOUT AND MERCHANDISE PRESENTATION

After reading this chapter, you will be able to discuss:

● The control function in a retail organization.

● Control standards.

● The analysis of control reports and their use as decision-making tools.

CHAPTER FIFTEEN

Merchandising Controls and Report Analysis

The word *control* has negative connotations when linked to restrictions of autonomy or creativity. However, controls are critical merchandising tools that provide information about current status and future planning while ascertaining that retailers do not waver from their charted course. Chapter 15 covers some of the ways that controls are used for effective decision making and for reacting to emerging problems.

CONTROL STANDARDS

Control involves measuring actual performance against goals or standards, and reacting to the causes of any deviations from those goals. Control is a three-step process that includes:

- Establishing goals or standards
- Measuring deviations of actual performance from standards
- Reacting to the deviations

Controls enable decision makers to react to problems before they become critical.

A control standard is a reference point or benchmark to measure performance. Plans are standards. A "$2.0 million sales goal for August," a "$25,000 open to buy for March," and "projected net income of 4 percent of net sales" are all standards. Like plans, standards are often based on comparable prior performance. "Last year's girls department sales during the week prior to school opening" is a standard for measuring "this year's girls department sales during the week prior to school opening."

The aggregate performance of similar business units is often used as a standard. The percentage sales increase (or decrease) for *all* stores in a chain can be used as a standard to measure the sales performance of *individual* stores. Penetration is a measure of the performance of a single business unit as a percentage of the aggregate performance of all similar business units.

A "4 percent penetration" can refer to the performance of a store that has generated 4 percent of the sales of all stores in a chain or a category of merchandise that has generated 4 percent of the sales of all categories in a department.

Internal standards are derived from data within an organization. Industry standards are derived outside an organization, often by a trade association. The National Retail Federation annually publishes the *Department and Specialty Store Merchandising and Operating Results*, or *MOR*, a listing of industry standards for maintained markup, markdowns, shortage, gross margin, and turnover, compiled by merchandise category and sales volume.

The validity of a comparison to a standard is based on the similarity of the standard to that which is being measured. To quote a trite but apropos cliché, the comparison must be "apples to apples and oranges to oranges." Comparing this year's July better sportswear gross margin to last year's September gross margin is an invalid comparison in that July gross margins are heavily eroded by end-of-season markdowns. Comparing the garden-shop sales of a full-line discount store to the sales of all garden shops in the chain is not as valid as a comparison to stores in the same geographic region. Regional weather conditions dramatically affect horticulture sales, making a comparison outside the region less valid than a comparison within the region.

A standard is sometimes validated by comparing actual performance to multiple standards. Assume that actual sales for a month are 20 percent under plan and 10 percent over last year. The 30 percent discrepancy between the comparisons to the two standards may be an indication that the plan for this year was unrealistically optimistic.

Multiple standard comparisons sometimes reveal problems veiled by a comparison to a single standard. Assume that a shoe store's actual December sales exceeded plan by 7 percent and last year's sales by 7 percent. The store manager was delighted by this performance until comparing the store's performance to the chain's performance. The manager found that the sales for all stores exceeded plan by 12 percent and last year by 14 percent. The store lagged behind the chain's performance relative to both plan sales and last year's sales by 5 percentage points.

Deviations

A deviation is a discrepancy between actual performance and a standard. If planned sales for a week are $2,000 and actual sales are $2,500, then there is a $500 deviation from planned sales. A deviation's direction is expressed by attributing negative values to deviations less than a standard and positive values to deviations greater than a standard. The direction of a deviation is a performance indicator. A +$500 deviation from planned sales is favorable, while a −$500 deviation is not. Not all positive deviations are

---

MULTIPLE MEASURES

It is often wise to review both dollar and percentage deviations together to determine the significance of the deviations. Consider a comparison of November's plan to actual sales for two outerwear categories in Table A. The +/− percent column shows a percentage shortfall in rainwear that is twice the percentage shortfall of wool coats. However, the +/− $ column indicated that the sales shortfall of wool coats is far more serious in terms of dollars than the sales shortfall of rainwear. Since wool coat sales were planned significantly higher than the rainwear sales, the −10 percent deviation from the wool coat sales plan represents a far greater sales deficit in dollars than the −20 percent deviation from the rainwear sales plan.

The situation is characteristic of a store in a northern climate where November sales projections for wool coats far exceed sales projections for lightweight rainwear. As depicted in Table B, the scenario would reverse itself in April when sales projections for rainwear exceed sales projections for wool coats. In this case, the −20 percent and $10,000 sales shortfall in rainwear would be more distressing than the −40 percent and $2,000 sales shortfall in wool coats.

Table A NOVEMBER

Category	Plan	Actual	+/− $	+/− %
Wool Coats	$100,000	$90,000	−$10,000	−10%
Rainwear	$10,000	$8,000	−$2,000	−20%

Table B APRIL

Category	Plan	Actual	+/− $	+/− %
Wool Coats	$5,000	$3,000	−$2,000	−40%
Rainwear	$50,000	$40,000	−$10,000	−20%

desirable, however. A +$500 deviation from planned expenses is not favorable, while a −$500 deviation is.

The degree of a deviation is expressed by dividing the deviation by the standard and multiplying by 100 to convert to a percentage:

$$percent \ of \ deviation \ = \ \frac{amount \ of \ deviation}{standard} \times 100$$

The +$500 deviation from plan sales represents a +25 percent increase over plan:

$$percent \ of \ deviation \ = \ \frac{+500}{\$2,000} \times 100$$

$$percent \ of \ deviation \ = \ 25\%$$

The resulting percentage expresses the degree of the deviation. A $500 increase on a $2,500 sales plan (+20 percent) is more impressive than a $500 increase on a $25,000 sales plan (+2 percent).

Control Objectivity

Qualitative controls measure performance descriptively; for example, a customer satisfaction survey that asks respondents to rate a store's customer service as excellent, very good, fair, or poor. Qualitative ratings are subjective in that one person's perception of "good" may differ from another person's. Quantitative controls measure performance numerically. Quantitative controls are objective. The calculation of a 5 percent increase over last year's sales will yield the same figure regardless of who performs the calculation.

Quantitative controls reduce the emotion in the communication between managers. A store manager may complain to a buyer that inventory is "low." The buyer may argue that the inventory is "not low." "Low" and "not low" are biased qualitative assessments. The store manager's assessment is biased by a single-store perspective. The buyer's assessment is biased by a multistore perspective. Each party should quantitatively define "low" and "not low" to resolve the dispute objectively. Comparing the store's stock-to-sales ratio to the chain's or comparing the percentage of inventory that the store owns to the percentage of the chain's sales that the store generates is a rational quantitative stance.

Control Intervals

Controls are established at specific time intervals such as hourly, daily, weekly, monthly, quarterly, seasonally, or annually. The frequency of a control is based on the likelihood and/or significance of deviations from standards. Inventory that turns 26 times a year requires more frequent monitoring than an inventory that turns only twice a year. Controls of fast-turning inventories must be established at short intervals to ensure that minimum stock levels are maintained and that replenishment orders are placed before stockouts occur. In general, controls should be established at intervals that will allow a timely reaction to meaningful deviations from standards.

Some controls involve multiple time intervals. Sales are often controlled by week, month, season, and year. Multiple time-interval comparisons broaden the perspective of an assessment. The trauma of a 50 percent deviation from plan sales for a week is diminished by the fact that sales are +20 percent over plan for the month, and +15 percent over plan for the season.

Control Levels

Controls are established at the same organizational levels as plans. In most retail organizations, sales and inventory are controlled by category, department, and division, as well as at store, district, and regional levels. Like plans, controls are used by managers relative to the nature and scope of their responsibility. A store manager may monitor a store's sales by category daily. A district manager may monitor total store sales daily. A regional manager may monitor total store sales weekly. The time constraints of the workday make it impossible for a regional manager of 100 stores to monitor daily the sales of every category in every store. Store managers can perform this task more effectively in that they have a narrower scope of responsibility.

REPORTS

Retail organizations compile various types of management reports that reflect the status of sales, inventory, and profitability by comparing actual performance to standards (last year, plan) for defined business units (store, category of merchandise) for specified periods (month, year). Some management report titles that are common to many retail organizations include Best Seller Report, Inventory Position Report, and Monthly Sales Report.

Compiling reports was once a labor-intensive, error-prone process that

---

WHAT ARE BESTSELLERS?

- Unit sales of 50 or more
- Dollar sales of $1000 or more
- Sell through of 30% or better
- In stock less than 4 weeks
- On hand of at least 10 units

---

involved tedious paper chasing. Today, computerized inventory management systems compile data into reliable, easily accessible, real-time reports that allow store managers to monitor best sellers and salespeople's productivity, and to locate merchandise for customers in other stores in the chain. Buyers rely on reports to review sales factors such as location, price, and vendor to make strategic merchandising decisions relative to reordering, transferring, or marking down merchandise. Computerization has facilitated inventory tracking at very precise levels. A men's dress-shirt inventory that was once manually tracked by units and store can be easily tracked by price, vendor, color, and sleeve and collar size.

Exception Reports

A wealth of readily accessible information has resulted in report proliferation in some retail organizations. To avoid this, some retailers generate exception reports that include only major deviations from standards, bypassing minor ones. A sales report may include only deviations that are 10 percent over plan and 10 percent under plan. Filtering out deviations, within a −10 percent to +10 percent range reduces the size of the report and the amount of time needed to review it.

Note that even "good" deviations (+10 percent to planned sales) should be included in an exception report. Because inventory allocations are predicated on planned sales, a store that is running significantly ahead of plan is likely to be underinventoried.

CHECKLIST FOR REVIEWING PROBLEM DEPARTMENTS

Is the percentage of stock appropriate to the percentage of sales? If not, how much stock must be obtained to reach an adequate level? Where will it come from? What is the on-order status?

Analyze the sales by classification. Are poorly performing classes adequately stocked? Is the stock in well-performing classifications depleted?

Are all classes productive? If not, should the non-productive classes be eliminated so that the productive ones can be further developed through additional floor space and inventory?

Is basic merchandise filled in? *Every* size, color, style?

Are groups broken? Is "piecy" merchandise frustrating customers, inhibiting presentation, tying up inventory dollars, and slowing your turnover?

What are the company's best sellers? Are they your best sellers? If not, why? Location? Stock level?

What are your competitors selling?

If stock levels are adequate, can you trade off slow-moving merchandise for more productive merchandise?

Are markdowns being taken in a timely manner? Have you taken a disproportionately large or small amount of markdowns?

Walk the floor. Has prime floor space been dedicated to your most productive classes, resources, and items? Have presentation standards interfered with moving goods quickly?

FIGURE 15.1
One retailer's checklist for reviewing sales and inventory reports.

REPORT FORMATS AND ANALYSIS

Though all reports are used to assess performance and as sources of information on which to effect decisions, report formats vary from one organization to another. Though most retailers generate reports of sales, inventory, and profitability, reports differ relative to the level of information, format, frequency, and application. The following are descriptions of actual reports obtained from several retail organizations. The company names have been changed to ensure the confidentiality of the information. The reports represent an infinitesimally small sample of the myriad of report types and formats used by retail organizations.

Turnover Report

Danielle's Department Store generates an annual turnover report for more than 500 categories of merchandise at its 12 specialty department stores. Figure 15.2 is a section of the 2007 report for the junior department's knit top category.

Features of the Report   The report includes this year's and last year's sales and average inventory by store and chain, and the percentage change to last year for each. Turnover for this year and last year is calculated by store and chain. Sales and turnover performance can be assessed by comparing a store's performance to the chain's. Turnover issues can be traced to sales and/or average inventory.

Observations   Assume that a 5.0 turnover is acceptable for the category according to industry standards. This year's Northfield sales increased by 4.6 percent, while inventory increased by 8.8 percent. Turnover decreased from 4.9 to 4.8. Though the 4.6 percent sales increase is a desirable result, the proportionately greater amount of inventory required to generate the increase negates the favorable judgment. The objective is to produce a sales

DANIELLE'S DEPARTMENT STORE

2007 Turnover Report

Department: Junior Sportswear
Category: Knit Tops
Division: Sportswear

	Chain	Westfield	Eastfield	Northfield
Average Inventory LY	$110,338	$ 8,933	$ 7,642	$ 9,651
Average Inventory TY	$118,431	$ 9,324	$ 6,371	$10,497
% Change Inventory	+7.3%	+4.4%	– 16.6%	+8.8%
Sales LY	$548,322	$43,165	$39,063	$47,671
Sales TY	$588,871	$28,160	$46,158	$49,880
% Change Sales	+7.4%	– 34.8%	+18.2%	+4.6%
Turnover LY	5.0	4.8	5.1	4.9
Turnover TY	5.0	3.0	7.2	4.8

FIGURE 15.2
2007 Turnover Report from Danielle's Department Store for three stores only.

increase with an equally proportionate inventory to yield the same turnover (4.9) or to produce a sales increase with a proportionately lower inventory to yield a higher turnover (greater than 4.9). The decrease in turnover is slight, however, and close to the 5.0 standard. Thus, the matter should receive little attention.

An additional 4.4 percent investment in inventory at Westfield resulted in a 34.8 percent decrease in sales and a dramatic decrease in turnover from 4.8 to 3.0. Westfield's sales performance (−34.8 percent) is inconsistent with the chain's sales performance (+7.4 percent), a 42.2 percent deviation (7.4 percent + 34.8 percent). The deviations are significant and worthy of investigation. If the sales decline is due to a permanent factor, such as the entry of new competition in the marketplace, then inventory allocations should be adjusted to reflect diminished sales. Assortments should be carefully edited so that only the best-selling resources and items are retained. If the sales decline is due to a temporary factor, such as a store renovation that disrupted business for a period, allocations should remain the same, anticipating that completion of the renovation will alleviate the store's lackluster sales performance.

Eastfield experienced an 18.2 percent sales increase and a 16.6 percent decrease in inventory, while turnover increased from 5.1 to 7.2. Unlike Westfield, Eastfield's sales and inventory are both headed in the right direction. This year's sales increase was achieved with a proportionately smaller inventory. The only cause for concern is that Eastfield's inventory may be turning too quickly, at 2.2 turns greater than the chain's 5.0. Remember that an excessively high turnover may be indicative of stockouts and/or broken assortments. Thus, Eastfield's inventory may need to be fortified by a generous infusion of merchandise to support an optimistically upward sales trend (18.2 percent) that far exceeds the chain's average (+7.4 percent).

Note that a $3,500 decrease in Westfield's average inventory and a $3,500 increase in Eastfield's average inventory would have yielded turnover figures close to the company's 5.0 standard (4.8 and 4.7, respectively). Balanced inventories among stores can be maintained by regularly monitoring inventory positions and by correcting inequities through the proper allocation of new shipments of merchandise. Some companies resolve inventory inequities among stores by transferring goods from overinventoried stores to underinventoried stores. Many companies avoid interstore transfers because of high processing and transportation costs and because transferred goods are dormant for the several days that they are in process.

Annual Review of Merchandising Statistics

Caitlin's Corner compiles an annual report of merchandising statistics for its 16 casual apparel stores. Figure 15.3 is the 2007 report.

Features of the Report   The report includes comparative percentages for this year's and last year's markdowns and gross margin for each store, as well as this year's employee discounts, shortage, and cash discount percentages. The report also includes turnover and an aged inventory indicator, the percentage of inventory over six months old, as well the par and median for each group of reported figures. In this case, the median is the middle number when the statistics are ranked from worst to best. The par is the middle number of the best half of the statistics when ranked from worst to best.

FIGURE 15.3
Annual Review of
Merchandising Statistics
for Caitlin's Corner.

CAITLIN'S CORNER

ANNUAL REVIEW OF MERCHANDISING STATISTICS

Men's Basics

	Mark Downs		Emp. Disc.	Short-age	Cash Disc. to Pur.	Gross Margin		Inventory Data	
	This Year	Last Year				This Year	Last Year	Turn-Over	Age of Inventory
1	4.2	3.5	0.5	0.9	8.0	49.3	49.7	4.6	27
2	8.4	7.7	0.7	2.6	—	45.0	45.4	3.7	05
3	10.7	9.3	0.8	3.4	7.9	43.9	45.3	4.3	26
4	10.0	13.6	0.7	5.6	5.2	43.9	45.3	3.5	33
5	6.2	5.5	0.7	2.1	7.9	47.8	48.5	5.4	—
6	8.6	11.6	1.2	2.4	7.7	46.9	46.8	4.9	07
7	6.4	10.3	2.0	0.7	7.8	48.1	44.7	5.5	17
8	7.5	18.9	1.5	2.1	6.0	43.0	37.2	3.2	23
9	12.8	6.6	1.1	2.8	7.6	45.6	48.5	6.6	11
10	3.9	4.3	0.9	0.5	7.8	49.6	48.4	6.4	01
11	4.6	6.1	0.8	5.5	8.2	45.7	46.3	7.7	04
12	4.5	7.5	0.8	1.7	6.8	46.8	44.1	5.6	—
13	14.1	19.2	0.9	2.5	7.7	44.6	42.5	3.3	04
14	3.9	5.5	0.6	3.6	7.6	48.1	45.9	4.3	20
15	7.5	7.3	0.7	0.6	7.4	47.9	47.7	5.4	23
16	9.5	9.0	1.3	2.4	8.3	45.9	46.5	5.7	07
PAR	4.5	5.5	0.7	0.7	7.9	48.1	48.5	5.7	04
MED	7.5	7.5	0.8	2.4	7.7	46.8	46.3	4.9	11

Léon Theremin invented radio frequency identification (RFID) in 1946 as an espionage tool for the Soviet Union. RFID is a method that uses radio waves to identify a product (or animal or person) with an attached or embedded mobile device called a tag. The data transmitted by the tag can provide product identification and location information relative to price, color, date of purchase, and so on. RFID is used in libraries, airports, warehouses, and retail stores for such things as pallet tracking, building access control, and item identification. RFID tags are commonly used in shipping container, truck, and trailer tracking. RFID is also used for car theft protection. A number of ski resorts, particularly in the French Alps, have adopted RFID tags to provide skiers hands-free access to ski lifts. Night clubs in Barcelona, Spain, and in Rotterdam, The Netherlands, use an implantable chip to identify their VIP customers, who in turn use the chip to pay for drinks. In-home uses of RFID, such as tracking the expiration dates of the food in refrigerators, have been proposed, but few have moved beyond the prototype stage.

In a typical RFID system, individual objects are equipped with a small, inexpensive tag. The tag contains a transponder with a digital memory chip that is given a unique electronic product code. The interrogator, an antenna packaged with a transceiver and decoder, emits a signal activating the RFID tag so it can read and write data to it. When an RFID tag passes through the electromagnetic zone, it detects the reader's activation signal. The reader decodes the data encoded in the tag's integrated circuit (silicon chip) and the data is passed to the host computer. Shelves in a Wal-Mart in Broken Arrow, Oklahoma, were equipped with readers to track the Max Factor's Lipfinity lipstick. Webcam images of the shelves were viewed 750 miles away by Procter & Gamble researchers in Cincinnati, Ohio, who could tell when lipsticks were removed from the shelves and observe the shoppers in action.

Since 2005, Wal-Mart has required its top 100 suppliers to apply RFID labels to all shipments. To meet this requirement, vendors use RFID printer/encoders to label cases and pallets. These smart labels are produced by embedding RFID inlays inside the label material, and then printing bar code and other visible information on the surface of the label. RFID tags are envisioned as a replacement for UPC barcodes, having a number of important advantages over the older technology. However, RFID may never completely replace barcodes, due in part to higher cost. It is more likely that goods will be tracked by pallet using RFID, and at item level with UPC barcodes. RFID has also been proposed for POS store checkouts to replace cashiers. However this is not likely without a significant reduction in the cost of current tags.

SOURCES

Weisman, R. (January 12, 2004). Boston's next exciting technology platform. *The Boston Globe*. pp. D1, 4; Garry, M. (November 24, 2003). New hope for source tagging? *Supermarket News*. pp. 77, 78; Marks, P. (March 20, 2005). Bye, bye, bar codes. *The Hartford Courant*. pp. D1, 2; Weisman, R. (December 25, 2004). Tracking a delay. *The Boston Globe*. pp. B5, 6.

Observations   Note that Store 8's gross margin improved greatly (37.2 percent to 43.0 percent) because of a dramatic decrease in markdowns from the second highest store (18.9 percent) to the median store (7.5 percent). Unfortunately, taking fewer markdowns has left Store 8 with a high percentage of aged inventory (23 percent), the fourth highest in the group. Stagnant merchandise has also caused Store 8 to yield the lowest turnover in the buying office (3.2).

Store 10 is the star. At 49.6 percent, Store 10's gross margin is the highest in the group because of a low markdown rate (3.9 percent), the lowest for the group. A low markdown rate at Store 10 has not resulted in a high percentage of aged inventory or slow turnover, however. Only 1 percent of Store 10's inventory is more than six months old. A 6.4 turnover exceeds par and is the third highest in the chain.

Stock-to-Sales Ratio Report

Tie One On compiles a monthly stock-to-sales ratio report for each of the five categories of merchandise sold by its ten fashion accessories pushcarts of trendy selections of scarves, hairgoods, sunglasses, and small leather goods. Figure 15.4 is April's report for all categories.

Features of the Report   The report includes the EOM and sales for each cart and the resulting stock-to-sales ratio. The report also includes each cart's EOM and sales penetrations. Based on the premise that penetrations of inventory should closely match penetrations of sales, the inventory position of each cart can be evaluated by comparing EOM penetrations to sales penetrations.

Observations   Note that the greatest discrepancies between EOM and sales penetrations are at Midway Plaza and Canyon Crest: 6 percent and 13 percent, respectively. Midway Plaza is overinventoried (high EOM penetrations relative to its sales penetration), while Canyon Crest is underinventoried (a low EOM penetrations relative to its sales penetration). Midway Plaza owns 11 percent of the EOM but generated only 5 percent of total sales. Canyon Crest owns only 10 percent of the EOM but generated nearly a quarter of the company's sales (23 percent). Comparing the problem cart's stock-to-sales ratios to the 6.4 aggregate stock-to-sales ratio further substan-

TIE ONE ON

STOCK-TO-SALES RATIO REPORT

April

	EOM		Sales		S/S Ratio
TOTAL CHAIN	$156.7	— %	$24.4	— %	6.4
Midway Plaza	$ 16.3	11.0%	$ 1.3	5.0%	12.5
Hamilton Heights	$ 12.4	8.0%	$ 1.1	5.0%	11.3
Bayshore	$ 15.6	10.0%	$ 2.2	9.0%	7.1
Long Beach	$ 12.4	8.0%	$ 1.4	6.0%	8.9
Town Center	$ 13.1	8.0%	$ 3.2	13.0%	4.1
Canyon Crest	$ 14.7	10.0%	$ 5.6	23.0%	2.6
Riverside	$ 10.3	7.0%	$ 1.3	5.0%	7.9
Eastridge	$ 21.3	14.0%	$ 3.6	15.0%	5.9
Chapel Hill	$ 22.5	15.0%	$ 3.1	13.0%	7.3
Fairfield Commons	$ 16.1	10.0%	$ 1.6	7.0%	10.1

FIGURE 15.4
Tie One On's April Stock-to-
Sales Ratio Report.

tiates the inventory inequity. Midway Plaza, with the highest stock-to-sales ratio (12.5), has nearly twice the proportionate amount of inventory to sales for all carts (6.4), while Canyon Crest, with the lowest stock-to-sales ratio (2.6), has less than half of the proportionate amount of inventory to sales for all carts. The inventory should be reallocated to alleviate these inequities.

Inventory Position and Sales

Monkeys & Pumpkins compiles a monthly report of stock-to-sales ratios and sales and inventory penetrations by category of merchandise for ten children's apparel stores. The report also includes month-to-date, season-to-date, and year-to-date sales compared to plan and last year. Figure 15.5 is a segment of the report for May for the infant layette category.

Features of the Report   The report lists the BOM, receipts, interstore transfers, markdowns, sales, and EOM for each store and the chain, as well each store's percentage of the chain's BOM, receipts, sales, and EOM. Like the previous report, the report is based on the premise that penetrations of inventory should closely match penetrations of sales. The inclusion of BOM, EOM, receipts, transfers, and markdowns in this report permits a careful analysis of inventory activity within the month. The report also includes

MONKEYS & PUMPKINS

May

INVENTORY POSITION AND SALES

	Total	%	Broadway %	Crossroads %	Village Square %	South Gate %	Ingleside %	Bel Air %	Buena Vista %
BOM	$227,525		14	14	18	14	9	14	16
Receipts	47,163		11	11	22	11	8	28	10
Sales	54,048		7	12	21	9	10	28	13
EOM Act	198,110		17	14	18	14	8	13	15
EOM Plan	159,100		12	12	23	12	9	16	16
S/S Act	4.2		6.7	4.1	3.0	5.1	3.1	1.6	4.2
S/S Plan	4.6		5.2	4.7	2.8	6.5	5.5	1.9	6.0

SALES TO DATE BY DEPARTMENT AND STORE

	Total	%	%	%	%	%	%	%	%
MTD last yr	$48,902	11	16–		21–	2–	18–	27	—
MTD plan	50,500	7	23–	6	12–	26	71	9	27
MTD this yr	54,048		7	12	21	9	10	28	13
STD last yr	143,151	29	5–	23	12	26	10–	33	—
STD plan	168,200	10	5–	2	8	31	39	12	2
STD this yr	184,854		9	11	25	9	8	28	10
YTD last yr	285,840	26	2–	19	19	6	12–	25	—
YTD plan	341,200	6	4–	9	16	15	2	12	22–
YTD this yr	361,221		9	11	26	6	7	29	10

FIGURE 15.5
A May Inventory Position and Sales report compiled by Monkeys & Pumpkins.

plan and actual stock-to-sales ratios for the month, and month-to-date, season-to-date, and year-to-date sales with percentage comparisons to plan and last year. The format facilitates a concurrent review of both inventory position and sales by store.

Observations   Broadway is overinventoried. The store owned 14 percent of the chain's BOM, received 11 percent of the chain's new receipts, but generated only 7 percent of the chain's sales. Broadway's EOM was planned at 12 percent of total, but the actual EOM was 17 percent of total. The store's 6.7 actual stock-to-sales ratio was the highest in the chain, considerably higher than the chain's 4.2 stock-to-sales ratio.

    Bel Air is underinventoried. The store generated 28 percent of the chain's sales, with only 14 percent of the chain's BOM. Though new receipts were generously distributed to Bel Air (28 percent), the allocations sold as rapidly as they arrived, leaving the store with only 13 percent of the chain's EOM. The store's 1.6 stock-to-sales ratio was the lowest in the chain, considerably lower than the chain's 4.2 stock-to-sales ratio.

Note Bel Air's sales growth. Month-to-date, season-to-date, and year-to-date sales are +27 percent, +33 percent, +25 percent to last year, respectively, the highest percentage sales increases of any of the stores. Note also that Bel Air's stock-to-sales ratio was planned at a modest 1.9, while the company's stock-to-sales ratio was planned at 4.6. The meager plan may have been the result of basing the plan on last year's inventory and sales. However, Bel Air's dramatic growth made last year's figures invalid benchmarks.

Sales and Stock-to-Sales Ratios

Shaun's Sporting Goods generates a monthly report of stock-to-sales ratios for more than 50 categories of merchandise common to most of its 28 stores. Figure 15.6 is the sleepwear department report for November.

Features of the Report   The report includes monthly sales for the category by store and total chain and percentage comparisons to last year. The report also includes the monthly stock-to-sales ratio for the category by store and last year's comparable ratio. Ranked percentage of sales increases/decreases and stock-to-sales ratios facilitate the assessment of individual store performance. The rankings range from 1, the best performer, to 23 or 24, the worst performer. Though there are 28 stores in the chain, only 23 have reported figures, since the other five stores do not carry the category. Par and median standards for percentage sales increases/decreases, and this year's and last year's stock-to-sales ratios appear at the bottom of the report.

Observations   Store 15 most typifies the November performance of a Shaun's Sporting Goods store. Last year's 5.1 stock-to-sales ratio defined the median, as did this year's 1 percent sales decrease, while this year's 5.4 stock-to-sales ratio came very close to the 5.1 median.

Store 28 produced the highest percentage sales increase for the month (28.3 percent, rank 1), but unfortunately, the store's monthly stock-to-sales ratio is the highest in the group (7.8 percent, rank 23). The positive perception of Store 28's sales increase is negated by the excessive amount of inventory that was carried to generate those sales.

SHAUN'S SPORTING GOODS

SALES AND STOCK-TO-SALES RATIOS

Department: 3300 Sleepwear
November

				MONTH STOCK-SALES RATIO			
				THIS YEAR		LAST YEAR	
Store	*($00) Sales*	*% Change*	*Rank*	*Ratio*	*Rank*	*Ratio*	*Rank*
1	3,474.9	2.0	11	6.8	22	7.1	22
2	1,616.0	19.2	2	5.8	17	8.9	23
3	710.6	−4.7	14	5.4	13	5.1	12
4	265.3	−11.6	18	4.7	8	4.7	8
5	672.5	−20.3	22	4.7	8	3.3	4
6	180.7	−17.4	20	4.0	3	2.5	1
7	401.3	2.2	10	5.1	12	5.0	11
8	174.7	5.7	6	5.4	13	5.1	12
9	532.8	17.3	3	3.8	2	2.9	2
10	485.3	−8.4	17	—	—	—	—
11	373.4	2.4	9	4.6	6	6.2	18
12	371.4	−7.6	15	4.8	10	5.4	15
13	309.3	−17.7	21	5.6	16	3.2	3
14	157.6	5.6	7	3.2	1	3.4	5
15	221.1	−1.0	12	5.4	13	5.1	12
16	—	—	—	—	—	—	—
17	66.2	−23.8	24	4.9	11	4.2	6
18	99.7	−12.8	19	6.2	19	6.2	18
19	154.5	−4.1	13	4.4	5	4.8	9
20	147.3	4.2	8	4.2	4	4.3	7
21	110.6	12.5	4	4.6	6	4.9	10
22	—	—	—	—	—	—	—
23	49.5	−20.5	23	6.5	20	5.8	17
24	—	—	—	—	—	—	—
25	49.2	6.3	5	5.9	18	6.7	20
26	—	—	—	—	—	—	—
27	29.6	−7.8	16	6.6	21	5.6	16
28	22.2	28.3	1	7.8	23	6.8	21
PAR		5.7		4.4		3.4	
MED	10,675.7	−1.0		5.1		5.1	

FIGURE 15.6
November Sales and
Stock-to-Sales Ratios
report for Shaun's
Sporting Goods.

Store 9 is a stellar performer. Monthly sales increased by 17.3 percent (rank 3), while the stock-to-sales ratio ranked second in the group. Though the stock-to-sales ratio increased from 2.9 to 3.8, the increase is consistent with the par increase from 3.4 to 4.4.

Store 6 is one of the poorest monthly sales performers (17.4 percent decrease, rank 20), but one of the best stock-to-sales ratio performers (4.0, rank 3). The "better than par" ranking is a dubious distinction, however. The poor sales performance may have resulted from inventories that were too low. A higher stock-to-sales ratio may have generated significantly greater sales.

Vendor Sales Report

Betty's Boutique compiles a weekly report of sales by major vendor for each of the 20 departments within its two women's specialty stores. Figure 15.7 is the Vendor Sales Report for the cosmetics department for week ending August 15.

Features of the Report   The report includes this year's and last year's sales by vendor, the percentage change from last year's sales to this year's sales, and sales penetration by vendor. The report also includes month-to-date, season-to-date, and year-to-date figures.

Observations   This week's Estée Lauder sales were 46 percent behind last year's sales for the same week. Though the immediate reaction is one of concern, further exploration reveals that last year's sales were unusually high because of a gift-with-purchase promotion not recurring until next

FIGURE 15.7
The Vendor Sales Report for the cosmetics department at Betty's Boutique.

BETTY'S BOUTIQUE
VENDOR SALES REPORT
Week Ending August 15

	WTD				MTD				STD				YTD			
	TY	LY	%	%	TY	LY	%	%	TY	LY	%	%	TY	LY	%	%
Estée Lauder	4.5	8.3	−46	32	9.6	8.9	+8	33	25.0	24.2	+3	28	150.1	140.5	+6	31
Clinique	4.5	4.2	+7	32	8.5	8.5	+0	29	28.0	27.1	+3	31	160.2	160.1	0	33
Elizabeth Arden	3.0	3.1	−3	21	6.2	6.2	+0	21	15.5	14.3	+8	17	90.4	88.8	+2	19
Lancome	2.0	2.5	−20	14	5.0	5.0	+0	17	20.8	19.8	+5	23	85.3	80.2	+6	18
TOTAL	14.0	18.1	−23	100	29.3	28.6	+2	100	89.3	85.4	+5	100	486.0	469.6	+3	100

week. Estée Lauder's sales penetration for the week is 32 percent, consistent with the line's month-to-date (33 percent), season-to-date (28 percent), and year-to-date (31 percent) penetrations. Lancôme sales are a greater concern to the buyer. The line's sales are 20 percent behind last year with no apparent justification. The line's sales penetration for the week is 14 percent, considerably lower than its month-to-date (17 percent), season-to-date (23 percent), and year-to-date (18 percent) penetrations. Reasons for the sales shortfall, such as low inventory or inadequate staffing, must be investigated.

Sales by Category

Steinert's compiles a monthly report of sales by department, classification, and store for the 50 departments in its ten updated misses apparel stores. Figure 15.8 is the dress department report for March.

Features of the Report   The report includes the department's actual and plan sales by store, a corresponding percentage comparison, and a plan and actual penetration of chain total. Departmental sales are broken out by classification for each store. Penetrations are computed for each classification as a percentage of total departmental sales and a percentage of total sales for the classification in all stores.

For instance, career dresses at Willow Station represents 32 percent of the total dress department sales in that store. The category represents 7 percent of the total sales for the category in all stores.

Observation   Special-occasion dresses is an important classification at Amity Plaza, generating about half (51 percent) of Amity Plaza's total dress business. The category represents only about a quarter (24 percent) of the total dress department sales in all stores. Though special-occasion dresses are a significant percentage of Amity Plaza's dress business, the category represents only 8 percent of special-occasion dress sales in all stores. The 8 percent penetration ranks at the low end of a range of penetrations that span from 5 percent to 20 percent. The importance of the category is dwarfed by the fact that Amity Plaza is a small store that generates only 4 percent of the company's total dress sales. Thus, special-occasion dresses are significant to the store manager of Amity Plaza, but Amity Plaza's special-occasion dress business is not as significant to the buyer of special-

STEINERT'S
SALES BY CATEGORY
March

	This Year	Plan		Career		Casual		Special Occasion		Suits		Petites	
	DOL	DOL	PCT										
Willow Station	10100	12600	20–	3230		1291		3036		1568		965	
	7%	9%		32%	7%	13%	7%	30%	9%	16%	8%	10%	5%
Amity Plaza	5381	5800	7–	1817		269		2760		282		253	
	4%	4%		34%	4%	5%	2%	51%	8%	5%	1%	5%	1%
Village West	4742	2900	64	1955		592		1642		551			
	3%	2%		41%	4%	12%	3%	35%	5%	12%	3%		
Cherry Creek	10553	10600		4549		101		3417		1146		1337	
	7%	7%		43%	9%	1%	1%	32%	10%	11%	3%	13%	7%
Bishop's Corner	22873	24400	6–	7734		3221		5508		4660		1748	
	16%	17%		34%	16%	14%	18%	24%	16%	20%	23%	8%	9%
University Place	18276	16900	8	7072		2855		2668		2036		3643	
	13%	12%		39%	14%	16%	16%	15%	8%	11%	10%	20%	18%
Hickory Hill	12280	13900	12–	3616		1325		3484		2003		1850	
	9%	10%		29%	7%	11%	8%	28%	10%	16%	10%	15%	9%
Lincoln Park	11939	11300	6	2555		1430		2194		1792		3966	
	8%	8%		21%	5%	12%	8%	18%	6%	15%	9%	33%	20%
Westwood Village	31716	33000	4–	11135		4598		6690		3972		5318	
	22%	23%		35%	22%	14%	26%	21%	20%	13%	20%	17%	26%
Chestnut Park	13268	12600	5	5834		1751		2589		1832		1261	
	9%	9%		44%	12%	13%	10%	20%	8%	14%	9%	10%	6%
TOTAL	141135	144000	2–	49503		17438		33994		19848		20312	
				35%	100%	12%	100%	24%	100%	14%	100%	14%	100%

FIGURE 15.8
Steinert's Sales by
Category for March.

occasion dresses, who is likely to favor the two stores that generate over a third of the category's sales: Bishop's Corner (16 percent) and Westwood Village (20 percent). The significance of the special-occasion category at Amity Plaza should stimulate a review of the assortment. Perhaps the dress department's total inventory is appropriate for a 4 percent dress store, but does the assortment reflect the fact that 51 percent of the store's dress business is special-occasion dresses, or that casual dresses, petites, and suits each only represent 5 percent of Amity Plaza's dress business? If inventory is allocated based on the total company's penetration of business by class (24 percent to special occasion, 14 percent to suits, and 14 percent to petites), then Amity Plaza may be overinventoried in petites, suits, and casual dresses, and underinventoried in special occasion.

Likewise, the petite category represents a third (33 percent) of the dress sales at Lincoln Park, but the category only represents 14 percent of total dress sales in all stores. If inventory is allocated based on the total company's penetration of business by class (14 percent to petites), then Lincoln Park may be underinventoried in this classification.

Sales performance for a single month is too narrow a time frame upon which to base decisions regarding a store's classification structure or allocation of floor space or fixturing. However, if April's category penetrations by store were to remain consistent with March, an analytical merchant might contemplate the following: Five percent of sales in a 4 percent dress store is hardly enough business to warrant carrying casual dresses, suits, and petites at Amity Plaza. If Amity Plaza's assortment is based on the sales, imagine how paltry the selections must be in those categories! Why not discontinue all three categories at Amity Plaza and devote the vacated space to special-occasion dresses? Though a business plateaus at some point, special-occasion dresses seems to have greater potential than casual dresses, suits, or petite dresses, making the expansion of the special-occasion dress category at Amity Plaza a prudent investment of space and inventory.

A similar thought process can be used to analyze Cherry Creek's dress business. If only 1 percent of the chain's casual dress business is generated by Cherry Creek, and if only 1 percent of Cherry Creek's dress sales are generated by the casual-dress category, then why carry casual dresses at Cherry Creek? It seems wiser to devote the casual dress classification's fixtures and inventory dollars to stronger sales-generating classifications, such as career and special-occasion dresses.

Style Status Report

Megan's Markdowns generates a weekly report of the distribution of specific style numbers among its ten off-price children's apparel stores. Figure 15.9 depicts the report for a cotton turtleneck for the week ending October 8.

Features of the Report The report includes a 12-week sell-through, the number of units sold in the past 12 weeks divided by the number of units received in that period. The report also includes rate-of-sale information by store and chain:

- STP is the number of units sold last week.
- S2W is the number of units sold during the prior two weeks.
- S4W is the number of units sold during the prior four weeks.
- S12W is the number of units sold during the prior twelve weeks.
- AWS is the average weekly sales computed by dividing the number of S12W by 12.
- OH is the units on hand.
- OO is the units on order.
- TWSO is the total weeks supply on hand, computed by dividing AWS by OH.

The TWSO for the chain is an important reference point for computing OP, or optimum stock, computed by multiplying the chain's TWSO by a

FIGURE 15.9
A Style Status Report from Megan's Markdowns.

MEGAN'S MARKDOWNS
STYLE STATUS REPORT
October 8

	STP	S2W	S4W	S12W	AWS	OH	OO	OP	TWSO	BAL
Willow Station	86	145	263	492	41.0	1108		697	27W	411–
Amity Plaza	63	121	220	378	31.5	547		536	17W	11–
Village West	42	76	128	226	18.8	429		320	23W	109–
Cherry Creek	74	129	245	438	36.5	722		621	20W	101–
Bishop's Corner	187	313	600	1157	96.4	1256		1639	13W	383
University Place	53	100	248	578	48.2	819		819	17W	0
Hickory Hill	103	182	338	585	48.8	1074		830	22W	244–
Lincoln Park	67	136	254	568	47.3	846		804	18W	42–
Westwood Village	205	350	602	1206	100.5	1093		1709	11W	616
Chestnut Park	74	119	228	536	44.7	1034		760	23W	274–
TOTAL	954	1671	3126	6164	513.7	8928		8928	17W	0

store's AWS. OP is the number of units that the store requires to match the chain's TWSO based on the store's AWS.

- BAL is the difference between OH and OP, or the number of units that should be transferred into a store (positive value) or out of a store (negative value) to match the store's TWSO to the chain's TWSO.

Observations   Willow Station, Village West, Cherry Creek, Hickory Hill, and Chestnut Park are overstocked; Bishop's Corner and Westwood Village are understocked. The inventory should be reallocated from the generously inventoried stores.

SUMMARY POINTS
- Control is monitoring or measuring actual performance or status relative to goals or standards.
- A control standard is a reference point, benchmark, or guideline used to measure performance.
- A deviation is the discrepancy between actual performance and a standard.
- Qualitative control measures are subjective. Quantitative control measures are objective.
- Controls are established at specific time intervals such as hourly, daily, weekly, monthly, quarterly, seasonally, or annually.
- Control levels parallel planning levels.
- A report is a compilation of timely information synthesized into a meaningful form.
- Most controls are generated by computerized systems that electronically transmit, process, and store timely information reliably and cost-effectively.
- Exception reports include major deviations from standards, bypassing minor ones.

KEY TERMS AND CONCEPTS

control	exception report	penetration
control standard	industry standard	qualitative control
deviation	internal standard	quantitative control

THINKING ABOUT IT

1. Identify the standards and the deviations in the eight reports that appear within the chapter (Figures 15.2 to 15.9).
2. Discuss the use of internal versus external control standards. What are the advantages/disadvantages of each?
3. Relate the importance of control systems to EDI.
4. Of the eight reports that appear within the chapter (Figures 15.2 to 15.9), which do you think best measure the performance of a buyer? Of a store manager?

TEAMING UP

1. Each member of the group should assume the role of manager of a Caitlin's Corner store. Each manager should decide what needs to happen to bring his or her store up to par. That is, determine which performance measures should increase, and which should decrease. Share the determinations with one another, and then decide which stores are already there, and which stores need the most work.
2. Each member of the group should assume the role of manager of a Monkeys & Pumpkins store. Each manager should determine if his or her store had enough BOM, receipts, and EOM to meet the store's "S/S Plan." Share these determinations with one another. Which managers seem to be getting the shaft from the buyer?

SEARCHING THE NET

1. Search for recent news coverage of a retailer's poor sales performance. What controls might have helped the retailer avoid this problem?
2. Search for a control report for a retail store or a trade organization for retailers. How does the report measure performance? What are the standards? How are deviations measured?

SOLVING PROBLEMS

1. At Danielle's Department Store (see Figure 15.2), what would have had to happen for this year's turnover to exactly match last year's? More or less sales? More or less inventory? How much and at which stores?
2. At Tie One On (see Figure 15.4), how would you reallocate the inventory to create a perfect match between EOM and sales?

3. At Monkeys & Pumpkins (see Figure 15.5), how would you reallocate "EOM Act" to perfectly match "S/S Plan"?

4. At Shaun's Sporting Goods (see Figure 15.6), what were this year's November inventories for each store? How would you reallocate the inventories to make the stock-to-sales ratio at every store perfectly (or almost perfectly) match the median?

USING EXCEL

1. Create a spreadsheet for the Turnover Report at Danielle's Department Store (see Figure 15.2).

2. Create a spreadsheet for the Annual Review of Merchandising Statistics at Caitlin's Corner (see Figure 15.3).

3. Create a spreadsheet for the Stock-to-Sales Ratio Report at Tie One On (see Figure 15.4).

4. Create a spreadsheet for the Inventory Position and Sales Report at Monkeys & Pumpkins (see Figure 15.5).

5. Create a spreadsheet for the Sales and Stock-to-Sales Ratio Report at Shaun's Sporting Goods (see Figure 15.6). Include a column for this year's inventory.

6. Create a spreadsheet for the Vendor Sales Report at Betty's Boutique (see Figure 15.7).

7. Create a spreadsheet for the Sales by Category Report at Steinert's (see Figure 15.8).

8. Create a spreadsheet for the Style Status Report at Megan's Markdowns (see Figure 15.9).

CHAPTER SIXTEEN

Store Layout and Merchandise Presentation

After reading this chapter, you will be able to discuss:

● The value of retail selling space.

● Strategies for store layout.

● Merchandise presentation.

● Fixturing and signage.

In large retail organizations, the task of creating attractive shopping environments is the responsibility of professionals with expertise in architectural and interior design, the building trades, and visual arts. Though not directly responsible for store planning, buyers and other merchandising executives play important consultative roles as sources of information on fashion trends, fixture and space requirements, and other merchandise-related topics. To interface with store planners and visual merchandisers, buyers need an understanding of fundamental store layout and merchandise presentation concepts. Chapter 16 covers some of these topics.

STORE PLANNING AND DESIGN

A store's physical appearance is an image component that conveys a message about offerings, pricing strategy, and market positioning. A prototype is a model store that combines elements of decor, lighting, fixturing, and signage to create a shopping ambiance consistent with the store's image and target customers. A prototype is a synthesis of standards for operational efficiency, merchandise presentation, and customer service. Though specialty stores are best known for their distinctive prototypes, model stores are developed within all retailing formats. The development of a prototype facilitates "cookie cutter" expansion whereby a large number of stores are opened in a short time.

Prototypes are often tested in several markets before being implemented, they are periodically reviewed for effectiveness. The cost of constructing a store can range from less than $100 a square foot to several hundred dollars. In conjunction with their "no-frills" strategy, most discounters execute simple store designs of vinyl tile floors, fluorescent lighting, and highly functional fixturing. In contrast, Ralph Lauren's museum-like flagship on New York's Madison Avenue is an example of a pricey store design.

FIGURE 16.1
A prototype combines
decor, lighting, fixturing,
and signage to create a
shopping ambiance
consistent with a store's
image and target
customers. Courtesy FRCH
Design Worldwide.

Prototype development is a store planning function. Some retailers operate an internal store planning department, while others contract professional design firms to develop prototypes. Many retail organizations combine the services of both an internal function and outside firms. The activities of store planning were once limited to allocating floor space, setting construction timetables, and selecting paint colors and wall coverings. Today, store planning is a far more comprehensive function that involves market research, merchandising strategies, space management, and interior graphics and lighting design. Updating and expanding existing facilities is also a store planning function. Renovations range in scope from replacing carpeting and a few fixtures to gutting and rebuilding entire stores. Store renovations have become more frequent as retailers attempt to keep pace with competition and fast-changing market conditions.

Computer-aided design and drafting (CADD) systems have helped to greatly reduce the time that it takes to design a 200,000-square-foot department store from four months to a week. CADD systems have a database of

FIGURE 16.2
Professional store
designers, such as
FRCH, develop retail store
prototypes. Courtesy
FRCH Design Worldwide.

design shapes, such as wall sections, fixtures, fitting rooms, wrap desks, and even images of folded sweaters that can be called from storage, thus eliminating the need to create unique images for each new project.

Visual Merchandising

Visual merchandising is the retail organizational function responsible for enhancing sales by creating visually appealing shopping environments. Storefront window displays were once the major responsibility of visual merchandising. Historically, windows have played an important role in the notoriety of many retailers. Animated Christmas windows at Lord & Taylor's Fifth Avenue store have become a New York tourist attraction. Avant-garde windows designed by Simon Doonan have reinforced the reputation of Barneys New York as being hip and high fashion. Visual merchandising responsibilities have expanded beyond window displays to include floor layout, the development of standards for merchandise presentation, and signage. Visual merchandising is also an influential voice in store design.

Layout

A strategically designed store layout combines the effective use of merchandise and aisles to draw customers through a store, maximizing their exposure to the store's offerings. A layout can increase the amount of time and money that customers spend in a store. Layouts should be flexible, allowing frequent moves as trends change, and as poor layout decisions surface.

SOURCE
Kuczynski, A. (July 6, 2006). Elegantly wrapped. *New York Times*.

ELEGANTLY WRAPPED

Henri Bendel is breathtakingly unlike any other department store in New York. Of the three Fifth Avenue mansions it occupies, two are neo-Classical landmarks: the former Rizzoli Building and the Coty Building, the front of which showcases a three-story cascade of 300 windows hand-cut in 1912 with etchings of poppies and vines by René Lalique.

Broad staircases usher customers from floor to floor at Henri Bendel. Balconies on each level of an atrium encourage visitors to visually plot out the next boutique they will visit. With its winding wrought-iron stair and balcony railings, and hand-painted domed ceilings, Bendel's interior invokes elements of both belle époque and art deco, signature themes of the great French couture houses of the last two centuries.

Three entrances allow shoppers to pass into the store through the consumer viaduct of their choice: directly into the four-story-high central atrium, through a cosmetics boutique, or straight into handbags. Bendel, whose parent company also owns the Limited and Victoria's Secret, does not offer the scope or variety of Bergdorf Goodman or Barneys. But the store makes do with what it has, arraying merchandise in rooms of residential scale, and even on the occasional stairway landing. Like all successful large stores, Bendel presents shoppers with an atmosphere of deliberate disorder, obliging them to travel through numerous galleries until they find what they came looking for, at which point they have also found something else to buy.

The Bendel layout is in constant flux, but generally speaking, in order to find Kevyn Aucoin, you have to pass through MAC and BeneFit. For lingerie by Hanky Panky and Princesse Tam-Tam, you must pass through the portals of custom-made jewelry, the Diane Von Furstenberg landing, and the cashmere department. To reach Missoni, you must make it through a gantlet of Cavalli, Collette Dinnigan, and Matthew Williamson. To go anywhere, you must pass through the extensive blue jeans department.

The great French stores of the nineteenth and early twentieth centuries were places for the lower middle class to aspire to become members of the upper classes: only women of elevated social standing had the time and money for the pleasure of idle shopping. In the twenty-first century, the elegant New York department stores are not unlike the French stores in their aspirational quality. The difference is that now, a store like Bendel's allows the nonfamous to dream of celebrity.

The value of selling-floor space is an important store layout consideration. Just as the value of a retail site is predicated on customer traffic, the value of space within a store is predicated on the number of customers that pass through or by the space. Consider the following: A four-level department store is connected on the second level to a single-level enclosed shopping center. A mall-level entrance is the only point of entry into the store. Assume that about 4,000 customers enter the store on an average day, and that typically about 25 percent of the customers are destined for each floor.[1] Centrally positioned escalators are the store's only people movers. Several assumptions can be made relative to the value of each floor as selling space based on the above information:

- The second level is the most valuable space in that all 4,000 customers who enter the store must pass through the second level.
- The third level is the next most valuable space in that an average of 2,000 customers pass through the third level on a typical day. This includes the 1,000 customers destined to the third level and the 1,000 customers destined to the fourth level.
- The first and fourth levels are the least valuable space in that only the 1,000 customers destined for these floors pass through them.

FIGURE 16.3
Avant garde windows have reinforced the reputation of Barneys New York as being hip and high fashion. Courtesy AP Photo.

As traffic carriers, aisles are an important factor in defining the value of selling space. Space that is close to an aisle is more valuable than space remote from an aisle. Aisles are classified according to their size and the amount of customer traffic that they carry. A major aisle, or *main aisle*, is a wide aisle that connects a store's extremes. Contrasting colors or floor compositions of wood, marble, carpeting, or tile are often used to define major aisles. A secondary aisle is a narrow aisle that interconnects major aisles, often carrying traffic through selling areas. Secondary aisles are often not as clearly defined as major aisles. A line of fixtures is sometimes used to define a secondary aisle.

A store's points of entrance affect traffic flow. Assume that the mall in the aforementioned example is expanded with a second level of stores, and that an additional mall entrance is opened to the third level of the four-level store. Assuming that the number of customers who enter the store from each mall entrance is evenly distributed, the value of the second floor will diminish and the value of the third floor will increase. The redistribution of traffic will effectively equate the value of the two floors. Direct entrances from parking lots and garages also enhance and/or balance store traffic.

Traffic is critical to the sale of certain types of merchandise. Recall from Chapter 6 that fashion goods often are purchased because of their aesthetic appeal. Fashion goods are best placed in heavily trafficked areas to maximize the exposure of their aesthetic qualities. In general, basic goods require less exposure than fashion goods.

Two terms that classify merchandise according to customer purchase habits are important to store planners. Purchases of destination goods are

PURVEYORS OF IMAGE AND AMBIANCE

Chipman Adams Architects has its roots in the early 1950s when Albert B. Chipman established one of the first professional architectural practices devoted to retail planning and design. In 1979, Chipman was joined by his son, John, and together they formed Chipman Design Ltd. As an architect with considerable experience on major projects in the United States and internationally, John Chipman's talents gave the firm an added dimension of expertise. Chipman Design expanded its base to include projects nationally from Puerto Rico to Alaska. Daryl Adams joined the firm in 1988 and the firm name was changed to reflect the new partnership.

The next 15 years brought national recognition to the firm and its staff increased to 60. A rapidly expanding corporate client base created the opportunity to open a West Coast office in Pasadena, California. In 2003, architect Joseph Defilippis joined

Chipman Adams following sixteen years with the McDonald's Corporation. At McDonald's, Defilippis was responsible for the traditional restaurant prototype, as well as the non-traditional restaurant design, completing many of the corporation's flagship locations throughout the United States.

Today, Chipman Adams provides a complete range of professional services including planning and programming, full architectural services and interior design. The company's three principals are members of the American Institute of Architects, and certified with the National Council of Architectural Registration Boards, holding individual licenses throughout the 48 contiguous states and Hawaii. Among the firm's current clients are Saks Fifth Avenue, Ulta Cosmetics, The Gap, Inc., along with numerous restaurants, resorts, and golf clubs.

SOURCE
Chipman Adams. (2006). About Us. www.chipman adams.com/about/history. asp.

planned. Purchases of impulse goods are unplanned. Big-ticket items, such as furniture, are destination goods. Less expensive items, such as candy, are often considered impulse goods. Destination goods are strategically located in remote areas to pull traffic through a store. As planned purchases, customers will seek them out. Impulse items are located in high-traffic areas to maximize their exposure. Some goods are destination/impulse hybrids. Cosmetics purchases are both planned and unplanned.

The characteristics of basic, fashion, impulse, and destination can be cross-linked to define four types of merchandise: fashion/impulse, basic/destination, basic/impulse, and fashion/destination. Note how these four types of goods are strategically located within a store:

• Fashion/impulse goods, such as fashion jewelry, are placed in high-traffic locations for visual prominence. Their aesthetic appeal stimulates unplanned purchases.

• Basic/destination goods, such as mattresses, are placed in remote locations. Because customers seek out basic/destination goods, they serve as magnets that pull customers through a store, thus exposing them to other merchandise. Public restrooms and sales support areas, such as giftwrap, are also customer destinations that pull traffic through stores.

• Basic/impulse goods, such as hosiery, are placed in high-traffic areas that are secondary to the more heavily trafficked areas in which fashion/impulse goods are placed.

• Fashion/destination goods, such as outerwear, are placed in locations that are less heavily trafficked than the locations of basic/impulse goods, but not as remote as the areas occupied by basic/destination goods. As destination items, customers will seek out fashion/destination goods. However, as fashion goods, they require semiprominent locations.

FIGURE 16.5
Strategically placed merchandise will pull traffic through a store's major aisle to maximize customer exposure to the store's offerings. Courtesy of the now defunct Ames Department Stores, Inc.

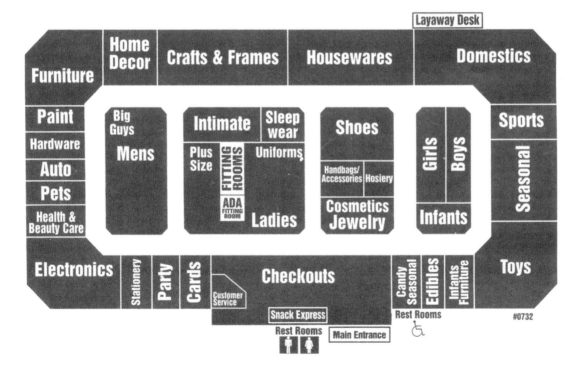

An adjacency is merchandise that is located next to other merchandise for customer convenience and to stimulate the sale of the adjacent goods. Hosiery is a good adjacency to shoes, and vice versa. Girls' sizes 4–6x are a good adjacency to girls' sizes 7–14 for the convenience of customers who straddle both size ranges. Private label goods often are placed adjacent to branded goods, hoping that customers lured to heavily advertised branded products will select the higher-margin private labels. Sometimes goods are exposed in more than one location, a practice called cross merchandising. In a department store, table linens can be cross-merchandised, or double exposed, with other household textiles products, as well as in the china and glass area. Store planners often are faced with deciding where to place goods that cannot be absolutely categorized as basic, fashion, impulse, destination, or any combination thereof. Some stores have experimented with moving hosiery from high-traffic main aisles to the less-trafficked innerwear areas, feeling that innerwear and hosiery makes sense as adjacencies. The result was disastrous for many of the retailers, who found that the hosiery sales generated by the innerwear adjacency did not compensate for the loss of impulse sales.

Manny's Men's Shop

To demonstrate these store layout principles, consider the case of Manny's Men's Shop, a chain of eight men's specialty stores departmentalized as follows:

- Clothing: suits, sport coats, dressy slacks, and outerwear
- Furnishings: dress shirts, ties, accessories (belts, small leather goods, jewelry), and basics (underwear, hosiery, pajamas, and robes)
- Sportswear: casual pants, knit and woven shirts, sweaters, casual outerwear, and activewear

The owner is considering a new location in an enclosed shopping center. The space is rectangular with narrow frontage, necessitating that the departments be aligned in a front/middle/back arrangement. The owner develops the following placement strategy:

- Clothing will be placed in the rear of the store. This is high-ticket destination merchandise that customers will seek. Higher-fashion sport coats will be placed at the front of the department to maximize their exposure.

• Sportswear will be placed in the front of the store. Visually exciting presentations of the store's most fashionable merchandise in this prominent location will lure customers from the mall and will stimulate impulse purchases.

• Furnishings will be placed in the middle of the store. This potpourri of categories is a good bridge between sportswear and clothing. Underwear and hosiery are a basic/destination, basic/impulse hybrid. As basic/destination goods, they do not warrant a prime location, but as basic/impulse goods, their sales will be enhanced by customer traffic en route to the clothing department. Shirts and ties are a perfect adjacency to suits in that suit sales will stimulate sales of shirts and ties.

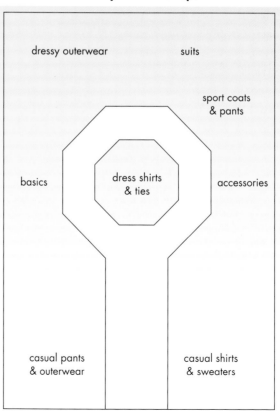

Manny's Men's Shops

FIGURE 16.6
The floor plan of Manny's
Men's shops.

FIXTURES

Fixtures are store furnishings used to present or store merchandise. Commonly called *racks* or *counters*, fixtures also include service desks, display props, and customer seating. Fixtures fall into several categories based on their use:

- Floor fixtures are free-standing units for presenting goods on the selling floor.
- Top-of-counter fixtures are units placed on top of counter-height fixtures (roughly 38 inches) to display goods such as carded earrings.
- Display fixtures are used to show goods not available for customer selection.
- Storage fixtures are used to store fill-in or backroom inventory.

Some fixtures are multifunctional. A floor fixture may have drawers for storing fill-in merchandise or understock. The storage function in fixturing has significantly diminished in importance as retailers endeavor to improve turnover by carrying lower inventory and less reserve stock.

Floor fixtures are classified according to customer accessibility. A closed-sell fixture restricts customer access to merchandise, requiring salesperson assistance for making selections. Easily damaged or highly pilferable big-ticket items, such as fine jewelry, are housed in closed-sell fixtures. An open-sell fixture permits customer access to merchandise, allowing selection without the salesperson assistance. Open-sell fixtures are far more common than closed-sell fixtures for two reasons:

1. Use of open-sell fixtures results in lower selling costs, since fewer salespeople are needed to service customers.
2. Customers are more likely to purchase goods that they can readily test, feel, or try on. Department stores are experimenting with open-sell fixtures for cosmetics, a product category sold entirely within closed-sell fixtures just a few years ago.

Several types of floor fixtures are designed for hanging goods:

- A four-way is a four-arm fixture, often made of chrome. Goods are hung on four-ways so that their most visually appealing side, typically the front, faces the customer.

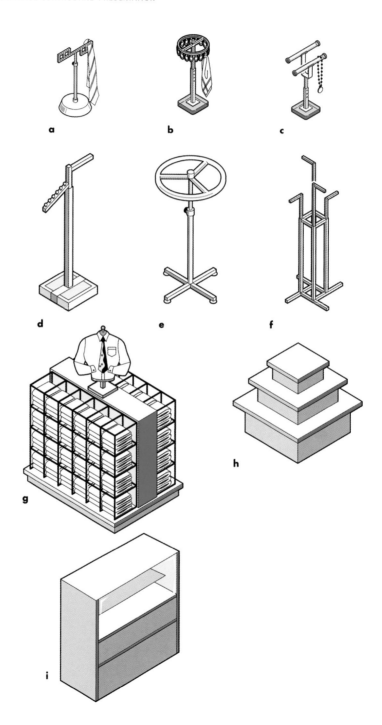

FIGURE 16.7
Types of store fixtures
include top-of-counter
fixtures (a–c); T-stands
(d); rounders (e); four-ways
(f); cubes (g); tier or
"Gap" tables (h); and
showcase (i).

- A T-stand is a two-arm version of the four-way, also used for facing-out merchandise.
- A rounder is a circular-shaped, rodded fixture. Rounders have greater capacity than four-ways or T-stands, and occupy proportionately less floor space. Rounders are used when facing out is not critical for aesthetics, as in the case of basic goods or clearance merchandise.

Other fixtures are designed for nonhanging goods, such as flat, packaged, or folded merchandise:

- A showcase is a closed-sell fixture used primarily in department stores for presenting high-ticket or fragile goods, such as jewelry and cosmetics.
- A tier table, commonly called a "Gap" table, is a shelved fixture popularized by the Gap, primarily used to present folded apparel.
- A platform is flat fixture raised a few inches from the floor often used to stack goods in large cartons, such as sets of dinnerware.
- Cubes are typically made of glass and used to present folded goods, such as shirts and sweaters.
- Lip tables, or *dump tables*, are used for haphazard presentations of clearance goods.

Floor fixtures are designed to maximize capacity, minimize the use of floor space, and attractively show merchandise. Mobility and flexibility are important fixture characteristics in that fixtures need to be moved and/or adjusted often to accommodate seasonal changes in merchandise assortments. Many department stores annually transform their female outerwear departments into swimwear departments, and then back again at the end of the summer. Fixtures must also accommodate changes in the merchandise itself, such as changes in

FIGURE 16.8
Open-sell fixtures permit customer access to merchandise allowing selection without salesperson assistance. Courtesy Fairchild Publications, Inc.

the physical dimensions of packaging. Modular fixturing has this adaptability in that individual units are designed to be used separately or configured into large groupings. Slatwall systems are another type of adaptable fixturing. Slatwall is a series of horizontal "slats" separated by grooves onto which chrome hardware, plexiglass, or glass fixtures can be easily mounted to shelve, peg, or hang goods.

Vendor Fixtures

A vendor fixture is a fixture supplied by a vendor to distinguish its brands from the competition, and to enhance consistent presentation of their product in all stores. Vendor fixtures run the gamut from corrugated cardboard, top-of-counter units to custom-designed fixtures for in-store shops of upscale brands, such as Ralph Lauren and Liz Claiborne. Inexpensive vendor fixtures are often provided without charge with a minimum order. More expensive fixtures are priced to cover the cost of production. Vendor fixtures are especially desirable for products not easily presented on conventional fixturing because of their shape or packaging. Vendor fixtures often include point-of-purchase (POP) signage or graphics linked to national advertising campaigns. Though vendor fixturing for hardlines is common, an increasing number of softlines vendors now offer fixture programs. Retailers must be conscious of the compatibility of vendor fixtures with other fixtures and the store's overall design. A selling area with an assortment of vendor fixtures may give a very disjointed visual impression.

MERCHANDISE PRESENTATION

Merchandise presentation involves the application of standards or techniques to show merchandise to maximize its attractiveness and to facilitate customer selection. Merchandise presentation involves grouping merchandise together on a fixture or within an area in the store based on one or more similarities.

Goods may be grouped based on common:

Merchandise Category   A presentation of a complete selection of a category or item uses the breadth and depth of an assortment to create a strong visual impression. Presentations by category facilitate customer selection when the item or category is the primary selection factor. ("Where are your socks?") Shorts, sweaters, and laptop computers often are presented by category.

Color   Merchandise of the same color is often presented together for impact. Color statements are often associated with a seasonal color trend or a holiday theme, such as red for Valentine's Day. Likewise, goods are often presented by design or print, such as paisley or stripe, to tie in with a seasonal fashion trend. Color presentations facilitate customer selection when color is the primary selection criterion ("I need a white blouse").

Colors within a multicolor assortment are arranged in vertical blocks. The visual impact of goods such as bath towels, knit shirts, and socks is maximized when the colors are arranged from left to right, warm to cool, light to dark.

Figure 16.10 is an example of a color spectrum used for color blocking. Note that the spectrum begins with white and ends with black. The warmest color is yellow and the coolest color is blue. Transitional colors (such as peach) bridge the colors from which they are derived (yellow and orange).

Fabrication or Composition   Goods are often grouped by fabric as part of a seasonal fashion statement or to create tactile statements, such as "soft dressing." Silk neckties, satin robes, and woven and knit tops are examples of goods presented by fabrication. Nonapparel goods are also presented by the material of which they are made, such as down pillows, silver-plated flatware, and leather handbags. Color, fabrication, and composition are sometimes linked, as in the case of straw hats, brass accessories, and sterling-silver jewelry. The presentation of fine jewelry by stone and metal effectively creates a color presentation: red (ruby), green (emerald), black (onyx), sapphire (blue), and sterling (silver).

Style   Merchandise is presented by style for customer convenience and visual impact. Goods often grouped by style include men's dress shirts (long sleeve and short sleeve), women's hats (narrow brim and wide

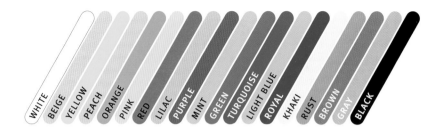

brim), and silk scarves (square and oblong). Vendor styles are also grouped together, such as Levi's 501, 505, and 550 blue jeans.

Price/Quality   Goods are grouped by price and/or quality to facilitate customer selection when an assortment has a wide range of quality or price points. A department store may group handbags as designer (Louis Vuitton, Gucci, and Fendi), bridge (Coach and Dooney & Bourke), better (Liz Claiborne), and moderate (Capezio).

Size   Merchandise is sized to facilitate customer selection. Sized merchandise is typically presented from small to large, left to right, top to bottom, front to back. In a sized presentation of denim jeans on a shelved wall, the pant with smallest waist and shortest inseam is at the upper left of the presentation, and the pant with the largest waist and longest inseam is at the lower right of the presentation. Sizing is often used to present broken assortments such as markdowns.

Vendor   A brand's complete assortment is often displayed as a unified presentation or "shop." The concept creates impact and strong brand identity and facilitates brand-driven purchases of goods, such as cosmetics. Vendor presentations are appropriate for presenting coordinated merchandise such as Liz Claiborne and Alfred Dunner sportswear. Vendors encourage this "shop within a shop" concept by supplying retailers with fixturing, signage, and floor plans.

   There are innumerable themes by which goods can be grouped together for presentation, such as end-use presentations that show customers how goods can be coordinated or used together. Examples include table settings

PRESENTATION STANDARDS FOR JEWELRY

- Present jewelry in shallow (third vision) showcases. Arrange merchandise from the front to back of the case. Create a balanced symmetrical look with a focal point in the middle of each case. Group sets and coordinating pieces together on ramped pads, encompassing a pair of earrings with a matching necklace. A coordinating bracelet or pin should be presented directly to the side to encourage multiple sales. Do not clutter the cases. Minimize duplication of styles in a case, and store duplicates in drawers directly below the presentation. Sales associates should sell from the drawers, not the case, unless the last piece is in the case.
- Use top-of-counter fixtures for earring presentations. Earrings should relate to the merchandise in the case below. Group earrings by "story," that is, pierced, clip-ons, vermeil drops, buttons, hoops, stone, and so on. Top-of-counter fixtures are limited to two per five feet of showcase and must be carefully placed to achieve a balanced look. Sparsely filled fixtures should be removed from the counter.
- Tailored goods are presented by vendor and identified with signage. Never mix vendors in a case. This merchandise is produced by story or look and must be presented in that fashion.
- Present fashion and designer jewelry either by vendor or look, with the exception of Dior, which is always presented by vendor.
- Feature fashion looks of sterling presentations. Use interesting pieces as a focal point.
- Display 14K earrings in boxes or within a case; 14K chains should be displayed on ramped pads according to type and size of chain. Do not angle necklaces. Display vertically or horizontally to the front of the case. Group together matching fashion sets and use display ramps, bangle holders, ring holders, and so on to enhance the presentation.
- Always present clearance jewelry on separate fixtures or promotional lip tables.
- Watches are presented by vendor and identified by signage. Swatch should have its own case. Better watches, such as Seiko and Citizen, can be presented together. Fashion watches, such as Guess and Fossil, may be presented together and should be set up by band color. Swatch should be merchandised by color in the suggested patterns. Citizen and Seiko should be presented on their own showcase pads.

FIGURE 16.11
Vendor shops within stores.
Courtesy Fairchild
Publications, Inc.

of china, crystal, and flatware; room settings of furniture; and layered apparel coordinates of jackets, pants, and tops. Lifestyle presentations are targeted to customers of a specific demographic or psychographic profile. A department store's junior and young men's departments are examples of lifestyle presentations. Music, color, and lighting distinguish these areas from the rest of the store.

The foregoing criteria for grouping merchandise are often combined in a hierarchy to create a standard for presenting merchandise. Men's knit polo shirts may be presented by:

- Vendor (Polo)
- Fabrication (interlock and mesh)
- Color (blocked on a wall left to right, warm to cool, light to dark)
- Size within each color (top to bottom, small to extra-large)

Though often associated with presentations of softlines, merchandise presentation standards are developed for accessories and hardlines as well. Crate & Barrel uses product color and style to create exciting presentations of housewares and decorative accessories. One jewelry store has experimented with a unique, customer-friendly approach for presenting jewelry. Jewelry stores typically present merchandise by metal and stone. This store presents goods by category, so that rings, watches, necklaces, and other items are grouped together regardless of metal or stone. The approach assumes that customers are more likely to shop by category ("I want to see a selection of rings") than by stone ("I want to see a selection of jade").

Retail organizations ensure consistent presentations within their stores by publishing merchandise presentation guidelines by category of merchandise in manuals distributed throughout the organization. Though the standards are based on a combination of objectives such as visual appeal, customer convenience, and ease of maintenance, balancing these objectives is sometimes a struggle. Most department stores present men's dress shirts in a vendor/color/size hierarchy, creating brand and color impact. However, some men consider size the primary criterion for selecting a shirt, and they are frustrated that shirt selections are not grouped together by size, regardless of brand or color.

SIGNS

Signs are a store image component that facilitate shopping by identifying merchandise by characteristics such as category, brand, size, style, and product features. Permanent signage is made of durable materials not intended for frequent change, such as exterior lighted signs and in-store signs identifying selling areas. Temporary signage is made of disposable material, such as paper or card stock, and is intended for frequent change. The most common forms of temporary signage include in-store signage on fixtures. Temporary in-store signs are important sales promotion vehicles that reinforce advertising, stimulate impulse purchase, and enhance customer convenience by calling attention to promotional events and prices. Fact tags, banners, and reprints of newspaper advertising are among the various forms of temporary in-store signage.

The most common uses of temporary and in-store signs are for the identification of:

- *Brand*—Jockey
- *Category or item*—Men's Crew Neck Sweaters
- *Shop-within-a-shop*—From Our Signature Room
- *Characteristics or features of merchandise*—Medium *or* 100% Cotton

FIGURE 16.12
Examples of temporary in-store signage.

- *Price*—25% off ticketed price
- *Promotion*—Anniversary Sale
- *Policy*—All Sales Final
- *Service*—Open a charge and receive 10% off your first purchase

Temporary in-store signs date back to 1929, when Milton Reynolds developed the concept of "talking price tags" to promote the sale of his Printasign machine. Today, computer sign-making systems transmit sign copy from central locations for printing at multiple store locations.

SUMMARY POINTS

- A prototype is a model store that combines elements of decor, lighting, fixturing, and signage to create a shopping ambiance consistent with the store's image and target customers.
- Visual merchandising is the organizational function responsible for enhancing sales by creating visually appealing shopping environments. The value of retail selling space is a function of customer traffic.
- A strategically designed store layout combines the effective use of merchandise and aisles to draw customers through a store to maximize their exposure to the store's offerings.
- Fixtures are store furnishings used to present or store merchandise.
- Merchandise presentation standards are techniques for displaying goods using the attributes of the merchandise to maximize its attractiveness and convenience of selection.
- Temporary in-store signage reinforces advertising, stimulates impulse purchases, and enhances customer convenience.

KEY TERMS AND CONCEPTS

adjacency	major aisle	slatwall systems
closed-sell fixture	modular fixturing	storage fixture
cross merchandising	open-sell fixture	temporary signage
cube	permanent	tiered table
destination goods	signage	top-of-counter
display fixture	platform	fixture
floor fixture	prototype	T-stand
four-way	rounder	vendor fixture
impulse goods	secondary aisle	visual merchandising
lip table	showcase	

THINKING ABOUT IT

1. Merchandise presentation standards have two objectives: to make goods visually appealing and to facilitate customer selection. Consider instances where these objectives conflict. That is, when does making merchandise look good simultaneously make it difficult to find an item within an assortment?

2. Visit the cosmetics departments at a local department store and full-line discounter. Compare the presentation of prestige and mass market lines. What are the differences?

3. Visit a local department store with open-sell fixturing in the cosmetics department. What type of customer do you think finds open-sell fixturing appealing? Will closed-sell fixturing in cosmetics departments become a thing of the past?

4. Walk the aisles of a local department store. How does the store's aisle configuration and layout of departments maximize the amount of time customers spend in the store?

5. Shop a store with an eye on signage. Is it helpful? Does it facilitate and/or stimulate purchase?

TEAMING UP

1. Each member of your team should visit a specialty store at a local mall. What do the elements of the store's decor tell you about the customer that the store is trying to attract? What about its displays? Signage? Merchandise presentation? Fixtures? Music? Share your observations

with the group, and collectively decide which store gets the prize for image making.

2. Each team member should shop a department at a local department store or full-line discounter with an eye on merchandise presentation. How are the goods presented? By category? Color? Fabrication/composition? Style? Price/Quality? Size? Vendor? How aesthetically appealing is the presentation? Are you compelled to buy? Look for a specific item. How easy is the department to shop? Look at adjacencies within the department. Do they make sense? Share your findings with the group, and collectively evaluate the store's merchandise presentation relative to aesthetics and "shopability."

3. Have each member of a team shop a store within a certain discounting format to evaluate its layout. Are destination items in a location that pulls customers through the store? Do the aisles do likewise? Are impulse items and fashion goods front and forward? (Even home improvement stores have fashion items!) Are assortments of goods easy to shop by color, style, composition, price, or other product attributes?

SEARCHING THE NET

1. Search for information on store windows. What types of stores do window displays? Where are they located? How important are windows as a promotional tool?

2. Search for information on architectural firms that specialize in designing retail stores. Examine their portfolios of clients and any visuals of their work. What types of stores are showcased? Are you impressed with the firms' work?

3. Search for information pertaining to vendor fixturing and point-of-purchase displays. Where is this type of vendor support prevalent? Does any program stand out as especially interesting?

GLOSSARY

acquisition the purchase of one organization by another, sometimes called a takeover.

additional markdown a percentage off the already marked down price.

additional markup a markup added to an existing markup to increase a retail price.

adjacency a product or product category strategically located next to another product or category for customer convenience and to stimulate sales.

advance dating delays the beginning of a payment and/or discount period until a specified future date. Also referred to as post or seasonal dating.

advertising conveys a message to a large group of people through a mass medium.

anchor a major shopping-center tenant.

anticipation an additional discount for paying an invoice prior to the cash-discount date based on the prevailing interest rate.

assets that which is owned by an organization.

average inventory the amount of inventory on hand within a period computed by dividing the sum of the beginning and ending inventories by two.

bait and switch the illegal practice of luring customers with a low-price advertised item with the intent of selling them a higher-price item.

balance sheet a statement of an organization's assets, liabilities, and owners' equity.

bankruptcy occurs when an organization becomes insolvent or incapable of paying its debts.

basic goods goods that remain the same from one season to another.

basic stock method an inventory planning method that asserts that a beginning-of-month inventory should equal planned sales for the month plus a basic inventory.

beginning-of-month (BOM) inventory the inventory on hand at the beginning of a month.

better line an apparel line priced at the upper end of a department store's selection.

bidding war a series of counteroffers by two or more parties interested in acquiring the same organization.

billed cost the cost of merchandise that appears on a supplier's invoice.

blind item an item for which consumers have no price reference.

book inventory a recorded perpetual inventory value.

bottom-up plan plans developed at the lower levels of an organization as building blocks of an organization-wide plan.

branch a microcosm of a large urban flagship store offering the same categories of merchandise but in limited selections.

brand a name and/or symbol associated with certain product characteristics, such as price, quality, fit, styling, and prestige.

brand-driven purchase a customer choice based primarily on brand.

brand extension using an existing brand name on a new product or product line to reap the benefits of the brand's reputation.

breadth the number of unique items, categories, styles, brands, sizes, colors, or prices in a merchandise selection.

broken assortment residual items within a group or set of related or coordinated merchandise.

bridge line an apparel line made with less expensive fabrics and fewer details than a designer's top-of-the-line creations.

budget, or mass market line a lower-priced apparel line carried in stores that include full-line discounters.

buyer a person who buys and prices merchandise for resale.

cannibalization results when a retailer spins-off a new merchandising concept too closely related to existing businesses, or when a chain opens new stores too close to existing stores.

case-packed goods prepacked merchandise with a standard assortment of sizes, colors, and styles.

cash dating payment arrangements with no provision for discount or payment periods.

cash discount a reduction in the amount due on an invoice when payment is made on or before a specified date.

cash discount date the expiration date of a cash discount period.

cash discount period a payment period that begins on the date that an invoice is issued and ends on the cash discount date.

cash flow the balance of cash coming into and going out of an organization.

cash on delivery (COD) cash payment is due upon the delivery of the goods.

catalog retailing a form of direct response marketing.

catalog showroom a nearly defunct type of discounter that sells consumer electronics, home accessories, sporting goods, toys and juvenile products, and jewelry by catalog and in a retail showroom.

category a group of related merchandise, sometimes called a classification.

category killer a discounter that offers a deep selection of branded merchandise in a single merchandise category at discounted prices, thus "killing" the category of business for other retailers.

category management managing a category of merchandise as an independent business unit.

central business district (CBD) an urban hub of commerce and transportation, commonly called downtown.

centralization performing functions for an organization's remote facilities from a single location, usually a corporate office.

chain two or more stores with the same ownership and identity.

classic a long-enduring fashion.

classification a group of related merchandise composed of subclasses.

clearance advertising features goods at discounted prices.

clearance markdowns price reductions that induce the sale of various types of residual or slow-selling merchandise.

closed-sell fixture a store fixture that restricts customer access to the merchandise, requiring salesperson assistance for making selections.

closeout store a discount store operated by a retailer to clear slow-selling or end-of-season merchandise from its regular-price stores.

cocooning a lifestyle trend associated with the increasing amount of time that people spend at home engaged in activities such as entertaining, exercising, or working.

commissionaire an agent who represents retailers that wish to purchase goods in foreign markets.

common carrier a trucker whose rates are based on established tariffs and schedules between designated points.

community center a shopping center with approximately 100,000 to 350,000 square feet of retail space often with a supermarket and full-line discounter as major tenants.

comparable refers to the factors that validate the comparison of current performance to past performance.

complementary stores stores that sell goods that complement each other.

component percentage a ratio that expresses an income-statement component as a percentage of net sales.

conglomerate an organization that unites the ownership of independently operated subsidiaries.

consignment goods goods not paid for by a retailer until they are sold.

consolidator a transportation intermediary that combines less-than-truckload (ltl) shipments from multiple shippers into truckload (tl) shipments.

consultant an adviser that offers expertise in a certain area on a fee basis.

consumer the ultimate user of a product or service.

consumer publication magazines and newspapers available to the public at newsstands.

contest a sales-promotion activity that requires participating customers to demonstrate a skill.

contract carrier provides services to individual shippers or groups of shippers based on individually negotiated agreements.

control monitoring or measuring actual performance against goals and reacting to the causes of any deviations from goals.

control standard a reference point or benchmark to measure performance.

cooperative advertising involves shared advertising expense between two marketing channel members.

corporate function performed within a company's central organization or corporate office.

cost the wholesale price paid to a supplier.

cost complement the difference between markup and 100 percent.

cost of goods sold includes payments to suppliers for merchandise, plus workroom and shipping costs, less discounts and returns to vendors.

cotenancy requirement a retailer's requirement of the presence of compatible tenants in a shopping center.

cross docking a logistical concept whereby a retail distribution center functions like a trucking terminal at which merchandise arrives from suppliers in one bay and is distributed to stores in another bay without any processing.

cross merchandising presenting merchandise in two or more locations in a store.

cubes a store fixture used primarily to present folded goods.

cumulative markup an aggregate percentage markup on goods with varying markup percentages.

current ratio the ratio of an organization's current assets to its current debts.

custom broker a licensed independent agent who represents clients in customs matters.

damage markdown a price reduction on goods after delivery from a vendor.

date of invoice the date that an invoice is issued.

dating the period allowed for the payment of an invoice.

days of supply the number of days an inventory will last if sold at a current rate of sale.

decentralization individual stores within a multistore organization are responsible for buying their own merchandise.

demographic segmentation the identification of markets by characteristics such as gender, age, education, and income.

department a group of related merchandise; a functional organizational unit that performs related activities.

department manager a person responsible for the merchandising and operational activities of an area in a store defined by department or division.

department store a retailer that caters to multiple needs of several groups of consumers that is most often an anchor of an enclosed shopping center.

depth the selection within an assortment of goods.

designer brand a designer name used as a brand name, also called a signature brand.

designer line the exclusive creations of a reputed apparel designer.

destination goods a consumer purchase that is typically planned.

deviation the discrepancy between actual performance and a standard.

direct competition occurs when stores offer the same merchandise to the same customers.

direct expense an expense attributable to a specific unit of business.

direct marketing a direct relationship between a retailer and a customer without the use of a retail facility.

direct response advertising catalogs, bill enclosures, and flyers sent directly to a store's customers.

direct response marketing uses a non-personal print or electronic medium to communicate with consumers.

direct sales force a manufacturer's sales staff that sells products directly to retailers.

direct selling selling one-to-one to customers using explanation or demonstration.

discontinued goods goods that will not be part of future assortments.

discount special price reduction in the cost of merchandise.

discounter a retailer that sells goods at prices lower than the conventional prices of other retailers.

display fixture a store fixture used to display goods not available for customer selection.

distribution center the location to which suppliers ship goods at which point they are unpacked, prepared for the selling floor, and redistributed to stores.

distributor allocates arriving shipments of merchandise to individual stores based on a store's capacity, current sales trends, and inventory levels.

district manager responsible for a group of

stores located within a defined geographic area.

diversification entering a new line of business that differs from present businesses.

diverter third-party wholesalers.

divestiture the sale of an organization's assets.

division a group of related departments; another name for a subsidiary.

divisional merchandise manager a person responsible for a merchandise division in a retail organization.

door-to-door selling the practice of canvassing customers at home.

drawing a sales-promotion activity in which participants register to win a prize.

e-commerce a popular form of electronic retailing in which a retailer operates a web site that allows customers to shop over the Internet.

economies of scale savings associated with conducting large-scale business.

electronic data interchange (EDI) an information-trading partnership between a retailer and a producer, sometimes extended to include a producer's suppliers.

electronic retailing a form of direct marketing that includes television shopping channels, infomercials, and online computer shopping services.

ending price point the highest price in a range.

employee discount a discount on employee purchases typical of the retail industry.

end-of-month (EOM) dating dating in which the payment and discount periods begin at the end of the month in which the invoice is dated, not the date of invoice.

end-of-month (EOM) inventory the inventory on hand at the end of a month.

ethnic segmentation the identification of ethnic groups as targeted markets.

everyday low pricing (EDLP) a value-oriented pricing strategy of offering merchandise at promotional prices on a day-to-day basis without the support of advertised sale events as promotional vehicles.

exception report a report that includes only major deviations from standards, bypassing minor ones.

exclusive line a product line developed by a reputed design company for exclusive distribution by a single retailer.

expenses occur in the day-to-day operation of an organization, including payroll, rent, utilities, advertising, and interest on debt.

external standard a benchmark derive from information external to an organization.

external theft shoplifting by people who are not employees of the organization.

extra dating adds additional days to payment and discount periods of an invoice.

factor a financial intermediary who buys manufacturers' receivables at discounted rates and then collects payment from retailers.

fad a fashion with a very short life cycle.

fair trade insulates small independent retailers from price competition with large chains that paid lower wholesale prices because of quantity discounts.

fall on the 4–5–4 calendar, the season that begins in August and ends in January.

family life cycle a sequence of family life stages based on marital status and the presence or absence of dependent children.

fashion a mode or expression accepted by a group of people over time.

fashion director a person responsible for providing buyers with information on dominant trends so that buyers can strategically select assortments.

fashion follower a trend-setter emulator.

fashion goods goods that change frequently.

fashion laggard a consumer who is either slow to adopt a fashion or slow to give it up.

fashion leader a trend-setter.

fashion life cycle the evolution, culmination, and decline of a fashion.

festival marketplace a shopping center of specialty stores, pushcart peddlers, and walkaway food merchants that is often a tourist attraction within a city's cultural and entertainment center. Also called an urban specialty center or festival marketplace.

field function performed in a remote or satellite operation away from the corporate office.

fill-in order an order to replenish sold-out sizes/styles/colors of a basic inventory assortment.

financial ratio an analytical tool based on the proportionate relationship between two balance sheet components.

first in, first out (FIFO) an accounting concept that assumes that goods acquired at the beginning of a fiscal period are sold before goods purchased later in the fiscal period.

floor fixture a free-standing store fixture used on the selling floor to present merchandise.

floor-ready merchandise (FRM) merchandise ready for selling-floor presentation upon arrival at a retail distribution center.

forecasting an attempt to predict trends or outcomes.

forecasting service an organization that studies prevailing socioeconomic and market conditions to predict trends as far as two years in advance of a selling season.

4–5–4 calendar an accounting calendar used by most retailers to structure their fiscal year.

four-way a four-armed store fixture used primarily to present apparel.

franchise a contractual agreement giving a franchisee the right to sell a franchisor's product line or service, subject to standards established by the franchisor.

free on board (FOB) a transportation term followed by indications of the point to which a supplier pays transportation charges, and the point at which the title of the goods passes from the supplier to the retailer.

free-standing stores stand-alone facilities with their own parking areas.

friendly suitor an acquiring company buying another company to give it financial assistance and growth.

friendly takeover the acceptance of acquisition of a company by another organization.

full-line discounter a discounter that offers a wide assortment of hardlines and softlines that includes private label goods and lower-priced brands not offered at department stores. Also called a general merchandise discounter.

general manager a person with the ultimate responsibility for the merchandising and operation of a store.

general merchandise manager a person who manages a group of merchandise divisions.

geographic segmentation the identification of markets by geographic region of the country.

gift with purchase (GWP) free premium with a purchase of goods.

gross margin the difference between sales and the cost of goods sold.

gross margin return on investment (GMROI) a measure of performance that combines gross margin and turnover.

gross sales net sales plus customer returns.

group buying pooling orders from many retailers to meet minimum order requirements or to take advantage of quantity discounts.

hardlines nontextile products.

high fashion apparel in the early stage of the fashion life cycle available through designers or exclusive stores.

hostile suitor an acquiring company being resisted by the company being acquired.

hostile takeover an acquisition resisted by the organization being acquired.

image the way a store is perceived by the public.

impulse goods unplanned purchases.

income statement a statement of revenue, expenses, and profit for a specific period.

indirect competition when stores offer the same merchandise categories but different prices and brands.

indirect expense an expense not attributable to a specific unit of business.

industry standard a benchmark derived outside an organization, often by a trade association.

initial markup the first markup added to the cost of merchandise to determine an original retail price.

initial public offering the first offering of stock on a public exchange.

institutional advertising image-oriented advertising that reinforces a store's position as a leader in value, service, fashion, selections, or prestige.

intermodal transportation combining two or more modes of transportation.

internal buyout the acquisition of an organization by its employees.

internal standard a benchmark derived from information within an organization.

internal theft shoplifting by employees.

inventory reconciliation an attempt to resolve large discrepancies between book and physical inventories.

invitation-only shopping events events designed to reward best customers while enticing them to buy by providing a club-like atmosphere, often including free food, merchandise giveaways, and discounts.

invoice a vendor's itemized statement of the goods shipped, their unit and extended cost, and any additional charges for transportation and/or insurance.

joint venture a foreign expansion strategy involving a partnership between a retailer and a foreign partner.

knockoff a less expensive imitation or copy of a successful branded product or product line.

landed cost the actual cost of an import that includes expenses for overseas buying trips, packing, shipping, insurance, storage, duties, and commissionaires' and customs agents fees.

last in, first out (LIFO) an accounting concept that assumes that goods acquired at the end of a fiscal period are sold before goods purchased earlier in the fiscal period.

lease department a retailer that operates as a department within another retail store.

leveraged buyout an acquisition financed through debt.

liabilities debts owed by an organization.

licensing an agreement that involves the use of a merchandising property in the design of a product or product line.

lifestyle center an open-air retail development of shops and restaurants designed to create a town-like atmosphere with sidewalks, ambient lighting, and park benches.

line function an organization's mainstream activities.

lip table a store fixture often used to "dump" clearance goods. Also called a dump table.

liquidity the likelihood of assets being converted to cash.

long-range plan an organizational plan that covers a three- to five-year period or longer.

loss results when expenses are greater than revenue and net income is negative.

loss leader an item priced below cost to generate store traffic.

loyalty program an individualized mass-marketing strategy of tracking customer purchases to anticipate their future needs.

maintained markup the difference between the cost of merchandise and the actual selling price.

major aisle a main aisle that connects a store's extremes.

major showroom building a building with showrooms for a particular merchandise category or group of related categories.

manufacturer uses labor and machinery to convert raw materials into finished products. Also called a producer.

manufacturer's outlet a discount store operated by a producer to unload overruns, irregulars, and slow-selling goods returned from department and specialty stores.

manufacturers' sales representative an independent sales agent who sells manufacturers' products within a defined geographic territory.

manufacturer-sponsored specialty store a store owned and operated by a manufacturer to sell its product line.

manufacturer's suggested retail price (MSRP) a retail price established by a producer.

markdown a downward price adjustment.

markdown cancellation a tactical markup.

market a place where buyers and sellers come together; a group of people with the desire and ability to buy.

market center a cluster of merchandise marts.

marketing channel the flow of goods from point of production to point of consumption. Also called the distribution channel or the distribution pipeline.

market segmentation the process of identifying niche markets undersatisfied or dissatisfied with current marketplace offerings.

markup the amount added to a wholesale cost to establish a retail price.

markup cancellation a tactical markdown.

mass fashion mass-produced fashions extensively distributed through multiple retail channels.

mass market a large group of customers with similar characteristics and wants.

mass market brand a brand intended for distribution to the mass market through moderate department stores and full-line discounters.

matrix a corporately derived list of preferred merchandise resources.

megabrand a brand that encompasses several related merchandise categories.

memorandum goods goods not paid for by a retailer until they are sold; however, the title of the goods passes from the vendor to the retailer when the goods are shipped, and then to the consumer at the point of sale.

merchandising in the apparel industry, planning, developing, and presenting a product line suitable for a business's intended consumers; in a retail organization, all of the activities associated with buying, pricing, presenting, and promoting merchandise.

merchandise mart a building that houses an entire market under one roof to facilitate one-stop shopping for retail buyers.

merchant-wholesale distributor a marketing-channel intermediary who buys goods from manufacturers and then resells them to retailers.

merger the combination of two or more companies to form a single organization.

minimum advertised price (MAP) the lowest advertised price allowed in a cooperative advertising agreement.

minimum order a dollar or unit amount that defines the smallest order that a vendor is willing to accept.

mixed-use center (MXD) a retail, office, parking, and hotel complex that sometimes includes a convention center and/or highrise condominium or apartment complex in one development.

moderate line an apparel line priced at the low end of a department store's selection.

modular fixturing adaptable fixturing that can be configured into large groupings.

neighborhood center a shopping center with approximately 30,000 to 150,000 square feet of retail space often with a supermarket or a large drug store as major tenants.

net income the difference between an organization's revenue and expenses.

net payment date the last day of the net payment period.

net payment period the payment period that begins on the cash discount date and ends on the net payment date.

net sales gross sales minus customer returns.

network marketing a strategy used by some direct selling organizations to reward sales reps for recruiting other sales reps with commissions based on personal sales as well as the sales of their "downline" of recruits.

niche brand a brand intended for distribution in a niche market.

niche market a small group of customers with characteristics that differ from the mass market.

off-price discounter a retailer that sells manufacturers' irregulars, seconds, closeouts, cancelled orders, and other retailers' end-of-season merchandise.

online retailing a form of electronic retailing in which a retailer operates a web site that allows customers to shop over the Internet.

open-sell fixture a store fixture that permits customers to make selections without the assistance of a salesperson.

opening price point the lowest price in a range.

open to buy the difference between planned purchases and merchandise on-order.

open to ship the number of units needed to meet a store's planned inventory projections.

organizational chart a diagram that depicts a company's corporate structure and lines of reporting and responsibility. Also called a table of organization.

outlet center a strip or enclosed shopping center with a tenant mix of factory outlet stores and off-pricers. Also called a value-oriented center.

out-of-home advertising billboard and transit advertising.

overage a discrepancy between a book and physical inventory where book is less than physical.

owners' equity the difference between an organization's assets and liabilities.

party plan a direct-sales strategy that uses the home of a host/hostess to demonstrate a product line to a group of invited customers.

past-due order an order that has not been received by the purchase order's specified delivery date.

pedestrian mall a shopping center with an open-air walkway between stores that is closed to vehicular traffic.

penetration the measure of a single business unit as a percentage of all similar business units.

percentage variation method an inventory planning method that asserts that a beginning-of-month inventory should be a percentage of an average inventory.

perishable goods merchandise with a limited shelf life or selling period.

permanent markdown markdown that will not return to a higher price at a later date.

permanent signage signs made of durable materials not intended for frequent change.

perpetual inventory system an inventory accounting system whereby the value of an inventory is maintained on a continual basis by adjusting a beginning physical inventory by purchases, sales, and price changes.

personal selling one-to-one interaction with a customer.

physical inventory counting and valuating inventory item by item.

plan purchases the amount of goods needed to ensure that inventory levels are appropriate for planned sales.

plan of reorganization (POR) a plan to reorganize a bankrupt organization so that it can become profitable.

planogram a visual model of product arrangements.

planner a person who projects sales and inventories based on an analysis of sales history, current market trends and an organization's performance objectives.

planning involves establishing an organization's goals or objectives and strategies to achieve them.

platform a store fixture used for stacking large packaged goods.

point-of-sale (POS) system a network of computerized cash registers linked to a central processing point called a back office.

positioning refers to the marketplace position that a product occupies relative to other products within the same category.

power center a shopping center with a tenant mix composed of big box discounters, such as category killers, warehouse clubs, off-pricers, full-line discounters, and supercenters.

predatory pricing a low-price strategy designed to put competitors out of business.

premium a product offered to customers without charge or at a very low retail price tied to a purchase within a product line.

preprinted insert marketing piece prepared by a retailer and sent to newspapers for insertion into the folds of a specific edition of the paper, often a Sunday paper.

preticketed merchandise goods ticketed by a supplier.

price-agreement plan a type of decentralized buying whereby a central buyer provides stores with a list of preferred merchandise resources from which stores directly order goods.

price lookup (PLU) a system file of stock-keeping units and prices that "looks up" a price at point of sale when a bar code or SKU number is entered into a POS terminal.

private buying office a buying office owned and operated by a single retail organization as an extension of its corporate merchandising function.

private carrier refers to an organization's internal fleet of trucks used to transport goods.

private company an organization whose stock is not traded on a public exchange.

private label merchandise goods that bear the name of a store, or a name used exclusively by a store, that are produced for the store's exclusive distribution.

producer converts materials and/or component parts into products.

product developer a person who establishes specifications for the design, production, and packaging of a retailer's private-label goods and then contacts producers to manufacture the goods according to these specifications.

productivity the number of units of output produced per unit of imput.

profit results when expenses are less than revenue and net income is positive.

promotional advertising commonly called "sale" advertising, features a retailer's regular offerings at discounted prices.

promotional markdown a price reduction on merchandise featured in promotional events, commonly called sales.

prototype a model store that incorporates an organization's standards for operational efficiency, merchandise presentation, and customer service.

proximo dating specifies the day of the following month by which a cash discount must be taken. Also called proximo dating.

psychographic segmentation identifying markets by lifestyles, values, and attitudes.

public company an organization whose stock is available to the general public and is sold or traded on a public stock exchange.

publicity "free advertising" through a mass medium in the form of news coverage.

pull strategy producer-sponsored advertising that stimulates consumer demand for a product.

purchase order a contractual sales agreement between a retailer and a supplier in which items of merchandise, prices, delivery dates, and payment terms are specified.

purchase with purchase (PWP) a paid-for premium with purchase of goods.

qualitative control a descriptive measure of performance.

quantitative control a numeric measure of performance.

quantity discount a reduction in cost based on the amount of merchandise purchased.

quota a restriction placed on the amount of merchandise that may be imported from a country within a time period.

raincheck allows a customer to buy advertised promotional merchandise at a later date at the sale price.

receipt-of-goods (ROG) dating delays the beginning of payment and discount periods until the invoiced goods have been received.

regional center a shopping center with approximately 400,000 to 800,000 square feet of retail space with two or more department stores as major tenants.

regional manager a person who supervises a group of district managers.

regular dating assumes that the date of invoice is the first day of the payment period. Also referred to as ordinary dating.

regular price an original price.

regular price advertising features premier assortments at conventional prices.

reporting service an organization that surveys and analyzes specific industry segments, reporting their findings to service subscribers.

resale price maintenance (RPM) a practice whereby a producer enforces the sale of its product line at manufacturer's suggested retail prices (MSRP).

resident buying office a marketing and research consultant that provides market information, merchandise guidance, and other services to a group of member or client stores.

retail merchandising all of the activities associated with buying, pricing, presenting, and promoting merchandise.

retail price wholesale cost plus markup.

retailer sells products and/or services to final consumers.

return to vendor (RTV) a damaged or slow-selling item returned to a supplier.

rounder a circular store fixture for hanging goods.

salaried buying office a buying office owned and operated independently of its member stores, also called a fee office.

sales per square foot a measure of productivity that reflects the amount of sales generated relative to the amount of retail space dedicated to sale of the goods.

sales promotion activities that induce customer traffic and sales by communicating information pertaining to a store's assortments, prices, services and other sales incentives.

seasonal discount a reduction in the cost of merchandise for orders placed in advance of the normal ordering period.

seasonal markdowns price reductions on goods remaining in stock at the end of a selling season.

seasonal merchandise goods in demand only at certain times of the year.

secondary aisle an aisle that interconnects major aisles, often carrying traffic through sitting areas.

secondary business district (SBD) a sub-shopping district in an outlying area of a city.

shopping center a commercial complex with on-site parking that is developed, owned, and managed as a unit.

shortage a discrepancy between a book and a physical inventory where book is greater than physical.

short-term plan an organizational plan that covers a period shorter than a year.

showcase a closed-sell fixture used primarily in department stores for presenting high-ticket or fragile goods such as jewelry and prestige cosmetics and fragrances.

showroom a setting where manufacturers, manufacturers' reps, wholesalers, or domestic or foreign importers present their product lines to prospective retail buyers.

slatwall system adapatable fixturing featuring a series of horizontal "slats," separated by grooves onto which chrome hardware, plexiglass, or glass fixtures can be mounted to shelve, peg, or hang goods.

softlines textile products.

source tagging adding antitheft or price tags to goods by the vendor before shipping to stores.

space management the strategic arrangements of products to maximize sales with a minimum investment of space and fixtures.

special events promotional attractions intended to create an exciting shopping atmosphere in a store.

special order an order placed for an individual customer.

specialty store a retailer that caters to the needs of a narrowly defined group of consumers with a single or limited number of product categories.

spring on the 4–5–4 calendar, the season that begins in February and ends in July.

staff function an advisory function that supports an organization's line functions and other staff functions.

stock-keeping unit (SKU) a unique item in an assortment distinguished from other items by characteristics such as brand, style, color, or size.

stock-to-sales ratio the proportionate relationship between a BOM and planned sales.

stock-to-sales-ratio method an inventory planning method that uses desired stock-to-sales ratios to plan beginning-of-month inventories.

storage fixture a store display fixture used to store fill-in or backroom inventory.

store image the way that a store is perceived by the public. A store's image positions the store in the marketplace, distinguishing it from its competitors.

store-level merchandise manager a person responsible for the merchandising activities of a store.

store operations the retail organizational function responsible for merchandising and operating stores. Also called store administration or store line.

stored value card a card that allows a holder to spend an amount embedded as the value of the card at the retail store of issue.

store planning a retail function responsible for planning new stores and renovating existing ones.

strip center a linear arrangement of stores connected by an open-air canopy, with off-street parking in front of the stores.

style refers to an item's distinctive characteristics or design features.

subclass a subdivision of a merchandise classification.

subsidiary an operating division within a conglomerate.

supercenter a combined supermarket and full-line discount store, also called a combination store.

superregional center a shopping center with more than 800,000 square feet of retail space and three or more department stores as major tenants.

syndicated buying office a buying office owned and operated by a retail conglomerate.

tactical price change a strategic markup or markdown that falls within a retail price zone defined at one end by a price with a standard markup and at the other end by a price with an inflated markup.

target marketing a response to the wants and needs of a niche market with a marketing strategy that may include a mix of products, services, or advertising.

tariff a duty levied by the U.S. government to restrict foreign competition.

temporary markdown a markdown that will return to a higher retail price at a later date.

temporary signage signs made of disposable materials intended for frequent change.

tiered table a store fixture for stacking nonhanging goods, commonly referred to as a "Gap" table.

time-series comparison a comparison of income statement components of two or more time periods.

top-down plan a plan that originates at the top of an organization.

top management functions that appear at the top of a table of organization.

top-of-counter fixture a store fixture for displaying goods on a countertop.

town centers shopping centers that evolved in towns and suburbs peripheral to cities, important for independently owned specialty stores and service retailers.

trade association an organization that represents the interests of a particular segment of industry supported by dues-paying members.

trade publication a publication for members of a specific segment of industry.

trade show a group of temporary exhibits of vendors' offerings for a single merchandise category or group of related categories.

trend implies the direction or movement of a fashion.

trend setter a person who buys fashion at the beginning of the fashion life cycle.

trickle-across theory proposes the existence of a horizontal adoption process across all socioeconomic groups. Also called the diffusion theory.

trickle-down theory proposes that the origins of fashion can be traced to upper socioeconomic classes and that lower socioeconomic classes imitate the fashions of the wealthy.

trickle-up theory proposes that fashions float up from lower socioeconomic groups to higher socioeconomic groups. Also called the status-float phenomenon.

T-stand a two-armed store fixture primarily used to present apparel.

turnover the number of times an average inventory is sold within a time period. Also called stockturn.

variety store a disappearing retail format commonly called a 5&10 or dime store.

vendor fixture a fixture supplied by a vendor to distinguish its products from the competition and to ensure consistent presentation in stores.

vendor matrix a list of preferred vendors selected at conglomerate level.

vendor partnership a collaboration between a retailer and a supplier that results in greater channel efficiency and better service to consumers.

vertical integration when an organization performs more than one marketing channel function.

visual merchandising a retail organizational function responsible for store decor, signage, display, fixturing, and standards for presenting merchandise.

warehouse club a discounter that sells a limited number of deep-discounted food and general merchandise items in a warehouse setting.

weeks-of-supply method an inventory planning method that asserts that the amount of inventory required to support planned sales for a week is based on the number of weeks that an inventory will last relative to a desired turnover and planned sales.

wholesaler facilitates the distribution process by buying larger quantities of goods from producers, and reselling smaller quantities to other channel members, a process called breaking bulk.

workroom cost a labor cost associated with altering, assembling, or repairing merchandise to make it ready for sale.

ENDNOTES

CHAPTER 1

1. U.S. Department of Commerce, Bureau of Economic Analysis.
2. U.S. Bureau of Labor Statistics.
3. Dicker, J. (November 6, 2005). Wal-Mart as the great divider. *The Boston Globe.* p. E12.
4. OneShare.com (2005). Home page. www.oneshare.com.
5. Gym-Mark, Inc. (2006). Gymboree: Our Company. www.gymboree.com.
6. Mazur, P. (1927). *Principles of Organization Applied to Modern Retailing.* New York: Harper & Brothers. p.66.
7. Ibid.
8. Donnellan, J. (1996). Educational requirements for management-level positions in major retail organizations. *Clothing and Textile Research Journal,* 14(1), 16–21.

CHAPTER 2

1. This description of a department store is consistent with the National Retail Federation's definition of a department store as a multidepartmental softlines store with a fashion orientation, full markup policy, carrying national branded merchandise and operating stores large enough to be shopping center anchors. By contrast, the U.S. Department of Commerce defines a department store as an establishment normally employing 25 people or more, having sales of apparel and softlines that amount to 20 percent or more of total sales, and selling each of the following lines of merchandise: furniture, appliances, radios, and TV sets; a general line of apparel for the family; household lines and dry goods. To qualify as a department store, sales of each of these lines must be less than 80 percent of total store sales. An establishment with total sales of $10 million or more is classified as a department store even if sales in one of the merchandise lines exceed the maximum percent of total sales, provided that the combined sales of the other two groups are $10 million or more. The U.S. Department of Commerce definition is slightly dated, written when standard department store offerings were limited to "radios and television sets," and when $10 million was considerable business.
2. Barbaro, M. (June 23, 2006). Lord & Taylor to remain on Fifth Ave. *The New York Times.* p. C1,7.
3. Hine, T. (March 13, 2005). We knew cities by their department stores. *The Hartford Courant.* pp. C1, 6.
4. Staff. (June 1, 2003). The department store: headed for the dustbin or ready to energize? *Display & Design Ideas.*
5. Reed, K. (February 13, 2005). The endangered department store. *The Boston Globe.* pp. C1, 6.

6. Khermouch, G. (December 1, 2003). It's not your mom's department store. *BusinessWeek.* pp. 98, 99.

7. Staff. (September 21, 1992). Discounting: Chronicles of its evolution. *Discount Store News.* pp. 49, 104.

8. Men's Wearhouse. (2005). Annual Report. http://library.corporate-ir.net/library/10/109/109554/items/200387/2005AR.pdf.

9. Home Depot. (2006). Our history. http://corporate.homedepot.com wps/portal/History.

10. Chain Store Guide. (2006). CSG Retail Locations Products. www.csgis.com/csgis-frontend/common/jsp/RetailLocations.jsp.

11. Staff. (May 2006). Outlet stores: Where to shop & how to save big bucks. *Consumer Reports.* pp. 19–24.

12. Talbots. (2006). About Talbots. www1.talbots.com/about/about.asp?BID=S2006197163136DZFEZFAD97.

13. Leckey, A. (January 16, 2005). Bang for the buck. *The Hartford Courant.* pp. D3, 4.

14. Reed, K. (September 6, 2004). Stopover and shop. *The Boston Globe.* pp. A1, 4.

15. HealthInsurance.info. (2006). Cole Vision. www.healthinsurance.info/providers/Cole-Vision.HTM.

16. Foot Locker, Inc. (2006). Our company. http://www.footlocker-inc.com/.

17. Beck, R. (July 18, 1997). Woolworth to close all its stores. (Springfield, Mass.) *Union-News.* pp. B7, B10.

18. Staff. (May 10, 2004). Ding-dong! Avon teens calling. *Examiner.* pp. 4, 5.

19. Norman, J. (December 18, 2005). Conquering the shoe business, party by party. *The Boston Globe,* p. C3; Schwab, E. (January 20, 2005). Party shopping. *The Boston Globe.* pp. H1, 4.

20. Direct Marketing Association. (2006). About DMA. www.the-dma.org/ aboutdma/.

21. www.searsarchives.com/catalogs/history.htm.

22. Ronco Corporation. (2006). History. www.ronco.com/rco_aboutus.aspx.

23. Aucoin, D. (June 8, 2006). Shopping's social value fading for those online. *The Boston Globe.* pp. A1, 6.

24. Best Buy. (2006). Introducing our new kitchen and laundry design center. www.bestbuy.com/site/olspage.jsp?id=pcmcat73800050017&type=category.

25. Grant, L. (December 3, 2004). Lands' end is an ultimate online model. *USA Today.* pp. 1b, 2b.

CHAPTER 3

1. Ghosh, A. & McLafferty, S. (Fall 1991). The shopping center: A restructuring of post-war retailing. *Journal of Retailing,* 67, 3. pp. 253–267.

2. Staples. (2006). Home page. www.staples.com.

3. Norman, A. (July 2006). California formula retail ordinances. A report by Sprawl-Busters, Greenfield, Mass.

4. Lockwood, C. (February 1998). Suburban Main Street gaining favor. *Shopping Centers Today.* pp. 23–24.

5. Thorson, R. (September, 12, 2004). Exit-ramp culture. *The Boston Globe.* p. C5.

6. www.icsc.org.

7. Weingarten Realty Investors. (2006). Home page. www.weingarten.com.

8. Webster defines a mall as a "shaded walk or public promenade" and a "shop-lined

street for pedestrians only." Thus, a mall is not necessarily enclosed. Bal Harbour Shops is an upscale, open-air shopping center located north of Miami Beach, Florida. The open-air pedestrian walkways that connect the stores at Bal Harbor Shops are closed to vehicular traffic.

9. Simon. (2006). Home page. www.simon.com.

10. Peachtree Center. (2006). Home page. www.peachtreecenter.com; John Portman & Associates, Inc. (2006). Mixed use. www.portmanusa.com/ mixed_use.html.

11. Garreau, J. (1991). Edge City: Life on the New Frontier. New York: Doubleday.

12. Wikipedia. (2006). Buckhead (Atlanta). en.wikipedia.org/wiki/Buckhead_%28Atlanta%29.

13. Condon, T. (January 16, 2005). Skywalk is not the ticket for New London. *The Hartford* (Conn.) *Courant*. p. C4.

14. Chelsea Premium Outlets. (2006). Home page. www.premiumoutlets.com.

15. Staff. (May 2006). Outlet stores: Where to shop & how to save big bucks. *Consumer Reports*. pp. 19–24.

16. International Council of Shopping Centers. (May 1994). *Research Quarterly*. Vol. 1, No. 1.

17. Diesenhouse, S. (November 20, 2004). Shopping malls a la Main Street. *The Boston Globe*. p. E1.

18. Grillo, T. (January 17, 2004). Something new in store. *The Boston Globe*. p. D9.

19. Altimari, D. (September 26, 2004). Mall plays rough on Blue Back. *The Hartford* (Conn.) *Courant*. pp. A1, A12; Mander, E. (May 1997). Regional malls: Aging or ageless? *Shopping Centers Today*. pp. 107, 110, 120.

20. Ghosh, A. & McLafferty, S. (Fall 1991). The shopping center: A restructuring of post-war retailing. *Journal of Retailing* 67, 3. pp. 253–267.

21. Many branches were in fact "twigs," stores that offered only a limited number of merchandise categories available in the flagship.

22. The Bergen Museum of Art and Science. (2006). Home page.www.thebergenmuseum.com.

23. Talisman Companies. (2006). Home page. www.talismancompaniesllc.com.

CHAPTER 4

1. Ableson, J. (September 10, 2006). Macy's has plans to woo Filene's fans. *The Boston Globe*. pp. D1, 2.

2. TSC Staff. (June 28, 2006). J. Crew IPO looks sharp. TheStreet.com. www.thestreet.com/stocks/retail/10294097.html.

3. Thomson Gale. (2006.) William Dillard II, 1945–. www.referenceforbusiness.com/biography/A-E/Dillard-William-II-1945.html.

4. Palmer, T. (March 1, 2005). Malls could get new stores or even housing. *The Boston Globe*. pp. D1,4; Lazaroff, L. (August 7, 2005). Investors are sold on Federated's shopping spree. *The Boston Globe*. p. D5; Marks, P. (February 13, 2005). Might Filene's morph into Macy's? *The Hartford Courant*. pp. D1, 2; Reidy, C. (February 28, 2005). Big retailers seen near $10.4b merger. *The Boston Globe,* pp. 1, 12.

5. MSNBC. (2006) www.msnbc.com/id/6509683; Bhatnagar, P. (November 17, 2004.) The Kmart–Sears deal. *CNNMoney.com*. http://money.cnn.com/2004/11/17/news/fortune500/sears_kmart; Sears Holdings Corporation. (August 17, 2006). Sears Holdings Reports second quarter results. www.searsholdings.com.

6. Bon-Ton Stores, Inc. (2006). Short history of the Bon-Ton. www.bonton.com/ investor_relations/companyhistory.asp.

7. Syre, S. (October 11, 2005). What can TJX do? *The Boston Globe.* p. E1.

8. Abelson, J. (February 7, 2006). In surprise move, Talbots to buy J. Jill. *The Boston Globe.* pp. E1,5.

9. Barbaro, M. (June 23, 2006). Lord & Taylor to remain on Fifth Ave. *The New York Times.* pp. D1, 7.

10. Blomberg, M. (January 29, 2006). For Filene's, the beginning of the end. *The* (Springfield, Mass.) *Sunday Republican.* pp. D2, 3.

11. Abelson, J. (February 7, 2006).

12. Limitedbrands. (2005). 2005 annual report. www.limited.com/investor/financial_performance/annual_report.jsp

13. Home Depot Companies. (2006). Expo Design Center. http://Corporate. homedepot.com/wps/portal/EXPO_Design_Center.

14. Pelham, T. (February 26, 2006). Battling Wal-Mart, et al., one customer at a time. *The Boston Globe.* p. L9.

15. Silverman, D. (October 30, 1997). Has expansion boon finally brought retailing to its knees? *Women's Wear Daily.* pp. 1, 10, 11.

16. Howe, P. (May 23, 2006). Wal-Mart to sell unprofitable chain of South Korean stores. *The Boston Globe.* p. E3.

17. Stabile, L. (October 5, 2003). H&M works out quirks. *The* (Springfield, Mass.) *Sunday Republican.* pp. E1,9; Wikipedia. (2006). H&M. www.en.wikipedia.org/ wiki/H&M.

18. Matchan, L. (November 3, 2005). Cheap thrills. *The Boston Globe.* pp. C 1, 6.

19. Hanrath, A. (February 8, 2004). Wal-Mart move into Mexico paying off. *The Boston Globe.* p. E3; Weiner, T. (December 6, 2003). Wal-Mart invades, and Mexico gladly surrenders. *The Boston Globe,* pp. A1,9.

20. ICSC. (April 18, 2006). Saks Fifth Avenue store to open in Shanghai. www.icsc.org/srch/apps/newsdsp.php?storyid=2148&region=main.

21. ICSC. (April 18, 2006) Gap Inc. to open 35 stores in Middle East. www.icsc.org/ srch/apps/newsdsp.php?storyid=2146&region=main.

22. ICSC. (March 23, 2006). Build-A-Bear Workshop heads to India. www.icsc.org/ srch/apps/newsdsp.php?storyid=2137&region=main.

23. Feinberg, P. (July 1998). Local partners key for overseas growth. *Shopping Centers Today.* p. 51.

24. ICSC. (June 15, 2005). India to have 250 shopping centers by 2010. www.icsc.org/ srch/apps/newsdsp.php?storyid=1911&region=main.

25. ICSC. (May 24, 2005.) Simon Property Group opens Hong Kong office. www.icsc. org/srch/apps/newsdsp.php?storyid=1893&region=main.

26. ICSC. (May 12, 2006). Vornado weighs international expansion. www.icsc.org/ srch/apps/newsdsp.php?storyid=2171&region=main.

27. Investorwords.com. (nd). Real estate investment trust. www.investorwords com/ 4060/real_estate_investment_trust.html.

CHAPTER 5

1. Wal-Mart. (2006). Wal-Mart facts. www.walmartfacts.com.

2. Abelson, J. (May 21, 2006). At Casual Male, big is big business. *The Boston Globe.* p. D3.

3. Aoki, N. (July 6, 2004). Casual Male's heavyweight hopes. *The Boston Globe.* pp. A11, 13.

4. Delaney, T. (August 24, 2003). Chasing gen-y shoppers. *The Hartford Courant.* p. D5.

5. Hill, A. (September 16, 2003). Teen Rooms. The (Springfield, Mass.) *Republican.* p. E3, 4.

6. Abelson, J. (March 5, 2006). Hot trend in fashion: maturity. *The Boston Globe.* pp. A1, 22.

7. Swartz, S. (January 29, 2004). Don't discount sex appeal of older women. *The (Springfield, Mass.) Republican.* p. E1; Staff. (September 28, 2004). Clothing retailers launch chains to cater to women 35 and older. *The Boston Globe.* p. F2.

8. Staff. (August 24, 2005). To woo baby boomers, Gap tries growing up. *The Boston Globe.* p. D2.

9. Barbaro, R. (June 23, 2006). Lord & Taylor to remain on Fifth Avenue. *The New York Times.* pp. C1, 7.

10. Koncius, J. (March 20, 2004). Clearing out the clutter. *The (Springfield, Mass.) Republican.* p. E3; The Container Store (2006). Home page. www.container store.com.

11. D'Innocenzio, A. (April 17, 2006). Revlon targets seniors. *Metrowest Daily News.* p. D3.

12. www.axiom.com/default.aspx?ID=2307&DisplayID=87.

13. shop.nordstrom.com/C/6002279/O~2376776~2374327~6002279?medium thumbnail=Y&origin=leftnav&pbo=2374327.

14. Staff. (June 10, 2006). Wal-Mart goes crunchy. *The Economist.* p. 62.

15. Farah, S. (July 9, 2006). Latino marketing goes mainstream. *The New York Times.* pp. D1, 5.

16. Staff. (March 15, 2004). Hispanic nation: Myth and reality. *BusinessWeek.* p. 28.

17. Lazarowitz, E. (October 10, 2004). U.S. apparel retailers go with a Latin accent. *The Boston Globe.* p. F3.

18. Marketing Trendz. (April 2, 2004.) Kmart bail-out plan includes multicultural ad campaign. www.marketingtrendz.net/m_bit_apr_02.htm.

19. Milpitas Square. (May 4, 1999). Home page. www.milpitasquare.com.

20. Barbaro, M. (December 7, 2005). Out of fashion. *The Boston Globe.* p. C1, 3.

21. Nayer, M. (November 6, 2006). It's not your mother's jewelry store. *The Boston Globe.* pp. D1, 5.

22. Staff. (August 24, 2005). From small-town to uptown. *The Boston Globe.* p. D4.

23. www.usatoday.com/money/industires/retail/2006–06–08-macys-shopping_x.htm.

24. Staff. (July 8, 2006). The ultimate marketing machine. *The Economist.* pp. 61–64.

25. web.lexis-nexis.com/universe/document?_m=cd21ebf88eedaccb391f00ad 9ecefdc4&.

26. Blomberg, M. (October 20, 2005). Retailers employ social conscience. *The (Springfield, Mass.) Republican.* p. C7.

27. Crowley, M. (February 2005). No-strings sex. *Reader's Digest.* pp. 33–35.

28. Staff. (January 14, 2005). Wal-Mart begin campaign to counter labor criticisms. *The Boston Globe.* p. F2.

29. www.retailology.com/macysnorthwest/about/diversity.asp.

30. www.federated-fds.com/company/starrewards.asp?print=yes.

31. www.fidelitysystems.co.uk/pdfs/loyalty.pdf.

32. Dash, E. (September 2004). The gift that keeps giving. *Inc. Magazine.* p. 32.

33. Abelson, J. (January 15, 2006). By invitation only. *The Boston Globe.* pp. L1, 5.

CHAPTER 6

1. www.smarterretail.com.

2. Aoki, N. (November 12, 2003). An alteration at Brooks Brothers. *The Boston Globe.* pp. E1,6.

3. Stein, B. (August 14, 2005). Hey guys, hairy knees are for the beach, not the office. The *New York Times.* p. BW3.

4. Aoki, N. (October 10, 2004). Creating a home office with Staples CEO. *The Boston Sunday Globe.* p. F2.

5. Pitts, Soni. (nd). "Taking Advantage of Trends: Cocooning." EzineArticles. com. http://ezinearticles.com?Taking-Advantage-of-Trends:-Cocooning &id=3431; Warner, M. (June 6, 2006). New frontiers in takeout. *The New York Times.* pp. C1, 10.

6. Stewart, D. (January 29, 2004). Waxing over meaning of metrosexual. *The* (Springfield, Mass.) *Republican.* p. E1.

7. www.smarterretail.com; Abelson, J. (February 20, 2006). Sniffing out new markets. *The Boston Globe. pp.* A10, 11.

8. Matchan, L. (April 10, 2003). Trends in design. *The Boston Globe.* p. H2.

9. en.wikipedia.org/wiki/Tickle_Me_Elmo.

10. Aoki, N. (November 12, 2003). An alteration at Brooks Brothers. *The Boston Globe.* pp. E1, 6.

11. Aoki, N. (August 28, 2003). Retailers ride a wave. *The Boston Globe.* pp. C1, 8.

12. Condenet. (2005). 1990s: Grunge, goth, gangsta and the rebirth of glamour. *Fashion Rocks.* www.condenet.com/promo/fashionrocks2005/loreal/1990s.html?page=1.

13. Caminiti, S. (March 18, 1996). Will Old Navy fill the gap? *Fortune.* pp. 59–62.

14. The trade name for costume jewelry.

15. Staff. (October 1994). Mail-order shopping: Which catalogs are best? *Consumer Reports.* pp. 621–626.

16. Mattlack, C., Tiplady , R., Brady, D., Berner, R. & Tashiro, H. (March 22, 2004). The Vuitton Machine. *Business Week.* pp. 98–102.

17. Springen, K. (March 20, 2006). White: So worn out. *Newsweek.* p. 10.

18. Holmes, S. (November 3, 2003). Nike's new advice? Just strut it. *Business Week.* p. 40.

19. Shartin, E. (April 5, 2005). Sports gear hits runway. *The Boston Globe.* pp. D1,13.

20. Aoki, N. (October 3, 2004). Reebok selling fashion over performance. *The Boston Globe.* pp. E1, 9.

21. Ibid. (October 3, 2004). Reeboks' new strategy: To be seen is to sell. *The Boston Globe.* pp. E1, 9.

22. Joe Boxer. (August 1, 2005). Our history. www.joeboxer.com/history_2001.html.

23. retro-fashion-history.com/html/1957_retro_fashion_history.html.

24. Kerber, R. (February 1, 2004). Titanium is hot, even if it's not always real. *The Boston Sunday Globe.* p. A1, 15.

25. Parr, K. (July 20, 1998). Buxton at 100: Building on history. *Women's Wear Daily.* p. 17.

26. Scelfo, J. Real fur is fun again. *Newsweek.*

27. Pemberton-Sikes, D. (March 3, 2006). *The Clothing Chronicles* 217.

28. Givhan, R. (July 4, 2004). De-Lovely designs. *The Hartford* (Conn.) *Courant.* p. H3.

29. Cassidy, T. (April 10, 2003). Who wants to be a millionaire. *The Boston Globe.* p. D3.

30. Muther, C. (July 6, 2006). 'Runway' is bringing fashion forward. *The Boston Globe.* pp. C1, 5

31. Horyn, C. (July 6, 2006) When Paris was all that mattered. *The New York Times.* p. E2.

CHAPTER 7

1. I.D. (2006). Packaging design distinction: Clinique Superbalanced Compact Makeup. *I.D. Magazine.* www.idonline.com/adr05/packaging_dd.asp.

2. LaFerla, R. (June 6, 2004).'Niche' scents bottle prestige. *The* (Springfield Mass.) *Republican.* pp. I1, I2.

3. Darnton, N. (August 1992). The joy of polyester. *Newsweek.* p. 61.

4. Google Finance. (2006). Liz Claiborne, Inc. www.google.com/finance?cid=338016.

5. Staff. (October 19, 2003). Levis: Name all that remains. *The* (Springfield, Mass.) *Sunday Republican.* p. A23.

6. Zellner, W. (December 15, 2003). Lessons from a faded Levi Strauss. *Business Week.* p. 44.

7. Morago, G. (November 6, 2005). H&M cries "Stella!" *The Hartford* (Conn.) *Courant.* p. H3.

8. Schrieves, L. (August 24, 2004). There's something about a retro '60s brand. *The Hartford Courant.* p. H3.

9. To, H. (nd). Coca-Cola: a value stock. *E-zine Articles.* http://ezinearticles.com/?Coca-Cola—A-Value-Stock?&id=19001.

10. Warnaco Group, Inc. (2006). Home page. www.warnaco.com.

11. Sara Lee Corporation. (2006). Home page. www.saralee.com/home.aspx.

12. Warnaco Group, Inc. (2006). Home page. www.warnaco.com.

13. Liz Claiborne, Inc. (2006). Home page. www.lizclaiborneinc.com.

14. Steinhauer, J. (June 7, 1997) Nike is in a league of its own. *New York Times.* June 7, 1997, p. 21.

15. Tode, C. (March 13, 1998). Diverters win battle, but the war rages on. *Women's Wear Daily.* p. 10.

16. Born, P. (March 4, 1994). May dropping Ultima, cites "diluted cachet." *Women's Wear Daily.* pp. 1, 11.

17. Jockey International, Inc. (2006). Corporate info: history. www.jockey.com/en-US/CorporateInfo/History/History.htm.

18. Ralph Lauren Media, LLC (2006). 1971. First women's line. http://about.polo.com/history/history.asp?year=1971.

19. Signature Eyewear, Inc. (2006). Home page. www.signatureeyewear.com.

20. Shartin, E. (November 4, 2004). Cheap chic. *The Boston Globe.* p. D3.

21. Smart Retail Solutions, Inc. (October 13, 2006). Smart Sign System. www.smartretail.com.

22. Federated Department Stores, Inc. (2006). Macy's Merchandising Group (MMG). www.federated-fds.com/support/mmg.asp.

23. www.fesslerusa.com.

24. Moretz Inc. (2004) Home page. www.moretzsports.com.

25. www.kellwood.com/brands.

26. Berner, R. (December 8, 2003). Race you to the top of the market. *Business Week.* p. 98.

27. Target.com. (2006). Our products. http://sites.target.com/site/en/corporate/page.jsp?contentId=PRD03–0005 3.

28. El Boghdady, D. (November 30, 2003). What's in a name? Retailers are hoping not much as they stock their toy shelves. *The Boston Globe*. p. H6.

29. VNU eMedia Inc. (October 6, 2003). E&P's annual holiday advertising forecast. *Editor&Publisher*. www.mediainfo.com/eandp/news/article_display.jsp?vnu_content_id=2006650.

30. Eddie Bauer. (2006). Company information. http://investors.eddiebauer.com.

CHAPTER 8

1. Frank W. Kerr Company. (nd). Home page. www.fwkerr.com.

2. Pfaff, Kimberly. (November 2, 2002). Nothing fancy: Christopher & Banks sells no-nonsense clothes for working women. *Shopping Centers Today*. ICSC.org. www.icsc.org/srch/sct/sct1102/page35.html.

3. Dallas Market Center. (nd). Home page. www.dallasmarketcenter.com.

4. Dallas Market Center. (nd). "New Buyer Kit." www.dallasmarketcenter.com/dmc/v40/index.cvn?ID=10047.

5. Berkery, Noyes & Co. (April 26, 2006). Forstmann Little to invest in ENK International. www.berkerynoyes.com/TransactionDetails.aspx?DealId=225&PageId=14.

6. All Candy Expo. (nd). Home page. www.allcandyexpo.com.

7. FFaNY. (nd). Home page. www.ffany.org; Shopa. (nd). *News Network*. www.shopa.org.

CHAPTER 9

1. If the average inventory for a year were computed by dividing the sum of the year's beginning and ending inventories by two, the resulting figure would not be a representative average. Using the average inventories for each month accounts for the dramatic inventory fluctuations that occur in a year. Ideally, an annual average inventory should be computed by summing each day's inventory and dividing by 365, just as an average daily balance is computed on a savings account or a charge account. However, most retailers do not maintain daily inventory balances, and the cost of generating this information would negate the value of it.

2. The data in this scenario has been manipulated to demonstrate dramatically the effect of average inventory on turnover. In real life, sales are never quite as predictable.

3. Outcalt, R., & Johnson, P. (January 1997). The diamond of doom. *Specialty Stores/The Business Newsletter*. p. 4.

4. For pedagogical reasons, assortment considerations other than size were ignored. Sport shirts require a broader range of styles and colors than dress shirts, a selection factor that increases their stock-to-sales ratio.

5. The machine takes up about 6 square feet.

6. Munk, N. (August 3, 1998). Gap gets it. *Fortune*. pp. 68–82.

7. Silverman, D. (October 30, 1997). Has expansion boon finally brought retail to a saturation point? *Women's Wear Daily*. pp. 1, 10–11.

CHAPTER 10

1. Capital Business Credit, LLC. (2006). Home page. www.capfac.com; America's Factors, Inc. (2006). Home page. www.americasfactors.com.

2. The large variances among stores for cost of goods sold, gross margin, and expenses are because of inconsistencies among firms relative to how they report certain operating expenses. For instance, some companies include occupancy costs in the cost of goods sold, thus maximizing cost of goods sold, and minimizing gross margin and expenses. Other retailers classify occupancy costs as a general operating expense, thus minimizing cost of goods sold, and maximizing gross margin and expenses. Net income is perhaps the only component percentage that can be compared across the board. In every case, the figure represents the before tax residual that results from deducting all costs and expenses from net sales.

3. It should be noted that in Chapter 9, discussion of turnover advocated using average inventory at retail to determine turnover. GMROI is based on average inventory at cost. Note that there are many variations of the GMROI formula. Some formulas include " × 100" in the gross margin portion of the formula, thus multiplying turnover by gross margin as a percentage of sales instead of as a ratio of gross margin to sales.

CHAPTER 11

1. Staff. (November 1990). Athletes' Foot steps up inventory control. *Chain Store Age Executive.* pp. 128–130.

CHAPTER 12

1. There was a 53.75 percent markup on the $9.25 ties, a 52.50 markup on the $9.50 ties, and a 51.25 percent markup on the $9.75 ties. The total of all three markup percentages is 157.50. This number divided by three is 52.5.

2. Goods damaged in delivery are the responsibility of either the vendor or the shipper and should be charged back to the vendor for credit.

3. Some retailers give no discount on sale or low-markup merchandise.

CHAPTER 13

1. DeGeorge, G. (June 9, 1997). Sunglass Hut is feeling the glare. *BusinessWeek.* pp. 89–91.

2. Reductions are included in the computation, since reductions reduce the value of the inventory.

CHAPTER 14

1. Units shipped times unit cost.

2. Time is expressed in days divided by 360.

3. Wikipedia. (2006). Wal-Mart. www.en.wikipedia.org/wiki/Wal-Mart.

4. Reda, S. (April 1994). Floor-ready merchandise. *Stores.* pp. 41–44.

5. Staff. (January 3, 2005). Estée Lauder. *Newsweek.* p. 133.

6. An in-stock position of 100 percent would mean an availability of *every* item *all* the time, resulting in excessive inventory and low turnover.

7. Staff. (December 8, 1991). Tracking fashion technology. *Discount Store News.* pp. A20–21.

8. Strunesee, C. (March 26, 1996). Dillard's leans on vendors to get with efficiencies. *Women's Wear Daily.* pp. 1, 4–5.

9. Rozhon, T. (July 15, 2005). Suppliers to Saks now want to see the receipts. *The New York Times.* pp. C1, 2.

10. Staff. (November 30, 1994). Wal-Mart cancel clause "grossly unfair" says court. *Women's Wear Daily.* p. 3

CHAPTER 15

1. The percentage of total inventory allocated to a store in a multiunit chain should not exactly match the percentage of the chain's total sales that the store generates. High-volume stores should own proportionately less inventory than low-volume stores, and thus have higher turnover and lower stock-to-sales ratios. Let us assume that in the case of Tie One On, the match between inventory and sales should be close, though not exact.

CHAPTER 16

1. This is highly unlikely in real life, but the assumption helps make a point.

COMPANY INDEX

SUBJECT INDEX